The Development of the Concept of Space in the Child

The Development of the Concept of Space in the Child

Monique Laurendeau
and
Adrien Pinard

INTERNATIONAL UNIVERSITIES PRESS, INC.

New York

Contents

v

The Development of the Concept of Space in the Child

Introduction

by Jean Piaget

In this book, Monique Laurendeau and Adrien Pinard combine two rarely compatible qualities which give it exceptional worth: a complete understanding of the hypotheses under consideration, and a continually alert critical sense which prevents them from adopting these hypotheses before having examined all possible objections and tested every conceivable interpretation. Dedicating an entire volume to a close examination of only five tests of the child's first spatial concepts might seem to be quite a challenge. On the one hand, the authors see these apparently limited problems as an opportunity to discuss the most comprehensive questions, such as the existence of stages of intellectual development, the internal consistency of the tests (a prelude to the problem of group structures), the *décalages* which disturb the synchronization between analogous developments, the existence of an initial topological structure, the role of cognitive egocentrism in the development of structures, etc.; in brief, the most general issues are raised through these particular experiments. On the other hand, precisely because these experiments are very limited, the authors can undertake an analysis in depth which overlooks no detail; they always consider the larger hypotheses, submitting them to a very rigorous control which is the more elaborate as its scope is limited. Indeed, in dealing with these general hypotheses, it is tempting either to find them interesting and accept them without question, or to misinterpret them and plunge into detailed criticisms which are easy because they are irrelevant or ignore the fundamental questions (an example of this is Dodwell's work, discussed in Chapter XVII). The great merit of this book, we must emphasize, is that, on

1

the contrary, the authors have thoroughly grasped the implications of the leading hypotheses and have submitted them to a relentlessly meticulous, careful, and objective examination. We must express our deep appreciation to Monique Laurendeau and Adrien Pinard for these two invaluable services which, by their very association, are both considered equally important.

One of the essential innovations of this work is that it involves a very large number of subjects (children from two to twelve years), all given the *same* tests, thereby permitting detailed analyses of internal consistency. The authors are right in pointing out (see Chapter XVII) the inadequacy of correlations even when these correlations are positive. In this case, the demonstration must rest on a scalogram analysis, and the authors' actual analysis is all the more convincing since its results are very significant when dealing with the homogeneous group of five spatial tests but lose significance when the heterogeneous spatial and causal tests are combined.

Let us now proceed from this problem of internal consistency to the main results obtained by Laurendeau and Pinard concerning the child's initial topological structures and spatial egocentrism, as well as the rather important gaps which they note—with very good reason—in our current knowledge of the nature of *décalages*. With regard to the first of these two points, the existence of initial topological structures having nothing to do with either metrics or the coordination of viewpoints is fairly normal; such forms of spatial organization express the most general properties of space and the properties most dependent on the conditions of the subject's own actions. But a frequent objection to this interpretation is the earliness of the distinctions between curvilinearity and rectilinearity which, from a mathematical point of view, is outside the field of topological concepts. In this respect, we must admire the subtlety of the authors' analysis, which shows that the young child discovers these distinctions through topological procedures proper to coordination of neighborhoods.

As for the question of spatial egocentrism, the authors' meticulous analysis (end of Chapter XVII) concludes "that at least in the development of spatial concepts, the egocentric attitude is regular enough to suggest that it reflects a genuine and consistent form of mental organization." Perhaps we should add one remark to this conclusion, because the term "egocentrism" (which we are using less and less) may lead to many ambiguities even in the specific area of epistemological egocentrism. This sort of concept includes two inseparable aspects, one positive and the other negative (or at least restrictive). This second aspect amounts to a lack of decentration, and this is what the authors have actually found in projective space, in the form of a systematic difficulty in freeing oneself from one's own point of view and coordinating it with others (the latter not even yet being considered as possible in the sense of "other," or different from one's own). But this negative aspect—that is, this lack of decentration and coordination—is inseparable from a very positive aspect which may be observed not only in the spatial area but in all areas on the preoperational level: this is the child's systematic attempt to understand a situation by assimilating it to what he already knows and to what seems to be directly given—that is, to the immediate aspects of his own action (including his own perspective, etc.). If we refer only to the negative aspects of egocentrism —that is, to the subjective distortions which it produces—it may indeed seem strange to speak of a "genuine and consistent form of mental organization." But let us consider the positive aspects which we observe in transitive motion, for example, where even very young subjects understand that a moving *A* pushes a moving *B* because they themselves have pushed *A:* in such cases the assimilation to the child's own action fulfills an indispensable cognitive function, and thus it is natural that the decentrations relative to this action appear only later on. In other words, since action plays an essential and central role in knowledge, the child must first make use of it before being able to locate his own action within the group of actions which present different characteristics or which must be imagined in different perspectives. It is this positive aspect that makes it legitimate to speak of a primitive "mental organization" whose dominant trait is the assimilation of reality to action—which is quite rational—but whose irrational concomitant is the primacy of the subject's own action and point of view, the only action and point of view he knows at first.

We now come to the crucial problem of *décalages:* the authors reproach us, both for making "too easy use" of them and for not providing a theory which allows "any systematic prediction." On the first of these two points, let us reply that Laurendeau and Pinard admit the frequency of such *décalages,* whose existence they say "is impossible to question," while many authors prefer to ignore them. Thus it would seem excusable to resort to them, and if resorting to the facts is certainly "easy," it is never "too" much so as long as we are unable to predict reality. It is the second question which is really the more crucial: is it possible, with the present state of knowledge, to provide a theoretical model of *décalages* which would compare with the one we can expect in the field of developmental stages?

All knowledge proceeds from an initially inseparable relationship between the subject, who builds structures through his actions, and the objects affected (with more or less efficient results) by these actions. Only when an adequate number of such actions or operations is known can we attempt to trace the laws of their development. And since logic is nothing but the formalization of the most general coordinations of actions and operations, the steps of this development should sooner or later take the form of a multilevel series or genealogy of prelogical or logical structures—which could eventually lead to the construction of a coherent theory and even to some predictions.

On the contrary, the *décalages* derive from the object's resistances, and the authors ask that we construct a theory of these resistances, as though this were an undertaking directly parallel to the one concerning the subject's actions and operations. It is an exciting project and it should certainly be considered. But we must remark at once that if the subject's actions always reflect intelligence (a condition which greatly facilitates the analysis), the object's resistances do not do so, and involve a much greater number of factors —whence two preliminary questions, one on the methods of approach and the other on the singularity or plurality of forms of *décalages*.

Concerning the methods of approach—granted that the subject is "intelligent" at all ages—we need only observe him and then multiply the tests to elicit the main facts: for example, Laurendeau and Pinard's very persistent analysis of just five of these tests shows that there is no basic contradiction between the adventurous "intuitions" of past investigators and the serious analyses of today's. On the contrary, the analysis of the *décalages* and thus of the object's resistances requires much more refined methods, since observation is no longer adequate for explaining a phenomenon which is, by its very nature, a kind of resistance to the subject's logic. Therefore, in order to explain these *décalages* it is necessary to isolate the factors by studying the development of a structure under rigorously controlled conditions, varying the conditions of acceleration and resistance in turn; the only way to throw light on this problem is to use the learning methods introduced in Geneva by Inhelder, Sinclair, and Bovet, and in Montreal by Laurendeau and Pinard—methods which consist of applying to learning the same factors effective in the child's spontaneous development. It would be premature to theorize before knowing the results of such studies.

As for the possible numerous reasons for the *décalages*, we can mention at least three categories, the last one being the most interesting but raising a host of other problems. The first of these categories refers to the conditions which favor or inhibit the functioning of thought and which often depend on the way the questions are asked. It is well-known, for example, that in a free interrogation, where the questions are modified as a function of the child's responses and where the examiner's art consists of following him rather than overdirecting him, there are considerable differences among psychologists: some will obtain only the *minimum* of what the subjects could offer, while others will stir up the subjects' interest and sometimes lead them spontaneously to reach the stage they were approaching. Such factors as interest, concreteness of the questions, etc., play an obvious role and often there is a *décalage* between, for example, the results of rigorously standardized interrogations and those of free interrogations.

A second category of factors, which are more important theoretically, concerns the relationship between the figurative aspects of the techniques used and the operative aspects of the problems to be solved. In order to determine the subjects' operational level we must, in effect, give them problems which cannot be solved by a simple perceptual reading: in this way, of course, the perceptual configuration of the material influences the resistance which has to be overcome, and the effect, though unpredictable, can vary considerably from one situation to another. We know that in physics, the most advanced of the experimental sciences and the one with the most highly developed theoretical models, the problems of friction are far from being entirely solved and still include numerous special cases even though all the factors are, as a rule, already known. The resistance of figurative aspects (perception, image, etc.) to operational manipulation raises problems which are similar in their complexity: we can understand the reasons for one or another local *décalage* after it has appeared, but we are at a loss to formulate truly general laws in this respect.

But the third category of factors is still more crucial. The reason why the object can resist the subject's operational structuring is that the object exists independently of him and because this independent existence is revealed in a series of causal reactions which are more or less understood by the subject. Thus, submitting these objects to a system of logical or mathematical operations, however simple these might be (seriations, classifications and inclusion, partitive addition, transitivity, conservation, etc.), requires that these structurings—and particularly the quantifications which they include—encounter no resistance in the causal relations which the subject attributes to these objects. We have only begun to analyze in any precise way the development of causality in the composition of motions and forces, etc., and the problem is unexpectedly rich and complex. Thus it is especially from this sort of analysis that we can hope to shed some light on this third category of *décalage* factors.

To give just one example, the fairly consistent *décalage* observed between the conservations (and transitivities, etc.) of quantity of matter, weight, and volume seems much more natural when we see these concepts operating in the causal explanations of children of four-five to twelve-fourteen years of age. Weight, in fact, plays a much greater causal role for the child than does quantity of matter, a role which is at first polyvalent (a "weight to pull," others "for pushing," "for holding," etc.): until about seven years, weight changes from one moment to another for a single object as soon as its spatial position and causal function are changed (even when its shape remains constant). In a glass of water, for example, the weight of a pebble is seen as varying according to whether it is at the bottom or at mid-height, etc. Furthermore, the weight of a suspended rod is seen as located at the end and, if the rod is placed obliquely, it is expected to fall along this inclination rather than vertically. In short, as our current studies on a great number of causal reactions seem to indicate, it is quite natural that the conservation of weight, barely acquired by seven to eight years in cases of simple changes in the object's position, is not discovered until later in cases of changes in shape (and much later still with changes in state, solid or liquid), while these factors do not produce similar *décalages* when applied to simple quantity of matter once it has been dissociated from weight.

As for the *décalage* between the conservation of weight and of volume, we must again refer to factors of causality, since the invariance or the variations in volume are related to rather late-appearing dynamic schemata (e.g., schema of the variable density of the parts of a substance, schema of pressure, etc.), which involve actions and reactions and consequently belong to formal-level operations. Further, if the seven- to eight-year-old child can reason on three-dimensional as easily as two-dimensional linear series, volume as such probably requires that the continuum be conceived as a "system of parts," a conception which also implies formal operations.

In a word, the *décalage* factors of this third category could not be very well defined without a rather clear knowledge of the multiple aspects we are currently studying in causality. This is why we cannot provide a theory of these *décalages* without a complete reorganization of our ideas about the development of causal explanations, a reorganization which is the object of our continuing efforts.

The various remarks presented here as an introduction seem to have moved farther and farther away from the object of the studies reported in a work which is strictly limited to space. But let us repeat that Laurendeau and Pinard's great merit is in having explored in depth a subject which was very small in terms of its initial dimensions, but which has led them to a clear discussion of very broad problems, and they have fully succeeded in this *tour de force*. It seemed appropriate to focus this introduction on these comprehensive issues, since the authors are admirable critics who allow no difficulty, visible or latent, to go undetected. When we compare their work with many others which debate our results superficially, lacking a real understanding of the general issues involved, we can only be pleased with the exceptional merit of a work which so beautifully combines experimental control and theoretical vision.

Chapter I

Theoretical and Experimental Context

In approaching the experimental study of the development of the child's concept of space, we confront a problem of definition: the question goes far beyond simple semantics, for from the beginning it entails considerations of an epistemological nature. Knowledge of space may in fact occur at different levels—levels which are not always easy to define or distinguish, and whose informational value may vary considerably. In attempting to resolve this basic problem, we run the risk of entering into fruitless debates on the "real significance" of one or another experimental study and of introducing even more confusion into a field which has already been rather poorly studied. Before defining the objectives or describing the general methodological aspects of the experiments discussed in this work—a discussion which will serve to introduce the chapters which follow—it would be helpful, then, first to review some basic distinctions which allow us to place the major works already published on the development of space into their proper perspectives. In addition, we must define the theoretical framework into which Piaget has placed the several studies replicated here.

PRELIMINARY DISTINCTIONS

Space has been and continues to be an area of investigation which is favored by psychologists interested in the question of knowledge. This consensus at the level of the object to be studied is today reflected in a mass of experimental works, whose conception and results are, however, still far from being in even relative agreement.

8

This lack of cohesion apparently stems from the fact that we do not always clearly recognize the various levels of knowledge implicit in the individual's (child's or adult's) contacts with the spatial dimensions of the world he inhabits. In fact, it is Piaget who deserves the credit for having introduced the fundamental distinctions which clearly seem to exist, first, between perceptual space and intellectual space, and, second, at the level of intellectual space itself, between sensorimotor and representational space.

PERCEPTUAL SPACE AND COGNITIVE SPACE

The first distinction, between perceptual space and cognitive space, is of primary importance and is related to Piaget's often-discussed distinction between perception and intelligence.[1] Piaget probably treats this question most specifically in his most recent book on the perceptual mechanisms (1961). In this work he proposes a distinction between the figurative and the operative aspects of knowledge, a distinction which is critical in all stages of development. If it is true that to know an object is to construct or reconstruct it, it follows that knowledge must include two aspects: first, an aspect which is essentially operative, related to the actions or operations by which the subject submits the object to the transformations necessary for its reconstruction, and, second, a figurative aspect, related to the direct or pictorial perception of the successive states or momentary configurations between which the transformational activities must intervene. The operative aspect is dependent upon intelligence at all levels, from the most rudimentary prerepresentational forms of sensorimotor activity to the most highly evolved internalized forms of operational thought. On the other hand, the figurative aspect is dependent upon perception (or on the mental image), whether it is a question of the primary effects of a single act of perceptual centering or a question of the secondary effects produced by increasingly complex perceptual activities.

Distinguishing in this manner the perceptual from the operative structures, Piaget nevertheless does not fail to emphasize the crucial fact that intelligence does not grow out of perception in a simple relational process, as though the perceptual structures could become intellectual structures by progressively enlarging and becoming more

---

[1] See especially Piaget (1947, 1950, 1955); Piaget and Inhelder (1948, 1963); Piaget and Morf (1958).

flexible. Between these two types of structures a reciprocal influence or functional interaction must operate; at all levels of development, the information provided by perception (or the mental image) serves as raw material for the intellectual action or operation, and, reciprocally, these intellectual activities exert an influence (direct or indirect) on perception, enriching and increasing the flexibility of its functioning with development. Space does not permit summarizing even the major differences and similarities which Piaget, through numerous and varied experimental studies, establishes between perception and intelligence. But it should be remembered that despite the reciprocal influences and fundamental analogies, intelligence remains distinct from perception and does not arise out of it. Intelligence and perception, both resulting from sensorimotor activity, represent two related but distinct aspects of knowledge of reality; while they always develop in a complementary fashion, they may often go in quite different directions.

This distinction of a dual system of knowledge applies, in principle, to all sectors of reality. There is, for example, a perceptual causality and a conceptual causality, a perceptual speed and a conceptual speed, etc. As far as the knowledge of space is concerned, which is the object of the present study, it is equally important to make a clear distinction between a *perceptual* space and a *conceptual* (or intellectual) space. There are a number of works[2] which examine the problems raised by the perception of space and spatial relations; among these we might mention the classic studies of the Gestalt theory (e.g., Koffka, 1935), the systematic research of Wapner and Werner (1957) on the development of space within the context of their "sensory-tonic" conception, the psychophysical interpretations of J. J. Gibson (1950, 1966), and the ingenious works of the transactionist school (Ittelson, 1960). We should above all point out the long series of experiments done by Piaget and his collaborators on the perception of topological relations (proximity, separation, continuity, etc.), projective relations (estimation of apparent size and shape, etc.), and the metric or Euclidian relations (perceptual coordinates, size constancy, etc.). Published in the *Archives de psychologie* beginning in 1942, these works have been assembled and summarized by Piaget in his recent volume on the

[2] See Wohlwill's (1960a) excellent summary of the genetic theories of perception.

perceptual mechanisms (1961). They indicate that spatial perception, in contrast to the concept of space, always retains an essentially relativistic character and is never completely freed from certain systematic distortions, precisely because of the irreversibility inherent in the perceptual structures.

SENSORIMOTOR SPACE AND REPRESENTATIONAL SPACE

According to Piaget's theory, the development of sensorimotor space occupies approximately the first two years of childhood and is one of the major achievements of sensorimotor intelligence. This space is progressively structured through an increasingly complex coordination of the child's actions and displacements and, consequently, enlists his perceptual functions as well as his motor functions. This space thus depends mainly on the operative aspect of knowledge and clearly exceeds the limits of mere perception, from which it draws its sustenance and its orientation. It is, in short, a space which is practical and experienced, perfectly organized and balanced at the level of action or behavior, even though the absence of the symbolic function still leaves the subject unable to imagine it or mentally to reconstruct it. Piaget has dedicated a substantial part of his works on the origin of intelligence (1936) and on the construction of reality (1937) to the development of this sensorimotor space in the child. It is also with this prerepresentational level that most of the ethologists and animal learning theorists are concerned in their work on the innate or acquired adaptation of the animal to its spatial environment.

The very important representational space which begins to develop in the child around the age of two years, with the advent of the symbolic function, has to be clearly distinguished from this sensorimotor space. In the domain of space, as in all other sectors of child thought (e.g., causality, time, etc.), there is a developmental phenomenon, often described by Piaget, which requires that the achievements attained at the level of practical and motor activity reassert themselves on the symbolic and conceptual level. Representational space is not a simple internalization nor a purely image reproduction of sensorimotor space. Already capable of dealing concretely with a practical space which has been progressively acquired during the first two years of his development, the child again finds himself at the beginning of the task as soon as the appearance of the symbolic function leads him to regulate his spatial behavior through a system of total representation of his displacements rather than according to simple motor expectations. By virtue of a fundamental *décalage,* the child must reconquer the obstacles already overcome on the plane of practical action, but this time on the level of representation. It is for this reason that perfect mastery of representational space—that is, the construction of operational space—is preceded by a long period during which the child's spatial representations are still subject to the distortions born of the irreversible and static character of intuitive or preoperational thought.

It is precisely this period, spread between the ages of about two and twelve years, which is the object of the present study. There are only a very few works which deal directly with tracing the steps of this evolution; more numerous are partial studies, limited to certain very particular aspects of the concept of space and almost never integrated into a comprehensive theoretical framework. Ames and Learned (1948), for example, studied the development of "verbalized" space in the child of about two to four years of age. They made a stenographic accounting of the use of terms having a spatial reference (e.g., "up," "down," "here," "there," "over," "between," etc.) by children engaged in spontaneous or induced play; they also used a series of individual questions covering the location of familiar persons or objects, previously visited places, different rooms of the house or of the residential area, etc. The results showed a fairly constant development, with age, in the frequency of certain terms (e.g., "up" and "down" are among the earliest to appear, and "between" and "outside" are among the last), as well as in the accuracy of responses to a questionnaire (e.g., "Where do you sleep?" gets an accurate response fairly early, while "Where is the kitchen?" is not answered correctly even at four years). Yet this study is limited to the purely verbal level of spatial intelligence and it is not always easy to distinguish what is dependent on mere information from what is more dependent on a real comprehension of spatial relations. In sum, as in other of the Terman or Gesell type of developmental scales, works of this nature are purely descriptive: they are not integrated into a larger theoretical context and are intended simply to catalogue the behavior spread through the age levels without trying to explain the mechanisms underlying the appearance and order of these various types of behavior.

Other works pursue more specific and more interesting objectives; nevertheless, their repercussions are more practical than theoretical and they deal even less closely with the problem of the development of space in the child. Thus Flickinger and Rehage (1949) report a group of studies designed to show that before the age of eleven or twelve years and even later, it is only with the greatest difficulty that children succeed in orienting themselves in space (cardinal points, positions of principal monuments in a city, relative location of neighboring towns, map reading, understanding geographical terms, etc.). Quite varied and often very ingenious, these studies are nevertheless motivated mainly by concerns of a pedagogical nature: they reveal the gaps inherent in the traditional teaching of geography, but they have no direct bearing on the specific problem of the conceptualization of space.

DEVELOPMENT OF REPRESENTATIONAL SPACE ACCORDING TO PIAGET

Piaget, in fact, seems to be the only investigator to have systematically studied the development of representational space in the child. It would be impossible to summarize the two volumes which are specifically concerned with this question (Piaget and Inhelder, 1948; Piaget, Inhelder, and Szeminska, 1948); but, because these works directly inspired the experiments reported here, it is necessary to review, at least in outline, the major points of Piaget's view of the child's spatial representations.

STEPS IN THE CONSTRUCTION OF REPRESENTATIONAL SPACE

Spatial representation derives from sensorimotor activity, to which it is added when the appearance of the symbolic function enables the child to act not only on objects which are real and physically present in his perceptual field but also on objects which are symbolized or mentally represented. Noteworthy, however, is the fact that the mental representation is not simply the mental recollection of the objects, nor even of the action exerted on them; in the truest sense of the word it is still an action, but an action which has been internalized—that is, an implicit action which is carried out in thought on the symbolized object. To phrase it differently, to recall an object mentally is to reproduce or to sketch this

object in thought, and this mental activity is not limited to representing an external action or the result of this action, but it actively
reconstructs it and extends it directly to the symbolic level. It is for
this reason, as Piaget asserts, that spatial representation is not a substitute for spatial action but is rather the symbolic and internalized
expression of it.

> To arrange objects mentally is not merely to imagine a series of
> things already set in order, nor even to imagine the action or arrang-
> ing them. It means arranging the series, just as positively and actively
> as if the action were physical, but performing the action internally on
> symbolic objects. This is why a child finds it quite easy to arrange
> counters on the table . . . [easier] than to imagine it, while at the
> same time he finds it easy to imagine he is triumphing over an op-
> ponent in a game but more difficult to defeat him in reality: spatial
> concepts are internalized actions (as are any logical concepts) whereas
> imaginary play is merely a substitute for actions [Piaget and Inhelder,
> 1948, p. 454].[3]

Representational space in the child, then, begins with the advent of the symbolic function and is developed progressively through
a long process of internalization; Piaget has attempted to trace the
successive steps of this process, from the as yet static and irreversible
representations of the intuitive or preoperational level (approximately two to seven years) to the mobile and reversible structures of
operational thought (seven to twelve years). The internalized actions
of the beginnings of symbolic thought are not immediately coordinated into a total system, nor do they have the mobility and reversibility which characterize the true mental operation. They are still
subject, for quite a while, to the limiting conditions of perceptual
or sensorimotor activity. These first representations evoke merely
the successive states or temporary configurations resulting from
simple physical actions which have already been carried out on real
objects. In the continuation of this process, but always at the preoperational level, these representations begin to refer to more complex physical actions and to coordinate among themselves to give
rise to certain rudimentary and isolated transformations, though
these transformations have no total structure and are not reversible.
It is not until the operational level (about seven years) that thought

3 The year refers to the original publication and the page number to the English
edition.

can disengage itself from the necessary limitations of the image: the internalized actions thus become completely mobile and reversible and are transformed into operations which are at first concrete (that is, dependent on the presence of manipulable objects, real or represented) and later formal and completely removed from real actions.

Between sensorimotor space and operational space, we must interject a preoperational space which Piaget calls *intuitive*, characterized by an internalization of spatial schemata already formed by sensorimotor intelligence—an internalization which is at first a purely static and fragmentary one and which becomes increasingly mobile and structured. This slow development covers the whole of early childhood, from about two to seven years, and culminates in the birth of operational space when articulation of the intuitive schemata acquires sufficient mobility and flexibility for the internalized actions to become fully reversible mental operations. Between sensorimotor space and operational space, then, the sequence is continuous: internalization of the spatial actions of the sensorimotor level gives rise to intuitive space, and the progressive mobility of the intuitive structures of the preoperational level eventually culminates in operational space. In sum, the development of representational space is a long progression from action to operation.

SPATIAL RELATIONS TO BE CONSTRUCTED

Analysis of space then leads Piaget to distinguish three major types of relations, based on the lessons of contemporary geometry, and to set about tracing their development in the child. First to be considered are the relations embodying *metric* (or Euclidian) space, which is based mainly on the concept of distance and in which the equivalence of figures depends on their mathematical equality. In *projective* space, on the contrary, it is the concept of the straight line which serves as the basis of spatial relationships, and it is perspective or the possibility of perspective transformation which insures the equivalence of figures. Finally, *topological* space depends on the purely qualitative relations (e.g., neighborhood, separation, ordinal relationship, closure, etc.) inherent in a particular figure: two figures are seen as equivalent when one is homeomorphous to the other by virtue of a simple continuous deformation excluding any tear or overlap. Thus Piaget asserts more than once (e.g., Piaget and Inhelder, 1948; Piaget, 1950) that the development of child space appears to reproduce the stages necessary for mathematical construction itself, wherein topological relations are the most basic —though the last to be discovered by mathematicians—and precede the projective and Euclidian structures which derive from them. Considering a group of experiments on the growth of these three types of spatial relationships, he concludes that topological representations are the first to evolve as mental operations in the child, while projective and Euclidian operations are created and appear only with a temporal *décalage*—a *décalage* which is considerable in comparison to the topological operations. These latter are limited to the inherent properties of a particular object (simple or complex) without further requiring that the subject locate the object in relation to others, neither in terms of a particular perspective or point of view (projective space) nor in terms of a system of axes or coordinates (Euclidian space). In all three cases, the first spatial operations available to the child between about six and nine years of age derive from representations which are increasingly better coordinated at the intuitive level, themselves deriving from sensorimotor actions and continually nourished by the child's perceptual activities.

Considering first the case of *topological* space, the elementary perception and active manipulation of relationships within the field —relations of separation, order, closure, etc.—serve as a point of departure to the structured representations of intuitive space up to the time when the first reversible and operational systems are established (generally around the age of seven years). These systems include partition and partitive addition (e.g., the concept of point and continuum), linear or cyclical ordering, reciprocity of neighboring areas, symmetrical relations, and multiplication of elements or relations. As concerns *projective* space, which adds to topological space the necessity of locating objects or the elements of a single object in relation to each other within a given perspective, the same general development occurs as in the case of topological relationships but with a slight temporal *décalage*. The child has already learned to manipulate certain projective relations at the level of perceptual activity and sensorimotor intelligence, as is seen in the very early development of size and shape constancy despite the distortions imposed by the variability of distances and perspectives. With the aid of the image representations of the intuitive level, coordination of the fragmentary projective relationships progressively acquires more flexibility and efficiency, but it requires another several years before an operational system of projective references can be organized which will assure the perfect coordination of perspectives and the reversibility of points of view. The topological operations already established are enriched by the addition of the projective relationships and assume new significance: for example, the intervention of perspective transforms the concept of linear order into a concept of rectilinear order (e.g., projection of the straight line) and the reciprocity of neighboring regions into the reciprocity of perspectives. There remains to be considered briefly the case of *Euclidian* (metric) space. Euclidian space also derives from topological space and is constructed parallel with projective space, from which it is distinct but to which it is closely related. While projective space is limited to coordinating different perspectives of an object and adjusts itself to these variations in apparent size, Euclidian space coordinates the objects among themselves with reference to a total framework or to a stable reference system which also requires a conservation of surfaces and distances. But it is quite clear that this conservation of Euclidian relations would not be possible without the concomitant structuring of projective relations: conservation of distances or of surfaces obviously implies reciprocity or symmetry of perspectives. It is for this reason that the development of Euclidian space is parallel to that of projective space. Already established during the first conquests of perceptual activity (e.g., visual reference systems, the first size and shape constancies, etc.) and practically organized at the level of sensorimotor intelligence (e.g., object permanence, detour behavior, labyrinths, use of instruments), Euclidian relations begin internalizing and coordinating at the intuitive level but for a long while remain subject to the distortions produced by the static and irreversible character of the image representations. It is only at the level of concrete operations that the first real conservations appear (e.g., surfaces, lengths, distances, etc.), and these conservations are required for the subsequent development of a space which is properly metric and quantified (e.g., measurement of length, surface, volume, etc.).

OBJECTIVES OF THE PRESENT WORK

Although summary, this account of Piaget's position on the development of space nevertheless suffices both to reduce somewhat the confusion surrounding this problem and to clarify the import of the present study by formulating its objectives.

Piaget's explanation has the great merit of being included in a complete theoretical system which supports it and of which it is also a principal element. This developmental analysis of space, based on ingenious experiments which are remarkable for their internal consistency, has been relatively little known and undisputed since its formulation. To what may we attribute this long silence? It should be pointed out that Piaget's works on the development of space, like the rest of his work, are not readily accessible. His style is both quite dense and very profuse, and he describes the most concrete observations (such as, for example, a child stringing beads or sucking his thumb) in as much detail as he discusses the most abstract problems (such as the primacy of the topological in mathematical thought). It is easy to understand that Piaget's frequent excursions into the realm of logic and epistemology, however necessary they may be for explaining the facts and constructing a complete theory of knowledge, may baffle the superficial reader, confuse the lazy reader, or irritate the hurried reader. The difficulties posed by the absence or inadequacies of translations, and by the still too-insular character of most national psychologies, only further complicate the situation.

Another factor which might somewhat explain the relative ignorance which surrounds the Piagetian theory of the development of space is the distrust shown in certain circles, notably in America, toward his experimental techniques. It has become the fashion to emphasize the overly free and suggestive character of his testing methods, the weakness of his samples, the paucity of his statistical analyses, the imprecision of his experimental conditions, etc. This is not the place to evaluate the truths and errors contained within these often severe and often even abusive criticisms. However, it is fair to mention that not all these criticisms are equally important, varying according to whether they are directed to the first or to the latest of Piaget's works or to his work on the development of perception. We should also point out that Piaget is, intentionally, uninterested in individual differences and the normative aspect of mental development. And, finally, some systematic replications[4] of some of his experiments, particularly those on precausality (Laurendeau and Pinard, 1962), on various aspects of operational thought (Elkind, 1961a, 1961b, 1961c, 1961d, 1962, 1964), and on sensorimotor development (Gouin-Décarie, 1962) have supported his initial conclusions; in many cases, the results which do differ from Piaget's may be explained by differences in materials, techniques of analysis, etc. We believe that the value of an experimental method is measured not by the abundance or subtlety of the statistical analyses it may favor but by the theoretical significance of the conclusions it may reach, and by the richness of the information it provides or the new hypotheses it suggests. In this respect, it would be futile to make any comparisons between Piaget's synthesis and the rather fragmentary studies which are currently flooding the journals.

Finally, one last factor deserves mention. If Piaget's works on the development of space have been relatively ignored, this may be because he has introduced some fundamental distinctions into this domain (e.g., perceptual space *versus* intellectual space, sensorimotor space *versus* representational space, etc.) which have uniquely upset the previously established knowledge and have led to the re-examination of a large body of experimental findings. Most of the works published in the area of space do not go beyond the level of perception or sensorimotor intelligence. This is particularly the case with the innumerable studies of the manipulation of spatial relations by the animal or the very young infant. The fascination with exclusively nonverbal techniques, stimulated by a concern for objectivity, leads investigators to question the use of problems or methods which require subjects to verbalize their solution procedures if they are able to do so. Resorting to increasingly impersonal or automated experimental methods may be seductive in its technical ingenuity. But in attempting to exclude systematically any verbal intervention on the part of the subject and the examiner as well, one eliminates the possibility of easily discovering the real level of functioning (e.g., perceptual, sensorimotor, intuitive, practical, etc.) which the subject relies on in solving the given problem.

---

[4] The major references to these works may be found in Becker (1962), Bell (1965), Brown (1965), Kagan and Henker (1966), Maccoby (1964), Reingold and Stanley (1963), and Wallach (1963).

To a certain extent, one eliminates even more surely any possibility of verifying the very existence of these different levels. In sum, rather than being dissipated, the initial confusion is being camouflaged by the trappings of objectivity, and "statistical significance" becomes a substitute for the psychological significance of the results.

Whatever may be the real importance of these different factors, there is no doubt that those of Piaget's works which are specifically concerned with the child's representation of space are still little known and rarely cited. Certain authors do not fail to make an occasional reference (e.g., Brown, 1965; Flavell, 1963; Russell, 1956), but very few are concerned with confirming or refuting them. The infrequent studies which are directly related to those of Piaget, such as the works of Dodwell (1963), Lovell (1959, 1961), or Lovell, Healey, and Rowland (1962) on the development of topological and projective space, as well as those of Meyer (1935, 1940) on projective space, will be discussed later when each of these particular aspects is examined.

Nevertheless, we must concede that Piaget and Inhelder's general conclusions on the development of space still await experimental confirmation. They depend too often on experimental facts which do not satisfy some of the scientific standards of uniformity of the testing methods (problematical in the work done in Geneva), the size and qualities (often not specified) of the samples, the equivalence (not guaranteed) of the groups selected to represent each age level, etc. The uneasiness caused by the lack of precision in these different methodological aspects of Piaget and Inhelder's research demands replication of at least a sample of these experiments in better-defined and more rigorous methodological frameworks. Furthermore, it sometimes happens that the facts accumulated in the course of their experiments do not merit the direct application of Piaget and Inhelder's conclusions. One notes that, for example, logical arguments (of disputable value, even by admission of the authors) may be substituted for the testimony of facts until experimental demonstration appears and can replace them. In this respect we should mention the allusions to the tenuousness of the ties which unite the multiple aspects of a single concept, or two different concepts, from a developmental point of view; these allusions are particularly frequent in the case of spatial concepts but appear in other contexts as well. In certain cases, the necessary relationship between two behaviors (or structures) is asserted, the first to appear being conceived as the prerequisite for the appearance of the second; in other cases, an absolute complementarity or continuous inter-actionism may be asserted, which leads to postulating an entirely concomitant development. We know that the tests designed by Piaget and Inhelder for examining the various aspects of the development of intellectual concepts were always administered to different groups of children. Consequently it was not possible to determine the presence or absence of concurrent processes which might reveal the actual degree of relationship between the different aspects of intellectual development. At most we could claim an agreement or an asynchrony in the average age at which different groups of children, each subjected to a different test, arrive at different phases in the development of each of these aspects. These chronological agreements might be valuable reasons for believing in the links between concepts, inasmuch as they may recur several times; it is still true, however, that these group comparisons will never be as strong as demonstrations based on longitudinal studies or on correlations drawn from the results of a single group of subjects submitted to a variety of tests.

It is within this dual perspective that the present study is situated. Some of Piaget and Inhelder's experiments on the development of space will be replicated in a new experimental context, requiring particularly a standardization of the materials and of the testing conditions, as well as the formation of subject groups representative of the general population. The new results generated in this more rigorous methodological framework will permit an evaluation of Piaget and Inhelder's general conclusions and of the criticisms directed against them. In addition, the several tests chosen will all be administered to the same group of subjects. It will thus be possible to study the genetic interdependence of the various aspects which they cover. To these general objectives is added also a detailed discussion of questions of a more limited scope which are raised with each experimental situation. Finally, although it is not one of the main interests motivating the present work, the normative dimension provided by analysis of the behavior of children of several successive ages in a series of operational tasks has every chance of attracting the attention of practicing psychologists, who have long been awaiting this complement in order to substitute (or simply add) these operational tests to the more traditional psychometric instruments which they are currently using.

EXPERIMENTAL PROGRAM

Devising an experimental program to cover the objective just formulated involved general decisions concerning both the choice of tests to use and the experimental procedure as a whole (subjects, experimental conditions, and analysis of results), as well as specific options regarding the nature of each of the tests used in the study. Only the former will be discussed in this chapter, which must serve as an introduction to all the chapters which follow. Discussion of the methodological aspects proper to each of the tests is covered in the chapters which deal specifically with them.

SELECTION OF THE TESTS

In testing Piaget and Inhelder's conclusions on the development of intellectual space, it was necessary to select a good sample of the tests which they themselves had used in studying this particular aspect of development. Two circumstances made this choice particularly difficult. For one thing, it was necessary to restrict the number of tests to a minimum because they had to be included in a group having a more general scope which demanded that all the important dimensions of intellectual development be explored. Yet the richness of the range of tests to be selected from was remarkable. In their studies on the construction of intellectual space, Piaget and Inhelder gave free rein to the ingenuity which they habitually show in designing their experimental techniques; this was required first because the construction of space is the fruit of a long genetic process which begins in the sensorimotor activities of the first months of life (Piaget, 1937) and which is not completed until adolescence (Piaget and Inhelder, 1948; Piaget, Inhelder, and Szeminska, 1948), and also because, at the level of representation alone, this construction covers three groups of concepts each of which defines a whole sphere in itself. It would have been unrealistic, in these circumstances, to think of testing all the genetic phases implicit in the structuring of space from the sensorimotor period up to the formal operations. The only area which will be explored here is the very crucial period running from the beginning of mental representation to the mastery of the first operations of conceptual intelligence. Thus the study will cover exclusively the evolution of intuitive space and the achievement of operational space.

This decision made, a group of both theoretical and practical considerations determined the selection of eight particular tests. Each test had to be able to reach one of the three crucial aspects of child space as directly as possible and at the same time lend itself to the transformations required by the standardization of the material and testing procedure, and to do so without introducing major technical difficulties or defeating its own end. Of these eight tests, two deal primarily with the development of topological space: the test of *Stereognostic recognition of objects and forms,* which theoretically should demonstrate the primitive character of topological relations over Euclidian relations, and *Localization of topographical positions,* which illustrates the shift from topological concepts to projective and Euclidian concepts. Three tests directly examine the construction of projective space: *Construction of a projective straight line,* which deals with the representation of the straight line, the basis of all projective space, the development of *Concepts of left and right,* which is related to the relativistic aspect of the points of view which are implicit in projective space, and the *Coordination of perspectives,* which describes the progressive coordination of the different points of view possible in a group of three objects. Finally, the last three tests investigate the formation of the first operational systems of Euclidian space: *Conservation of length, Conservation of distance,* and *Conservation of surface,* whose acquisition is presupposed in the subsequent development of metric and fully quantified space. It should be noted, however, that these last three tests are not integrated into the present work but will be presented in a later study covering the general problem of those invariants in thought which are the conservations. They are mentioned here only to prevent the reader from thinking that the range of the tests is grossly incomplete. The detailed descriptions and accounts of the theoretical bases of each of the five tests included in the present study are contained in the chapters which follow.

EXPERIMENTAL PROCEDURE

If we may refer the reader to a previous work on the development of causal thinking (Laurendeau and Pinard, 1962), the expla-

nation of the experimental procedure may be reduced to a minimum. The subjects, the experimental conditions, and the methods
of analysis are the same in both cases and are fully described in the
work just cited. It should suffice here to summarize only the major
points.

Subjects were 50 children at each of the chronological ages between two and 12 years inclusive, distributed at six-month intervals
up to the age of five years and at twelve-month intervals after that
point. At each age level, subjects were distributed according to sex,
father's occupation, and level in school (or number of children in
the family in the case of the preschool children), so as to reproduce
exactly the proportions established by the French Canadian population census for the city of Montreal. In the preceding study on causal
thinking, only children between four and 12 years were examined,
because of the almost exclusively verbal nature of the questionnaires
used at that time. In the present study, the use of concrete material
and the simplicity of the instructions and the questionnaires made
most of the tests accessible to much younger children. Furthermore,
given the fact that several of these tests (such as *Construction of a
projective straight line, Stereognostic recognition of objects and
shapes,* and even the *Localization of topographical positions* test)
deal with spatial concepts which have already begun to develop before the age of four years, the examination had to begin at the earliest ages, even at the risk of later having to ignore results which may
be judged too inconsistent. Table 1 shows the distribution of subjects of preschool age, and Table 2 shows the distribution of the
school-age subjects.

The experimental conditions were also identical to those in the
experiments reported in the earlier study on causal thinking. The
five tests included were administered individually. They were scattered, in no particular order, within a longer series of 27 tests spread
across several successive testing sessions. The examiners were all
graduate students in psychology, specifically trained in this sort of
testing. Children of preschool age were examined at home, and the
others were tested in school.

For each of the five tests, the *analysis of the results* includes two
principal measures. The first deals with determining the relative
difficulty of the problems (or questions) in the test and allows us to

Table 1

Distribution of preschool subjects by age, sex, father's occupation,* and number of children in the family (N=400)

Age	Number of children in the family	Occupational category												Total	
		1		2		3		4		5		6			
		F	M	F	M	F	M	F	M	F	M	F	M	F	M
2:0	1	1	1	0	1	1	0	2	3	1	0	0	1	5	6
	2	2	2	1	0	1	1	4	4	0	1	1	0	9	8
	3+	3	1	1	1	0	1	5	7	1	0	1	1	11	11
2:6	1	1	1	0	1	1	0	2	3	1	0	0	1	5	6
	2	2	2	1	0	0	1	4	4	0	1	1	0	8	8
	3+	3	1	1	1	1	1	5	7	1	0	1	1	12	11
3:0	1	1	1	1	0	1	0	2	3	1	0	1	0	7	4
	2	2	2	0	1	0	1	4	3	0	1	1	0	7	8
	3+	1	3	1	1	1	1	7	6	0	1	1	1	11	13
3:6	1	1	1	1	0	1	0	2	2	1	0	0	1	6	4
	2	2	2	0	1	0	1	3	4	0	1	1	0	6	9
	3+	2	2	1	1	1	1	7	7	1	0	1	1	13	12
4:0	1	1	1	0	1	0	1	2	2	0	1	1	0	4	6
	2	2	2	1	0	0	1	4	3	1	0	0	1	8	7
	3+	2	2	1	1	1	1	7	7	1	0	1	1	13	12
4:6	1	1	1	1	0	0	1	2	2	0	0	1	0	5	4
	2	1	2	1	0	0	1	3	4	1	0	1	0	7	7
	3+	3	2	1	1	1	1	7	7	1	1	0	2	13	14
5:0	1	1	1	0	1	1	0	2	2	0	0	0	1	4	5
	2	1	2	1	0	0	1	3	3	1	0	1	0	7	6
	3+	3	2	1	1	1	1	7	8	1	1	1	1	14	14
6:0	1	1	1	0	0	0	1	1	2	0	0	0	0	2	4
	2	2	2	0	1	1	0	3	3	0	1	1	0	7	7
	3+	3	3	2	0	0	2	8	7	1	1	1	2	15	15

*Classification in six categories: 1. Proprietary, managerial, professional; 2. Clerical; 3. Commercial, financial; 4. Manufacturing, mechanical, construction, transportation, communication; 5. Service; 6. Laborers.

regroup these problems into hierarchical categories which then delimit the various stages or levels of development. The methods applied to this part of the analysis of results are extremely simple: they almost always consist of percentage calculations and the application of the usual statistical tests to determine the significance of the observed difference. The second measure deals directly with classifying the protocols into stages or levels of development which are as homogeneous as possible. For a description and discussion of the methods applied in this second measure, the reader is referred to the previously cited work on causal thought. Suffice it to mention that in each test, the age of accession to each stage of the scale can be determined only if the distribution of median ages corresponding to each of these stages allows us to assume transitivity. The age of

Table 2

Distribution of school-age subjects by age, sex, father's occupation,* and level in school (N=300)

Age	Sex	Occupational category						School grade							Un-graded	Total
		1	2	3	4	5	6	1	2	3	4	5	6	7		
7:0	F	6	2	2	12	1	2	14	11							25
	M	6	1	2	12	2	2	15	10							25
8:0	F	6	2	2	12	1	2	2	13	10						25
	M	6	1	2	12	2	2	2	14	9						25
9:0	F	6	2	2	12	1	2	0	3	13	9					25
	M	6	1	2	12	2	2	1	3	12	9					25
10:0	F	7	2	2	12	1	2		1	4	13	8				26
	M	5	1	2	12	2	2		1	4	11	8				24
11:0	F	6	2	2	12	1	2			1	5	12	7	0		25
	M	6	1	2	12	2	2			2	5	11	6	1		25
12:0	F	6	2	2	12	1	2			0	2	5	11	6	1	25
	M	6	1	2	12	2	2			1	2	6	10	5	1	25

*See footnote to Table 1.

accession is defined as the age at which at least 50 per cent of the subjects are found for the first time in the distribution.

In addition to this specific study of the five tests individually, we include a final broader study, based principally on a hierarchical analysis of both the interdependence of the various concepts reached by the five tests and their relationship to the various aspects of pre-causal thought.

Chapter II

Stereognostic Recognition of Objects and Shapes: Presentation of the Test

The first of the five tests seeks to demonstrate the development of the most elementary concepts of topological space and particularly the genetic primacy of these concepts in relation to Euclidian concepts. This chapter begins with some considerations of a theoretical nature and includes a detailed description of the experiment and an analysis of the results.

THEORETICAL CONTEXT

In studying the development of topological space, Piaget and Inhelder (1948) used several complementary techniques, each designed to investigate a particular aspect of topological representation: direct or inverse reproduction of a linear or cyclical row of beads (relationships of neighborhood and order); practical recognition of knots (relationships of covering); unlimited division and reconstruction of a figure or a line (concept of point and continuum); tactile recognition of objects and shapes (general topological relationships of all kinds); etc. After several preliminary experiments it was this last technique which was finally selected. The test itself is not enough to demonstrate the development of real topological operations, but the discrimination of Euclidian relations, whose progressive development may be traced through this test, implies the application of exploratory procedures which themselves presuppose an operational sort of coordination. Furthermore, the technique has the triple advantage of (a) permitting investigation of some of the most general types of topological relationships, (b) demonstrating the role of the image in the transition from perception to representation, and (c) clearly illustrating the difference between topological and Euclidian relationships. Finally, it is relatively easy to standardize the administration and scoring of the test: the materials and instructions are quite simple and the analysis of the protocols does not require the additional evaluation of the children's drawings, which is most instructive but quite difficult.

The technique proposed by Piaget is not a novel one, although he used it in the investigation of completely new theoretical problems. To cite one example among many, by 1933 Cutsforth had used stereognosis in determining the relative importance of tactile and visual elements in normal adult perception. The subjects were to try to adjust the dimensions of a movable rectangle to match those of other rectangles which they could touch but could not see. The method of exploring the rectangle which was touched was sometimes left very open and at other times limited to simple prehension. Cutsforth concluded from his experiments that, in a seeing subject, perception is never exclusively tactile and is never completely separable from visual perception. The stereognostic technique has been used by other authors as well, and with younger subjects, but the objectives are almost never of a developmental nature and most of the time are limited to the purely perceptual level. Thus Strauss and Lehtinen (1947) were interested in tactile perception of the figure-ground relation in children suffering from cerebral lesions, while Ross (1954) sought to determine the degree of "completion" which certain geometric figures must have before children (also with cerebral lesions in this case) are able to recognize them by touch. More recently, Hermelin and O'Connor (1961) and, following them, Medinnus and Johnson (1966), compared normal and retarded children, in mental age between about four and eight years, in a task of tactile and visual recognition of shapes which were completely foreign to the subject's experience (Greek and Russian letters or blocks with undefined shapes). In some of the subjects, both exploration and recognition used the same sensory modality (tactile or visual); in the others, the shape first explored by touch had to be recognized by sight or, conversely, the shape first explored visually had to be recognized by touch. The results show no significant differences between normal and retarded subjects, nor between the various experimental conditions, except in the case of exclusively stereognostic recognition (from tactile to tactile), where the retarded children, contrary to all expectations, are superior to the normals. The authors suggest that the results are explainable by the fact that, in their experience, the translation of the tactile into the visual (or its converse) does not require verbal decoding, and they emphasize the possibility that the development of stereognosis, as compared with visual development, may be relatively intact in the mentally retarded.

The work of Worchel (1951) on spatial perception in blind subjects (those born blind and those blinded after birth), as compared with seeing subjects, deserves special mention. For example, Worchel asked his subjects to sketch or to recognize by touch from among other figures some blocks of a simple geometric shape (e.g., square, circle, triangle, ellipse, crescent, parallelogram, etc.) which they had previously touched. The subjects were between the ages of eight and twenty years (average age fifteen years). The results indicate a clear superiority of the seeing subjects over the blind subjects in general, and in particular a superiority of those blinded later over those born blind in the ability verbally to describe or graphically reproduce shapes. These conclusions clearly suggest the importance of the role of visual imagery, an importance which is further confirmed by the subjects' own introspective reports as well as by the strong correlations which were observed, among the blind children, between the age when blindness began and the accuracy of verbal or graphic responses. Purely tactile recognition, on the other hand, is almost perfect in the blind children as well as in the seeing subjects: this lack of difference between the two groups may be partially explained by the relatively higher age of the subjects and by the inherent simplicity of a simple tactile matching which does not necessarily imply a representational intermediary. It is possible that the solution is found at the simple level of perceptual activity without requiring that tactile or visual imagery play a decisive role, though it may intervene by chance. It is interesting to note also that the most difficult shapes to reproduce, for the blind as well as the seeing subjects, are the parallelogram, the ellipse, and the crescent; the easiest for the seeing is the square, and for the blind subjects the square and the circle. Worchel got very similar results with a slightly different technique requiring the subject to recognize by touch the aggregate shape resulting from joining two incomplete shapes which he had touched at the beginning.

In the same context, Hatwell (1959) compared blind and seeing subjects, aged from six to seventeen or eighteen years, who were asked to recognize by touch, from among three or four others, a more or less complex geometric shape (e.g., squares, circles, etc., each shape capable of being used individually or variously combined with the others). The material included two series of 10 shapes each: one was of small dimensions (2 x 2 cm.) and the forms were glued to a small board; the other was larger (4 x 4 cm.) and only the outlines of these shapes were delineated, in a raised relief similar to that of the Braille method. The results of this experiment are less clear than Worchel's, but Hatwell's analysis is remarkable in its finesse and perceptiveness. Hatwell observes that in fact the blind subjects as a whole are superior only in recognizing the larger shapes, but that even this difference is insignificant in the case of the subjects blind from birth. The superiority of the blind subjects is thus due primarily to the success of the children blinded later. To what can these apparently erratic findings be attributed? The fact that the superiority of blind subjects appears only in the case of the larger forms would seem to arise from the blind children's greater training in coordinating their tactile exploration procedures, especially when the stimuli are presented in the familiar Braille method; but this factor alone is not enough and must be backed by the role of visual imagery—the superiority of the later-blinded subjects over those blind from birth, and the absence of any superiority of the subjects blind from birth over the seeing subjects, would testify to this. When it is a question of the small forms, on the other hand, tactile exploration is equally available to the seeing subjects and the blind children, and all significant differences then disappear. Worchel had observed the same phenomenon elsewhere. In the case of the later-blinded subjects, as Hatwell carefully points out, visual imagery does not necessarily intervene at the very moment of the test, since there had been a span of five years between the onset of blindness and the administration of the test (blindness began at about four years). We should rather consider that during the two years preceding blindness the visual imagery facilitated the structuring of the child's first spatial representations. When tactile organization alone becomes available, it is then more easily integrated into the visual systems already established; thus the child who is not blinded until relatively long after birth has resources which are not available to the child who is blind from birth.

Hatwell also required his subjects to reproduce, using material which can be fastened to a wooden board (e.g., sticks, etc.), certain patterns which the subjects had been able to touch immediately before or 30 seconds before. Results obtained by this method seem to confirm the complementary roles of visual imagery and tactile exploration. Here again the children who have been blind from birth are clearly at a disadvantage in relation to the later-blinded children, which again illustrates the importance of the role of visual imagery. Nevertheless, if we compare the seeing subjects with the blind subjects in general, or the seeing subjects and those blinded after birth in particular, the differences are not significant, revealing the importance of tactile exploration in a situation where manipulation of the material must rely solely on tactile indices.

Moreover, in the course of a complementary experiment reported by Hatwell in the same work, a new group of seeing subjects, aged seven and one-half years on the average, had to recognize the same forms as in the first experiment after having felt them beforehand; but the subject must now visually find the shapes from among a choice of others glued to a board (small shapes) or outlined in black and white (large shapes). The results obtained on these subjects are immediately superior to those of the blind or the seeing subjects of the first experiment. The translation from tactile to visual, which is necessary in this condition, undoubtedly stimulates tactile exploration and facilitates recognition. The method of reproduction, replicated exactly with these new subjects except for the removal of the screen, again yielded clearly superior results.

Finally, Hatwell completed her study with a special analysis of the *square* and the *rhombus,* comparing the abilities of seeing and blind subjects to reproduce these shapes, by graphic sketch or by means of the sticks used in the above experiment, when the shapes had been touched beforehand. The results showed that for all subjects, accurate reproduction of the rhombus comes much later than that of the square, and seeing subjects are always superior to blind ones.

The major interest of these works on stereognostic perception in the blind (see also Ewart and Carp, 1963) is to demonstrate the complementary roles of visual imagery and tactile exploration in the normal person. They serve also to confirm in another way the results of research done on normal children and adults focusing on the problem of intersensory transfer in the construction of mental images, a problem which seems noticeably to preoccupy contemporary Soviet psychology (see E. Gibson, 1963; Zaporozhets, 1965). The stereognostic method is thus quite appropriate to the study of the child's spatial representations; it is for this reason that Piaget uses it, but he uses it for ends heretofore completely ignored and derives results whose theoretical significance has long escaped—and continues to escape—the attention of several specialists in the field. At first, stereognosis was for Piaget simply an excellent instrument of developmental analysis; while it is used particularly with relatively older subjects, or with pathological cases, Piaget is more interested in the normal development of the child's spatial representations, and does not hesitate to trace the evolution of stereognosis back to the very beginnings of infancy. Further, this interest in the developmental aspect is not limited to the simple declaration of a progressive improvement in tactile recognition with age, as seen in Worchel's and Hatwell's correlations among relatively older subjects; rather, Piaget undertakes a qualitative analysis of child space and introduces into it modern geometry's distinction between topological and Euclidian relations. He then proposes the hypothesis that the psychogenesis of the child's spatial relations, rather than recapitulating the historical evolution of geometry (which proceeds from Euclidian to topological), must instead reflect the very structure of mathematical thinking in which topological relations form the basis and starting point of projective and Euclidian relations. Such a hypothesis considerably changes the significance of the usual studies; these have almost all been based on the postulate of the primacy of Euclidian relations, as is evident in the predominant use of geometric shapes whenever anyone in either animal or human psychology wants to study the ability to discriminate spatial relations. Finally, for Piaget, stereognosis is not always limited to the simple translation from tactile into visual perception, a phenomenon which is rather early in appearing and which Piaget has been able to demonstrate as developing well before the appearance of representational thought in the child—coordination of prehension and vision, studied at the sensorimotor level of intelligence (Piaget, 1936), provides numerous examples of this. But if a child is asked to sketch, or visually to recognize from among others, or even to identify verbally a more or less complex shape which he has previously touched, stereognosis then requires the intervention of a visual image (or at least a tactilokinesthetic one) which will both control the tactile exploration and supplement the graphic, visual, or verbal behavior. Thus joined to the symbolic function, stereognosis becomes a phenomenon which goes far beyond any simple practical adaptations of sensorimotor intelligence and the immediate tactile or visual matching to which purely perceptual activities may give rise. It is this shift from tactile perception to representation in which Piaget is directly interested in his experiments on stereognosis, and it is this shift as well which leads him to use stereognosis in studying the development of representational space in the child.

Piaget's technique is quite simple (see Piaget and Inhelder, 1948, pp. 31ff.). The child is placed behind a screen which prevents his seeing the objects that he touches while allowing the investigator to observe his exploratory tactile procedures. The child is asked to recognize, in turn: a series of common objects which he has felt but not seen (e.g., comb, key, pencil, etc.) and whose duplicates are then shown to him, as well as a series of cardboard shapes: simple symmetrical shapes (e.g., circle, square, ellipse, triangle, etc.); more complex but still symmetrical shapes (e.g., stars, semicircles, etc.); asymmetrical but rectilinear shapes (e.g., unequal quadrilateral, etc.); and shapes of a topological nature (e.g., closed or covered rings, entwined rings, etc.). The child must feel these objects or shapes and then identify them from among others or from various sketches presented to him. In some cases he is also asked to sketch the shape he has just felt. The examiner almost never intervenes except to sustain the child's motivation and encourage him to make his responses more accurate. The size of the shapes is but slightly specified by Piaget; judging by the few specifications given, however (e.g., the square at 10 cm. to a side and the circle with an 11.5 cm. diameter), they surely could not be held in a child's hand. Nor is the number of subjects indicated. As for the age of the subjects, the examples reported indicate an age spread of from about two to seven years.

The results seem to show that the progression of stereognosis can be defined by a succession of three principal stages, omitting stage O (under about two and one-half years) where experimentation is virtually impossible. At stage I (up to around three and one-half or four years), children at first recognize only familiar objects (substage IA), then are able to discriminate certain geometric shapes (substage IB), but must base these discriminations solely on topological relationships (e.g., the circle is distinguished from the open ring but not from the square). Exploration remains completely passive. In stage II (from about four to seven years), Euclidian relations are gradually differentiated. The child begins by distinguishing curvilinear from rectilinear shapes but confuses them with each other (intermediate stage between IB and IIA). A little later, he is able to recognize certain more precise Euclidian relations which at first are very simple (substage IIA: e.g., circle *versus* ellipse, square *versus* rectangle) and become more complex (substage IIB: e.g., recognition of rhombus and trapezoid). During this second stage, exploration is more and more active, although it is still rather empirical and tentative. Finally, at stage III (around seven years), the most complex shapes (e.g., various stars and crosses) are recognized, and the subject is able to coordinate all the Euclidian dimensions (size, angles, slopes, etc.). Exploration becomes more systematic and reveals the operational character of the mental activities directing it. It is interesting to note also that a second of Piaget's tests, requiring the child to draw by sight a series of patterns (of Euclidian or topological characteristics, or a combination of the two), strongly supports the order of succession of the stages as it is observed in the stereognostic tests.

Piaget sees this group of experiments as proof of the genetic primacy of topological representations over Euclidian representations. He sees, in addition, a further argument in favor of his hypothesis that the mental recollection of an object may not be simply the passive copy of it but rather a reconstruction of it which is internalized but active. Strictly speaking, the child can recall internally only what he is capable of executing externally, so that representation does not come directly from the object but rather from the actions, coordinated among themselves, which the subject carries out on this object. In sum, if representation of topological relations is earlier than that of Euclidian relations, this is basically because the actions dealing with topological relations (e.g., surrounding, enclosing, overturning, overtaking, etc.) are easier to coordinate among themselves than are the actions dealing with the Euclidian relations (e.g., aligning, measuring, maintaining direction, establishing reference points, etc.).

Of all Piaget's experiments on the concept of space, the tests of stereognosis have been the most frequently replicated. Already applied several times in various areas, the technique itself is particularly attractive because of its simplicity and the richness of the information which it can provide to anyone who can use it effectively. Yet the theoretical importance of the conclusions which Piaget draws from his experiments demands complementary studies which can confirm their accuracy and generality. Thus Page (1959) replicated the experiment on stereognosis in order to verify the order of succession of the stages which Piaget established. He used nearly the same forms as Piaget (although he complicated them a bit, particularly at the level of Euclidian relations), and he found the same stages in a group of 60 children from 2:10 to 7:9 years of age. He observed only that the dissociation of curvilinear and rectilinear shapes, which is important in Piaget's progression, was not as frequent in these subjects. As a whole, however, Page's conclusions confirm the primitive character of topological relations, whose mastery is easier at all ages but particularly so between the ages of two and four years.

Other authors are more reticent. What seems to preoccupy them the most, in all Piaget's works, is the imprecision of his experimental techniques, the smallness of his samples, and the frequent introduction of concepts or theoretical models borrowed from disciplines outside psychology. Thus Lovell (1959), replicating some of Piaget's experiments on the concept of space, lists his grievances and asks in particular whether Piaget's early interest in zoology and his growing interest in symbolic logic and mathematics have not had a determining influence on his conception of the child's mental structures. Lovell adds, perhaps a little maliciously, that the child as conceived of by Piaget would have been completely different without this initial zoological orientation and without the recent progress in certain branches of mathematical thought.

That this influence existed is undeniable; but the problem remains entirely one of whether this influence has been harmful or beneficial. It would be disastrous if, instead of providing reference frameworks for a better-directed observation and for an interpretation which is better integrated into a total system, it had had the effect of systematically distorting the observations and interpretations to the point of negating an important area of psychological realities, or of giving these realities a significance outside their real meaning. Undoubtedly it is this last possibility which disturbs Lovell. He wonders, in effect, whether the topological relations which Piaget speaks of are really topological in the mathematical sense of the term, and whether resorting to a topological language is not merely a means of translating into more precise terms certain relations which the child comes to perceive or conceive in Euclidian space and which are rather vague to begin with. In other words, Piaget would have introduced into the perceptual or mental structure of the child a coherence and a systematization which in fact do not exist. The objection is not a new one. It reflects the tendency, so rampant in developmental psychology, to conceive of mental development as a gradual accumulation of knowledge beginning with a state of initial ignorance, or as a growing differentiation of mental structures which are at first confused and quite vague and later become increasingly precise and elaborate. Thus, in the domain of causality, rather than accepting the hypothesis of a precausal thinking characteristic of the child (Piaget, 1926, 1927; Laurendeau and Pinard, 1962), there is a preference for an interpretation holding that knowledge of the external world, at first rudimentary and undifferentiated, gradually becomes more complex and elaborate, without requiring a qualitative transformation of mental structures or a break in the developmental continuity (Bruce, 1941; Huang and Lee, 1945; Klingberg, 1957). In sum, in whatever sector is considered, there is a reluctance to admit that mental functioning obeys different laws in the child and in the adult; and, to explain the difference observed in the child, such authors would rather speak of incomplete, embryonic, or as yet undifferentiated structures. This view undoubtedly reflects the influence of traditional empiricism, whose heritage still weighs heavily on developmental psychology. The child's mind is conceived of as unformed matter on which the acquisitions of experience are accumulated and articulated; this view leaves no room for the possibility of evolution creating successive levels of integration, each characterized by its own laws and the levels coordinated among one another by the continual restructuring of previous acquisitions.

Whatever may be the more general problem, the replication of Piaget's tests on stereognostic recognition, with subjects from about three to eight years of age, led Lovell to doubt the truly topological character of the child's first spatial representations. His uneasiness is inspired by two groups of facts observed in the course of his experiment. The first concerns the extreme rarity of the child's spontaneous verbalizations during his tactile exploration, as well as the baffling paucity of explanations provoked by the examiner. Compared with children studied by Piaget, Lovell's subjects are extremely stingy in commentary and their explanations may be summarized in the purely tautological *"Because I think it's like that"*— whence the impossibility of knowing, for example, whether the confusion of the circle and the square is due to the fact that both are closed figures. In sum, the child's behavior does not always directly reflect the type of mental representations on which it is based, and the investigator is forced to infer them from the purely statistical analysis of the successes and confusions.

It is in just this analysis that Lovell finds a further reason for questioning the primitive character of topological representations. The results show that in fact the curvilinear Euclidian shapes (circle, ellipse, regular and indented semicircles) are no more difficult to recognize than shapes which are really topological (open ring, entwined rings, etc.). The statistically significant overall difference observed between recognition of Euclidian shapes and recognition of topological shapes centers mainly on the presence of rectilinear Euclidian shapes, which remain confused among themselves for some time although they are soon distinguished from curvilinear shapes. It can be seen that these results partially fit those of Page (1959), discussed above, insofar as the precociousness of the rectilinear-curvilinear distinction is concerned. Lovell also replicates other experiments of Piaget's, such as drawing geometric shapes, making knots, reproducing a linear or a cyclical order, and constructing a projective line. The results of these replications will be discussed in detail in Chapters V and VII; in general, Lovell's conclusions fairly clearly support Piaget's, even though the variability of the results is much greater at all age levels. But the crucial point, which he again raises in his conclusions, concerns the genetic priority of topological relations over projective and Euclidian ones. The results of his own experiments on tactile recognition, in particular, are far from confirming Piaget's basic hypothesis. According to Lovell, it is not the so-called topological character of these shapes which facilitates their recognition but rather the presence of certain characteristics of Euclidian space itself, such as voids, corners, holes, points, projections, depressions, etc. The argument is a specious one and poses a number of problems; discussion of these issues is better left until after the presentation of the present experiment's results.

We must finally point out an ingenious experiment of Fisher (1965), who is certainly among those writers most reluctant to accept Piaget's conclusions. Fisher does not challenge the fact that young children can more easily recognize shapes of a topological than of a Euclidian character (or linear shapes, in Fisher's own phrase), but he does not accept the interpretation which Piaget gives this fact. According to him, there would exist no primacy of the topological over the Euclidian: the easier recognition of topological shapes would be tied mainly to a process of verbal mediation, the child simply having more words with which to identify (or classify) topological shapes, whose configurations have a greater variety than do linear forms. This explanation is suggested to him from reading the protocols reported by Piaget and by Page, where he notes that children much more easily recognize shapes to which they can attach the name of a concrete object.

To test his hypothesis, Fisher gave an arbitrary name (meaningless syllable) to each of the topological and linear shapes included in his experimental material and required his subjects to learn these names, presenting them first in an exclusively visual manner before proceeding to stereognosis. The control-group subjects did not learn these arbitrary names; the stereognosis experiment was, however, preceded by a visual presentation of the shapes so that at the beginning of the experiment the degree of familiarity with these shapes would be about the same for both the control subjects and the experimental subjects. The results showed that the control-group children, who were submitted to experimental conditions which were as similar as possible to those of Piaget's subjects, like Piaget's subjects recognized topological shapes more easily than linear shapes. On the other hand, in the experimental group, linear shapes were more often recognized than were topological shapes. Recognition of these topological shapes seemed even more difficult in this case than when the stereognostic experiment was not preceded by learning the arbitrary names, which led Fisher to think that, for topological shapes, this learning was harmful precisely because the new name interfered with the name which the child has already spontaneously assigned to the object.

Fisher's results, then, seem to confirm his hypothesis. Nevertheless, before accepting it and certainly before following his suggestion to replace topological primacy by Euclidian primacy in describing the development of intellectual space, it seems essential to consider some basic questions and to go on to some further verifications, some of which may be most elementary. In particular, it is difficult to see why Fisher has not profited from this design also to ask the children which names they spontaneously assigned to the various shapes presented to them. With this information he would have been able to determine the fullness of the vocabulary relating to the two families of figures and would have provided a less indirect and consequently less ambiguous proof than the one he proposes. The ambiguous nature of this proof is, among other things, due to the fact that no one knows either the factors which might have intervened in the course of the learning process or the real effects of this learning on the stereognostic experiment. In this respect it would have been useful for Fisher to report the results of this preliminary phase of the learning procedure, for they would have helped in the retention or discarding of some of the rather trite explanations which naturally come to mind. Thus, to hold to a single example, we do not know whether the children that Fisher studied showed the same difficulty in associating the arbitrary names to the linear figures and to the topological figures. Possibly, the fact that the children experienced difficulty in learning the names of the linear figures resulted in more frequent presentation of these figures. Thus, the figures may have become more familiar and, consequently, more accessible to tactilovisual recognition. As for the effects of this preliminary learning on the stereognostic task, we may still ask whether this stereognosis experiment, when it immediately follows a memorization task using the same material, is not still largely influenced—despite all the precautions taken by the examiner—by the prevailing conditions of this first memorization task; the child's effort might be oriented more toward verbal identification than toward visual recognition of forms which he has previously touched. Finally, even if the preceding objections were shown to be unfounded and if an irrefutable proof of the existence of a direct relationship between verbal identification of gometric shapes and their stereognostic recognition were provided, there would still remain the question of the meaning of this relationship and the need to explain why, in their spontaneous development, children know how to identify (or name) shapes of a topological nature earlier than they do linear forms. Confronted with a perfect correlation between the ability to name the figures and the ability to recognize them through stereognosis, we could undoubtedly conclude, as Fisher does, that it is because it can be named (classified, identified) that a figure is easy to recognize. But we could just as convincingly hold that if a figure can be identified by a name, it is because it has geometric qualities which are simple and easy to picture, such as the topological characteristics of opening, closure, continuity, etc. In other words, if it could be shown that the young child really has more words for designating shapes of a topological nature than for Euclidian shapes, this would not be enough to prove that this possession of a vocabulary is what is facilitating the recognition of the figures. It would be at least equally tenable to suppose that it is the particular attention which the child accords these topological characteristics which leads him to perceive numerous nuances between the figures defined by these relations and to adopt a differentiated vocabulary; this vocabulary would have a precision of which he is apparently not capable at the level of Euclidian shapes if he has not grasped the differences between, for example, the circle and the square, or the rectangle and the triangle.

On the whole, the criticisms which are periodically formulated regarding Piaget's theory seriously question two particular aspects of it: the chronological primacy of topological differentiations over Euclidian differentiations, and the authenticity of the child's first topological discriminations. It is to test the legitimacy of these criticisms that we have replicated these experiments with a large group of subjects and under conditions which are as rigorous as possible.

DESCRIPTION OF THE TEST

The *Stereognostic recognition of objects and shapes* test consists of three phases; only the major points will be summarized here, as the details are presented in the Appendix.

FIRST PHASE: RECOGNITION OF COMMON OBJECTS

In the first phase, the child must recognize by touch, without seeing them, a series of 11 familiar objects presented to him in turn
behind a screen which he can move his hands behind. On the first
trial the objects are presented in the following order: (1) *comb*,
(2) *key*, (3) *wooden block*, (4) *penny*, (5) *safety pin*, (6) *ball*, (7) *pencil*, (8) *pair of scissors*, (9) *spoon*, (10) *button*, (11) *glass*. The child
must simply name the object he has touched. During the second trial
(order of presentation: 1, 9, 7, 11, 5, 3, 4, 2, 6, 8, 10), he must identify the same objects, but this time by pointing them out on a card
which pictorially represents all of them. More accessible to the
younger subjects (2:0 years and 2:6 years at the most), whose verbal
expression is frequently still clumsy, this second technique seems
more apt to reveal the child's actual abilities (Benton and Schultz,
1949). Furthermore, the use of this nonverbal technique with very
simple objects prepares the subject for the two subsequent phases by
familiarizing him with establishing the relationship between the
object he has felt and its pictorial representation.

At the beginning of the study, the test included a third trial
(order of presentation: 1, 4, 7, 11, 10, 2, 6, 8, 5, 9, 3) in which the
subject was required to select the duplicate of each object from
among the group of 11 objects placed before him on the table. This
third trial was intended to control for the difficulty which the
graphic representation risked raising (e.g., imperfection of the picture, reduced scale, translation of the three-dimensional into the
two-dimensional, etc.). But examination of the first subjects very
soon demonstrated the futility of this third trial, which considerably prolonged the experiment without being very instructive. The
successes were never any more numerous than in the preceding trials
and became even less frequent as the monotony of the task and the
build-up of fatigue led the subjects to refuse to finish this last trial
and induced them to play with the material without any concern
for the instructions.

SECOND PHASE: RECOGNITION OF SHAPES
OF A TOPOLOGICAL CHARACTER

The material of the second phase consists of different shapes (see
Figure 1: first series), distinguished from each other by topological
or Euclidian relations, and presented in the following order on the

first trial: (1) *square,* (2) *disk with one hole in the center,* (3) *closed ring,* (4) *irregular cross,* (5) *triangle,* (6) *open ring,* (7) *rectangle,* (8) *Greek cross,* (9) *circle,* (10) *open rectangle,* (11) *four-cornered star,* and (12) *disk with two holes.* The child touches these figures

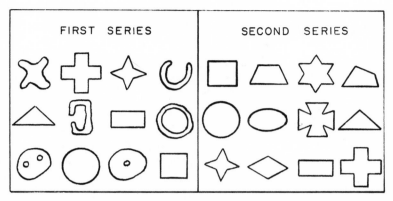

Figure 1. Shapes used in the *Stereognostic recognition of objects and shapes* test. Dimensions are proportional to those of the *circle* (diameter: 7.5 cm.).

in turn, without seeing them, and each time he must designate, on a card which pictures all of them, the one that he has just touched. In a second trial (order of presentation: 1, 10, 3, 5, 12, 6, 11, 2, 4, 7, 9, 8), the subject must choose from among the duplicates of these 12 figures, laid out before him on the table in the same order as on the card of the preceding trial. This second trial is not intended to facilitate recognition of shapes by using a less abstract method. Results of preliminary tests, confirmed by the main experiment, showed that in fact children have no more difficulty in discriminating pictures of the figures than they do the figures themselves. In fact, the second trial serves simply to test the consistency of the choices made in the first trial, and replacing the sketch card by the figures themselves helps diminish the monotony inherent in the repetition of a single task.

THIRD PHASE: RECOGNITION OF SHAPES
OF A EUCLIDIAN CHARACTER

The third phase consists of a series of 12 geometric shapes (Figure 1: second series) to be recognized by touch and presented in the following order on the first trial: (1) *circle*, (2) *Maltese cross*, (3) *square*, (4) *ellipse*, (5) *four-cornered star*, (6) *rectangle*, (7) *triangle*, (8) *irregular quadrilateral*, (9) *Greek cross*, (10) *trapezoid*, (11) *six-cornered star*, and (12) *rhombus*. The child must again recognize them on a sketch card where they are all pictured. In a second trial (order of presentation: 1, 7, 3, 2, 6, 11, 10, 9, 4, 5, 12, 8), the choice is from among the duplicates of these 12 figures which are spread out in front of the child.

Characteristic of this last phase of the experiment is thus the use of shapes whose topological differences are reduced to a minimum and which are distinguished particularly by their Euclidian or metric attributes (e.g., length of sides, size of angles, number of elements, parallelism of the sides, etc.). Half of these figures are borrowed from the preceding series and are compared this time with new figures; the advantage of this inclusion is to illustrate the importance of the available choices in recognizing a shape. The 12 patterns used in this third phase should be able to verify the successive stages which Piaget sensed in the construction of Euclidian relations: first is a gross distinction between curvilinear and rectilinear figures, soon followed by a differentiation of the circle and the ellipse but as yet with no differentiation among rectilinear forms; recognition of the simplest angular figures then follows (e.g., square, rectangle, triangle), then various types of crosses; finally comes the distinction of the most complex quadrilaterals such as the rhombus, the trapezoid, etc.

CHARACTERISTICS OF THE TEST

Like those of Lovell (1959) and Page (1959), the general technique is inspired largely by that of Piaget and Inhelder. It holds to that basic principle but is distinguished from it by certain important points which should be discussed here. In the first place, the possible choices are not limited solely to several figures or objects which conform to the most typical of the children's mistakes, as in Piaget's technique and probably those of Lovell and Page; on the contrary, for each object he has touched, the subject must choose from among all the objects of the series concerned. The procedure has the drawback, particularly among the youngest subjects, of favoring a certain type of randomness because the child's restricted field of attention keeps him from simultaneously considering all the choice elements presented to him. This drawback is compensated for not only by the simplification of the practical conditions of the test, but especially by the specifications of a theoretical nature which the procedure of constant choices makes possible. In fact, the difficulty inherent in the recognition of an object depends equally on the very structure of that object and on the diversity and complexity of the different objects from among which it must be recognized. And if we want to evaluate the relative difficulty of several figures, we must standardize the choices.

The present technique is further distinguished from Piaget's in that the choice objects or figures remain open to the subject's view for the duration of the experiment. Whereas Piaget withdraws the object from the child's hand each time, just when he is to recognize it from among several others, the method used here allows the subject the possibility of directly coordinating his tactile and visual exploratory procedures. It does not change the main point of the task, which is to translate the tactile into the visual; but it does economize on the purely memory-related objects and stimulates tactile exploration in children who, through distraction or carelessness, might otherwise be content with looking for the global characteristics of the shape they have touched and would thus find themselves helpless before a subtler choice.

In the particular case of the second phase, three points should be noted. First, the group of 12 shapes includes both shapes which are predominantly topological and others which are predominantly Euclidian. This mixture is intentional. The most direct and most valid way to establish the relative difficulty of the different types of figures is to require the subject to compare each one with all the others at one time. It will be noted also that, for each of the elementary relations considered, the method always presents at least two shapes with the same topological attribute (e.g., closed ring and the disk with one hole in the center), which are not distinguishable without taking account of their metric relations (e.g., size of the internal space). Thus the procedure seems particularly able to reveal any possible *décalage* between the moment when the child restricts himself to considering the topological relations (and thus confuses the objects) and when he becomes able to manipulate the metric relations (and thus correctly identifies each of the shapes). Finally, and above all, the fact should be mentioned that the experiment does not cover the entire range of topological relations. The relations of neighborhood, for example, are not systematically exploited. And the relations of covering do not appear at all, for lack of any easy way of integrating them into the particular experimental schema. The graphic representation of covering (e.g., two intertwined rings) was shown to be very ambiguous during a preliminary test. The ambiguity does not arise from the complexity of the topological relation expressed by this covering; rather, it is inherent in the graphic symbolism itself, as is seen in the ease with which children manage to establish the difference between two partially superimposed rings and two intertwined rings, when the choice must be made from the duplicates of these objects rather than on the basis of a graphic sketch.

A last difference between the present technique and that of Piaget deserves particular attention because of the effects it could have on the validity of later comparisons. This difference concerns the size of the objects used in the last two phases of the test. As far as it is possible to judge from the scanty indications provided by Piaget, the sizes of his materials are considerably greater than those of the materials used here. The same remark should probably be made in the cases of Lovell and Page, who never give specifics on this subject. Thus, the circle used by Piaget has a diameter of 11.5 cm., while here it is only 7.5 cm.; similarly with the square, which in Piaget's test is 10 cm. on a side and is here reduced to 6.2 cm. Further, Piaget's material is cut from thin pliable cardboard, whereas here it is made of cardboard 3 mm. thick and absolutely rigid. It is difficult to foresee the consequences which such differences could have for the difficulty of the task; from all appearances, we may well imagine that the exploratory procedures necessary for the recognition of a shape differ appreciably according to whether the shape can be held in the child's hand or whether it more or less denies this possibility. In the first case, it may suffice to close the hand over the figure to grasp its major characteristics, whereas, in the second case, a more overtly active and systematic exploration seems necessary.

Does this difference in size necessarily lead to differences in the quality or level of the spatial relations which the subject is able to grasp? In principle it would seem not. Because he is working with smaller figures, the child will undoubtedly be able to acquire immediately a greater number of tactile indices and thus construct an image of the figure he has touched with a minimum of exploration. However, we cannot conclude *ipso facto* that the primitive or elementary character of the child's first mental representations would disappear at the same time; if this were the case, it would then be necessary to explain the children's initial errors as a failure in tactile exploration, without being able to recognize in this a real level of mental development. But it is just as possible that facilitating the exploration could, instead of changing the quality of the spatial relations worked out by the child, have no effect other than to accelerate the rhythm of his successive acquisitions without upsetting their logical sequence. Be that as it may, it must be admitted that the use of smaller figures has the disadvantage of concealing the real quality of the tactile exploration. The subject who merely closes his hand over the figure is not necessarily passive; at a certain level of development, the perceptual synthesis can be immediate without overtly betraying itself through a detailed examination of outline and surface. On the other hand, the advantage of the smaller materials is in minimizing the possibility of attributing the child's errors to a simple lack of tactile exploration and in allowing us to see them as a real difficulty in mental representation.

In sum, then, the experiment includes three sections. The first is concerned with the recognition of common objects and is designed particularly to determine whether even the youngest children understand the nature of the task required of them and whether they already know how to make the tactilovisual coordination implicit in a test of stereognosis. The last two sections study the same mechanism by using more and more abstract figures and are intended to delimit the content of the child's spatial representations as well as to retrace the principal steps of their development.

Not all the subjects of the sample were subjected to all three sections. At the age of 2:0 years, for example, it was futile to administer the last two sections, since the child at this age is barely able to recognize some of the common objects of the first section and quickly loses interest in a rather long and unexciting task. At 2:6 years, only the first two sections were administered to the subjects: the second is still almost inaccessible to children at this age and the third is a fortiori much too difficult. From 3:0 years onward, subjects were given all three sections of the test; by 4:0 years the first section was discontinued, since children at 3:6 years had been shown to be capable, as we shall see later, of recognizing almost all of the common objects. Between 4:0 and 12:0 years, therefore, subjects worked on only the last two sections.

Except in rare cases, the various sections of the test were never administered in immediate succession, but they were always given in the 1, 2, 3 sequence. In most cases, especially in the youngest subjects who were easily discouraged by the repetition of too-similar tasks, the three sections were included in three different groups of tests administered in as many separate sessions. If occasionally it was necessary to present more than one section in a single session, the sections were separated from each other by completely unrelated tests.

Chapter III

Stereognostic Recognition of Objects and Shapes: General Analysis of the Results

Examination of the results of the *Stereognostic recognition of objects and shapes* test includes two critical steps. The first is limited to a statistical analysis of a general nature and has two objectives: comparison of the present results with those obtained by other investigators (Lovell, 1959; Benton and Schultz, 1949; etc.) who hold to this sort of general analysis, and the discovery of rather widespread and characteristic types of responses in the children, to serve as a basis for working out a developmental scale. The second step, reported in the following chapter, is derived from the first but is more directly based on the detailed examination of the individual protocols and describes the different levels or stages which mark the evolution of stereognosis.

The general analysis touches two principal aspects: the relative difficulty of the items of the test, and a detailed study of the errors.

RELATIVE DIFFICULTY OF THE ITEMS

The major question to be directly examined deals with Piaget and Inhelder's central hypothesis about the chronological order of the child's acquisitions: after the recognition of common objects, which from the start is the easiest discrimination, would come discrimination of topological relations, followed by discrimination of metric or Euclidian relations. Table 3 gives the level of difficulty of each item of the test and provides a preliminary answer to the question. The table totals the correct responses yielded for each item in

Table 3

Number of successes at each age level and for each of the items contained in the three sections of the *Stereognostic recognition of objects and shapes* test*

Item	2:0	2:6	3:0	3:6	4:0	4:6	5:0	6:0	7:0	8:0	9:0	10:0	11:0	12:0
							Chronological age							
Ball	44	71	95	97										
Spoon	39	74	98	97										
Glass	36	70	93	98										
Comb	39	69	94	89										
Pencil	29	63	90	96										
Pin	30	60	88	87										
Penny	27	62	82	85										
Block	31	50	78	87										
Scissors	24	52	84	82										
Key	14	29	58	61										
Button	14	20	40	47										
Closed ring		17	46	52	60	77	80	92	93	99	98	100	99	99
Open ring		9	40	45	63	75	88	87	85	89	88	96	95	97
Open rectangle		9	38	39	48	62	77	82	92	95	94	98	100	100
Disk (1 hole)		20	54	54	57	67	78	93	94	97	100	98	98	99
Disk (2 holes)		10	30	47	52	67	75	90	93	91	94	97	99	100
Irregular cross		11	19	35	38	39	49	67	71	75	77	88	94	94
Circle		14	38	60	68	85	91	97	98	100	100	99	100	100
Square		9	25	37	49	53	66	81	87	96	96	99	99	100
Rectangle		9	27	40	56	70	82	93	91	99	98	100	99	100
Triangle		7	40	41	55	62	81	91	92	99	99	99	100	100
4-cornered star		10	37	44	48	66	82	88	83	86	88	96	100	98
Greek cross		5	35	31	43	56	67	89	88	94	90	100	97	99
Circle			49	60	66	91	96	97	97	99	100	100	100	100
Ellipse			31	36	54	78	86	92	93	98	99	100	100	100
Square			22	30	47	66	72	79	83	96	94	97	96	98
Rectangle			26	39	54	77	83	95	94	99	97	100	99	99
Triangle			21	33	44	60	77	88	88	96	97	95	99	99
4-cornered star			18	33	33	55	61	73	79	92	92	99	100	100
6-cornered star			14	29	28	43	47	61	71	91	94	95	96	98
Maltese cross			27	38	39	59	72	74	69	92	96	97	99	99
Greek cross			16	23	40	35	51	63	72	85	83	90	94	97
Irregular quadrilateral			12	19	17	30	43	61	68	80	85	91	93	97
Trapezoid			8	11	14	23	39	68	59	82	85	89	93	97
Rhombus			12	8	18	25	42	53	63	79	83	89	95	96

*The two trials in each of these sections are combined. N=50 per age level.

the two trials. As each age level has 50 subjects, the maximum possible number of successes is always 100. Note, however, that the difficulty is rarely the same in the two trials, the second ordinarily yielding a greater number of correct responses than the first. These variations can be explained by a number of factors (e.g., learning effect, substitution of the object's duplicate for a simple graphic sketch, rejection of the second trial by the youngest subjects, etc.); as they do not appreciably affect the relative difficulty of the items, it is not necessary to single out each of these factors at this time. The combined results of the two trials of each section fully suffice to provide the elements of the solution to the problem.

In the first place, it is clear that the recognition of common objects is much easier than that of the more abstract shapes, whatever these may be. Between 2:6 and 3:6 years, for example, where it is possible to compare directly the difficulty of the common objects with that of the first series of shapes, the average success rate is 74.1 per cent in the first case and only 30.1 per cent in the second. In fact, by 2:6 years, nearly all the common objects are recognized by at least 50 per cent of the children, a finding which immediately confirms the results of other authors (Piaget and Inhelder, 1948; Benton and Schultz, 1949; Fisher, 1965).[1] Of all the objects involved, only the *key* and the *button* seem to pose any particular difficulties, undoubtedly because both have unusual patterns and do not form a part of the child's everyday experience as much as do the other objects. For these two objects, moreover, the number of successes increases considerably on the second trial (the average success between 2:0 and 3:6 years changes from 28 to 53 per cent for the *key* and from 22 to 40 per cent for the *button*), as though visual presentation of the duplicate of the object he has touched helped the child to construct an image which tactile exploration alone does not easily allow him to do.

The relative difficulty of the various abstract shapes poses a more delicate problem. The major hypothesis to be investigated is the genetic priority of topological relations over Euclidian relations in the child's construction of space. To this end, it is hardly instructive to compare the average success rates with each of the two series of shapes (77.6 per cent for the first against 69.4 per cent for the second,

---

[1] For reasons which are not clear, Lovell (1959) makes no mention of the results obtained in his experiment on the recognition of common objects.

between 3:0 and 12:0 years), since both series include shapes which may be differentiated by topological and Euclidian means. Would it be more worth while, then, to ask, as Lovell does, whether the relative difficulty of the shapes is the same at all ages? For the ages between 3:0 and 6:0 years, comparable to those of Lovell's subjects and undoubtedly the most critical ages, the rank correlations spread between .78 and .95 and are thus at least at the same level as the correlations which Lovell obtained (.73 to .81). But these results are not much more interesting than the others; although they show in fact that the easiest or the most difficult shapes are appreciably the same at each age level, we nevertheless have no conclusions about what characterizes the easiest or the most difficult, nor consequently about the relative difficulty of shapes of a topological character and shapes of a Euclidian character. To answer this question we can again resort to a procedure which Lovell used, and simply compare the average success with the two groups of shapes, without going further than subdividing the groups themselves into more restricted families (e.g., curvilinear, rectilinear, etc.). Applied to the age levels which more or less correspond to those of Lovell's subjects (i.e., from 3:0 to 6:0 years), this analysis shows that the eight shapes of a topological character from the first series (*open ring, open rectangle, closed ring, disk with one hole in the center, disk with two holes, irregular cross, Greek cross,* and *four-cornered star*)[2] are correctly

2 In a preliminary analysis of the results (see Pinard and Laurendeau, 1966), all the cruciform figures had been arranged, with the *circle,* the *square,* the *rectangle,* and the *triangle,* among the figures whose topological characteristics are always the same (closed solid figures) and which can be distinguished from each other only by considerations which refer to Euclidian geometry or metrics. It was found, however, that this classification, while it conforms to the definitions of scientific geometry, does not at all correspond to the psychological reality. Detailed examination of the children's errors and analysis of the results of a complementary experiment in which subjects were required to sketch the objects they had touched (rather than simply to recognize them from among several others) showed in fact that the crosses and stars are considered to be open figures, or figures with noncontinuous borders. In fact, this phenomenon is not at all surprising. The projections and depressions which mark the outline of the cruciform figures are particularly emphasized in every case, and the fact that these various crosses are cut from hard cardboard favors even more the impression of discontinuity. We find also, in the materials used here, other figures for which the mathematical definition does not agree with the classification proposed to describe the psychological reality. The *open ring* and the *open rectangle* are also, in strict topological geometry, continuous-border figures, since we cannot avoid giving thickness to the figures once we use solid material instead of a simple pencil stroke or drawing. And we should not be surprised to see the children placing these figures among the open shapes; this absence of mathematical rigor would not be enough to challenge a priori the real topological nature of the considerations which are the basis of such responses.

identified 59.3 per cent of the time, and that the four metric shapes in the same series are correctly identified at 62.0 per cent. The difference is not significant (Mann-Whitney U test). Adding the shapes of the second series to those of the first, the percentages become respectively 53.8 for the 12 topological shapes (four crosses are added to the eight topological figures of the first series) and 53.3 for the 12 shapes of a Euclidian character. If we now distinguish, in this second group of 12 shapes, the curvilinear *(circle, ellipse)*, the simple rectilinear *(square, rectangle, triangle)*, and the most complex rectilinear shapes *(trapezoid, rhombus, irregular quadrilateral)*, the proportions of success are 70.8 per cent for the first, 57.3 per cent for the second, and 27.9 per cent for the last. Considering the group of topological shapes in this series, we arrive at three levels of difficulty whose differences are significant at the .01 level (Mann-Whitney U test): the curvilinear shapes come first as the most easily recognized, then the simple rectilinear shapes and the topological shapes, and finally the complex rectilinear shapes, which are clearly the most difficult of all. These results compare fairly well with Lovell's and, like his, they differ from the predictions made from Piaget's hypothesis. Recognition of curvilinear shapes is easier (or earlier) than that of topological shapes. Further, certain intracurvilinear and intrarectilinear distinctions *(circle* versus *ellipse, square* versus *rectangle,* etc.) are at least as early as recognition of topological characteristics.

Nevertheless, in spite of its merits, this technique of analysis is powerless to reveal the real importance of the responses of a topological nature or the possibility of a developmental primacy of these responses in relation to responses of a Euclidian nature. It ignores a considerable group of responses which are relevant to topology— this is the case with all errors where the child confuses two topologically similar but metrically different shapes (e.g., confusion of the *circle* and the *square,* the *circle* and the *ellipse,* the *square* and the *trapezoid,* etc.). If we are content with merely counting the cases of perfect recognition, the errors are equalized by wrongly holding as equivalent the confusion engendered by neglect of the Euclidian relations alone (e.g., *circle* versus *square*) and the confusion due to a neglect of relations which are both Euclidian and topological (e.g., *square* versus *closed ring*). This limitation of the technique does not wholly invalidate Lovell's analysis. It is still true that, if discrimination of topological relations is prior to that of Euclidian relations, shapes which are predominantly topological should be recognized earlier. But such an analysis remains most superficial and equivocal because nothing can be concluded about the real *décalage* which may exist between discrimination of topological relations and discrimination of Euclidian relations.

In the present study these flaws have even more serious consequences and they negate any value which statistical analyses based on such a method might have. It should be noted that, for most of the topological relations studied here, the material includes at least two shapes which are perfectly homeomorphous among themselves (e.g., *closed ring* and *disk with one hole in the center, open ring* and *open rectangle,* and various *crosses*), whose differentiation must therefore be based solely on a consideration of metric characteristics such as size, openings or internal spaces, etc. In sum, to require perfect recognition of these so-called topological shapes is to demand that the subject recognize the metric relations which are not separable from the topological characteristics, a method which is equivalent to restricting the analysis to these single metric relations. Under these conditions, it is not difficult to understand why the comparison reported above between success with topological shapes and success with metric shapes remains basically an equivocal one. Whether or not the differences observed are statistically significant, they have no real psychological significance because the analysis is centered exclusively on the metric aspect of the figures and does not meet its principal objective at all.

A more sophisticated technique is required. It is necessary to avoid any sharp distinction between the two groups of shapes—between those of a topological character and those of a metric character. In actuality, any figure necessarily possesses both of these types of properties: it is quite evident that a figure is never homeomorphous or heteromorphous in general, but that it is always so in relation to another figure, and it is no less apparent that even two homeomorphous figures can also be defined in Euclidian terms. The real problem, then, consists of discovering whether the child's responses, correct or incorrect, are based on the simultaneous consideration of topological and Euclidian relations or whether discrimination of topological relations is genetically prior to that of Euclidian relations. It is for this reason that it seems crucial to analyze the child's mistakes as well as his successes: the child who confuses, for example, the *closed ring* with the *disk with one hole in the center* is undoubtedly committing a metric "error," but this confusion is at the same time a topological "success." Only this type of analysis can reveal the actual level of the child's responses.

EXAMINATION OF ERRORS

The principle of the method is a simple one. It consists of taking the total responses given by children at all ages and identifying the different levels of functioning which these responses reflect. Tables 4 and 5 present the raw data required for this analysis. The results obtained with the first series of shapes (Table 4) are surely the most instructive: the shapes in this series were selected specifically to reveal the *décalage* which may exist between responses based on topology and responses relying more on metrics. These results are the only ones we will consider at this point in the analysis. Those of the second series (Table 5), specifically constructed to evaluate the discrimination of metric relations, are reported here only for reference; their real significance will not be seen until later, when we begin to refine the developmental scale that is to be worked out.

Examination of Table 4 immediately suggests one conclusion. Far from being randomly distributed, the responses continually center on certain selected figures, varying according to which figure was touched beforehand. The phenomenon is clearly apparent in the case of the crosses and the stars: when the figure which is selected is not the correct one, it always belongs to the same family as the figure that was touched. Similarly, the *open ring* and the *open rectangle* are quite frequently confused. The *rectangle* and the *square* also give rise to clear reciprocal confusions; and thus it is with other figures as well.

From this group of raw data, it remains to derive certain rules or constants which may serve to evaluate the individual protocols and above all to verify the hypothesis holding that topological discriminations are earlier than Euclidian discriminations. For this we could resort to a purely empirical procedure. Beginning with a comparative analysis of the errors, or a correlation of these errors with age, we might try to separate, at least roughly, the responses which may be explained by chance and those which reveal various

Table 4

Number of responses* to each shape in the first series of the *Stereognostic recognition of objects and shapes* test (Ages: 2:6 to 12:0 years; N=600)

Figure touched	Figure chosen												
	A	B	C	D	E	F	G	H	I	J	K	L	None
A. Circle	1,050	18	43	10	7	9	8	8	8	6	15	26	92
B. Closed ring	29	1,012	36	21	46	48	5	4	9	6	13	11	60
C. Disk (1 hole)	53	45	1,009	48	6	12	10	7	8	0	16	14	72
D. Disk (2 holes)	36	16	162	945	9	8	6	9	6	5	11	5	82
E. Open ring	15	28	13	16	957	133	14	3	7	8	11	7	84
F. Open rectangle	17	52	13	17	112	934	11	9	12	9	15	13	84
G. Irregular cross	15	5	14	12	11	21	757	111	208	32	25	9	80
H. Greek cross	17	8	14	10	8	12	77	894	116	11	30	16	87
I. 4-cornered star	12	4	8	10	8	7	119	42	926	41	20	12	91
J. Triangle	12	7	14	10	8	19	30	27	77	966	34	15	81
K. Rectangle	22	4	15	9	11	26	8	20	16	39	964	65	101
L. Square	37	13	32	9	14	23	16	25	27	35	88	897	84

*The two trials are combined.

Table 5

Number of responses* to each shape in the second series of the *Stereognostic recognition of objects and shapes* test (Ages: 3:0 to 12:0 years; N=600)

Figure touched	Figure chosen												
	A	B	C	D	E	F	G	H	I	J	K	L	None
A. Circle	1,055	46	7	17	3	8	3	3	6	2	7	3	40
B. Ellipse	91	967	14	11	10	8	4	4	9	13	7	11	51
C. Rectangle	10	21	962	33	17	11	9	9	13	19	22	20	54
D. Square	15	21	58	880	18	21	8	19	14	29	44	28	45
E. Triangle	6	19	14	15	897	22	26	37	9	49	20	40	46
F. Maltese cross	6	6	9	7	4	861	61	91	81	10	8	6	50
G. 4-cornered star	7	5	3	8	11	81	835	139	29	8	4	15	55
H. 6-cornered star	7	12	9	5	5	96	169	767	39	12	11	11	57
I. Greek cross	5	10	13	12	6	209	50	47	749	10	20	11	58
J. Irregular quadrilateral	10	18	24	24	152	18	16	17	13	696	87	61	64
K. Trapezoid	6	28	37	32	69	19	15	19	13	147	668	79	68
L. Rhombus	9	22	22	30	86	20	30	23	14	148	68	663	65

*The two trials are combined.

and consistent tendencies in the children. But this blind treatment of the raw frequencies would hardly be instructive and again could only lead to equivocal conclusions, and this for quite simple reasons. In the first place, it should be noted that equal frequencies may have completely different meanings. The concentration of errors around certain figures can be explained in several ways, depending on the figures. In some cases this concentration clearly reveals the existence of a level of conceptualization which is still limited to topological relations. The frequent confusion of the *open ring* and the *open rectangle,* for example, is explainable both by the ability to recognize certain qualitative characteristics and by the inability to estimate their respective proportions. In other cases the confusions seem to be due to totally different causes. Thus the choice of the *disk with one hole* for the *disk with two holes,* inexplicable in topological terms and having an unexpectedly high frequency, is probably the result of a too-hasty exploration which would overlook certain details, particularly the smallest ones. The fact that the reverse confusion (choosing the *disk with two holes* for the *disk with one hole*) is about four times less frequent confirms this interpretation. Even with an equal amount of concentration it would be unwise to classify errors which are so radically different into one group.

In the second place, the converse situation is also possible. Two apparently very different frequencies could have the same psychological significance, the difference then being explicable by reasons which are irrelevant to the task itself. The problem is that the choices which the child makes, for each of the figures used in the test, are not directly comparable to each other for the simple reason that the number of figures with attributes similar to the figure which he has touched is not the same in all cases. Thus, in the hypothesis where solutions of a purely topological level really exist, the child who touches the *closed ring,* for example, really has only two possible choices (the *disk with one hole* and the *closed ring* itself), the other figures all being heteromorphous to this closed ring. On the other hand, when he touches the *star* or the *Greek cross,* the same subject may be equally attracted to at least three figures (*irregular cross, four-cornered star,* and the *Greek cross*), or perhaps to five (since the *open rectangle* and the *open ring* belong to the same family). Even if Piaget's hypothesis of the primacy of real topological representations had to be abandoned in favor of Lovell's hypothesis of the primacy of certain characteristics of metric space (e.g., points, projections, curvilinearity, etc.), this phenomenon would still confuse the significance of the observed frequencies: the whole figures are more numerous than the pierced ones, the figures with a regular outline are more frequent than those with projections and indentations, etc. This phenomenon has two correlative effects. First, it facilitates success on items for which the choice is limited to a minimum number of "attractive" or equivalent figures, and at the same time it removes any absolute value of the observed frequencies. This is why two different frequencies may have the same real importance and, conversely, why two unequal frequencies may refer to clearly different types of behavior.

For want of specific hypotheses to investigate, a simple empirical analysis of this sort may perhaps be the only solution, despite the difficulties which have been mentioned. But this is not the case here. For this reason, rather than trying to discover homogeneous response categories from a blind analysis of the raw data, it is more important to proceed directly to a verification of the hypotheses which provided the basis for the experiment.

TOPOLOGICAL RELATIONS

The major hypothesis to be tested is Piaget's hypothesis that the child's spatial representations are topological before they are Euclidian. The way to test this hypothesis is to analyze the responses given by children who are as yet incapable of correctly identifying the figures they have touched; the method should reveal: (1) whether confusions of a topological nature are frequent enough to constitute a unique group in relation to other confusions, and (2) whether this unique sort of error, given that we could demonstrate its existence, characterizes a specific level of development.

In answering the first of these two questions, it suffices to regroup the results in Table 4 (p. 56) so as to classify into one group the errors in which the figure chosen has the topological characteristics of the figure that was touched—these errors thus considered as successes at the topological level—and, in a second group, all errors which are different from these. Table 6 gives the results of this regrouping for each figure of the first series. We note immediately (second and third columns) that the errors of the first type are, in general, less frequent than those of the second. In other words, when

Table 6

Actual and theoretical distributions of errors in the first series of abstract shapes in the
Stereognostic recognition of objects and shapes test, according to whether the errors respect
(topological successes) or ignore (topological errors) the topological characteristics of the
figures that were touched (Ages: 2:6 to 12:0 years; N=650)

| Figure touched | Total errors | Distribution | | | |
| | | Actual | | Theoretical | |
		Topological successes	Topological errors	Topological successes	Topological errors
Disk (2 holes)	273	0	273	0.0	273.0
Disk (1 hole)	219	45	174	20.0	199.0
Closed ring	228	36	172	21.0	207.0
Open ring	259	157	102	94.0	165.0
Open rectangle	282	144	138	102.5	179.5
Irregular cross	463	351	112	168.0	295.0
Greek cross	319	213	106	116.0	203.0
4-cornered star	283	176	107	103.0	180.0
Circle	158	47	111	43.0	115.0
Rectangle	235	126	109	64.0	171.0
Square	319	160	159	87.0	232.0
Triangle	253	61	192	69.0	184.0
Total	3,291	1,516	1,775	887.5	2,403.5

the child cannot identify a figure, he shows no preference for the
figures which are homeomorphous to the figure he has touched. This
first statement thus seems to invalidate Piaget's hypothesis. However,
before concluding anything of this sort, it is important to remember
that certain factors naturally tend to conceal, in the calculations,
the real importance of behavior based on topological considerations.
The analysis effectively excludes all the successes (or choices of the
correct figure) of which a considerable proportion (unfortunately
impossible to determine with any certainty) may very well be based
on topology. Furthermore, in the choices which were possible, the
number of figures homeomorphous to the figure which was touched
each time is always less than that of the heteromorphous figures: in
the case of the *disk with two holes,* there is not a single homeomorphous figure, and for all 12 figures, the number of homeomorphous
figures is nearly three times smaller than that of the others. It is
true that this disproportion should not, in principle, influence the
subjects' responses if they are really using topological relations to
recognize the figures they have touched. Whatever the number, the
heteromorphous figures would not be able to retain the children's
attention in these cases. Let us nevertheless suppose that some of
the subjects have effectively reacted in this fashion and are always,

or nearly always, led to select shapes which are homeomorphous to the figure they have touched and that other children, being younger, less interested, etc., have made much more uncertain choices in which the heteromorphous figures clearly predominate because of the nature of the material. We see at once that the response grouping of these two categories of subjects would lead to a more or less equal division of the homeomorphous and heteromorphous choices, and that the resulting data would lose all significance because they would not describe the underlying reality. One of the simplest means of knowing whether such interferences are present in the results given earlier is to calculate the theoretical division of the errors, supposing that the children are never guided by the topological characteristics of the figures. This would lead us to suppose that when they cannot recognize the figure they have touched, the children choose any one of the figures open to choice, the effects of chance leading them to prefer the homeomorphous shapes to the others with a frequency which is exactly proportional to the frequency with which these shapes are represented in the group of figures. Calculations deriving from this hypothesis are given in the right-hand portion of Table 6: for each shape in the first series, the total number of observed errors is divided according to the number of homeomorphous and heteromorphous figures contained in the 11 incorrect choices, with the exception of the figure which is identical to the figure that was touched, since the analysis covers only the errors. Comparing these theoretical frequencies with the frequencies which were actually observed, we soon see that, as a whole, these errors implying shapes which are homeomorphous to the figures that were touched (or topological "successes") are actually nearly twice as numerous as the hypothesis concerning the random division of errors would predict (1,516 versus 887.5). For all the figures considered together and for each of them in particular, the actual and theoretical distributions of the errors almost always differ significantly from each other (chi-square test, .01 level), the only exceptions being related to the *disk with two holes,* the *circle,* and the *triangle.* Thus it is quite obvious that, at least for some children, the errors are not randomly distributed but are guided by a search for homeomorphism. This analysis is, of course, very weak and tells us nothing about the details of the facts. Among other things, it does not allow us to determine the actual proportion of subjects who consider the topological characteristics of geometric figures. Furthermore, it presupposes an equivalence of the figures in each group when in fact they are not necessarily equally attractive. Among the figures heteromorphous to the *circle,* for example, detailed analysis of the responses shows clearly that the closed figures are preferred to open ones. But this technique at least has the important merit of establishing a common basis of comparison which takes account of the variability of choices available for each figure. Even with so gross a method of analysis, the predominance of errors of a topological kind over other errors is clear. There is no doubt that consideration of topological relations agrees with a well-defined tendency in children who are still unable to identify correctly the figures they have touched.

But we must now reply to the second question and see whether these topological errors are found indiscriminately at all ages, or whether they appear rather at an intermediate level, between the level when responses are accurate and the one at which the errors do not even reach the topological level. This is really the only way directly to test Piaget's hypothesis of the genetic primacy of topological over Euclidian space. The frequency of topological errors alone has only secondary importance. Whatever it is, we would not be able to infer from it the existence of a real step in the development of child space if these errors at the topological level were shown to be contemporary with or even later than the others. To study this crucial aspect of the problem, it is necessary to redistribute the two types of errors just identified, by age levels and for all the figures in the series. Table 7 (second and third columns) shows the results of this redistribution. If we compare the frequency of each type of error, it is easy to see the relative importance of the two categories of behavior depending on the different levels. Up to 4:6 years, the errors constituting topological successes are appreciably fewer than other errors. After 5:0 years, the comparison favors the responses of the topological level from the start, and this disproportion is accentuated at later ages: already twice as numerous as the others at 6:0 years, these topological responses are six times as much more at 9:0, 10:0, 11:0, and 12:0 years. In sum, beginning at about five years, the child who fails to identify the figure he has touched prefers a figure which is homeomorphous to that one, so that his mistake in a very real sense constitutes a topological success. Finally, to

Table 7

Actual and theoretical distributions of errors by age level in the first series of abstract shapes of the *Stereognostic recognition of objects and shapes* test, according to whether the errors respect (topological successes) or ignore (topological errors) the topological characteristics of the figures that were touched (N=50 per age level)

		Distribution			
		Actual		Theoretical	
Age	Total errors	Topological successes	Topological errors	Topological successes	Topological errors
12:0	14	13	1	4.0	10.0
11:0	20	16	4	5.0	15.0
10:0	30	26	4	8.0	22.0
9:0	77	65	12	20.0	57.0
8:0	80	66	14	21.5	58.5
7:0	133	90	43	36.0	97.0
6:0	147	96	51	40.0	107.0
5:0	272	154	118	74.0	198.0
4:6	397	175	222	107.0	290.0
4:0	522	209	313	141.0	381.0
3:6	624	255	369	168.0	456.0
3:0	593	227	366	160.0	433.0
2:6	382*	124	258	103.0	279.0
Total	3,291	1,516	1,775	887.5	2,403.5

*The decrease in the total number of errors at 2:0 years is explained by the very high number of responses (43 per cent) among subjects at this level in which no specific shape was chosen.

specify better the time when topological responses become dominant, at least for an appreciable number of subjects, we must again redistribute the errors observed at each age level as a function of the inherent probabilities of the experimental material (see the fourth and fifth columns of Table 7) and compare these theoretical figures with the actual data. This time, by the age of 3:0 years the number of topological responses observed is significantly more important than in the chance distribution (chi-square test, .01 level), and this predominance holds for all later age levels. On the other hand, it is only at 5:0 or 6:0 years that the total number of errors decreases markedly, this decrease reflecting the appearance of Euclidian or metric considerations which gradually enable the child to locate, from among all the figures homeomorphous to the figure he has touched, the one that corresponds to it in all respects. In sum, the total of these results shows that before the age of 3:0 years the children's responses are rarely correct (11 per cent correct responses) and the errors do not yet derive from topology—choices of any one of the figures presented to them are made on a chance basis. From 3:0 to

4:6 years, successes are still rare, even though their number gradually increases (percentages going from 36 to 65 between 3:0 and 4:6 years), and the confusions concerning the figures homeomorphous to the figures which were touched are more numerous in the actual distribution than in the theoretical one. From 5:0 or 6:0 years, the number of successes rises again (76 per cent at 5:0 years, 88 per cent at 6:0 years, etc.) and the rare mistakes are, in absolute as well as in relative terms, more often topological successes than topological failures. Piaget's hypothesis thus seems to be supported: after a period when the child makes no systematic discriminations (before 3:0 years), there is a stage lasting about two or three years during which a concern with Euclidian and metric relations dominates his behavior but sometimes gives way to errors, most of which are then classified as topological successes; this again seems to indicate the predominance of topological relations.

CURVILINEAR-RECTILINEAR DIFFERENTIATION

The analysis up to this point is not sufficient to support or invalidate the hypothesis of the primacy of topological over Euclidian concepts in mental development, since it considers all the Euclidian or metric relations as a bloc; Piaget, on the contrary, distinguishes several categories of difficulty among these, one of them being characterized by the differentiation of curvilinear and rectilinear shapes. This distinction derives from Euclidian geometry and, according to Piaget, it would be the first to be formed in the child who is already able to discriminate topological relations. In his developmental scale, Piaget reserves no specific level for it; but he recognizes its early arrival since he locates it between his stage IB (where recognition of topological relations predominates) and his stage IIA (where the first discriminations of Euclidian intracurvilinear and intrarectilinear relations begin). In this perspective, the curvilinear-rectilinear distinction normally presupposes the previous mastery of topological relations, so that we should be able to observe a *décalage* between these two levels of functioning. However, Lovell (1959), replicating Piaget's experiment, does not find this *décalage*. He states that identification of curvilinear shapes is not much more difficult than that of shapes labeled topological, even though the discrimination of various rectilinear shapes is found to be more complex and later in arriving. Page (1959) also observes, with Piaget's technique, that children hardly ever confuse curvilinear and rectilinear shapes.

Can the present results provide any new angles to the solution of this problem? Let us examine the effects of regrouping the errors observed in the first series of abstract shapes when it is done as a function of a new dichotomy in which the responses either respect or do not respect the curvilinear or rectilinear shape of the figure that is touched. Tables 8 and 9 give these results, first for each of the shapes in the series and then for each age level. In both cases, the actual distribution of errors can be compared with the theoretical distribution which, as before, is based on the probabilities inherent in the experimental material. But we should note that, in these various classifications, the *open rectangle* is considered as a figure with both rectilinear and curvilinear borders. Seemingly contradictory, this categorization simply reflects the basically ambiguous nature of this shape, which has rounded corners but rather straight sides. It necessarily follows that all confusions which include the *open rectangle,* either as the figure which is touched or as the figure which is selected, are automatically classified in the group of curvilinear-rectilinear successes. In other words, whatever the quality of the out-

Table 8

Actual and theoretical distributions of errors in the first series of abstract shapes in the *Stereognostic recognition of objects and shapes* test, according to whether the errors respect or ignore the curvilinear-rectilinear distinction (Ages: 2:6 to 12:0 years; N=650)

		Distribution			
		Actual		Theoretical	
Figure touched	Total errors	Curv.-rect. distinction	Curv.-rect. confusion	Curv.-rect. distinction	Curv.-rect. confusion
Disk (2 holes)	273	237	36	149.0	124.0
Disk (1 hole)	219	174	45	119.5	99.5
Closed ring	228	185	43	124.5	103.5
Open ring	259	219	40	141.0	118.0
Open rectangle*	282	282	0	282.0	0.0
Irregular cross	463	78	385	252.5	210.5
Greek cross	319	185	134	145.0	174.0
4-cornered star	283	122	161	128.5	154.5
Circle	158	95	63	86.0	72.0
Rectangle	235	166	69	107.0	128.0
Square	319	198	121	145.0	174.0
Triangle	253	272	81	115.0	138.0
Total	3,291	2,113	1,178	1,795.0	1,496.0

*The open rectangle is both curvilinear and rectilinear (see discussion in text).

Table 9

Actual and theoretical distributions of errors by age level in the first series of abstract shapes
in the *Stereognostic recognition of objects and shapes* test, according to whether the errors
respect or ignore the curvilinear-rectilinear distinction (N=50 per age level)

| | | Distribution | | | |
| | | Actual | | Theoretical | |
Age	Total errors	Curv.-rect. distinction	Curv.-rect. confusion	Curv.-rect. distinction	Curv.-rect. confusion
12:0	14	6	8	7.0	7.0
11:0	20	12	8	11.0	9.0
10:0	30	14	16	17.0	13.0
9:0	77	39	38	42.0	35.0
8:0	80	40	40	44.0	36.0
7:0	133	71	62	72.5	60.5
6:0	147	95	52	80.0	67.0
5:0	272	178	94	148.0	124.0
4:6	397	259	138	216.5	180.5
4:0	522	343	179	284.0	238.0
3:6	624	420	204	340.0	284.0
3:0	593	394	199	324.0	269.0
2:6	382*	242	140	209.0	173.0
Total	3,291	2,113	1,178	1,795.0	1,496.0

*See footnote to Table 7.

line of the figure which is confused with the *open rectangle,* the
response is never judged incorrect in relation to the elementary Euclidian distinction between curvilinear and rectilinear. This risk may
undoubtedly seem great, in these circumstances, of biasing the result
of the response grouping by introducing a special category for which
there can be no errors. However, in reworking the calculations, excluding for a while all responses in which the *open rectangle* is involved, no important difference is found. It thus seems in no way
detrimental to retain the data resulting from the classification of all
responses made by the subjects, the main advantages of this option
being that the comparison of the findings of this section of the
analysis with those of all the others is made simpler and perhaps
more valid.

The facts emphasized in Tables 8 and 9 seem clearly to confirm
the conclusions of Lovell and Page. For nine shapes out of 12, the
actual distribution of errors clearly favors the figures having the
same outline quality as the shape that was felt by the subject. Apparently excepting the *open rectangle,* whose special case was just
discussed, the only shapes for which this distribution is not significantly different from the chance distribution are the *circle* and

the *four-cornered star* (chi-square test, .01 level). On the other hand, analysis of the same results as a function of the various age levels (Table 9) shows that, from the age of 2:6 years and up to 6:0 years, children have a marked preference for figures having the same kind of border as the shape they have just touched. After the age of 6:0 years and at all later ages, the curvilinear-rectilinear distinction is much more irregular: successes and failures are numerically equal, approximately corresponding to the probabilities inherent in the material. At first this deterioration of the curvilinear-rectilinear distinction is not easy to understand; it is less so as this differentiation is established extremely early and seems even earlier than the differentiation of topological relations. If it were so basic to the child's spatial representations, it would seem that it should be respected at all times. But it must be remembered that at the age levels where the curvilinear-rectilinear distinction seems to deteriorate in terms of the quality of the errors that are committed, the absolute number of these errors is markedly less than at preceding levels, perhaps because the subjects then begin to deal with metric considerations. It is not impossible that the attention paid to an analysis of size of the figures, and also to their topological qualities (this preoccupation seems to prevail up to the age of 12:0 years), causes the subject to forget for a moment the basic distinction between curvilinear and rectilinear; but these oversights are exceptional, since the total number of perfect identifications of shapes (i.e., the successes), which demand the curvilinear-rectilinear distinction, is very high at age levels above 5:0 or 6:0 years.

Be that as it may, the main lesson to be drawn from these findings is the extreme precociousness of the curvilinear-rectilinear distinction. By the age of 2:6 years, in fact, subjects who make mistakes prefer a rectilinear figure when the shape they have felt is rectilinear and, conversely, a curvilinear figure when the shape touched is curvilinear. This differentiation is so predominant that it often operates regardless of topological equivalencies (see Table 4, p. 56) whose primitive character was just demonstrated. Should we conclude that the curvilinear-rectilinear dichotomy in the child's stereognostic representations is at least as primitive as the various dichotomies dealing with the topological relations of opening and closure, of full and empty, etc.? If this must be the case, we would have to hold that all these discriminations are psychologically equivalent. But before accepting this conclusion, it is necessary to examine the real interaction of these two types of discrimination.

TOPOLOGICAL RELATIONS AND THE
CURVILINEAR-RECTILINEAR DISTINCTION

To determine the nature of this interaction, the most direct procedure is again to regroup the original results, coordinating the *homeomorphous errors* versus *heteromorphous errors* dichotomy and the dichotomy of *presence* versus *absence of the curvilinear-rectilinear discrimination*. The simultaneous consideration of these two dimensions, whose results are given in Table 10 for each abstract shape of the first series, generates four different types of behavior depending on whether or not the curvilinear-rectilinear discrimination is respected in the choice of figures homeomorphous or heteromorphous to the figure that was touched. One fact stands out clearly in this table: there is a rather loose connection between the recognition of topological relations and the curvilinear-rectilinear distinction. In only 41.8 per cent of the cases (857+519 out of 3,291 errors) does the child's response either agree with both types of differentiation simultaneously or neglect them both. This percentage is significantly lower (chi-square test, .01 level) than that furnished by the calculation of the inherent probabilities of the choices (50.7 per cent). Nevertheless, it should be recognized that the data resulting from joining these two extreme response categories do not give a completely fair picture of the facts. In actuality, the calculated proportion is as low as it is because the children so seldom choose figures which respect neither the topological nature nor the outline quality of the shapes they have touched. Even if they fairly well avoid this particular type of error and even if they show a clear preference for figures conforming to the two types of relations simultaneously (the difference between the real and the theoretical frequencies for each of these error categories taken individually is significant at the .01 level), most of their responses are found rather in the other two categories and these are due to focusing on only one of the two types of relations distinguished here. When the child's response is limited to the discrimination of either one or the other of these two aspects, it is the curvilinear-rectilinear distinction which, in absolute terms, seems to be preferred (1,256 versus 659). But we need only compare the real and theoretical frequencies of

Table 10

Actual and theoretical distributions of errors in the first series of abstract shapes in the *Stereognostic recognition of objects and shapes* test, according to whether the errors respect (C-R dist.) or ignore (C-R conf.) the curvilinear-rectilinear distinction in the choice of figures homeomorphous (topological successes) or heteromorphous (topological errors) to the figure that was touched (Ages: 2:6 to 12:0 years; N=650)

		Distribution							
		Actual				Theoretical			
		Topological successes		Topological errors		Topological successes		Topological errors	
Figure touched	Total errors	C-R dist.	C-R conf.	C-R dist.	C-R conf.	C-R dist.	C-R conf.	C-R dist.	C-R conf.
Disk (2 holes)	273	0	0	237	36	0.0	0.0	149.0	124.0
Disk (1 hole)	219	45	0	129	45	20.0	0.0	99.5	99.5
Closed ring	228	36	0	149	43	21.0	0.0	103.5	103.5
Open ring	259	147	10	72	30	47.0	47.0	94.0	71.0
Open rectangle*	282	144	0	138	0	102.5	0.0	179.5	0.0
Irregular cross	463	32	319	46	66	84.0	84.0	168.5	126.5
Greek cross	319	128	85	57	49	58.0	58.0	87.0	116.0
4-cornered star	283	49	177	73	34	51.5	51.5	77.0	103.0
Circle	158	0	47	95	16	0.0	43.0	86.0	29.0
Rectangle	235	104	22	62	47	43.0	21.0	64.0	107.0
Square	319	123	37	75	84	58.0	29.0	87.0	145.0
Triangle	253	49	12	123	69	46.0	23.0	69.0	115.0
Total	3,291	857	659	1,256	519	531.0	356.5	1,264.0	1,139.5

*The open rectangle is both curvilinear and rectilinear (see discussion in text).

the two types of response to see that the discrimination of topological relations is relatively much better established than the curvilinear-rectilinear differentiation.

Analysis by age levels of the real and theoretical proportions of
each of the four possible types of error[3] (see Table 11) illustrates the
same phenomena in a different way. By the age of 2:6 years and at
all subsequent age levels, the figures conforming simultaneously to
the topological characteristics and the curvilinear-rectilinear distinction are preferred, while figures conforming to neither of these relations are systematically avoided. In both cases, and at all age levels,
the difference between the actual and the theoretical frequencies is
significant (.01 level). On the other hand, errors based exclusively
on consideration of topological relations become prevalent at the
age of 3:0 years and remain so up to the ages of 10:0 to 12:0 years.
Errors caused by an exclusive concern with the curvilinear-rectilinear relation are never significantly more numerous in the actual
distribution than in the theoretical one. Up to 6:0 years these errors
are about equally frequent in the two distributions and, starting
at 7:0 years, they become significantly less frequent in the actual
distribution (.01 level). In sum, between the recognition of topological relations and the curvilinear-rectilinear differentiation, there
seems to be a *décalage* which in all cases gives priority to the topological relations. Either the children may in fact recognize the two
types of relation at once, and their errors are then explained by a
neglect of the metric aspects of the figures; or they may focus their
attention on only one of the two types of relations and thus always
show a preference for the topological relations, as if these relations
were the more basic or at least the first to attract their attention.
This *décalage* becomes even more important during the course of
development so that, after 7:0 years, it is quite unusual to find responses in which the outline qualities are considered while the
topological relations are not.

While they support Piaget's hypothesis, these findings allow us
to understand why Lovell (1959) was led to challenge the genetic

[3] Always done by means of chi-square, this analysis implies, successively for each
type of error, the comparison of actual and theoretical frequencies of the error category
considered each time and those of the other three categories put together. So that the
theoretical frequencies are always large enough to permit the use of chi-square, the
ages of 10:0, 11:0 and 12:0 are grouped together.

Table 11

Actual and theoretical distributions of errors by age level in the first series of abstract shapes in the *Stereognostic recognition of objects and shapes* test, according to whether the errors respect (C-R dist.) or ignore (C-R conf.) the curvilinear-rectilinear distinction in the choice of figures homeomorphous (topological successes) or heteromorphous (topological errors) to the figure that was touched (N=50 per age level)

		Distribution							
		Actual				Theoretical			
		Topological successes		Topological errors		Topological successes		Topological errors	
Age	Total errors	C-R dist.	C-R conf.	C-R dist.	C-R conf.	C-R dist.	C-R conf.	C-R dist.	C-R conf.
12:0	14	5	8	1	0	2.0	2.0	5.0	5.0
11:0	20	8	8	4	0	3.0	2.0	8.0	7.0
10:0	30	10	16	4	0	5.0	3.0	12.0	10.0
9:0	77	29	36	10	2	12.0	8.0	30.0	27.0
8:0	80	26	40	14	0	13.0	8.5	31.0	27.5
7:0	133	42	48	29	14	21.5	14.5	51.0	46.0
6:0	147	50	46	45	6	24.0	16.0	56.0	51.0
5:0	272	87	67	91	27	44.0	30.0	104.0	94.0
4:6	397	103	72	156	66	64.0	43.0	152.5	137.5
4:0	522	121	88	222	91	84.0	57.0	200.0	181.0
3:6	624	154	101	266	103	100.5	67.5	239.5	216.5
3:0	593	136	91	258	108	96.0	64.0	228.0	205.0
2:6	382*	86	38	156	102	62.0	41.0	147.0	132.0
Total	3,291	857	659	1,256	519	531.0	356.5	1,264.0	1,139.5

*See footnote to Table 7.

primacy of topological relations. This is because, apart from restricting his analysis to the correct answers, he never took into account the limitations imposed by his experimental material. The response choices offered by this type of experiment are such that, if the child bases his response on a consideration of topological relations, he often finds himself opting *ipso facto* for a figure having the same type of borders (curvilinear or rectilinear) as the figure he has touched. The experiment reported here showed how the influence of this factor may be misleading. As long as the two types of differentiation are considered separately and, above all, each time the frequencies themselves are considered without reference to the inherent probabilities of the material, the curvilinear-rectilinear differentiation seems from the start to dominate the discriminations of a topological nature. Yet as soon as the interaction of these two types of discrimination is determined, the primacy of topology is confirmed. It goes without saying that these refinements in the analysis would be superfluous if the *décalage* between the discrimination of topological relations and the curvilinear-rectilinear distinction were very extensive. But all the evidence suggests that it is rather slight and for this reason, when certain flaws in the experimental material have the effect of masking this *décalage,* only a more stringent analysis can succeed in bringing it to light. The experimental material used here is surely not balanced enough to allow us to determine the exact size of the *décalage* separating the two types of discrimination. Thus, for example, the topological or Euclidian relations that define the various shapes are not always found in an equal number in the choice figures, so that it is necessary, in distinguishing the chance responses from the truly motivated responses, to compare the obtained frequencies with those furnished by a probabilistic analysis of the available choices. While it permits us to see the presence or absence of particular tendencies in the responses, this statistical detour does not, however, tell us anything about the relative importance of the observed tendencies. Despite this gap in the method, it is still easy to see that the *décalage* between the topological discriminations and the curvilinear-rectilinear differentiation is not sharply brought out. By the age of 2:6 years, in fact, the number of errors in which these two types of discrimination are simultaneously respected already exceeds that of the probabilities inherent in the material. By this time the child can refer, at least occasionally, to the quality of the outline of the shapes he has felt. Although curvilinear differentiation may appear very early, it is nevertheless dependent on successful discrimination of topological relations.

If we now try to understand why the curvilinear-rectilinear differentiation appears so early, in comparison to all the other Euclidian or metric relations, it may be necessary to hold that the topological relations contribute directly to this differentiation without, however, completely explaining it. The relations of neighborhood, which are undoubtedly the earliest of all the topological relations, can in fact be an extremely important discriminating factor in the case of the curvilinear and rectilinear shapes. If we compare the succession of points which form respectively the perimeter of a rectangle or a square and that of a circle, it is quite certain that the relations of neighborhood (or of proximity) between these points are not qualitatively homogeneous. When the figure is rectilinear, the motions of tactile (or visual) exploration and the mental anticipation accompanying these movements must abruptly change direction where the sides come together while, when the figure is curvilinear, the exploratory activity and the motor anticipation can play out in a more continuous fashion, without shocks or discontinuities. In sum, at equal proximity, the neighborhood of two points does not necessarily have the same significance. Moreover, certain partial characteristics of the figures, such as the presence of angles, have a polysensory value in the sense that they reach tactile perception as well as kinesthetic or superficial pain perception. It is surprising, in this respect, to note that recognition of angles is not an analytical phenomenon. The child does not arrive at it by a decomposition and reconstruction of intersecting straight lines; he recognizes them in a bloc, so to speak, as Piaget had already observed with the sketch technique (Piaget and Inhelder, 1948, pp. 89-93); the spontaneous remarks of children who, touching the triangle, will say, for example, *"it's a house," "a point," "a roof,"* etc., testify to this as well. It is thus the intervention of these topological aspects which would favor the curvilinear-rectilinear relation as regards other relations of a Euclidian nature, and this is true to the extent that these aspects are more or less emphasized depending on the nature of the shapes which are compared each time. For example, the *circle* is less differentiated from the *square* than from the *Greek cross,* and an analysis of the errors (see Table 4, p. 56) shows precisely that confusions of the *circle* and the *square* are at least twice as numerous as of the *circle* and the *Greek cross*. Even though these considerations of a topological nature can explain the unique character of the curvilinear-rectilinear relation among the other Euclidian relations, it would be wrong to suppose that they are the only ones which intervene in the curvilinear-rectilinear distinction. The inadequacy of the topological aspects is in fact unequivocally apparent in the *décalage* which separates the distinction of topological relations and that of the curvilinear-rectilinear relations, a *décalage* which is attested by the frequency of the errors to which the curvilinear-rectilinear distinction may give rise once the purely topological relations have been mastered.

Chapter IV

Stereognostic Recognition of Objects and Shapes: Analysis by Stages

The construction of a developmental scale derives directly from the general analysis described in the preceding chapter. This comparative analysis of the children's responses was able to single out the principal tendencies which seem to characterize the development of stereognostic representations. From these indications, it is now possible to try to identify the general levels of this development and to see at what average age the children attain each of these levels.

CONSTRUCTION OF A DEVELOPMENTAL SCALE

The scale describing the development of stereognosis is based on the major conclusions of the preceding analyses. Recognition of common objects is the most primitive; following this is the recognition of certain topological relations such as the distinction of open and closed, complete and pierced figures, etc. The differentiation of curvilinear and rectilinear figures follows closely on that of the topological relations and can, consequently, be assimilated into the same level. Finally, consideration of purely metric relations (size, slopes, spread of angles, number of components, etc.) does not appear until last, as indicated particularly by the difficulty with the figures of the second series of abstract shapes, which are nearly all homeomorphous among themselves and are nearly all rectilinear.

Evaluation and classification of the individual protocols requires first a translation of these general conclusions in terms of developmental stages. The problem is not simply to construct a scale which will reproduce the three major steps of the phenomenon under con-

75

sideration. There must also be included some intermediate levels in order to increase the discriminative value of the scale. And above all, each level must be defined objectively enough to allow unequivocal assignment of the individual protocols to them. Before presenting the results of this classification and going on to a detailed description of the stages, it is necessary to summarize the principles and criteria which helped in the construction of the scale.

RESPECTIVE USE OF THE THREE SECTIONS OF THE TEST

Although the three sections of the test were designed to study the development of stereognosis, each one deals with a particular aspect of this unique phenomenon. The first section, for example, directly examines the ability of the child to recognize a group of common objects by touch. The second uses abstract figures, but these figures are selected to show whether the child is able to discriminate certain elementary relations of a topological nature (heteromorphous and homeomorphous figures) or of a Euclidian nature (curvilinear and rectilinear figures). Finally, the third section, consisting of geometric figures which are almost all homeomorphous to each other and are nearly all rectilinear, seeks mainly to point out the discriminations of a more complex Euclidian or metric nature. Thus the very structure of the test decides the method to be used in classifying the protocols. When it is a question of specifying to what extent a child can recognize common objects, only the results obtained in the first section will be considered. Similarly, in determining the child's ability to identify the elementary relations of a topological or Euclidian nature, only his results in the second section will be used. Finally, only the results of the third section will be used to discover at which level a child is located regarding discrimination of complex Euclidian or metric relations.

In the case of the common objects, such a method is apparently the only one possible, but the procedure may be disputable in the case of the geometric shapes, since there is no clear division between the second and third sections. To a certain extent, the second section can give rise to discriminations of a metric kind (e.g., *square* versus *rectangle; closed ring* versus *disk with one hole)* and, conversely, the third section can lead to simple elementary topological discriminations (e.g., *circle* versus *square; four-cornered star* versus *square).* Are we then justified, when classifying the protocols, in holding exclusively to the second section in evaluating the discriminations of elementary or topological relations, and exclusively to the third section in evaluating the discrimination of metric or complex Euclidian relations?

The procedure is justified first by the nature of the test. The second section in fact includes some figures (the *circle* and the *disk with two holes*) which are the only ones with certain particular elementary characteristics (continuous surface and curvilinear border; double perforation): of all the other figures open to the child's choice, there is not one which has the same elementary characteristics and which is distinguished from the first only by Euclidian or metric characteristics. It necessarily follows that recognition of these two figures may be interpreted in topological or elementary terms as well as in Euclidian terms. There is nothing which permits us to determine at which level the child's identification is located. Similarly, in the third section, the strictly topological properties are more often held constant: the only relations capable of lending themselves to discriminations of a primitive level are the elementary relations defining the curvilinear or rectilinear and the open or closed figures. But if these elementary relations were studied in the same way as those in the third section, it would be necessary to increase the number of curvilinear figures (the series has only two) and especially to expand the range of topological relations. Thus, in classifying the protocols, it is better to ignore the errors of a topological or elementary type that the third section may give rise to, because the inadequacy of the information provided by this section makes interpretation of this type of error difficult if not impossible. In sum, each section is designed to reach a particular aspect of the recognition of geometric shapes, and each must be considered in its proper perspective.

Moreover, it is not at all obvious how it could be logically defensible to use the same series of figures to study errors of an elementary type and errors of a metric type at the same time, given that any error of the first type involves *ipso facto* an error of the second (e.g., confusion of the *open rectangle* and the *closed ring*) and that consequently errors of a metric nature are necessarily of an equal or greater number than elementary ones. Proceeding in this manner, one would find himself assuming that metric discriminations are contemporary with or later than elementary discriminations, and would lose all possibility of verifying, from the developmental point of view, the relative earliness of these two types of discriminations. From all evidence, it is necessary to resort to different series of figures to distinguish these two aspects in classifying the protocols.

EVALUATION OF THE PROTOCOLS

A protocol's score depends primarily on the number of objects or shapes with which the subject succeeded in each of the three sections considered individually.

A. *In the first section,* an object is held to be correct when the subject correctly names it (first trial) or points to it (second trial). On the first trial, it is not necessary for the child to give the exact name of the object. In order to minimize the importance of language in an experiment which is not intended to determine its scope, the subject is required only to let the examiner know that he recognizes the object that he touched, whether he uses verbal expression or gestures (e.g., touching the *key,* saying that it is *"for the door,"* or even simply pointing to the door in the room; touching the *comb,* making the gesture of combing his hair; touching the *pin,* saying *"prick-prick";* or saying *"for milk"* in touching the *glass;* etc.)

The successes are compiled separately for each of the two trials, and the better of the two classifies the subject. This method avoids penalizing children who are still unable to express themselves verbally and those who are discouraged by the prospect of a second trial. In sum, the number of correct objects determines the subject's rating in the recognition of common objects.

B. *In the second section,* evaluation of the protocols follows the same general principle. When the figure designated by the subject has the same elementary attributes as the shape, the choice is considered correct. It is not necessary for the shape that was touched to be correctly identified; a metric error constitutes a success at what we call the "elementary" level if the selected figure has the same topological characteristics (opening, perforation, etc.) and the same sort of outline as the shape that was examined. Thus the child who touches the *four-cornered star* and who indiscriminately designates the *star* itself, the *Greek cross,* or even the *open rectangle* scores a success of the elementary type because he always chooses an open form with rectilinear borders. Table 12 presents, for each figure of the series, the responses (+) which the subject can make without losing credit for a success at the elementary level.

Table 12

Distribution of all possible responses, in terms of successes (+) or errors (−), to each of the shapes (A to L) in the first series of abstract shapes in the *Stereognostic recognition of objects and shapes* test

Figure touched	Figure chosen in response											
	A	B	C	D	E	F	G	H	I	J	K	L
A. Disk (2 holes)	+	−	−	−	−	−	−	−	−	−	−	−
B. Disk (1 hole)	−	+	+	−	−	−	−	−	−	−	−	−
C. Closed ring	−	+	+	−	−	−	−	−	−	−	−	−
D. Open ring	−	−	−	+	+	+	−	−	−	−	−	−
E. Open rectangle*	−	−	−	+	+	+	+	+	−	−	−	−
F. Irregular cross	−	−	−	+	+	+	−	−	−	−	−	−
G. Greek cross	−	−	−	−	+	−	+	+	−	−	−	−
H. 4-cornered star	−	−	−	−	+	−	+	+	−	−	−	−
I. Circle	−	−	−	−	−	−	−	−	+	−	−	−
J. Rectangle	−	−	−	−	−	−	−	−	−	+	+	+
K. Square	−	−	−	−	−	−	−	−	−	+	+	+
L. Triangle	−	−	−	−	−	−	−	−	−	+	+	+

*The open rectangle is both curvilinear and rectilinear (see Chapter III).

Contrary to the method applied in the first section, the two trials are no longer considered separately here: a shape is considered as failed when, after having felt it, the child on one or the other of the two trials (or both) designates a figure which does not have the same elementary characteristics. The number of successful figures (the maximum possible being 12) determines the subject's rating in the recognition of elementary relations.

At this point we must justify the decision to hold topological discriminations and the curvilinear-rectilinear discrimination as equivalent and to classify as successes at the elementary level only responses in which these two types of relation are simultaneously respected. The decision would seem to fit rather poorly with the findings of the general analysis of the responses, where we observed a *décalage* between these two types of differentiation. But it will be remembered that this *décalage* was due to a statistical correction which was designed to control for the influence of the experimental material on the apparent difficulty level of the various types of discrimination. At the level of the actual frequencies, the curvilinear-rectilinear differentiation was shown to be, in fact, more often correctly made than was the discrimination of topological relations. The limited number of problems presented to each child does not justify transposing the statistical correction, which was applied to the analysis of the responses of the entire group of subjects, to the level of individual protocols. In classifying the protocols, it is therefore necessary to keep to the actual frequencies, any kind of *décalage* then being masked by the fact that the different types of relations which are compared are not equally represented in the experimental material. Thus it is because the experimental device used here is not specific enough to distinguish them, and not because they are in fact undifferentiated, that these two types of discrimination are held to be equivalent in this analysis.

C. *In the third section,* evaluation of the protocols poses no particular problems. To be correct, each figure must be correctly identified both times it is presented to the subject, a criterion requiring perfect discrimination of Euclidian or metric relations.

In sum, *mutatis mutandis,* the same criterion applies to all three sections of the test. In the first section, a protocol's score depends on the number of objects correctly named or designated by the subject. In the second and third sections, the score depends on the number of figures which always yield successes of the elementary (second section) and metric or Euclidian types (third section). One may ask whether the criterion adopted is the best suited to identifying the actual level of the child's stereognostic representations. Particularly in the second section, and even in the third, might it not have been preferable to base it either on the number or on the quality of geometric relations distinguished by the child or, more simply, on the number of responses respecting the geometric relations of the figure that was touched?

The *first* of these two methods would require finding the number of geometric relations (topological or Euclidian) which the child is able to recognize systematically in each of these sections of the test. In the second section, analysis of the responses made by a subject to all of the 12 figures could show, for example, that the subject can recognize only the topological relations of opening or closure and that he confuses the others (e.g., whole figures and empty figures, curvilinear and rectilinear figures, etc.). Similarly, in the third section, this analysis could reveal that a particular subject discriminates only certain Euclidian relations (such as the slope of angles, parallelism of sides, etc.) and fails to discriminate others. In this type of analysis, only the geometric relations which the subject could respect for all figures in a given family, without exception, would be considered as correctly mastered. Compared with the present method, which allows for partial successes, this technique would certainly be more rigorous. It would also perhaps answer more directly the questions of anyone who is interested in knowing the specific content of the child's stereognostic representations. Despite this advantage, however, the procedure has two major drawbacks which advise against its use. In the first place, the test would become much less discriminating, considering the limited number of relations which are involved in the second section (opening-closure, empty-full, curvilinearity-rectilinearity) as well as in the third (size of sides and angles, number of sides and angles, parallelism of sides), and also the huge individual differences in the number of responses where these relations are not respected (some children could make a single error of each type and thus be classed among those in whom these errors are prevalent). The classes established by such a technique would thus be made up of very heterogeneous elements, and the classification would lose much of its value. The only means of increasing the homogeneity of the classes would be to form subgroups based on both the quality and the frequency of errors, which would be, in effect, to adopt the present method. The second drawback to a technique based exclusively on the quality of the subject's discriminations is that it ignores the relative difficulty of the figures used in the test. It is inevitable that some of these figures are easier to recognize than others. In the third section, at the level of metric relations, these differences in difficulty are manifest: identification of the *square* and the *rectangle*, for example, is much earlier than that of the *rhombus* and the *trapezoid*. Even in the second section, at the level of elementary topological relations, it is logical to suppose that an analogous phenomenon holds. If we require all figures of a single family to be correctly identified before granting the mastery of the geometric relation common to all of them, the discriminative value of the test is further reduced. In fact, although at first it seems quite promising, this method does not seem well adapted to the present findings.

A *second* possibility may be suggested. Rather than taking up the number of correct figures of each section, why not simply count the number of the subject's successes—that is, the number of responses in which he respects the geometric relations of the figure he has examined? We would thus be able to locate each protocol on a clearly marked scale whose lowest level would be defined by a certain number of purely chance successes and whose highest level would correspond to the total of the items presented to the subject (24 in each section). Assuming that we would want to add to this purely metric classification a qualitative study of the mechanisms underlying the development of the child's performance, it would be necessary only to make a detailed analysis of the successes and failures at each level of the scale in order to identify their general causes. Seductive in its simplicity, this method nevertheless faces an insurmountable obstacle. The impossibility of controlling for the influence of chance in the child's responses would involve an artificial increase in the number of successes and would deprive the scale of any psychometric or even psychological value. The intervention of these fortuitous factors, inevitable in experiments of this type, is seen here in a particularly selective and capricious fashion. The fact is that the characteristics found by tactile exploration of the figure may vary considerably from subject to subject, and the number of figures sharing the same common property discovered during the exploration also varies from figure to figure. From this comes the impossibility of determining the proportion of successes attributable to chance factors or of insuring that the intervention of these factors, in two equivalent results, is identical or even comparable. Consequently, if each level of the scale thus combines quite disparate behaviors, it is difficult to see how subsequent analysis of these behaviors could identify the true dimensions of the process under consideration.

Based instead on the number of figures correctly identified by the child in each section, the technique adopted here is judged as preferable to the two preceding techniques. It is less rigorous than the first, but it is more discriminating and takes into account the relative difficulty of the figures. It is actually more rigorous than the second technique, and thus appreciably lessens the importance of chance successes.

ALLOCATION OF THE STAGES

The protocols are first classified into three general stages corresponding to the three levels of conceptualization outlined in the general analysis made in the preceding chapter. The subject who recognizes only common objects is classified in stage 1. He is placed in stage 2 if he is also able to discriminate the elementary topological relations, and in stage 3 if he distinguishes the Euclidian relations as well. The number of objects or figures correctly identified in each section of the test establishes this first classification. However, further to reduce the danger of identifying accidental successes as real ones, the subject must have succeeded with at least three objects in the first section, five figures in the second section, and seven figures in the third before it may be concluded that he has arrived at the beginning of the stage concerned. The choice of these criteria, whose systematic application must occasionally risk overindulgence or too much stringency, was not made arbitrarily. As we shall see later in the description of the stages, it is in fact only when the child no longer confuses at least the criterion number of objects or shapes that any consistency or regularity appears in the protocol: thus a minimum structuring of stereognostic representations is seen in the child, representations which are, depending on the case, relative to the recognition of common objects, to elementary relations of a topological type, or to Euclidian relations.

The first classification into three general stages is hardly adequate. Given that each section of the test has 11 to 12 objects or figures to recognize, it would not be sufficiently discriminating to classify into a single stage subjects who succeed with three to 11 objects or with between five and 12 geometric figures. Thus it is necessary to refine the main classification by adding intermediate stages in which subjects are grouped together who have already gone beyond a lower stage without having yet reached the fullness of the subsequent stage. Thus stage 1, characterized by the recognition of at least three common objects, is subdivided into two substages depending on whether the subject succeeds with between three and seven (substage 1A) or with from eight to 11 (substage 1B). Similarly stage 2, requiring both recognition of at least eight common objects in the first section and elementary success with at least five figures in the second, has two substages depending on whether the subject succeeds with from five to eight (substage 2A) or from nine to 12 (substage 2B) of the geometric figures of this second section. Finally, stage 3, which adds the solution of at least seven figures of the third section to the success criteria of eight objects and nine figures for the first two sections, is divided into two substages depending on whether the number of perfectly identified figures is from seven to 10 (substage 3A) or rises to 11 or 12 (substage 3B). These points dividing the principal stages are justified mainly by the concern with increasing the discriminative values of the test. Table 13 summarizes the numerical criteria used in classifying the protocols.

Table 13

Number of successes required in each of the three sections of the *Stereognostic recognition of objects and shapes* test for classifying the subjects in each of the stages and substages of the scale

Section of the test	Assigned stage						
	0	1A	1B	2A	2B	3A	3B
1. Common objects	0-2	3-7	8-11	8-11	8-11	8-11	8-11
2. Abstract shapes (series 1)	0-4	0-4	0-4	5-8	9-12	9-12	9-12
3. Abstract shapes (series 2)	0-6	0-6	0-6	0-6	0-6	7-10	11-12

Largely arbitrary in respect to the substages, this classification can be valuable only insofar as it satisfies the conditions of transitivity on which it is based. The advance to stage 2B, for example, first requires success with at least nine of the figures of the second section; but at the same time it assumes recognition of the common objects of the first section (at least eight out of 11) and a failure with the figures of the third (less than seven successes). Tables 14 and 15 show that the criteria adopted insure a clearly transitive classification. In Table 14, for example, which distributes the 150 subjects from 2:6 to 3:6 years according to their ratings on the first two sections of the test, there is no exception. In other words, none of the 150 subjects succeeds with a minimum of five abstract shapes without being able to recognize at least eight of the common objects. Table 15, on the other hand, shows the analogous results obtained from the 600 subjects from 3:0 to 12:0 years who have taken at least the last two sections of the test. It is obvious that exceptions to the transitivity rule are very infrequent: only eight subjects were

Table 14

Distribution of subjects according to number of successes (from 0 to 12) in sections 1 and 2 of the *Stereognostic recognition of objects and shapes* test (Ages: 2:6 to 3:6 years; N=150)

Section 1: common objects	Section 2: abstract shapes												
	0	1	2	3	4	5	6	7	8	9	10	11	12
0	3												
1	0												
2	2												
3	1												
4	2												
5	2												
6	3	1	0	1									
7	5	0	0	1									
8	12	5	3	2	0	0	1	0	0				
9	5	2	6	2	3	3	1	2	1				
10	10	4	2	6	2	10	1	3	2	1	1	1	0
11	4	2	4	4	3	5	6	2	2	3	0	1	2
Total	49	14	15	16	8	18	8	7	5	4	1	2	2

able to recognize at least seven figures of the third section before succeeding with at least nine figures of the second. Thus, combining all the indications of these two groups of results, it seems that the criteria adopted for delimiting the substages increase the discriminative value of the test without upsetting the order of succession of

Table 15

Distribution of subjects according to the number of successes (from 0 to 12) in sections 2 and 3 of the *Stereognostic recognition of objects and shapes* test (Ages: 3:0 to 12:0 years; N=600)

Section 2	Section 3												
	0	1	2	3	4	5	6	7	8	9	10	11	12
0	17	2	0	1									
1	7	2	0	3									
2	6	4	2	2	3								
3	10	3	3	2	1	0	1						
4	8	1	5	0	1	4	0						
5	6	5	4	6	4	1	1						
6	3	2	6	3	3	3	1	2					
7	3	1	4	1	5	2	2	0					
8	1	3	4	4	9	9	2	5				0	1
9				1	4	9	5	2	4	3	1	1	3
10	0	1	0	3	3	4	15	13	8	10	7	5	12
11	1	0	0	1	2	5	5	7	8	13	10	3	26
12	1	0	0	0	1	3	5	9	4	11	23	12	142
Total	63	24	28	27	36	40	37	38	24	37	41	21	184

the levels as established by the analysis described in the preceding chapter. The great majority of protocols are easily classifiable into one or the other of these levels. Rather than changing the criteria that we have selected, it seems more useful to avoid classifying those eight subjects who do not follow the rule. In any case, it is significant that these exceptions are mainly in the youngest subjects, whose reactions are never predictable, and that even these exceptional protocols reflect a certain internal consistency since, for the most part, the number of Euclidian successes does not exceed the number of successes of the elementary type. In sum, if we did not hold to a rigid and systematic application of the numerical criteria, most of the subjects would be easily classified, given that the exception generally depends on a single extra error or success. The importance of these exceptions is further reduced by the observation that they are frequently due, as indicated by the examiners' remarks, to factors which are extrinsic to the task itself (e.g., temporary fluctuations in interest, fatigue due to administration of a particular section at the end of a session, etc.).

DISTRIBUTION OF SUBJECTS ON THE DEVELOPMENTAL SCALE

Excluding a stage 0 characterized by total incomprehension of instructions or absolute inability to recognize objects or shapes, the development of stereognostic representations in the child includes three successive stages, each subdivided into two substages. In the first stage, children are able to recognize only one part (substage 1A) or almost all (substage 1B) of the common objects but fail utterly in identifying the abstract figures of the last two sections.[1] The second stage includes subjects who, recognizing the common objects, show success of an elementary type (discrimination of topological relations or curvilinear-rectilinear differentiation) in the second section but without yet distinguishing the more complex Euclidian relations or the metric relations implicit in the figures of the third section. These subjects are placed in substage 2A or 2B depending on the number of figures that they do not confuse. Finally, at the third stage, the

---

[1] Also classified at substage 1B are the some 30 subjects of 4:0 years who, without having taken the first part of the test (common objects), still do not satisfy the minimum criterion required at the next stage.

child becomes capable of taking into account the metric relations as well, as shown by his success with the figures of the last section. This third stage includes two substages depending on whether the child can recognize only the simplest figures, such as the *circle, ellipse, square, rectangle, triangle,* and the *crosses* (substage 3A), or whether he has mastered a variable number of more complex figures (substage 3B).

Table 16 shows the distribution of the subjects according to age and the stages where they are located. It will be noted first that, of the 700 subjects tested, only 15 are not classified, either because the test was not completed satisfactorily (seven subjects) or because the protocols are among the exceptions just discussed (eight subjects). All the others are distributed along the scale in a progression, the regular sequence of median ages attesting to its transitivity. All distributions differ significantly from one another (Kolmogorov-Smirnov test, .01 level), with the exception of those at stages 0 and 1A which are both severely truncated. And as the sequence of the ages of accession to each stage indicates, recognition of common objects is already apparent at 2:4 years (substage 1B), whereas discriminations of the elementary type, in the case of the geometric figures, are not mastered before the age of 4:6 years (substage 2B). Finally, discriminations of a Euclidian nature are much later (8:2 years for substage 3B), except for the simplest figures which the child already discriminates before 6:0 years (substage 3A is achieved at 5:8 years). The differences between girls' and boys' results, at each age level and at all ages considered together, are not significant (Kolmogorov-Smirnov test, .01 level).

These findings confirm both the existence of a level of conceptualization of a topological type and the developmental primacy of this level in relation to that of the purely metric representations. Close to 25 per cent of the subjects are classed in stage 2; this is a considerable proportion if one remembers that the development of stereognosis is relatively rapid, as we can see in the early accession to the beginning of stage 3. Furthermore, the genetic primacy of topological over Euclidian representations is obvious if we compare the ages of the subjects located respectively at stages 2 and 3. We note, finally, that despite the almost purely quantitative and somewhat arbitrary character of the criteria distinguishing the substages, the divisions between these intermediate stages are rather clearly

Table 16

Distribution of subjects by age and by stage in the *Stereognostic recognition of objects and shapes test*

		Stage — Frequencies								Stage — Cumulative percentages					
Age	N	Unclassified	0	1A	1B	2A	2B	3A	3B	1A	1B	2A	2B	3A	3B
12:0	50							5	45					100	90
11:0	50							10	40					100	80
10:0	50	1					2	11	37				100	96	74
9:0	50	1				2	3	14	30			100	96	90	61
8:0	50					3	4	19	27			100	100	92	54
7:0	50	2			2	3	11	19	15		100	96	90	68	30
6:0	50	2			1	6	7	26	8		100	98	86	71	17
5:0	50	1			4	14	10	18	2		100	92	63	42	4
4:6	50	1			11	15	15	8	0		100	78	47	16	0
4:0	50	1			15	23	9	2			100	69	22	4	
3:6	50	1		1	22	21	4	1		100	98	53	10	2	
3:0	50	3		2	28	14	3			100	96	36	6	0	
2:6	50	4	5	12	27	2				89	63	4	0		
2:0	50		21	15	14					58	28	0			
Total	700	15	26	30	124	100	68	133	204						
Median age*			2:1	2:3	3:1	4:0	4:11	7:1	10:0						
Age of accession											2:4	3:6	4:6	5:8	8:2

*The ages indicated are the median ages of each distribution, with the frequencies at each age level (excluding the unclassified subjects) transformed into percentages.

marked. Taking into account the relative ease of the test, each of these substages combines a sufficient proportion of subjects, and the constant progression of the median age testifies to the real developmental nature of the phenomenon.

DETAILED DESCRIPTION OF THE STAGES

Only a detailed description of the stages can indicate the full significance of an analysis of this sort, and we must now illustrate, with examples, the specific criteria distinguishing the stages of the scale. The inclusion of protocols typical of each stage both supports and clarifies the definition of the stages and, better than any purely theoretical description, illustrates the mechanisms at work in the reasoning processes of children at any given level.

STAGE 0: REFUSAL, INCOMPREHENSION, OR INABILITY TO RECOGNIZE EVEN THE COMMON OBJECTS

In order to reveal the first manifestations of such an early phenomenon as stereognostic representation, it was necessary to begin the examination at the age of about two years, or just when the child's first mental representations begin to be structured. At this age, however, the child does not easily accept undergoing a rather long experiment, particularly when he must manipulate objects without seeing them. We also had to expect most of the youngest children to be unable to give the task the necessary attention and interest. It is surprising, then, to note that despite these expectations, less than half (42 per cent) of the children of 2:0 years refused to take the test or were unable to recognize at least some of the objects they touched. As early as the age of 2:6 years these instances were exceptional (11 per cent) and disappeared completely by 3:0 years. Only three subjects absolutely refused to take the test and their behavior may be explained by their fear of putting their hands behind a screen. While it did not always lead to a flat refusal, this fear was frequently encountered and in some cases produced an anxiety resulting in tears. But the ingenuity of the examiner (e.g., replacing the screen by a book which was familiar to the child; letting him feel the objects under the table, under the child's skirt, in a bag, behind his back, etc.) was usually enough to overcome the most fearful resistance and to allow the test to continue.

In most of the cases included at stage 0, the child agrees to feel the first objects presented by the examiner, but he then simply holds the object in his hand without going on to any active exploration of it. If he does not succeed in identifying the object he has touched, it is not because he does not know its name, since he immediately names it when he sees it and his parents report that the objects are familiar to the child. Nor is it because in the second trial he must recognize them only from a smaller-scale sketch, since he can point out the correct one if he can see the object at the same time. Basically what he fails to do is to translate the tactile into the visual (or verbal). The child does not try to construct an image or a mental representation of the object he has touched, or if he does try to do so he is unable to. It may be that he simply does not know that such a thing is possible. In any case, the child is not able to coordinate his tactile and visual impressions. Thus, when the examiner insists, the child does not so much try to explore the object as to bring it into his visual field. Kept from using this spontaneous gesture, he soon tires of exploring the objects without being able to see them and, usually at the fifth or sixth item, simply refuses to continue the experiment. The patience and ingenuity of the examiner can sometimes overcome this opposition, but the child still does not change his exploratory procedures. Even if he has tried all the objects, which is rare at stage 0, the child at this level usually recognizes only one of the 11 objects, or two at the most. The most frequently recognized objects are the *comb,* the *ball,* and the *penny.* In addition to the fact that these objects come rather early in the series of items presented to the child and are thus less susceptible to refusal, they undoubtedly require less tactile exploration, either because of their greater familiarity, because of their smaller size as is the case with the *penny,* or because of the homogeneity of their internal structure, as is the case with the *comb* and the *ball,* all of whose parts are more like each other than are those of the *key* or the *scissors,* for example. In any case, a recognition which is limited to one or two objects still seems too fragile and unstructured to be unequivocally considered as a beginning of stereognostic representation.

At stage 0, presentation of more abstract shapes is completely futile. Deprived of any concrete significance for the child, these geometric figures hold no interest for him and, if it has not already happened with the common objects, the mere presentation of a card describing the figures of the first geometric series leads to a refusal on the child's part. The examiner can go no further than the very first items.

STAGE 1: RECOGNITION OF COMMON OBJECTS BUT NOT OF GEOMETRIC SHAPES

Stage 1 is characterized both by a progressive structuring of stereognostic representations relevant to the common objects and by an inability to recognize geometric shapes. The stage is divided into two levels depending on whether the number of objects recognized is between three and seven (substage 1A) or from eight to 11 (substage 1B).

While it is undoubtedly rather artificial, this division introduces a certain break into a development which would not appear to have clearly defined levels. It should suffice to study the results given in Table 17 to be convinced of this. There is an appreciable increase in

Table 17

Distribution of subjects in stages 1A and 1B by age and by number of objects recognized in the better of the two trials in the first section of the *Stereognostic recognition of objects and shapes* test

Age*	N	Number of objects recognized								
		3	4	5	6	7	8	9	10	11
2:0	29	0	4	2	6	3	6	6	2	0
2:6	39	1	1	2	3	5	8	8	9	2
3:0	30				1	1	9	5	8	6
3:6	23				1	0	3	5	7	7
Total	121	1	5	4	11	9	26	24	26	15

*Subjects 4:0 years old or more did not take this part of the test.

successes with age and a certain tendency of the subjects to identify correctly eight to 10 objects; but there is nothing in the numerical increase which suggests the existence of a continuity solution or a clear qualitative transformation. However, we should not neglect the considerable difference separating the two extreme poles of this scale. Among the subjects able to recognize a greater number of objects, tactile exploration is barely more systematic than in the others, nor is it enough to assure the identification of more abstract geometric shapes; but the speed with which most of the subjects learn to recognize the objects after the first contact shows that this exploration is surely more efficient and calls up more flexible and better structured anticipatory schemata. These qualitative differences are not clear enough, however, to justify establishing a very refined scale; the apparent discriminative value of such a scale would risk being based on accidental or circumstantial factors or, in any case, on factors foreign to the test's objectives. In order to minimize the artifices inherent in the application of an exclusively numerical criterion, we should rather hold to a simple dichotomy dividing the subjects of this stage into only two groups depending on the number of objects which are correctly identified. The distribution of successes clearly shows that the criterion adopted here (more or less than eight figures out of the 11) is neither absolute nor magical. Particularly in the borderline cases (seven or eight out of 11), the interpretation of individual protocols requires a great deal of caution.

Except for this numerical difference, substages 1A and 1B are perfectly comparable. For the whole stage, analysis of the errors shows that the *key* and the *button* are from the beginning the least well-recognized objects. These two items, which account for 47 per cent of the errors, have special difficulties: the *key* is of an unusual variety, and the *button,* presented after the *penny* which has nearly the same dimensions, is often confused with it. The other three most frequently missed objects (28 per cent of the errors) are the *pin* and the *scissors,* which maternal solicitude probably keeps the child from exploring on his own, and the *wooden block,* whose shape is easily assimilated into various objects available in the child's everyday experience (e.g., boxes, candies, rubber erasers, etc.). Thus it is because of unforeseeable difficulties with these different items that the subject is not required to recognize more than eight objects out of 11 to be classed at stage 1B, that is, at the level where perfect recognition of common objects is given him.

The reader will recall that in this first section of the test the results are totaled separately for the two trials and that the better of the two scores classifies the subject. In fact, of the 121 subjects at stage 1 who took this part of the test, 60 obtained almost the same results (except for one object) on the two trials. It is interesting to note, in this respect, the relation which seems to exist in the child between the ability to name an object and the ability to recognize its graphic representation. For most of the objects, the subject who is able to point out the correct sketch is usually also able to name the object which is represented (and he names it unnecessarily while he is pointing to it); conversely, the subject who can name the object he has touched is able to recognize it on the card.[2]

Furthermore, 31 subjects are superior in the first trial and 30 in the second; but, in the first case, 13 of these subjects refused to take or to complete the second trial. Fatigue accumulated during the first trial and lack of interest in a task which is hardly a fascinating one in itself are perhaps responsible for this refusal. When the first trial actually does show a higher score, we may note a difficulty in grasping the relationship which must be established, in the second trial, between tactile exploration of an object and selecting the object on a card which depicts it. In fact it is not unusual to find a subject who feels an object and succeeds in recognizing it, since he gives it a name or has previously done so, but who selects none of the objects on the card or chooses randomly, or always the same object, etc. In sum, he proceeds as in the first trial, without paying attention to the card which he sees, considering it superfluous, either not looking at it, turning it upside down, throwing it on the floor, etc. It is possible that the subjects are puzzled by the variety of the drawings presented to them or by the difficulty in recognizing certain specific drawings, like the *ball,* whose three-dimensional aspect is rather poorly conveyed in the graphic design, or the *penny* and the *button,* whose dimensions are nearly the same and which are not easy to distinguish without close examination of the internal detail of the drawings. But these various factors do not mean that the second trial is more difficult than the first, since 60 subjects had the same result in the two trials and 30 subjects were superior in the second. Basically, the factors just mentioned have an unpredictable effect, depending on the individual case, and it is undoubtedly more valuable to retain both trials of the test and then to classify each subject by his score in the better of the two. We can thus avoid penalizing the subjects who are less able to express themselves verbally and at the same time lay the groundwork for the subsequent two sections of the test where the children must refer to pictorial representations.

Insofar as recognition of geometric shapes is concerned, the subjects of stage 1 are unable to discriminate even the most elementary relations of the second section. In many children, despite all the

---

[2] This observation seems to confirm, at least for the common objects, Fisher's (1965) position discussed above, according to which the recognition of an object would depend on the ability to name it; but in fact there is still nothing that allows us to determine the direction of the causality which may link these two behaviors.

efforts of the examiner, merely the sight of the screen used in the first section produces a flat refusal. Others, less reluctant, agree to attempt the first items but, discouraged by the difficulty of the task and the unusual or overabstract character of the figures, soon refuse or maintain an uninterested randomness (e.g., the subject explores neither the object nor the card and randomly designates any of the figures). The items which are actually attempted are then too few to allow us to determine the strategies which the child has adopted. Finally, some subjects attempt every item or at least attempt a sufficient number to allow an analysis of the protocols; but the analysis then reveals that the most elementary geometric relations are not respected and that the child consistently confuses curvilinear and rectilinear figures. If occasionally certain topological relations seem to be discriminated (e.g., choosing the *square* for the *rectangle,* or vice versa; choosing the *closed ring* for the *disk with one hole,* or vice versa), the effect of chance is undoubtedly at work, since only a few moments later the same figures are involved in a topological or curvilinear-rectilinear confusion. The following case is a good example of this.

42 (2:6):[3] Names no object in the first trial but then correctly designates the *comb, spoon, glass, pin, penny,* and *scissors.* The *pencil* and *wooden block* puzzle him, leaving him unable to choose any of the objects on the card. He chooses the *spoon* in response to the *key,* the *penny* in response to the *button,* and the *button* in response to the *ball.* To the geometric shapes in the second section he gives the following responses:

Figure Touched	Figure Chosen	
	First trial	Second trial
Square	Disk (1 hole)	None
Disk (1 hole)	Circle	Disk (1 hole)
Closed ring	Closed ring	Open ring
Irregular cross	Circle	Rectangle
Triangle	Star (4 corners)	Closed ring
Open ring	Open rectangle	Closed ring
Rectangle	Rectangle	Disk (1 hole)
Greek cross	Disk (2 holes)	Star (4 corners)
Circle	Disk (1 hole)	Disk (1 hole)
Open rectangle	Open rectangle	Open ring
Star (4 corners)	Closed ring	Disk (1 hole)
Disk (2 holes)	Circle	Closed ring

3 The first figure indicates the number of the protocol within the age group, and the second one, in parentheses, the child's age in years and (:) months.

This child is placed at stage 1A because he succeeds with six common objects and systematically misses every figure in the second section. The *closed ring,* for example, is correctly identified the first time the subject touches it but is then confused with the *open ring* (topological error). The *square* is assimilated to the *disk with one hole,* which is both a topological and a curvilinear-rectilinear error. And again, the *disk with two holes* leads to the choice of the *circle* and the *closed ring,* which might suggest a simple failure of exploration; but this explanation does not hold when, while feeling the *circle,* the child twice designates the *disk with one hole* and thus ignores the topological relations. We could go on with the analysis of this protocol by showing that, for each figure, sometimes the curvilinear-rectilinear distinction, sometimes the purely topological relations, and sometimes both at once, are ignored.

There is also the phenomenon, rather frequent among the youngest subjects, of limiting the choices to a restricted number of figures. In the case just cited, the *circle,* the *closed ring,* and the *disk with one hole* are clearly selected. This phenomenon, however, does not always have the same significance. In some subjects it may reflect simply an attitude of perseveration or of "anythingness," as suggested by a monotonous repetition of the same figure chosen up to five or six times in succession. In other subjects, as in the protocol previously cited, the repetitions are less systematic and are always interspersed with different responses, which themselves may frequently recur. The choice of these privileged figures clearly demonstrates the difficulties with these first levels. The child assigns a preference to a group of simple or familiar figures (usually the *circle,* the *square,* or the *triangle)* or, on the contrary, he may prefer a group of unusual figures (for example, the perforated or open figures). Unable to form a complete enough mental image of the figure he has felt, one subject may rely on partial indices (e.g., points, curves, solids, etc.) which he recognizes with no other complications in any simple figure. Another may retain, from his initial tactile perception, a global impression of uniqueness or unusualness, which he will find again in the visual examination of certain figures that clearly have the same characteristics.

In sum, children at stage 1 usually miss all the abstract figures of the second section and do not respect even the most elementary topological relations. There are, however, especially at stage 1B, a certain number of subjects who are able to succeed with at least one, and sometimes two, of the figures in the series. In other words, for these figures the subject's responses never include a confusion of the elementary type (curvilinear versus rectilinear figures, homeomorphous versus heteromorphous, notched versus unnotched). Below are two examples from the 1B level.

40 (3:0): By naming them, can recognize the *comb*, the *wooden block*, the *penny* ("*a nickel*"), the *pin* ("*a spin*"), the *ball*, the *pencil*, the *scissors*, the *spoon*, and the *glass*; he misses only the *key*, which he sees as a hammer, and the *button*, which he compares to a penny. In the second trial, he correctly points out the *comb, spoon, pencil, glass, pin, penny, key, ball*, and *scissors*. In response to the *wooden block* and the *button*, he designates the *penny* both times. In the first series of abstract forms, his responses are the following:

Figure Touched	Figure Chosen	
	First trial	*Second trial*
Square	Triangle	Rectangle
Disk (1 hole)	Disk (2 holes)	Disk (1 hole)
Closed ring	Disk (2 holes)	Open ring
Irregular cross	Irregular cross	Star (4 corners)
Triangle	Star (4 corners)	Star (4 corners)
Open ring	Open ring	Closed ring
Rectangle	Circle	Star (4 corners)
Greek cross	Star (4 corners)	Star (4 corners)
Circle	Disk (1 hole)	Circle
Open rectangle	Greek cross	Closed ring
Star (4 corners)	Irregular cross	Star (4 corners)
Disk (2 holes)	Triangle	Closed ring

34 (3:6): Correctly names the *comb, key, wooden block, penny, pin, ball, pencil, scissors, spoon*, and *glass* ("*bottle*"). In the second trial he identifies all the objects except for the *penny*, for which he selects the *button* while saying "*one cent.*" The first series of abstract forms had the following responses:

Figure Touched	Figure Chosen	
	First trial	*Second trial*
Square	Rectangle	Square
Disk (1 hole)	Closed ring	Closed ring
Closed ring	Open rectangle	Open rectangle
Irregular cross	Irregular cross	Rectangle
Triangle	Greek cross	Triangle
Open ring	Disk (2 holes)	Open ring
Rectangle	Open ring	Rectangle
Greek cross	Star (4 corners)	Star (4 corners)
Circle	Disk (1 hole)	Circle
Open rectangle	Disk (1 hole)	Rectangle
Star (4 corners)	Star (4 corners)	Greek cross
Disk (2 holes)	Closed ring	Disk (1 hole)

Despite a perfect success rate with the common objects, these subjects still cannot really master the relations of the elementary level. The only success is with the *square* and the *Greek cross,* in the first subject, and the *square,* the *disk with one hole,* the *Greek cross* and the *four-cornered star* with the second subject; none of these forms is ever placed among figures of a different topological or curvilinear-rectilinear group.

In the subjects at stage 1 who are capable of a minimum of success at the elementary level, there is no particular tendency to recognize certain types of relationships over others. The *open rectangle* and the *open ring* are perhaps more often correct than the other shapes; between them they account for 29 per cent of all successes observed at stage 1. These results, however, do not mean that the topological relation of opening, common to both figures, is more striking or earlier recognized than the others. They may be explained instead by the fact that the *open rectangle,* considered both as a curvilinear and as a rectilinear figure, cannot produce errors at the level of the curvilinear-rectilinear distinction, whatever may be the figure that is compared with it: the probability of a correct solution is thus increased. The special situation of the *open rectangle* reciprocally influences the success rate with the *open ring,* since these two shapes tend to be confused most of the time. Finally, it should be noted that the *irregular cross* is very rarely recognized by children at stage 1 (only three successes out of a total of 200). The explanation of this phenomenon is linked to the fact that the various types of relations are unequally represented in the experimental material. The figures with which the *irregular cross* is most often confused—the *Greek cross* and the *four-cornered star*—are both rectilinear figures. Thus each time the child relies exclusively on the topological characteristic of the opening which defines the *irregular cross,* his chances of committing an error of the curvilinear-rectilinear type are extremely high.

As far as the figures of the third section are concerned, it is not surprising that subjects at stage 1 are still less able to recognize the more difficult Euclidian relations which are the object of the analysis at this point. Most of the children are completely incapacitated by the more abstract figures and retreat to refusal or indifference. The protocols of children who agree to take at least part of the test despite everything usually abound in all sorts of errors, excluding those errors of the elementary level which are not considered at this stage in the analysis since the material is not adequate for studying them. In fact, at stage 1, this part of the test introduces no new elements, as is seen in the responses of subjects whose earlier protocols were discussed above and whose responses to the last section are given below.

40 (3:0): Responses to the third section:

Figure Touched	Figure Chosen	
	First trial	*Second trial*
Circle	Irregular quadrilateral	Star (4 corners)
Maltese cross	Star (6 corners)	Star (4 corners)
Square	Ellipse	Star (6 corners)
Ellipse	Ellipse	Ellipse
Star (4 corners)	Star (6 corners)	Star (4 corners)
Rectangle	Ellipse	Star (4 corners)
Triangle	Star (6 corners)	Star (6 corners)
Irregular quadrilateral	Ellipse	Star (4 corners)
Greek cross	Star (6 corners)	Star (4 corners)
Trapezoid	Trapezoid	Ellipse
Star (6 corners)	Star (6 corners)	Star (4 corners)
Rhombus	Star (6 corners)	Rhombus

34 (3:6): Responses to the third section:

Figure Touched	Figure Chosen	
	First trial	*Second trial*
Circle	Circle	Maltese cross
Maltese cross	Maltese cross	Star (4 corners)
Square	Triangle	Rhombus
Ellipse	Star (4 corners)	Circle
Star (4 corners)	Star (6 corners)	Ellipse
Rectangle	Star (6 corners)	Rectangle
Triangle	Triangle	Ellipse
Irregular quadrilateral	Star (6 corners)	Triangle
Greek cross	Irregular quadrilateral	Trapezoid
Trapezoid	Rectangle	Square
Star (6 corners)	Rhombus	Maltese cross
Rhombus	Star (4 corners)	Greek cross

It is not necessary to emphasize further the inability of subjects at this stage to recognize systematically even the simplest Euclidian or metric relations in the third section. Of the 67 subjects who took this section in its entirety, 28 did not succeed with one of the 12 figures of the series, 31 succeeded with one or two, and 18 with more than two. The most frequently recognized shapes are the *circle,* the *ellipse,* the *rectangle,* and the *Maltese cross.* But since some of these figures most often produce the most elementary topological errors in the second section, and with the same subjects, it is hardly possible to see any proof of real recognition in these scattered successes, which might well be attributed to chance.

STAGE 2: RECOGNITION OF RELATIONS OF AN ELEMENTARY TYPE (TOPOLOGICAL SUCCESSES AND THE CURVILINEAR-RECTILINEAR DISTINCTION)

To the recognition of all or nearly all of the common objects of the first series, subjects at stage 2 add a growing ability to identify the elementary topological relations which define the abstract figures, and to distinguish curvilinear from rectilinear shapes. From this point on, these subjects can respect these relations unequivocally for at least five of the 12 figures in the second series.

Like the preceding stage, stage 2 is subdivided into two substages according to whether the number of correct figures (topological successes) is between five and eight (substage 2A) or between nine and 12 (substage 2B). This distinction does not represent a basic qualitative difference; almost entirely quantitative, it divides the number of possible successes into two nearly equal parts. The results in Table 18, which distributes the subjects at stage 2 according to the number of correct figures in the second section, clearly show the impossibility of any more logical division in this growing process, but this may be useful to anyone desiring to increase the accuracy of his interpretations and diagnoses. It may seem too lenient to reduce the number

Table 18

Distribution of subjects in stage 2 by age and by number of correct shapes (at the elementary relations level) in the second section of the *Stereognostic recognition of objects and shapes* test

Age	N	Number of correct shapes							
		5	6	7	8	9	10	11	12
2:6	2	1	1						
3:0	17	7	4	2	1	2		1	
3:6	25	10	4	5	2	3		0	1
4:0	32	5	5	5	8	3	5	1	0
4:6	30	5	4	4	2	5	6	3	1
5:0	24		2	2	10	3	3	3	1
6:0	13		1		5	0	3	2	2
7:0	14				3	2	5	3	1
8:0	4				0	0	2	0	2
9:0	5				2	2	0	0	1
10:0	2						1	1	
Total	168	28	21	18	33	20	25	14	9

of required successes to nine out of 12 for the subject to be conceded the mastery of the elementary topological relations. But, in fact, 32 of the 59 subjects who succeed with only nine, ten, or 11 of the figures in the series make only one or two errors out of a total of 24 responses (12 figures presented twice each) and the others never make more than five. Thus it is not unreasonable to think that these infrequent mistakes are much more the result of temporary distractions than of an underlying inability to recognize the elementary geometric relations.

Apart from this *décalage* in the number of successful figures, the subjects at stage 2A do not greatly differ from those of stage 2B, except in the tactile exploratory procedures. At stage 2A exploration is still quite passive and is usually limited to one part of the surface or outline of the figures. In the case of some figures, such as the *disk with one hole* where he may happen to put his finger in it, the child seems temporarily surprised and then begins a more interested and more intensive examination. But most of the time the exploration remains rather superficial: the child feels the figure with one hand or with both hands in succession, but lacks any real coordination. At stage 2B the examination is more active: the child explores contours and surfaces and attempts to locate the critical indices. As for the quality of the discriminations, subjects at stage 2 are remarkably similar. The common objects of the first section are usually all recognized, and errors, where they occur, are of the same type as at stage 1. To illustrate the type of successes observed at the present stage, two examples should do. The first gives the responses of a stage 2A subject to the first series of abstract figures.

40 (4:0): Responses to the second section of the test:

Figure Touched	*Figure Chosen*	
	First trial	*Second trial*
Square	Square	Square
Disk (1 hole)	Circle	Disk (1 hole)
Closed ring	Disk (1 hole)	Closed ring
Irregular cross	Star (4 corners)	Star (4 corners)
Triangle	Triangle	Triangle
Open ring	Open ring	Open ring
Rectangle	Square	Square
Greek cross	Greek cross	Star (4 corners)
Circle	Circle	Square
Open rectangle	Open rectangle	Closed ring
Star (4 corners)	Irregular cross	Star (4 corners)
Disk (2 holes)	Irregular cross	Disk (1 hole)

This child manages to succeed, at least at an elementary level, with six of the 12 figures of the series: the *square, closed ring, triangle, open ring, rectangle,* and *Greek cross.* These figures are always recognized or, at least, are never confused with figures of a different family. In this protocol, as generally with all subjects at the same stage, confusions of a curvilinear-rectilinear type (e.g., *irregular cross* versus *four-cornered star, circle* versus *square*) are no less frequent than the confusions pertaining to the purely topological relations of opening and closure (e.g., *open rectangle* versus *closed ring, disk with one hole* versus *circle*) or of solid and void (e.g., *disk with one hole* versus *circle*). Even when the number of successes exceeds the number of failures, the errors still have the same character, as seen in the following example taken from the protocol of a stage 2B subject.

11 (5:0): Responses to the second section of the test:

Figure Touched	Figure Chosen	
	First trial	Second trial
Square	Square	Square
Disk (1 hole)	Disk (1 hole)	Disk (1 hole)
Closed ring	Closed ring	Closed ring
Irregular cross	Triangle	Irregular cross
Triangle	Triangle	Triangle
Open ring	Open ring	Open ring
Rectangle	Square	Rectangle
Greek cross	Star (4 corners)	Irregular cross
Circle	Circle	Circle
Open rectangle	Open ring	Open ring
Star (4 corners)	Star (4 corners)	Star (4 corners)
Disk (2 holes)	Disk (1 hole)	Disk (2 holes)

Even though this child manages to discriminate nine of the 12 figures of this series, he nevertheless continues occasionally to confuse the curvilinear and rectilinear figures (e.g., *Greek cross* and *irregular cross*) or open and closed figures (e.g., *irregular cross* and *triangle*).

The question naturally arises whether the different elementary relations exploited in this series of geometric forms are all of equivalent difficulty. Table 19 provides the necessary elements for the solution of this problem. For each figure in the series, the frequency of successes at the elementary level obtained by stage 2 subjects is reported (i.e., the responses in which a figure is never confused with another of a different family), distributed according to the number

Table 19

Distribution of all successes of stage 2 subjects for each shape of the second section of the *Stereognostic recognition of objects and shapes* test: subjects regrouped according to total number of successes in the section

Figure	Number of successes in section 2								Total	Average per subject (T/168)	% of successes (T/1,348)
	5	6	7	8	9	10	11	12			
Open ring	12	16	17	32	17	24	14	9	141	.839	.105
Rectangle	22	10	14	26	17	24	14	9	136	.810	.101
Closed ring	10	14	15	25	17	23	14	9	127	.756	.094
Circle	14	15	11	23	19	21	14	9	126	.750	.094
Disk (1 hole)	12	16	7	26	19	23	13	9	125	.744	.093
Open rectangle	14	10	10	24	19	23	14	9	123	.732	.091
4-cornered star	16	10	13	19	12	18	12	9	109	.649	.081
Square	9	8	10	19	16	24	14	9	109	.649	.081
Greek cross	10	6	9	22	13	24	14	9	107	.637	.079
Triangle	10	5	10	21	16	20	13	9	104	.619	.077
Disk (2 holes)	6	11	7	21	13	18	12	9	97	.574	.072
Irregular cross	5	5	3	6	2	8	6	9	44	.260	.033
Total	140	126	126	264	180	250	154	108	1,348		
Number of subjects	28	21	18	33	20	25	14	9	168		

of successes per protocol. Thus the *open ring* is correct 12 times among the 28 subjects having a total of five successes each, 16 times by the 21 subjects with six correct solutions, and so forth. All told, this figure is correct 141 times for the 168 stage 2 subjects. The 12 figures in the series are thus arranged in order of difficulty according to the number of successes with each. The next to last column of the table (T/168) shows the proportion of subjects who succeed with each figure, and the last column (T/1,348) gives the proportion of successes of each figure in the total of all observed successes. Still rather crude, this compilation clearly illustrates the absence of any specific tendency in the stage 2 subjects' responses. Some open figures, for example, are among the easiest shapes (e.g., the *open ring*), and others are shown to be quite difficult (e.g., the *Greek cross* and the *irregular cross*). Similarly, the empty, full, curvilinear, rectilinear, etc., shapes are distributed throughout the range of difficulty. Thus no single type of relation seems actually to dominate the spatial representations of children at this level.

It is true that this analysis, limited to cases where all elementary relations are simultaneously respected, may give a distorted picture of the facts. Among other things, it allows the assumption that all the elementary relations defining each shape are equally likely to be noticed (or ignored) by the child; and this is not what a more detailed analysis of the errors reveals. For some shapes, like the *irregular cross*, for example, the curvilinear-rectilinear relation is the only one which is not respected in the great majority of errors (144 times out of 176), the subjects selecting either the *Greek cross* or the *four-cornered star*. For other shapes, on the other hand, errors are almost always due to a neglect of topological relations only, the figure chosen by the child having the same type of borders as the shape he has touched: the *disk with two holes* and the *closed ring*, for example, lead to errors of an exclusively topological nature (101 times out of 105 in the first case and 45 times out of 49 in the second). Yet far from being an argument modifying the conclusions drawn in an analysis of the successes, this variability in the errors is, on the contrary, a further reason for granting the nearly total equivalence of the various types of relations in the spatial representations of the child of this level. If, in fact, each in turn can dominate the child's discriminations, it is because they are of nearly equal importance, and the temporary priority of one or another is linked to accidental or secondary factors (e.g., occasional passive exploration or simply a too-hasty examination, etc.).

The progress in stage 2 in the discrimination of elementary relations does not yet involve the mastery of Euclidian relations (size of angles, of sides, of openings, etc.). The child who in the second section already confuses the *closed ring* and the *disk with one hole,* the *open rectangle* and the *open ring,* etc., will now confuse, in the last series, the *square* and the *rectangle,* the *circle* and the *ellipse,* etc. Because his mental representations are still at the topological level, then, he will behave similarly with the more complex forms of this last series. Particularly at the 2A level, where successes of the elementary sort are still very fragile, most children will still make very primitive errors (e.g., confusion of curvilinear and rectilinear figures, open and closed figures); this is clear in the following example, taken from the protocol of a subject at stage 2A.

44 (4:0): Responses to the last section of the test:

Figure Touched	Figure Chosen	
	First trial	*Second trial*
Circle	Ellipse	Rectangle
Maltese cross	Circle	Maltese cross
Square	Circle	Maltese cross
Ellipse	Star (4 corners)	Ellipse
Star (4 corners)	Circle	Trapezoid
Rectangle	Rhombus	Rectangle
Triangle	Maltese cross	Triangle
Irregular quadrilateral	Maltese cross	Trapezoid
Greek cross	Circle	Trapezoid
Trapezoid	Ellipse	Star (6 corners)
Star (6 corners)	Maltese cross	Star (4 corners)
Rhombus	Trapezoid	Rectangle

This sort of protocol is not unusual. Even at stage 2B, where the mastery of elementary relations is already acquired, the confusions are still numerous; but from this point on they are linked to the Euclidian or metric characteristics which distinguish the members of a single family. Thus the *crosses* are confused with each other because of their common character as open figures; also confused are the *triangle,* the *square,* the *rectangle,* and all the *other quadrilaterals* because of their common character as closed rectilinear figures; etc. The following protocol is especially typical of the behavior at this level: the number of figures which are correctly identified is still quite limited, but the metric errors are almost always successes of an elementary type.

13 (6:0): Responses to the last section of the test:

Figure Touched	Figure Chosen	
	First trial	Second trial
Circle	Circle	Circle
Maltese cross	Maltese cross	Star (6 corners)
Square	Rectangle	Rectangle
Ellipse	Ellipse	Ellipse
Star (4 corners)	Star (4 corners)	Star (6 corners)
Rectangle	Rectangle	Rectangle
Triangle	Rhombus	Rhombus
Irregular quadrilateral	Triangle	Rhombus
Greek cross	Maltese cross	Greek cross
Trapezoid	Triangle	Rhombus
Star (6 corners)	Maltese cross	Star (4 corners)
Rhombus	Irregular quadrilateral	Triangle

In this group of responses, only the *circle,* the *ellipse,* and the *rectangle* avoid any confusion and the child commits no errors of the elementary type. On this point, it is true, the example given here is unusual. More often, in fact, stage 2B subjects still occasionally confuse the curvilinear with the rectilinear, the open with the closed, etc.

At the 2B level, the responses to the first series of abstract figures are sometimes so accurate that it is tempting to interpret them as proof that the child is already capable of metric discriminations; but the near-complete failure with the figures of the last series shows that this is not at all the case. The following example clearly illustrates this paradox.

37 (4:0): Responses to the first, and then to the second, series of abstract shapes:

Figure Touched	Figure Chosen	
	First trial	Second trial
Square	Square	Square
Disk (1 hole)	Disk (1 hole)	Disk (1 hole)
Closed ring	Closed ring	Closed ring
Irregular cross	Star (4 corners)	Irregular cross
Triangle	Triangle	Triangle
Open ring	Open ring	Open ring
Rectangle	Rectangle	Rectangle
Greek cross	Greek cross	Greek cross

Circle	Circle	Circle
Open rectangle	Open rectangle	Open rectangle
Star (4 corners)	Star (4 corners)	Greek cross
Disk (2 holes)	Disk (1 hole)	Disk (2 holes)

Circle	Circle	Circle
Maltese cross	Maltese cross	Star (4 corners)
Square	Square	Trapezoid
Ellipse	Rectangle	Ellipse
Star (4 corners)	Star (4 corners)	Star (4 corners)
Rectangle	Rectangle	Rectangle
Triangle	Triangle	Triangle
Irregular quadrilateral	Triangle	Rhombus
Greek cross	Maltese cross	Greek cross
Trapezoid	Triangle	Trapezoid
Star (6 corners)	Star (6 corners)	Maltese cross
Rhombus	Triangle	Triangle

Although he manages to give 21 good responses out of 24 in the first of the two series, the child misses eight of the 12 figures of the last one and even reverts to some errors of the elementary type, such as the confusion of the *ellipse* and the *rectangle*.

As a whole, subjects at stage 2 indicate that they can discriminate elementary relations in the case of at least five of the 12 figures of the first series; but metric successes are still very infrequent in the second series, particularly at substage 2A where most of the children (79 per cent) have no more than four successes (see Table 20). At substage 2B, where the successes at the elementary level appear in nine of the 12 figures, Euclidian and metric successes are more numerous and more systematic than at the preceding substage, but nevertheless they never exceed six, barely half the figures in the last

Table 20

Distribution of subjects in stages 2A and 2B according to the number of successes accumulated in the third section of the *Stereognostic recognition of objects and shapes* test

Stage	N	Number of successes						
		0	1	2	3	4	5	6
2A	98*	13	11	18	14	21	15	6
2B	68	2	1	0	5	9	21	30
Total	166	15	12	18	19	30	36	36

*Two subjects 2:0 years of age, classified at stage 2A, did not take this third part of the test.

section. The most frequently recognized figures among stage 2 subjects are, in order, the *circle* (130 times), the *rectangle* (91 times), the *ellipse* (86 times), the *triangle* (67 times), and the *square* (61 times). With the exception of the *ellipse,* they are all included among the forms of the second section of the test and, consequently, they have perhaps acquired a familiarity which favors their recognition. For the child who can already distinguish the curvilinear from the rectilinear, in fact, identification of these figures is relatively simple and entails none of the dangers of confusion which the multiplicity and complexity of the other figures in the series may entail. Analysis of later stages shows that these figures are always the most easily recognized, strongly suggesting that the successes at the present level are not necessarily fortuitous. They are, however, too infrequent to define a real advancement in the child—that is, an advancement which is not exclusively due to greater and greater mastery of the elementary relations of this level.

STAGE 3: RECOGNITION OF EUCLIDIAN AND METRIC RELATIONS

Accession to stage 3 is marked by success, at the elementary level, with at least nine of the 12 shapes in the second section, and by a gradual mastery, at the level of Euclidian and metric relations, of the 12 forms of the last section. The protocol is placed at stage 3A or 3B depending on whether the number of figures correctly identified in this last section is between seven and 10 or reaches 11 or 12. In every case, however, the child's exploration is clearly active, curious, and systematic.

Just as in the preceding levels, the subdivision of this stage into two substages does not really correspond to a qualitative difference in the subjects' behavior, even though at this level we find what we have searched for in vain in the previous levels, namely, a certain regularity in the order of acquisitions. Studying the results in Table 21 which give the frequency with which each shape of the third section is solved by stage 3 subjects (once these have been regrouped according to the number of correct responses in the protocols), we note the existence of at least three homogeneous families of shapes which could serve to delimit steps in the development of Euclidian or metric representations. First are the shapes which are both simple and symmetrical *(circle, rectangle, ellipse, square),* whose recognition began to generalize at substage 2B and for which errors after this

Table 21

Distribution of all successes of stage 3 subjects for each shape of the third section of the *Stereognostic recognition of objects and shapes* test: subjects regrouped according to total number of successes in the section

Shapes	Number of successes in section 3						Total	Average per subject (T/337)	% of successes (T/3,580)
	7	8	9	10	11	12			
Circle	30	25	37	40	21	183	336	.996	.094
Rectangle	30	24	37	40	18	183	332	.983	.093
Ellipse	28	23	37	40	19	183	330	.977	.092
Triangle	21	20	33	39	21	183	317	.938	.088
Square	24	23	29	37	19	183	315	.932	.088
Maltese cross	20	19	32	34	20	183	308	.912	.086
4-cornered star	12	21	28	33	19	183	296	.876	.083
6-cornered star	9	12	29	36	20	183	289	.855	.081
Greek cross	13	11	23	30	17	183	277	.820	.077
Trapezoid	5	8	20	28	20	183	264	.781	.074
Irregular quadrilateral	6	7	14	30	18	183	258	.764	.077
Rhombus	12	7	14	23	19	183	258	.764	.072
Total	210	200	333	410	231	2,196	3,580		
Number of subjects	30	25	37	41	21	183	337		

point are unusual. Following these is the family of *crosses* and *stars* whose mastery, added to that of the simple rectilinear shapes, would indicate arrival at stage 3A. Finally, recognition of complex quadrilaterals, by far the most difficult, marks the end of this development. Now, even though such a hierarchy seems indisputable at the level of analysis of the responses of all stage 3 subjects, at the level of protocol analysis these tendencies are not clear enough to justify using these qualitative criteria in establishing these various levels of mastery. In fact, if it is unusual to find errors with simple symmetrical figures, it is, on the contrary, extremely common to find in a single protocol errors in the cruciform figures and other errors with the complex quadrilaterals. This phenomenon occurs 103 times in the 133 subjects who made two or more mistakes. Even in the children who make only one mistake, the complex quadrilaterals, although the most difficult of all the shapes, are missed only six times, while the cruciform figures are missed eight times and the simple symmetrical figures seven times. In sum, the hierarchy of difficulty resulting from the global analysis of the successes is not clear enough to determine qualitatively distinct levels. Rather, we should treat these different groups of figures grossly and be satisfied with a purely quantitative criterion to mark the difference between children who, beyond recognizing simple symmetrical geometric shapes, begin to recognize the crosses and complex quadrilaterals (substage 3A: seven to 10 successes) and those who manage to master these shapes completely (substage 3B: 11 or 12 successes).

In conclusion, despite the limitations of the stereognostic method in general and of the particular technique used in this study (e.g., the imprecision of the role of the child's exploratory procedures, the relative scarcity and ambiguity of the topological relations treated here, etc.), the analysis by stages refines the results discussed in the preceding chapter and again confirms Piaget's conclusions. From the criteria derived from the quantitative analyses done previously, and taking account of the particular objectives achieved by each section of the test, it has been shown to be possible to establish a scale of three general stages describing the evolution of the child's stereognostic representations. During the first stage, reached by the age of two and one-half years, the child can recognize commonly used objects but systematically fails to distinguish the most elementary abstract shapes, and his errors do not respect even the topological characteristics of the shapes involved. The second stage, fully attained by four and one-half years, is characterized by the child's ability on the one hand to respect the topological character of the shapes he has touched (the errors being at least "topological successes"), and on the other hand to distinguish curvilinear from rectilinear forms, a distinction in which the topological relations of continuity, neighborhood, etc., seem to play an important role. It is not until the third stage, which begins around six years and is fully attained by eight years, that the distinctions made by the child go beyond the elementary level of topological successes to be linked more and more with the Euclidian or metric characteristics distinguishing the abstract shapes. Each of these three general levels is subdivided into two substages whose distinction, based as it is on purely quantitative criteria (number of successes typical of the particular stage), nevertheless lends a necessary degree of refinement to the general scale.

Thus this test of stereognosis may help to clarify the difficult problem of the child's first spatial representations and, to a certain extent, confirm the genetic primacy of the topological over the Euclidian. The gaps in the technique, however, demand a certain reserve, and before saying anything definitive about Piaget's hypotheses we must first examine the findings of other tests, particularly the test of the *Construction of a projective straight line,* which deal with some complementary aspects of the child's spatial representations.

Chapter V

Construction of a Projective Straight Line: Presentation of the Test

The *Construction of a projective straight line* is the second test used in studying the child's spatial representations. The first of the three chapters covering this test includes two parts—the location of the problem in its theoretical context and a detailed description of the test itself. The subsequent two chapters present the findings of the experiment, first in a general analysis (Chapter VI) and then in an analysis by stages (Chapter VII).

THEORETICAL CONTEXT

The construction of a straight line is one of the techniques used by Piaget and Inhelder (1948) to illustrate the shift from topological representations to projective and Euclidian representations in the child's conception of space. The problem presented to the child would appear to be quite simple: it consists of constructing as straight a line as possible between two fixed points, using about 10 matches, each of which is vertically planted in a small disk of modeling clay.

Even though the perceptual identification of an already-established straight line is attainable by the child at a fairly early age, the mental representation of this same straight line is much later in appearing because the child must be capable of mentally constructing or reconstructing it. Particularly when this construction cannot depend on perceptual indices (e.g., following the edge of a rectangular table; placing the elements along an existing straight line which serves as a guide; etc.), it is impossible for the child to

111

make this construction without resorting either to operations of a *projective* nature, which are translated externally into a sort of aiming behavior, or to operations of a *Euclidian* nature, which may manifest themselves in several different forms (e.g., tracing an imaginary line with the finger, straightening a curved line by pressing the hands together, using the forearm to guide the construction, etc.) but always consist of looking for the shortest distance between the two points or of holding constant the direction imparted by the movements of construction.

The efficacy of the projective method, then, implies the composition of a space structured along the total of possible perspectives which could be established between the objects and the subject. In fact, as long as the child has not reached the point of differentiating and coordinating the many points of view of visual space which the observer's displacements would necessarily entail, he cannot understand the usefulness of placing himself in the extension of the straight line which he is to construct in a way which would control its rectilinearity; nor can he immediately select, from among all possible perspectives, the preferential position which will assure the successive masking of the most far-removed elements by those closest to him as the construction progresses. Likewise, resorting to Euclidian methods presumes the representation of space structured along a system of coordinates. In order to succeed in consistently following the same direction or systematically searching for the shortest route between two points, the child must, in effect, be able to guide himself along converging referent axes which determine the relative position of individual elements in a space common to all of these elements.

Results obtained by Piaget show that these two types of operations are complementary to one another and develop simultaneously in the child. In constructing his straight line, it is not unusual for a single child to resort successively or even simultaneously to these two procedures. Yet it is not before the age of six or seven years—that is, before the beginning of operational thought—that the child is able to allow the intervention of elements of projective or Euclidian geometry, rudimentary though these may be, into his spatial representations. Undoubtedly he will know how to distinguish a straight line from a curved or broken one well before this period.

He will also be able to draw a straight line on paper provided that he can sketch it in a single stroke and not have to locate it between two selected points. But, as soon as the instructions impose a precise direction on the child's efforts and as soon as they require him to construct the straight line through a succession of elemental movements (e.g., lining up a series of units to represent a line of telephone poles), the preoperational character of the methods which the child uses are betrayed by the preponderance accorded to the topological relations of simple contiguity, as well as by the difficulty which he shows in freeing himself from the perceptual suggestions offered by certain elements in the situation, such as, in particular, the contours of the table on which he is working. One child will, for example, go to great trouble to juxtapose the elements to see that all the bases touch each other in pairs, but without any concern for conserving a single direction, producing in the end a curved line which is rarely oriented, even as a whole, in the specified direction. Another child will be able to construct a straight line only if he can place the elements near the edge—or sometimes even on the edge —of a rectangular table, but he will lose all of this if deprived of this perceptual cue. Thus the oblique line which must be constructed by joining the mid-points of two adjacent sides of a table may assume all kinds of shapes: two segments of a line closely reflecting the right angle formed by that corner of the table; a curved line which is at first headed in the right direction but quickly deviates toward the apparently irresistible edge of the table; an arc of a circle, whose end points effectively mark the two points to be joined but whose central portion is still drawn to the edge of the table; etc. In sum, for lack of a total structure (projective or Euclidian) which might direct his construction movements, the preoperational child must rely solely on the topological relations of neighborhood and order. He moves step by step, making sure that each new element is juxtaposed to the preceding one, but he does not see the need for and is not able to coordinate these successive movements in a single total structure in order to maintain a constant direction and reach his goal. Given that he can already recognize a perceptual straight line, the child is not completely oblivious to the failure of his approach; but, being unable to imagine these lines and thus to anticipate them or to reconstruct them mentally, he is deprived of the internal structures he would need to guide his constructions and to resist the suggestion of the perceptual straight lines which are already present in his visual field.

Thus it is understandable to want to include this problem in a study designed to verify not only the succession of stages in the development of spatial representations as Piaget sees them, but in particular the developmental primacy of the topological over the projective and Euclidian. Results obtained in the test of stereognosis, analyzed in the preceding chapters, have already demonstrated the earliness of the topological discriminations in the child. But the fact that the differentiation of certain Euclidian characteristics, such as curvilinear or rectilinear geometric figures, was shown to be almost as early as the topological discriminations seemed at first to weaken the hypothesis of topological priority. Rather than reject this hypothesis, however, it seemed preferable to retain it at least provisionally, even though we had to give this synchronism an interpretation in which the curvilinear-rectilinear differentiation does not necessarily require the Euclidian distinction of straight lines and curves as such, but may be partially explained by recognition of certain partial topological characteristics (notably neighborhood) which are common to rectilinear and curvilinear figures, though functionally different in each of them. For this reason it should be interesting to compare the results obtained in the stereognosis test with those of a test of construction of a straight line, in order to see to what extent these new results confirm or disprove the first interpretation. In this last test, representations of a topological nature cannot alone insure the rectilinearity of the line to be constructed. Thus if construction of a straight line is not later than the curvilinear-rectilinear distinction, we would have to admit that this differentiation no longer has anything to do with topology and would at the same time have to reject the more general hypothesis holding that the child's first spatial representations are essentially topological. If, on the other hand, construction of a straight line is not possible for the child until several years after the curvilinear-rectilinear differentiation, and if analysis of this *décalage* shows that it is not a question of a simple horizontal *décalage* (analogous to those which the comparison of this test with the tests of *Coordination of perspectives* and *Localization of topographical positions* could demonstrate), we could see it as support of the interpretation that the curvilinear-rectilinear differentiation is partially based on topological factors and as a confirmation of Piaget's general hypothesis of the primacy of topological representations.

A comparison of this sort between results of two analogous tests *(Construction of a straight line* and *Sketch of geometric figures)* provides Lovell (1959) with a further reason for doubting Piaget's conclusions. In the first place, he insists on the earliness of success with the test requiring construction of a straight line following Piaget's own technique. Of his 30 youngest subjects (3:7 to 4:0 years), the great majority (93 per cent) are capable of lining up perfectly, or nearly perfectly, 10 matches when the construction can closely (about 2.5 cm.) follow the edge of a rectangular table. These perceptual cues very soon cease to be necessary; more than half (57 per cent) of his 35 subjects of from 4:7 to 5:0 years manage to construct a straight (or nearly straight) line joining the mid-points of two adjacent sides of a rectangular table, and a comparable proportion (53 per cent) of the same group (though we do not know how many of the same subjects are involved) succeed in constructing the straight line which forms the chord of an arc on a circular table. In sum, the age of approximately six or seven years to which Piaget assigns the mean success with these problems is seen by Lovell as much too late, and—at the risk of giving undue weight to Lovell's remarks—is based much more on the need for theoretical clarity than on empirical observations. In the second place, Lovell observes in many of his subjects (all those under six years) the presence of aiming behavior and manual procedures of straightening and reference—behavior and procedures which Piaget considers the most accurate indices of the ability to use projective and Euclidian relations. These first two groups of facts which Lovell observes clearly seem to be incompatible with Piaget's results, and we must see to what extent they will be confirmed in the present experiment.

The factor which seems to encourage Lovell to challenge the topological character of the first spatial representations comes from his observations, contradicting those of Piaget, to the effect that construction of a projective straight line is much earlier than the ability to draw even the most elementary rectilinear figures such as the square and the rectangle. In order to be able to construct a straight line, the child must be able to imagine it, and the greater difficulty which arises when he then tries to reproduce graphically a rectilinear figure cannot be attributed to the fact that representation of the Euclidian characteristics of space is much later in arriving than the representation of topological characteristics. Without explicitly stating it, Lovell leaves it understood that this *décalage* indicates that a child's ability to imagine space can vary considerably depending on the nature of the tests that are used and on the motor difficulty of certain modes of expression, such as graphic design. The particular influence of this last factor certainly should not be ignored. Lovell's argument would be much less vulnerable, however, if he had compared the construction of a straight line and its graphic design not with even so elementary a rectilinear figure as the square, rectangle, or triangle, but with a pure and simple straight line drawn between two points or with a series of points marked out in a straight line between two others. It is one thing to coordinate a group of straight lines into angles and parallels, and quite another to coordinate a group of points following an order of succession in a constant direction. Only this last graphic activity, which is logically implicit in the first, directly compares with the construction of a straight line by means of lining up matches. The horizontal *décalage* which might exist between drawing a simple straight line between two points and drawing a rectilinear figure could be important in explaining the difference in difficulty which Lovell observed between constructing a straight line with vertical matches and the graphic reproduction of rectilinear figures. It is helpful, in this respect, to emphasize the analogous *décalage* which Lovell points out between drawing a rectilinear figure and reproducing this same figure with horizontal matches or sticks: it is clearly simpler to coordinate already-made straight lines than to have to construct them first and coordinate them later.

Be that as it may, it is for these reasons that Lovell refuses to grant that Piaget's distinction between a topological level and a Euclidian level of spatial conceptualization in the child has been proved. We must examine his conclusions more closely in the light of the findings of the present experiment where we observe, significantly, that construction of a straight line is much later than Lovell's results would predict. Before going on to an examination of these results, however, we must describe the technique which was used and the nature of the problems presented to the subjects.

DESCRIPTION OF THE TEST

The materials consist of two thin pieces of plywood, one of which is rectangular (26 x 35 cm.) and the other of which is circular (diameter 34 cm.), two small toy houses (1.5 x 2 cm. at the base) marking the two end points of the line to be constructed, and eight miniature lampposts (8 cm. high, weighted at the bottom by a lead disk which both keeps them from tipping and facilitates the child's manipulation of them). The test is divided into two parts, each of which contains three problems. The subject must construct, each time with the eight lampposts placed in a random order in front of him, a straight line between the two houses which the examiner has placed on the plywood base at different points for each of the six problems (see Figure 2).

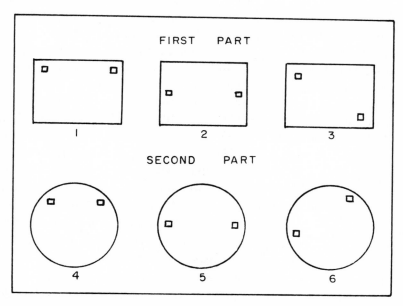

Figure 2. Bases (rectangular and circular) on which the subject must construct his straight lines in the *Construction of a projective straight line* test. The small squares indicate the position of the miniature houses in each problem.

In the first part, the subject must construct his straight line on the rectangular base. The houses are first placed at about 2 cm. each from the longer side nearer the subject (problem 1) and then at 2 cm. from the center of each of the smaller sides of the rectangle; thus in each problem they are separated by a distance of about 30 cm. Finally (problem 3) the houses are placed in two opposite corners of the rectangle, at about 3 cm. from the edge, the distance between them being about 35 cm. Thus each of the problems presents the subject with a task of different difficulty. In the first, the line to be constructed is parallel to one of the sides of the rectangular base, and the immediate surroundings are a valuable perceptual cue. This parallelism continues into the second problem, but its index value is undoubtedly reduced since the line must be constructed farther from the sides of the rectangle. In the third problem, on the other hand, the subject must be able to free himself from the attraction of the sides of the rectangle in order to construct his straight line.

In the second part of the test, which immediately follows the first, the houses are placed on a circular base. The value of this technique, already used by Piaget and adopted by Lovell,[1] is in demonstrating the influence which is exerted on the child's constructions by the neighboring perceptual contours and, in particular, in revealing whether the child finds it more difficult to free himself from a rectilinear contour than from a curvilinear one. In order to hold the testing conditions constant—the test was administered at home in the case of the preschool children and at various schools with the older ones—it was necessary to replace the circular table which Piaget had used by a simple circular piece of wood, asking the examiners always to make sure that this piece projected over the edge of the examining table so as to minimize the chances of interference. The three problems presented to the child in this second part (see Figure 2) are a fairly exact copy of the first three. They require the child to construct three successive straight lines between the two houses; the houses are spaced first (problem 4) some 20 cm. apart on a small segment of the arc perpendicular to the child's plane of vision, then (problem 5) at about 30 cm. along a diameter still perpendicular to the plane of vision, and finally (problem 6) at some 25 cm. on a larger chord of the arc but this time on the oblique in terms of the plane of vision.

[1] Dodwell (1963) also adopted this test in an experiment done to test Piaget's more general hypothesis concerning the developmental synchronism between several different concepts. Dodwell's results will be discussed later (Chapter XVII) with the comparison of the five studies presented in the present work.

The instructions are extremely simple (see details in the Appendix). Before beginning the test, the examiner makes sure that the child can perceptually recognize a straight line among a group of various lines (curved, winding lines, zigzags, etc.) which he draws on paper in front of him. He then tells him, for example, the story of two men who each own a house and who decide to install a row of lampposts between their two houses to light up the path. The child is then asked to arrange these lampposts himself, always taking care to *"make a very straight line between the two houses, a line starting at one house and going in a straight line to the other."* The examiner must absolutely refrain from tracing with his finger or from suggesting by any gesture the imaginary line along which the child must place his lampposts. The instructions specifically forbid this in order to avoid the child's being able to orient his construction along a purely static image of a line which he would have just seen and would not have to construct on his own. If the child's behavior shows that he has not understood what is asked of him (e.g., constructing a straight line between the houses but perpendicular to the expected direction; placing the lampposts all around the board with no concern for the houses; etc), the examiner's intervention must be limited to asking whether the line *"goes from one house to the other, whether there is a different way to make a straight road between the two houses,"* etc.

Aside from the difference in detail pertaining, for example, to the material utilized or the exact length of the line to be constructed, the method described above replicates the main points of Piaget's method, with the exception that the examiner does nothing which could lead the child to discover the aiming behavior which he has not spontaneously adopted. According to Piaget, the spontaneous or even induced use of this procedure, which for the subject amounts to placing himself in the extension of the line he is to construct, indisputably testifies to his ability to coordinate projective relations. From this comes Piaget's addition, at the end of the test, of a special section in which he asks his subjects to straighten a curved line of items arranged on the table and suggests that they change position, and thus their perspective, asking them to specify which position they feel is best for lining up the items. The inefficacy of these suggestions, as seen in the examples reported by Piaget and confirmed here during some preliminary trials, shows that we may dispense with this section in a test which is already too long for the children. Where they do not spontaneously adopt an aiming behavior in the course of their free constructions, it is very unusual to find children who are capable of efficiently using this procedure under the examiner's pressure alone. It often happens that even children who have successfully used Euclidian procedures (e.g., tracing an imaginary line, lining up the elements by bringing the hands together, etc.) then begin to doubt their own methods when new ones are suggested by the examiner.

Chapter VI

Construction of a Projective Straight Line: General Analysis of the Results

As in the preceding test, the results lend themselves to two kinds of analysis. The first is a gross, global analysis, centered directly on the problems themselves in an effort to determine their nature and relative difficulty. Derived from the first, the second is an analysis by stages (see Chapter VII), centered rather on a study of the protocols and designed to determine the different levels of conceptualization to which the protocols belong as well as the ages corresponding to each of these levels.

The present chapter is restricted to the global analysis, and its main objective is to establish the relative difficulty of the different problems in the test. Before presenting the results of this analysis, we must accurately define the criteria which were applied in scoring the problems. This first scoring is quite important, since it considerably influences the value of the analysis of protocols by stages which is dealt with in the following chapter.

SCORING OF PROBLEMS

The test seeks mainly to measure the ability to construct a straight line between two points. In order to prove that he has this ability, the child must show that he can, by whatever method he uses (projective or Euclidian), arrange a group of elements in a single constant direction without doing anything which might change the conditions of difficulty of each problem. This is the general principle which served to establish the scoring criteria. Figure 3 illustrates the principal criteria of failure and success, the

121

main points of which are outlined below; the figure uses concrete examples taken from the protocols themselves and intentionally selected from among the most contentious.

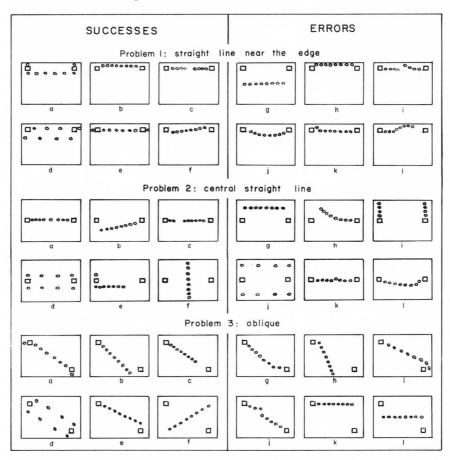

Figure 3a. Examples of responses considered as successes and as errors in the six problems of the *Construction of a projective straight line* test.

RESPONSES SCORED AS INCORRECT

A. A curved or twisting line: a single poorly aligned element suffices to define a line as winding, even if this single differing element is the last one placed into position (see Figures 3a and 3b —1k, 2k).

B. A straight line constructed under conditions which could

change the difficulty of the problem: e.g., in problem 1, constructing a straight line on the very edge of the rectangular base rather than at a distance of at least 2 to 3 cm. from this edge (e.g., 1h); in prob-

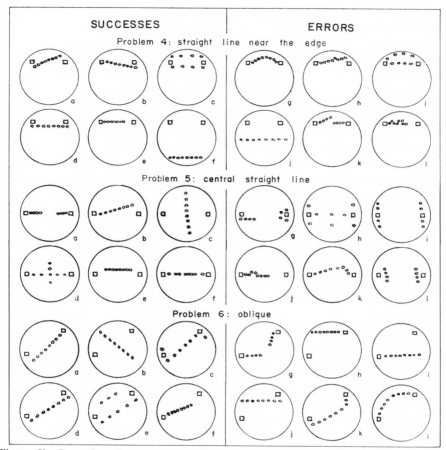

Figure 3b. Examples of responses considered as successes and as errors in the six problems of the *Construction of a projective straight line* test.

lem 4, constructing a straight line close to the diameter of the circular base rather than on the small chord of the arc near the circumference (e.g., 4j); etc.

C. A configuration in which the elements are scattered with no effort toward symmetry, either randomly on the base (in small groups or singly) or around the two houses, or even between them.

D. Refusal to attempt the problem despite the examiner's insistence.

RESPONSES SCORED AS SUCCESSES

A. A straight line which perfectly respects all the conditions of the instructions.

B. A straight line which, while disregarding certain points in the instructions, nevertheless respects their main purpose and is not constructed under conditions which change the level of difficulty of the problem. Points considered as extra considerations are the following.

1. *Equalization of intervals.* Even though most of the subjects do this spontaneously, equalization of the intervals is not necessarily required (e.g., 2a, 5f).

2. *Use of the entire space.* The instructions suggest covering the whole distance between the two houses (*"make a straight line which goes from one house to the other"*); but many subjects systematically make their straight lines by bringing the lampposts together so that the space is not completely filled. The straight lines are thus constructed either as single short segments in the middle of the space (e.g., 5e) or brought close to one of the houses (e.g., 3c, 4e, 6f), or as two still smaller segments (of an equal or unequal number of elements), each being near one of the houses (e.g., 1c, 2c, 5a) or parallel to each other (e.g., 1d, 2d, 4c, 6e). These behaviors are frequent even in the oldest subjects and are often accompanied by projective or Euclidian procedures. Although in principle it is easier to align closer elements than to align separated elements, we must not see this, as Piaget used to do, as proof of an inability to use projective or Euclidian methods.

3. *Use of all the lampposts.* The instructions do not require the use of all the lampposts. Some subjects have so much space between the first few that they do not need more than five or six to cover the whole distance. The extras are then ignored or placed somewhere around the base, and not necessarily in an extension of the straight line (e.g., 1a, 1e, 6c).

4. *Perfect orientation of the straight line.* It often happens that the line the child constructs starts at one house but does not exactly reach the other, missing it by several centimeters (e.g., 1f, 2b, 3b, 3e, 4b, etc.). Such a line is accepted provided it is perfectly straight, the

deviation is not extreme (e.g., 3h and 6h are rejected, while 3b and 6a are accepted), and the flaw in the orientation is not due to the attraction exerted by perceptual indices like the edge of the rectangular table, even when the construction is done on a circular base which is on a rectangular table (e.g., 6i, 6j). This criterion is probably the most difficult to apply; but even at the risk of increasing the possibilities of error in the scoring, it seems fairer to count these lines with a good over-all orientation and perfect rectilinearity as correct.

5. *Order of construction of the straight lines.* It is not necessary for the lines to be constructed in the order implied in the instructions. Assuming, for example, that the child constructs a central straight line in problem 1 (e.g., 1g) and a straight line near the edge in problem 2 (e.g., 2g), these two straight lines are both considered incorrect at their respective levels, but the two problems are scored as successes despite their reversal: the straight line 1g is considered good for problem 2 and the straight line 2g is correct for problem 1. The test is not intended to discover whether the child is able to construct his straight lines in the order desired by the examiner, but simply to find out whether he is capable of constructing them at all.

6. *Uniqueness of the line.* Some subjects refused to construct just a single row. Probably out of a concern for realism, they made a double row by placing the lampposts *"like the ones in town, on both sides of the street."* They then placed them either exactly opposite each other (e.g., 3d, 4c) or interspersed (e.g., 1d), and the two parallel lines could be of equal or unequal length (e.g., 6e). When the constructions respect the main point of the instructions (rectilinearity, location, and orientation of the whole group), they are considered as correct. Furthermore, the value of a double row may depend on the problem in which it is constructed (e.g., line 2i is acceptable in problem 1 but not in problem 2 because the latter requires a distance from the sides).

7. *Location of the straight lines between the two houses.* Having poorly understood the instructions requiring the construction of the straight line "between" the two houses, some children choose to make a straight line perpendicular to the imaginary line joining the houses and equidistant from each (e.g., 2f, 3f, 5c, 6b). This kind of line is accepted when it satisfies the other conditions.

In sum, the scoring of each problem is both lenient and severe. It is lenient in that it does not penalize subjects who ignore certain implicit requirements of the instructions, when it seems fair to consider these as secondary or as dealing with factors irrelevant to exploratory ability. On the other hand, it is severe insofar as the main condition is concerned, that is, the rectilinearity of the line to be constructed and the specific difficulty of each of these problems.

These scoring criteria were jointly determined by the authors after several preliminary attempts which were felt to be inadequate. All protocols were then scored by them, problem by problem, according to these criteria. A second rating, relying on the same criteria, was then made by a third person who was experienced in child testing techniques but ignorant of the results of the first scoring. Comparison of these two independent scores reveals distinct agreement: the percentage of disagreement between the two is only 4.99.

RELATIVE DIFFICULTY OF THE PROBLEMS

In order to determine the level of difficulty of the problems, it suffices to determine the age at which each is correctly solved, according to the criteria just defined. This order of difficulty will later serve to delimit the principal steps that describe the development of the child's first projective (and Euclidian) representations. Even at this crude level of analysis, examination of the difficulty of each item will provide crucial elements for comparison with the (often divergent) findings of Piaget and Inhelder (1948) on one hand and Lovell (1959) on the other.

Table 22 gives the percentage of subjects who succeeded on each of the six problems at each of the 12 age levels between 2:0 and 10:0 years. Beyond the age of 10:0 years the test becomes too easy and loses its usefulness. In principle, the number of children examined is 50 in each age group, except at 10:0 years where six subjects did not take the test because of a technical problem in organizing the sessions. Subjects not classified into stages (see the following chapter, p. 136) are excluded even from this analysis of individual problems.

Examination of the results shows that the six problems of the test are split into two groups of unequal difficulty. The first includes problems 1, 2, 4, and 5, which are all of appreciably equivalent difficulty, considering the median age when successes appear or the

Table 22

Percentage of successes* at each age level and for each problem in the *Construction of a projective straight line* test

			Rectangular base			Circular base		
Age	N	Not classi-fied in stages	1 Straight line near the edge	2 Central straight line	3 Oblique	4 Straight line near the edge	5 Central straight line	6 Oblique
10:0	44	6	95	92	84	89	95	89
9:0	50	8	79	90	71	79	86	76
8:0	50	3	83	87	64	81	89	83
7:0	50	8	69	76	69	76	76	64
6:0	50	10	75	65	30	63	65	40
5:0	50	14	61	58	17	47	44	22
4:6	50	12	37	29	16	18	39	8
4:0	50	3	13	21	0	4	15	2
3:6	50	3	26	19	0	9	26	9
3:0	50	3	11	4	2	6	11	2
2:6	50	1	6	6	0	0	4	0
2:0	50	1	0	0	0	0	4	0
Median age			7:3	7:6	8:2	7:8	7:5	8:1
Age of accession			5:0	5:3	7:0	5:6	5:5	6:5

*The percentages are computed only for the subjects classified in the scale.

age at which the percentage of successes reaches 50 (age of accession). Subjects manage to construct a central straight line as easily as a marginal one, and can do so independently of the rectangular or circular nature of the base. The second group (problems 3 and 6) is much more difficult: the median age of success is at least five months higher and the age of accession about one year higher than the corresponding ages in the first group. Construction of oblique lines is thus not within the child's capacity as early as that of other lines, but it is hardly important whether the base is circular or rectangular. If we now compare the developmental curves of each of these problems, the preceding remarks are confirmed. The Kolmogorov-Smirnov test reveals that the growth of success differs significantly (at the .01 level) when the problems of the first group are compared to those of the second, with the exception of problem 4 which differs significantly from problem 3 but not from problem 6. Furthermore, the difference between the growth of success with the problems of a single group is never significant. When the time comes to design a developmental scale, these results will be of primary importance. At the present level of analysis, these results raise at least three questions whose examination may help to clarify the mechanisms implicit in constructing a straight line and to explain the differences between Piaget and Inhelder's results and those of Lovell.

In the first place, one may ask why constructing a straight line near the edge of a circular base (problem 4) presents no more difficulty than the central straight lines (problems 2 and 5) or constructing a straight line at the edge of a rectangular base (problem 1). It is logical to suppose that the immediate environment of a curvilinear contour exerts a distorting attraction on the child's construction, an attraction which is reduced in constructing the straight line in the middle of a circular base and is totally nonexistent in the case of constructing the two lines on the rectangular base, where the more or less immediate vicinity of a rectangular edge should facilitate the child's task. The results obtained suggest a tendency of this sort (see Table 22: total successes and median age), but the difference is not great enough to be significant. Should we necessarily conclude that the child's constructions are not influenced by the perceptual quality of the neighboring contours? The fact that the great majority of failures in problem 4 are characterized by a bending of the lines suggests the contrary. The equivalence of this problem to the other three of its group reflects, rather, the fact that the circular base is always placed on a rectangular table. Even if the examiner is careful to place it far from the edge of the table, to reduce the influence of the rectilinear contour, this influence continues to be exerted to a great extent. As Figure 4 illustrates, the arrangement leads to a

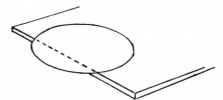

Figure 4. Arrangement of the circular base in problems 4, 5, and 6 of the *Construction of a projective straight line* test.

broken straight line which the child easily sees as unbroken and which may readily serve as a perceptual guide, since the subject's construction must be made precisely in the extension of this straight line. In sum, the principal objective sought in using a circular base has effectively miscarried for technical reasons.

The second question is the counterpart of the first and concerns the difficulty posed by the construction of two oblique lines (problems 3 and 6). The oblique line to be constructed on the rectangular base is not much more difficult than the other. Nevertheless, given the possibility of interference due to the nearness of deviant perceptual contours, it seems a priori more difficult to construct an oblique on a rectangular figure than on a space defined by a uniform curvilinear outline free of any diverging straight lines. This is why we should expect the construction of an oblique on a large chord of an arc of the circular base to be no more difficult than constructing a straight line along a diameter of the same base. Here again, however, the experimental material can explain the results. Although the construction is done on a circular base, this base is placed on a table whose rectilinear contours are always liable to exert a positive or negative influence on the child's work—whence the nearly equal difficulty of problems 3 and 6 (negative influence of rectilinear contours) and the unequal difficulty of problems 5 and 6 (positive influence in 5, negative in 6). Moreover, problem 4 is clearly of intermediate difficulty: easier than problem 3 where the distorting influence of rectilinear contours is maximal, it is located midway between problem 6 and problems 1, 2, and 5 without differing significantly from either. All told, the technique of the circular base does not at all fulfill its objective. Yet it is not useless, for it contributes at least to increasing the reliability of the test. An interpretation is more accurate when it can draw on the results obtained from six problems rather than only three and when these problems are presented in a different enough manner to avoid the impression of unnecessarily repeating the same problem. If we wanted to study directly the difficulties involved with the perceptual neighborhood of curvilinear outlines, we would have to modify considerably the present technique and resort, for example, to one of the following means: using a circular table à la Piaget and Lovell; increasing its size so as completely to cover the work table; placing the circular base on the floor of the examining room; etc. But most of these modifications would be either inadequate to eliminate completely the rectilinear references, or impractical in a standardized test which is administered both at home and at school.

The last question to be discussed is undeniably the most important. The question asks why the construction of a straight line is not possible for the child at an earlier age. If the ages of accession reported in Table 22 are comparable to those found by Piaget, they nevertheless show a marked delay in comparison with Lovell's results. Particularly in the case of the straight line to be constructed at the edge of a rectangular table, the successes do not reach 50 per cent before the age of 5:4 years, while Lovell's subjects, before the age of 4:0 years, manage the straight line in a proportion of 53 per cent (and even 93 per cent if the criterion of success admits certain irregularities). As concerns the obliques, also, the results reported here are different from Lovell's, even though the *décalage* is less sharp. While Lovell's subjects succeed in constructing perfect obliques at 32 and 36 per cent between 5:0 and 5:8 years, comparable percentages (30 and 35) are not attained before the age of 6:0 years in this experiment.

It is not easy to explain these differences. One might first think that the relative quality of the subjects is the determining factor. But the groups of children tested here constitute samples which exactly represent the general population from which they are drawn and which should not have an undue proportion of children who are less gifted than average. Furthermore, there is nothing to support the assumption that Lovell's subjects were above average in ability. On the contrary, he expressly states that, in relation to the English population, his subjects were below average. Perhaps we should speculate that the differences are due to the scoring procedure. But Lovell mentions that his scoring criteria were strict, even at the risk of crediting the subject with errors which were really made by the examiner in recording the responses. The criteria applied here are certainly no more rigorous: they require the absence of any curve or twist in the child's constructions but are more lenient on several other points, such as the precise orientation of the lines, the order of the successful constructions, use of the entire space, etc. Although Lovell is quite sparing with details concerning his scoring criteria, we may accurately assume that his evaluation of the protocols is more strict than the scoring procedure applied here and thus would not account for the apparent precociousness of his subjects. Another factor which might influence the results is the nature of the experimental materials. We know that Lovell, like Piaget, used matches planted vertically in balls of modeling clay rather than the miniature lampposts used in the present test. It is not impossible that manipulation of the miniature lampposts presents more difficulty than the matches, especially among the very young children. But this would have to be proved, and even assuming that it were true, this factor would be largely compensated for by the fact that, for an equal number of elements to line up (eight in both cases), Lovell's subjects had to construct considerably longer lines than in the present test (ratio of 1.5 to 1 for the edge line and 2.0 to 1 for the obliques). It is logical to assume, other things being equal, that a straight line is much more difficult to construct when the elements are spaced apart, for the subject is less aided by the elementary relations of proximity.

It remains to be asked whether the earliness of the successes observed by Lovell could not depend on characteristics of the test and, specifically, on the instructions given the subject. For lack of precise indications in this respect, we are reduced to conjecture. It seems that it may be worth while to raise the question whether Lovell's directions specifically forbade the examiner to trace an imaginary line with his finger in full view of the subject. The examiner may spontaneously resort to this very simple gesture in order to make the child understand what is required of him. It is undeniable that this gesture economizes on verbal explanations and is quite effective, as the results of some preliminary trials showed. But this efficacy is won at the price of serious theoretical concessions whose consequences might escape the attention of the unprepared examiner and which seriously compromise the interpretation of the results. In tracing the imaginary line with the finger in full view of the child, the examiner is doing more than expressing a purely verbal instruction; he changes the basis of the problem, whose solution may be then located at a purely intuitive or preoperational level, particularly in the simplest cases. This procedure provides the child with a partial solution to the problem: he is given a perceptual model which he can internalize as is, without having to reconstruct it, while the very movement of tracing an imaginary straight line already presumes the capacity for such a reconstruction and is itself classified among Euclidian solution procedures. For this reason, as Piaget and Inhelder emphasize (1948, p. 196), the immediate mental representation resulting from models already formed in the perceptual field, however useful it may be to the child, still retains the fragility of purely intuitive or static images. It is still subject to the perceptual conditions of the moment, and especially to interferences which might be produced by the simultaneous presence of diverging perceptual models, and cannot free itself of these before the child is capable of projective or Euclidian operations.

Assuming, therefore, that Lovell's instructions authorize or even invite the examiner to trace with his finger or to suggest by gesture the straight line which the subject must construct, the significance of his findings is considerably clarified. If the successes are so early in the case of straight lines parallel to the edge of the table, it is because the subject can order his construction according to a mental image whose elaboration implies no more than the internalization of a perceptual model supplied by the examiner and whose conservation is easier when it is supported and favored by the perceptual configurations present at the time (parallelism of the edges of the table). If, on the other hand, the success with the oblique is much later than with the straight lines parallel to the sides, reflecting a *décalage* which is more accentuated than the analogous *décalage* observed here, it is because the pictorial representation of the imaginary line traced by the examiner is much more precarious since it is in conflict with the immediately perceived—and more salient—diverging straight lines in the child's visual field. An analogous conflict between the imaginary straight line and the curve perceived by the child may also explain the considerable difference which Lovell observed between success with straight lines parallel to the edge of a rectangular table and success with straight lines constructed on a circular table.

Thus it is not impossible that Lovell's results may be explained in this manner. Even supposing that his examiners refrained from illustrating the verbal instructions with concrete gestures, we should at least like to see Lovell place as much emphasis on recognizing (and explaining) the difficulty with the obliques as he places on pointing out (without explaining) the ease with straight lines parallel to the edge of the table. The *décalage* observed between these two types of problems is so great that we are correct in enquiring about the equivalence of the procedures required to resolve them and, in particular, about the truly projective or Euclidian quality of the earliest solutions.

Chapter VII

Construction of a Projective Straight Line: Analysis by Stages

The analysis by stages is based on the results of the preceding analysis and is, in various ways, its necessary complement. It is necessary first to an understanding of the intellectual mechanisms implied in the construction of a straight line. A simple age distribution of successes and failures with each problem is superficial and impersonal; only an examination of the protocols, by analyzing the various failures and successes and the behavior leading to them, can demonstrate the intuitive or operational character of the solutions which the child brings to the problems in the test as a whole. Nor can individual analysis of these various problems determine the age at which construction of a straight line is really accessible to the child—that is, the age at which the child can construct it independently of favorable conditions such as the absence of diverging straight lines in the visual field, the presence of a previously constructed model, etc. If the percentage of success observed with each problem can barely contribute to clarifying the major developmental aspect, it is for the very simple reason that we cannot specify to what extent these percentages, calculated separately for each problem, refer to the same subjects each time. Thus, without analyzing the individual protocols, it is impossible to evaluate the quality of the various methods used by the child, to distinguish the intuitive from the operational (projective or Euclidian) solutions, or to determine with minimum accuracy the age at which the child becomes capable of this latter type of solution. Finally, we may emphasize the importance of the analysis by stages when the time comes to compare the child's ability to construct a straight line, as studied in

133

this test, with his ability to distinguish curvilinear from rectilinear figures as studied in the preceding test on the child's stereognostic representations. In order to be useful, such a comparison must be made between the ages when these two abilities are respectively acquired and mastered. Only an analysis by stages can establish this comparison if we wish to avoid having accidental successes—or successes due to primitive solution procedures—fog up the picture and weaken the significance of the conclusions.

ESTABLISHMENT OF A DEVELOPMENTAL SCALE

The proposed stages derive from the findings of the preceding analyses. Given that the six problems of the test are split into two different levels of difficulty (problems 1, 2, 4, and 5) versus problems 3 and 6), a primary classification of the protocols into three principal stages appears. In the *first* stage, children are incapable of constructing even the easiest straight lines and consequently miss every problem. The *second* stage includes children who can construct straight lines parallel to the edge of the rectangular base (problems 1 and 2) or to the rectangular table on which the circular base is placed (problems 4 and 5), but who fail to construct the obliques (problems 3 and 6). Finally, in the *third* stage, children master even the oblique lines.

To increase the sensitivity and homogeneity of the classification it is necessary to subdivide these principal stages into a certain number of substages, each one corresponding to a group of more limited and more specific behaviors. Thus, before stage 1 itself we must have a stage 0 that groups together all subjects who simply refuse to take the test or who, either through lack of understanding of the instructions or inability to follow them, never manage to arrange the elements along even a curved or winding line and are content to place them in separate groups with no concern for order or symmetry. On the other hand, as soon as they succeed in constructing a curved or twisting line at least once, they are classified in stage 1 even if the rest of the protocol shows stage 0 characteristics. This first stage is divided into two substages according to whether the number of lines constructed is less than four out of six (substage 1A) or at least four (substage 1B). In neither case, however, are the lines straight.

Similarly, stage 2, characterized by success with at least one straight line parallel to the rectilinear sides and by a failure with the two obliques, includes two substages depending on the quality of the failure with the oblique. The subject is classified in substage 2A when this failure reflects an inability to free himself from the attraction of the diverging lines of the visual field. He is classified in substage 2B when at least one of the two obliques is not subject to the influence of these perceptual indices but nevertheless has certain irregularities (twists, deviations) which reveal a failure to resort to projective or Euclidian construction techniques. Finally, stage 3, where even the obliques are mastered, also has two substages depending on whether the subject can construct only one of the two (substage 3A), or both (substage 3B).

DISTRIBUTION OF SUBJECTS ON THE DEVELOPMENTAL SCALE

Once this developmental scale was established, after numerous trials which were required for delimiting the substages, all protocols were jointly examined and classified by the two authors into one or another of these stages and substages, with the exception of those of children who did not follow the instructions. Rather than trying to construct at least the required lines, as most of even the youngest children did (more or less clumsily), these subjects seemed to see the experimental material as an opportunity to make their own constructions regardless of the instructions. This attitude is recognizable in the way the subjects respond to some or all of the problems: a regular arrangement of the lampposts on the base; systematic arrangement around the two houses; decorative motifs which are independent of the two houses; identical construction in all six problems without regard for the houses (e.g., a central straight line, double row, central ring, etc.). How can we explain this type of behavior, which appeared especially between 4:6 and 7:0 years? It may be a question of an intentional refusal to follow the instructions, since this is likely in children of this age who are already watchful of their autonomy, who are inclined to demonstrate creativity or fantasy in their activities, and who are still more or less ignorant of school discipline. It is also possible that this apparent disobedience is a symptom of an actual inability which the child is aware of and which he seeks to disguise under the cloak of play and fantasy rather than betray himself by a simple refusal or by clearly incorrect constructions, as the youngest children often do.

It is not easy to decide between these two explanations, as each undoubtedly contains an element of truth. When the child's attitude is not contradictory during the course of the test, and when he invariably gives the same solution to each problem, we should probably interpret this as an intentional refusal to follow the instructions and to make a real attempt. The fact that these subjects systematically reproduce the same construction—a construction which is sometimes remarkable in its symmetry and even its rectilinearity—suggests that their refusal does not necessarily hide a real inability. On the other hand, when these aberrant behaviors are seen only with certain problems it is easier to discriminate the child's real capabilities; but a child's occasionally resorting to whimsical behavior, oblivious to the instructions, may influence the whole protocol and indirectly complicate even the interpretation of problems which he seems really to have tried to solve. To settle the question of whether the children are simply rebelling against the instructions or are perhaps unable to follow them, we should also consider their verbal explanations. Many will voluntarily admit that they did not construct straight lines, but will justify themselves by remarks of this sort: *"it's too easy to make a straight road"* (!); *"a really straight road isn't pretty"; "it's better to put the lights right next to the house, it lights them up better"; "we should keep some lights for the others, too";* etc. Whatever it is, in order to avoid compromising the analysis of the results by these difficulties in interpretation (relative difficulty of the problems, developmental curves, etc.), it is better to eliminate all the equivocal protocols, including those where only certain problems are in question. Of the 594 subjects studied, 72 were eliminated in this way. As Table 22 shows (p. 127), these subjects were found at almost every age level, but for the most part they were between 4:6 and 7:0 years. The distribution of these subjects by socioeconomic level—the main selection criterion—is not significantly different from the distribution of the whole group (see Table 23). Thus, eliminating these subjects does not introduce a systematic bias into the results of the analysis.

A second classification of all protocols, independent of the first, was then made by the same judge who had replicated the scoring of

Table 23

Comparative percentages of all subjects (2:0 to 10:0 years) and of subjects not classified in the *Construction of a projective straight line* test, for each of the six occupational categories

Subjects	N	Occupational category*					
		1	2	3	4	5	6
Total group	594	22	7	8	49	6	8
Unclassified subjects	72	27	7	4	47	8	7

*See Tables 1 and 2.

the individual problems. The over-all disagreement between the two classifications is 8.40 per cent. Still rather low for such a difficult classification, the importance of this disagreement is further reduced if we note that, of the 39 protocols which were classified differently by the second judge, only one is removed by three levels (out of the seven levels in the scale), three are two levels removed, and the other 35 are only one level different. Furthermore, of the 72 protocols eliminated in the first scoring, 67 were eliminated in the second, which rejected only six of the protocols retained by the first. Considering all of these disagreements, we may state that the great majority (about 82 per cent) concern the evaluation of the obliques. The second scoring seems to be much stricter than the first in defining as imperfect those lines which the first scoring procedure had attributed to imperfections in the examiner's transcriptions. This kind of ambiguity undoubtedly would have been less frequent if the examiners had known from the beginning how important the obliques would be in the developmental scale. Be that as it may, the disagreements have but little effect on the total distributions or on the indices which are sought (median age and age of accession), since the disagreements are often balanced by each other.

The scale is divided into seven levels along which we may distribute all the protocols except those which were impossible to classify using the present criteria. Table 24 gives the results of this distribution. The figures are based on the first scoring procedure. The only significant difference which the second procedure would entail would concern the age of accession to the last level of the scale (substage 3B) which would be about nine months less than that presented here. The results in Table 24 indicate first that there is not one exception in the order of progression of median

Table 24

Distribution of subjects by age and by stage in the *Construction of a projective straight line* test

Age	N	Unclassified	Stage												
			Frequencies							Cumulated percentages				
			0	1A	1B	2A	2B	3A	3B	1A	1B	2A	2B	3A
10:0	44	6					3	4	31				100	92
9:0	50	8				2	3	12	25				95	88
8:0	50	3				2	2	17	26				96	91
7:0	50	8				3	5	12	22			100	93	81
6:0	50	10			3	6	11	12	8			93	78	50
5:0	50	14			6	8	10	10	2		100	83	61	33
4:6	50	12	3	4	7	10	6	7	1	92	82	63	37	21
4:0	50	3	2	9	18	12	5	1		96	77	38	13	2
3:6	50	3	1	13	8	17	4	4		98	70	53	17	9
3:0	50	3	5	9	20	8	3	2		89	70	28	11	4
2:6	50	1	9	18	16	5	1			82	45	12	2	
2:0	50	1	24	18	5	2				51	14	4		
Total		72	44	71	83	75	53	81	115					
Median age*			2:3	2:10	3:5	4:1	5:3	6:9	8:7					
Age of accession										—	2:10	3:10	4:11	5:11

*See footnote to Table 16.

ages. The distributions of each stage are significantly different (at the .01 level, except between stages 0 and 1A where the significance level is .025: Kolmogorov-Smirnov test). Examination of the ages of accession to different stages also shows that the ability to construct even one of the straight lines parallel to the straight edge of the table is not acquired before the age of 3:10 years (stage 2A) and that the oblique is not mastered before 5:11 years (stage 3A). This shows that the ability to construct a straight line is not really acquired until about six years, since before this minimum age the child is unable to line up a series of elements without relying on perceptual or at least intuitive models. Mastery of the oblique is crucial, in this respect, because it implies an emancipation from the interference due to the proximity of diverging straight lines and normally presupposes the intervention of projective or Euclidian procedures.

Examination of the same table shows that children of 3:6 years are slightly superior to children of 4:0 years. It seems impossible to find a logical and decisive explanation of this phenomenon, which leads to the irregularity of the percentage curve in certain stages. Perhaps it may be attributable to the fact that disobedience of the instructions, so frequently observed after 4:6 years, has already begun to appear by 4:0 years; but, because this disobedience is still neither systematic nor blatantly evident, the subjects involved are not considered impossible to classify and their protocols are thus added to those already assigned to lower stages.

Finally, there is no significant difference (Kolmogorov-Smirnov test, .01 level) between results obtained on boys and on girls.

DETAILED DESCRIPTION OF THE STAGES

In order to determine the real significance of these numerical results, it is necessary to analyze each level of the scale individually. Only a detailed description of these stages, illustrated with examples, can isolate their principal characteristics and reveal the intellectual mechanisms underlying each level of conceptualization.

STAGE 0: REFUSAL, INCOMPREHENSION, OR INABILITY TO CONSTRUCT EVEN A CURVED OR TWISTING LINE

The primitive character of this stage, where the oldest children are no more than 4:6 years, is seen either in the refusal to take the test or in the absence of any linear construction at all (even curved or twisting). However, subjects who reject the test altogether are very infrequent (only five), which attests to the interest the children have in it. Most of them try at least some of the problems before declining, and nearly half of them attempt all six. But not one of them gives any indication that he is able to construct even a single line. The response always consists of placing the elements here and there on the base without any concern for order or symmetry.

As figure 5 (I and II) shows, the child will prefer to place the lampposts in the space separating the two houses in order to follow the instruction asking him to *"make a straight line between the houses,"* or *"a very straight road which starts at one house and goes to the other."* He thus arrives at configurations of elements which are sometimes quite far apart (see especially I) or sometimes much closer together (see especially II). Other children will not even follow this much of the instructions and will place the lampposts either near one or both of the houses (IIIa or IIIb), in a limited area of the base but without concern for the houses (IIIc), or finally over the whole surface in a purely arbitrary and random manner (IIId).

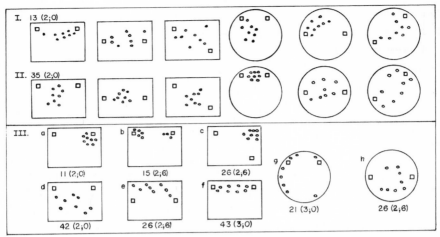

Figure 5. Examples of protocols (complete: I and II; excerpts: III) from stage 0 of the *Construction of a projective straight line* test.

There is no doubt that these various behaviors are extremely primitive. They are characterized by the intervention of the most elementary topological relations of neighborhood or proximity. The child places the lampposts side by side, or around the houses, and can thus manage to construct groups or configurations of varying density and shape; but he is still far not only from the projective or Euclidian line, but even from the purely topological line. Construction of such a line in fact implies much more than the representation of simple relations of proximity. To these elementary relations, which are common to all of the child's constructions, he necessarily adds the more specific relations of continuity and particularly of order or spatial succession which constitute the basis of the topological line. Undoubtedly it is because they cannot coordinate these very simple relations that some children cannot construct even a twisting line. In any case, whether the primitive behavior is explained by a failure to understand the instructions or by a complete inability to follow them, it has not yet reached stage 1, which is reserved for subjects who are capable of at least the representations or anticipations necessary for constructing a topological line. These protocols must also be distinguished from those which are impossible to classify: in the latter case, the subject's various constructions (e.g., systematic repetition of a single line in all six problems; ordered and symmetrical arrangement of elements not in linear succession; etc.) may be explained equally well by a deliberate refusal to follow the instructions as by an actual inability.

Finally, in certain subjects at the intermediate level, it is not easy to make the distinction between the simple configurations of stage 0 and the topological lines of stage 1. Even in a collection of randomly placed elements it is sometimes possible to recognize or perceptually to isolate fragments of a curved or twisting or even of a straight line. Figure 5 gives examples of this (see especially IIIe, IIIf, IIIg, and IIIh). In judging these ambiguous problems, we may refer to the rest of the protocol or to the sequence adopted by the child in positioning the elements. If the rest of the protocol shows almost the same type of construction without discernible lines, or if the child's sequence is neither ordered nor systematic, it is probable that the partial sequences or the line fragments are the result of chance, and the protocol then belongs to stage 0.

STAGE 1: LINEAR CONSTRUCTIONS WHICH ARE OF A PURELY TOPOLOGICAL NATURE BUT ARE NEVER STRAIGHT

Subjects at this level understand the instructions and openly try to conform to them. They are characterized mainly by the ability to construct a line, that is, a series of items distributed so that they follow each other in a relationship of sequence or spatial succession. But they never manage to make a straight line, not even in the easiest cases where the construction must be parallel to one side of the rectangular base. All the lines are twisting or curved, and they may be formed of one or more than one segment; in the latter case, however, the segments are never placed in each other's extensions nor parallel to each other. When the construction requires the child to ignore the straight lines or curves present in his visual field, the influence of these diverging lines is still felt: thus the oblique to be constructed on the rectangle becomes a more or less sinuous line running along one of the sides, or a pronounced curve bending toward the two adjacent sides. The lines to be constructed on the circular base clearly reflect the distorting influence of the neighboring borders, whenever the lines are not simply twisted. Figure 6 gives several examples of these various constructions.

Compared with the preceding level, the behavior at this stage shows considerable progress. The child is no longer content with forming groups or collections based solely on relations of neighbor-

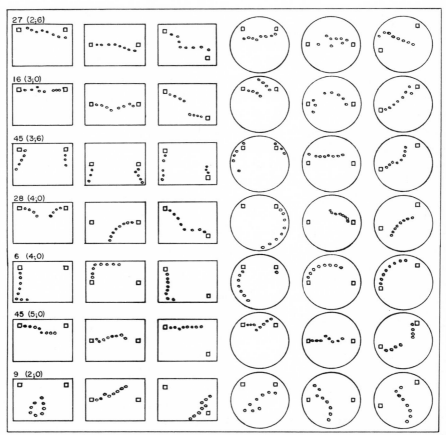

Figure 6. Examples of protocols from stage 1 of the *Construction of a projective straight line* test.

hood; he is now capable of constructing at least a line, which pre-supposes a minimum of coordination between these elementary neighborhood relations and the other less simple relations of continuity and order (or spatial succession). However, despite this flexibility in his mental representations and anticipations, the child is still powerless to impose a constant direction on his movements. Still unable to rely on projective or Euclidian reference schemata, the child cannot imagine, or anticipate, the whole of the line which he is asked to construct. He must proceed bit by bit and, so to speak, shortsightedly—whence the importance of the perceptual models which he both depends on and is victimized by, but which he cannot even systematically imitate. Whence also the topological character of his lines, made up of elements progressively distributed, without a total plan, and following only the elementary relations of proximity and spatial succession. It is not surprising that under these conditions the child's linear constructions are all curved or twisting and are not always oriented in the direction requested by the examiner, even in a very general sense. The last protocol included in Figure 6 gives clear examples of topological lines which start almost anywhere, are constructed without concern for the total effect, and are consequently subject to all sorts of chance distortions from the successive neighborhoods. Nor is it surprising that many of the subjects at this level do not even attempt to straighten their lines. Unable to imagine a real straight line, they assume that their construction is rectilinear and they often affirm this with a conviction which could be shaken only by a comparison of their line with a previously constructed straight line (a comparison which would not, however, provide them with a means of correcting their own lines). Other subjects, more hesitant and certainly more docile, will try to adjust their lines but will not succeed because, since they are unable to consider the total group of elements, their corrections are fragmentary and deal only with pairs of neighboring elements individually.

The difference between substage 1A and substage 1B is, above all, a quantitative one. The protocols are classified in 1A or 1B depending on whether the number of linear constructions made by the child is less than or at least equal to four. This demarcation point, besides dividing the number of possible solutions into two equal parts, also delimits to a certain extent two different levels of behavior. The protocol fragments reported in Figure 7 illustrate these qualitative differences. On one hand, the linear constructions or topological sequences of substage 1B are generally better defined and better arranged than those of substage 1A (compare examples a, b, d to examples g, h, j in Figure 7). On the other hand, even in the case of responses characterized by the absence of any linear construction, the configurations of substage 1B are already more structured than those of substage 1A (compare examples i, k, l with c, e, f).

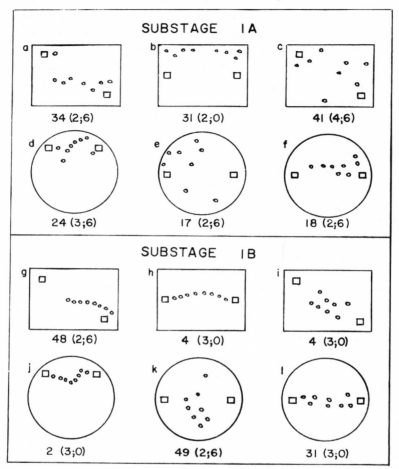

Figure 7. Excerpts of protocols illustrating the differences between substages 1A and 1B of the *Construction of a projective straight line* test.

STAGE 2: SUCCESS WITH STRAIGHT LINES PARALLEL TO
SIDES, BUT FAILURE WITH OBLIQUES

It is at stage 2 that the ability to construct a more or less straight line is seen for the first time; it should still be specified—and this specific is extremely revealing—that these successes are limited to straight lines parallel to the rectilinear contours already present in the visual field. This parallelism is evident in the case of the marginal straight line (problem 1) and the central straight line (problem 2) which are constructed on the rectangular base. This is undoubtedly why both can be resolved without one seeming more difficult

than the other despite the slight difference in distance which separates the two from the edge of the rectangle. As for the straight lines
on the circular base, parallelism does not exist as such; but if the
last two problems in this section (problems 4 and 5) are shown to be
as easy as the two corresponding problems in the first section, this
is probably due to the fact that the circular piece is placed on a
rectangular table and, consequently, the proximity of parallel rectilinear contours is not really eliminated. It is striking to note that
several children, when asked to construct an oblique on a circle
(problem 6), repeat almost exactly the angular lines or the straight
lines parallel to the rectilinear sides of the base which had already
been constructed in response to problem 3 (oblique on a rectangle),
an action which unequivocally betrays the persistent influence of the
rectilinear contours beyond the circular base. Figure 8 gives some
typical protocols of stage 2.

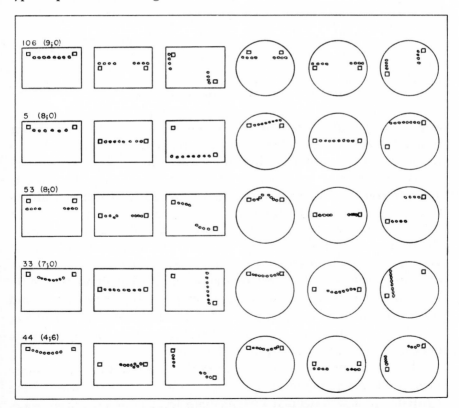

Figure 8. Examples of protocols from stage 2 of the *Construction of a projective
straight line* test.

In sum, children at this level succeed with at least one of the straight lines parallel to the sides but miss both of the obliques. This failure with the obliques is not necessarily of the form which we note in the examples just cited. Some subjects revert to the primitive behavior proper to the earlier stages: simple refusal, figurative groups, topological lines, etc. As Figure 9 illustrates, other subjects

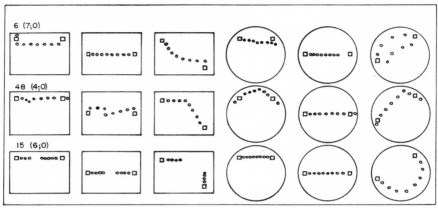

Figure 9. Protocols from stage 2 illustrating various types of errors on problems 3 and 6 of the *Construction of a projective straight line* test.

attempt to join the two houses by a straight line, but the line curves under the distorting influence of the neighboring rectilinear contours or of the immediate curvilinear contours (in the case of constructing a straight line on a circular base). Even when the subjects are able considerably to free themselves from this perceptual attraction, the linear constructions always have irregularities which the subjects are powerless to correct since they are unable to exploit the projective or Euclidian properties of the straight line. It is significant here that only two of all the subjects at this stage use procedures of this sort. The first uses an aiming behavior in two problems (problems 4 and 5), which he immediately solves; the second tries to straighten two of his lines (problems 3 and 5) by bringing his hands together, but he still fails on both problems because he does not apply this technique to the entire line.

The main interest of stage 2, from the viewpoint of the development of the representational straight line, is to demonstrate the existence of a well-defined intermediate level between purely topological constructions and operational constructions. The fact that subjects at this level can solve only straight lines parallel to the rectilinear sides and systematically fail with the obliques indicates that the spatial representations implicit in these linear constructions are still dependent on the perceptual factors of the moment. As soon as the subject can no longer guide his activity by a rectilinear model already present in his perceptual field, he is powerless to provide himself with this model. This is because a mental representation of a straight line, when it is not the simple copy of a straight line which is immediately or was just previously perceived, presupposes an activity of mental construction of which the child is not capable without a system of projective or Euclidian relations. We see here the basic distinction between the static and passive representations of preoperational thought, still subject to perceptual influences, and the mobile and active representations of operational thought, finally freed from these influences. It is for this reason that constructing a straight line parallel to a visible rectilinear contour assumes no more than the passive imitation of a model which already exists, while constructing a straight line which is slanted in relation to the perceived models implies a real activity of internal reconstruction. Failure to distinguish these two levels of mental representation risks considering solutions which in fact do not go beyond the purely intuitive or preoperational level as operational solutions. Thus, for example, Lovell (1959) may be justified in conceding to the child the ability to construct a straight line quite early; but before granting the child the absolute mastery of the straight line, we must wait until he proves able to construct an oblique. The present results show that there is about a two-year lapse between the ability to construct a straight line parallel to the sides and the ability to construct an oblique. This *décalage* is easily understood if we see that in constructing a straight line without relying on an immediately perceived (or intuitively imagined) model, and despite the obstacles of diverging perceptual models, the child must be able to coordinate and anticipate his successive movements within a larger plan whose elaboration necessarily assumes the use of projective or Euclidian representations. Certain spontaneous remarks of the children clearly reflect the precariousness of the mental representations at this level. In problem 6, for example (see Figure 10), one child (subject 9, at 4:0 years) makes a perfect straight line which starts at one house but remains in a horizontal direction (perpendicular to his plane of vision). Surprised that his line does not reach the second house, he is quick to say: *"when the houses are placed like that, you have to make a round line to get to the other house."* As this child feels that a straight line cannot become oblique without ceasing to be straight, we are justified in questioning his ability spontaneously to imagine the straight line joining the two houses.

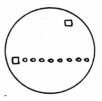

Figure 10. Protocol excerpt from subject 9 (4:0) in the *Construction of a projective straight line* test.

If behavior characterized simultaneously by failure with the obliques and success with the straight lines parallel to the rectilinear contours were not so frequent or so systematic, we might try to explain the *décalage* by incidental factors such as a fluctuation in the child's efforts, inconsistency in his temporary interests, attention span, etc. As we shall see in a moment, these factors can account for the fact that the subjects do not necessarily succeed with all straight lines parallel to rectilinear contours (problems 1, 2, 4, and 5) whose difficulty is, however, nearly equal. But the *décalage* in question here is much more basic. All subjects at stage 2 (128, representing 25 per cent of the subjects classified on the scale) succeed with at least one of the parallel straight lines but consistently fail with both obliques. Of the 256 failures recorded for problems 3 and 6, 57 per cent unequivocally show complete submission to the perceptual suggestion of the neighboring contours, 13 per cent reflect still more primitive behavior (simple refusal or formation of clusters), and only 30 per cent indicate a freedom from perceptual contours, although the constructions are still sinuous or irregular. If these perceptual elements play such a role in the construction of obliques, it is logical to suppose that they intervene even more in the case of straight lines parallel to rectilinear contours. Without having universal effectiveness, this intervention nonetheless demonstrates the intuitive or preoperational character of successes typical of this level.

Like the preceding stage, stage 2 is divided into two substages. Yet the criterion that determines this subdivision is not a quantitative one as it was in the first stage. It is based on the nature of the failures recorded for the oblique lines rather than on the number of successes with the straight lines parallel to the rectilinear sides. The choice of this latter criterion might seem indicated, given that the four straight lines in question (problems 1, 3, 4, and 5) are of equivalent difficulty—at least for the whole sample taken together— and that success with any one of these lines does not automatically entail success with the others. Whence the possibility of distributing the subjects into two subgroups according to whether they solve only one or two, or more than two, straight lines out of four. Considering the facts in a developmental perspective, we also observe a rather marked difference in age between these two groups of subjects (see Table 25). But, despite its real merits, this quantitative criterion was not used, and for two complementary reasons.

Table 25

Distribution of subjects at stage 2 by age and by number of successes with the four easiest problems (1, 2, 4, and 5) of the *Construction of a projective straight line* test

Age	Number of successes				Total
	1	2	3	4	
10:0		1		2	3
9:0		1	3	1	5
8:0	1	1	1	1	4
7:0	3	2	1	2	8
6:0	4	3	7	3	17
5:0	7	3	3	5	18
4:6	8	4	3	1	16
4:0	11	4	1	1	17
3:6	13	6	2		21
3:0	8	3			11
2:6	4	2			6
2:0	2				2
Total	61	30	21	16	128
Median age	3:11	4:3	5:9	6:0	

The first reason depends on the fact that the four problems concerned are of nearly equivalent difficulty. In seeking to discover the child's ability to construct a straight line at this level of difficulty, the question whether this child can do so only once or more than once is not of primary theoretical interest and thus can be ignored. Speaking strictly in terms of the level of spatial conceptualization, the main point is to require that the child manage at least once to overcome the difficulties which mental representation of the straight line may pose in a given perceptual context. If these difficulties are basically the same in a group of problems, as is the case here, successes are equivalent or interchangeable at least in the sense that not one of them requires a different level of mental functioning. Thus it is permissible to assume that a distribution of subjects according to the number of solutions to the problems would refer much less to intrinsic differences in ability than to temporary fluctuations in efficiency. When we know the children's difficulty with sustained attention, we can understand that they are not systematically able to solve all the problems of a single level and that this sort of inconsistency, as Table 25 shows, is found especially among the youngest subjects. Such an interpretation, however, assumes that failures on these four problems among stage 2 subjects are distributed nearly equally among the problems without any noticeable bias, since the problems are of the same difficulty throughout the sample. Now, if we compare the results given in Table 26, we note that the number of

Table 26

Number of errors in each of problems 1, 2, 4, and 5 of the *Construction of a projective straight line* test for all stage 2 subjects divided into two groups according to their total successes (1-2 or 3-4) with the four problems

Total number of successes	N	Problems			
		1	2	4	5
1-2	91	54	54	77	58
3-4	37	3	6	8	3

failures is approximately the same in the four problems. Analysis of these differences indicates that only problem 4 is significantly more difficult than the others (McNemar test: .01 level). In sum, at least three of these four problems are of equivalent difficulty and, if the youngest children can solve one without solving the others, perhaps it is simply because the efforts and interests of these children are still subject to temporary fluctuations.

Yet the main reason why the quantitative criterion was not retained is that the subdivision of a stage must depend as much as possible on the quality of the intellectual processes typical of that stage. The preceding analysis clearly demonstrated that the mental representations available to children at this level are not yet free of the perceptual configurations of intuitive or preoperational thought. It is this fragility or passivity of mental imagery which explains both the child's relative ease at solving a straight line parallel to neighboring rectilinear contours and his utter inability to construct a straight line which slants in relation to these contours. This is why the criterion adopted for subdividing the present stage is based on the nature of the failures recorded on oblique lines, since the quality of the mistakes is the most instructive indication of the child's ability to free himself from the perceptual or intuitive constrictions of this level. Thus the subjects are divided into two subgroups. The first consists of children whose failure with the oblique visibly reveals the distorting influence of the diverging contours when it does not simply take the form of the still more primitive behavior of the earlier stages. The second group includes all subjects whose "oblique" constructions seem, in one problem, to remove themselves from this perceptual context but are still subject to irregularities (twists, slight curves, or major flaws in the general orientation) which undeniably reflect a persistent inability to use projective or Euclidian procedures.

The distribution of subjects at stage 2 by a qualitative criterion satisfies the requirements of a developmental study. Referring to the results in Table 24 (p. 138), we observed that in fact the median age of subjects at substage 2A (poorer solutions) is at least one year less than that of subjects at substage 2B (better solutions). However, this distribution does not agree with that yielded by the quantitative criterion just discussed. Although each of these classifications is tied to the chronological age (tau = .46 for the quantitative criterion and .36 for the qualitative), there is no possibility of a single classification based on both at once. The results given in Table 27 indicate that despite a certain amount of overlap (tau = .24), the subjects are

Table 27

Distribution of stage 2 subjects in the *Construction of a projective straight line* test according to two possible criteria (numerical or qualitative) for division into substages

| Numerical criterion | Qualitative criterion | | Total |
	Inferior solution	Superior solution	
1-2 successes	60	31	91
3-4 successes	15	22	37
Total	75	53	108

divided differently depending on which criterion is used. Since we must choose between the two, preference should go to the one which divides the subjects along the dimension most directly related to the nature of the test. As we have just shown, the qualitative criterion better satisfies this theoretical requirement because the classification to which it leads emphasizes, above all, the child's ability progressively to leave his intuitive and preoperational modes of spatial representation. That the correlation between this criterion and the numerical criterion is a weak one is not at all paradoxical. It clearly illustrates the fragility of the child's success and of his intuitive solution procedures. If the failures recorded in constructing the obliques can be explained by the intuitive character of spatial conceptions at this level, it is not surprising that the child can construct a straight line parallel to neighboring rectilinear contours; but neither is it surprising that, given the fragility of these intuitive procedures and the variability of the child's efforts, the correlation between the number of successes with the parallel straight lines and the quality of failures with obliques is rather low.

Taking account of these various considerations, subjects at stage 2, already able to construct one or more straight lines parallel to the rectilinear contours of the table (problems 1, 2, 4, and 5), are divided into two substages according to the quality of their solutions to problems 3 and 6. At substage 2A, failure on these two problems is reflected in an apparent inability to resist the perceptual suggestions of the diverging contours, or by a regression to still lower behavior (simple refusal, or formation of figural groups). Figure 11 gives some typical examples from this level. At substage 2B, on the other hand, solutions are already more advanced. As Figure 11 illustrates, the subject still misses the two problems involved; but he manages at least once (subjects f, g, and h), if not both times (subjects i and j), to construct a line whose obvious obliqueness testifies to a certain independence from the surrounding perceptual contours but whose lack of straightness or orientation still indicates a lack of projective or Euclidian construction procedures. Comparing the protocols reported in this figure, we immediately note the superior quality of the "obliques" constructed by subjects at substage 2B. In cases where the line strongly deviates from its objective (subject g, for example), we may suspect that the subject is still a victim of the attraction exerted by the edges; because the line is never even par-

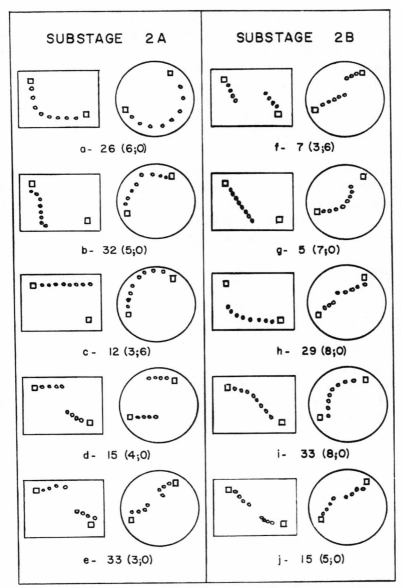

Figure 11. Protocol excerpts illustrating the differences between substages 2A and 2B of the *Construction of a projective straight line* test.

tially parallel to the edges and since it is rigorously straight in spite of everything, however, it seems that the failure depends much less on an excessive submission to perceptual indices than on an as yet imperfect mastery of projective (or Euclidian) methods. Unable to found his linear constructions on a comprehensive projection which would include both his own body and the two objective reference points in a single perspective, the subject restricts himself to lining up the elements as a function of his own body, starting from a single objective reference point. It is this residual egocentrism which keeps him from locating the two reference points in relation to each other (and both in relation to himself) and from choosing, among all possible perspectives, the only one which could effectively coordinate all three elements of the total projection.

Finally, we must emphasize that, of the 53 subjects at substage 2B, 28 still submit at least once to the attraction of the base contours. However, nothing suggests that this influence differs depending on whether the base is rectangular (problem 3) or circular (problem 6), since the 28 subjects are distributed in an exactly equal number in both cases.

STAGE 3: MASTERY OF THE OBLIQUE

Stage 3 is characterized by the mastery of the oblique line. At least one time out of two, the child at this level is able to construct an oblique in the desired direction and with no deviation whatever. As examination of Figure 12 shows, the obliques may differ in how

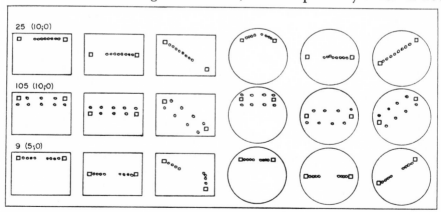

Figure 12. Examples of protocols from stage 3 of the *Construction of a projective straight line* test.

they conform to the instructions (e.g., short lines, parallel rows, double sections, etc.); in every case, however, the elements are correctly aligned and are placed along the imaginary line joining the two houses. To make this construction, the subject may resort to several strategies whose projective or Euclidian characteristics are undeniable: aiming behavior; preliminary tracing of imaginary lines; subsequent straightening of the elements which were at first arranged rapidly and carelessly, by bringing the hands together or by spontaneous use of another object (e.g., a pencil); etc.

Before going further in the analysis of the behavior proper to this level, it is important to note that at stage 3 is found the same phenomenon observed in the preceding stage, regarding the relationship between the quality of the obliques and the number of straight lines which the child succeeds in making parallel to the sides. Rather paradoxically, even a perfect solution of the oblique by the stage 3 child does not necessarily presume the solution of the other straight lines (problems 1, 2, 4, and 5), which we have seen to be easier. Table 28 shows that among subjects capable of constructing obliques

Table 28

Distribution of subjects* according to their number of successes at each of two levels of difficulty (oblique or parallel to the sides) of the *Construction of a projective straight line* test

Oblique	Parallel to the sides					Total
	4	3	2	1	0	
2	86	23	5	1		115
1	21	27	20	8	5	81
0	16	21	30	61	198	326
Total	123	71	55	70	203	522

*Excluding the 72 subjects who were not classified in the developmental scale and the six subjects of 10:0 years of age who did not take the test.

a rather considerable number still lack one or more of the straight lines parallel to the sides (and five subjects fail with all of them). Does this lack of transitivity significantly compromise the value of the classification? The question arises especially in the most extreme cases where the mastery of the oblique alone, with failure on the other five problems, sufficed to classify the subject at stage 3—that is, at a higher level than that to which a subject is assigned when he succeeds with the four straight lines parallel to the sides but misses the two obliques. At the strictly theoretical level, it is undeniable that the validity of a hierarchical classification ideally presumes a perfect transitivity. But analysis of human behaviors, particularly when one hopes to go beyond simple numerical series and to order them according to the very quality of the mental processes underlying them, does not easily accommodate itself to these theoretical exigencies. Examination of the results reported in Table 28 shows that in fact of the 196 subjects classified at stage 3 for having solved at least one of the two obliques, only five (3 per cent) missed all of the other straight lines, 107 (54 per cent) solved them all, and 157 (80 per cent) solved at least three out of the four. When we consider the whole group (522 subjects), as we would have to do in order to evaluate the degree of transitivity of the total classification, the proportions change considerably: only 1 per cent of the subjects (five out of 522) completely escape the transitivity rule; 83 per cent (433) conform perfectly to it, and 10 per cent (50) have only slight exceptions to it, these last subjects never solving an oblique without solving at least three of the other four straight lines. Particularly if we consider that these four problems are of nearly equivalent difficulty and that the child's temporary interest and efforts are naturally subject to chance fluctuations, these results seem consistent enough to justify the importance which is accorded the success with obliques in the behavioral sequence.

It remains to examine the sort of progress which has taken place in the spatial representations of children reaching this last level of success with the oblique. Analysis of the behavior proper to the preceding stage revealed a progressive liberation from the perceptual indices which could facilitate the construction of straight lines parallel to rectilinear sides and complicate the construction of obliques. At substage 2B especially, imperfection of the obliques seems much less dependent on the distorting influence of neighboring contours than on the inadequacy of the projective or Euclidian procedures employed by the child. If this interpretation is correct, it is logical to suppose that accession to stage 3 marks the appearance of the first projective and Euclidian operations necessary for the perfect construction of the oblique. In principle, this shift from the intuitive to the operational is manifest in the use of aiming behavior, which includes the subject himself and his two objective reference points in a single perspective, or in alignment (or straightening) behavior guided by objective reference frameworks (e.g., tracing an imaginary straight line, placing the elements at an equal distance from the sides of the base, bringing the hands together, etc.). We should thus expect these means of construction to be unusual at stage 2 and massively apparent at stage 3. It is unfortunate, then, that the examiners did not deem it necessary to note systematically on each protocol the presence or absence of these projective or Euclidian techniques. Most of the examiners, probably thinking that the quality of the lines was enough to determine the level of mental functioning, were generally satisfied with carefully indicating the location of the elements as arranged by the child. But in spite of this, we should point out that among the 128 protocols assigned to the second stage, only two (1.5 per cent) include an observation to the effect that the subject resorted to projective or Euclidian methods. At stage 3, on the contrary, 24 per cent of the protocols (47 out of 196) include the same observation, and it is still necessary to point out that the presence of these more highly evolved techniques is noted in 30 per cent (34 out of 115) of the subjects capable of solving both obliques, while the corresponding proportion among those who solved only one of them is only 16 per cent (13 out of 81). Incomplete as they are, these results at least give a valuable indication that the progress observed at stage 3 presupposes the intervention of the first projective or Euclidian operations.

Considering also the nature of the task imposed on the subjects, it is difficult to imagine otherwise. When the straight line must be parallel to a neighboring rectilinear contour, the child may take advantage of these perceptual indices and line up the elements without having to go beyond a purely intuitive or preoperational level of mental representation. When the straight line must be slanted in relation to the neighboring contours, the child must resist the now distorting influence of these perceptual indices and, outside of supposing against all the evidence that the child's successes are always due to chance, construction of a perfect oblique necessarily implies the use of projective or Euclidian techniques. We also observe a considerable improvement, in stage 3 subjects, even in the construction of straight lines parallel to rectilinear sides (problems 1, 2, 4, and 5). From 29 per cent at the preceding stage, the percentage of subjects able to solve at least three of the four problems now reaches 80. To explain this abrupt increase, we may first note that the older child of stage 3 is capable of more sustained and consistent attention. We can also clearly see—and this second factor, rather than excluding the first, may be its principal cause—a valuable indication that the stage 3 child can finally resort to more highly evolved and thus more efficient construction techniques. Mastery of the first projective and Euclidian operations, which are both more stable and more flexible than the intuitive representations of the preoperational level, would have a double effect: it would favor a success with the first oblique lines in freeing the subject from his perceptual bondage, and would at the same time consolidate the ability to construct straight lines parallel to rectilinear contours by straightening the positive role of the perceptual indices. Such an interpretation is quite consistent with the results obtained by Piaget and by Lovell. The former, in fact, finds perfect agreement between success with the obliques and resorting to operational procedures. The latter, furthermore, first observes that solution of the obliques appears toward the age of six years and then points out—without, however, establishing any link between these two observations—that aiming behavior is not generalized before the age of six years, even though it may be encountered before them.

Like the preceding stage, stage 3 is divided into two substages. Substage 3A, several examples of which are given in Figure 13, in-

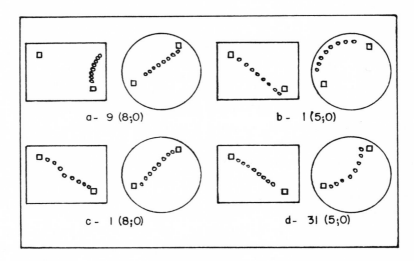

Figure 13. Excerpts of protocols from substage 3A of the *Construction of a projective straight line* test.

cludes subjects who manage to construct only one of the two obliques. The other oblique is never solved, but most of the other straight lines are. In most cases (78 per cent), the failure is reflected in the construction of a slightly irregular or curved oblique (see subjects c and d) while, in the others, the failure is still due rather to the distorting attraction of the neighboring contours (subjects a and b). If we now examine the results in detail, we note that the oblique on the circular base is solved more often than the first (62 per cent versus 38 per cent). This difference may raise doubts about the operational character of the children's procedures. Given that the projective and Euclidian operations are in principle independent of any perceptual configuration, we may ask why the stage 3A subjects seem to have more difficulty with problem 3 than with problem 6. The major explanation may be related to the fact that these children have not yet fully reached the operational level. They are able to use projective or Euclidian procedures, which is a step above the preceding stage; but their use of these procedures is still clumsy and uncertain, a clumsiness and uncertainty which may explain the occasional stumbling over the strongest perceptual suggestions. It is also possible, for the same reason, that the discovery of these operational techniques occurs only in the course of the test and thus favors the solution of the oblique on the circular base. Finally, it is possible that the subject does not immediately show the need to use these techniques and that he begins to doubt the value of his first responses when the examiner questions him each time with the usual question: *"Is your line really quite straight?"*

Substage 3B is characterized by perfect success with both obliques. Use of this purely numerical criterion to distinguish substages 3A and 3B might seem to contradict the principles which determined the subdivision of stage 2. We emphasized at that time the drawbacks of adopting an exclusively numerical criterion because such a criterion is likely to give relatively too much importance to accidental factors (e.g., temporary fluctuations in interest, variability of effort, etc.), which are irrelevant to the very structure of the task required of the child. This danger is a real one. If we were able to avoid it in the case of stage 2 it was because we could choose between a numerical and a qualitative criterion. In the present case, the qualitative criterion which we had hoped for turned out to be either theoretically valuable but impractical because of gaps in the test (e.g., the child's use of Euclidian or projective construction procedures when the examiner did not always note their absence or presence), or practical but with no real theoretical value because they did not reveal intellectual progress (e.g., spacing or contracting the elements; perfect orientation or slight deviation from the objective, etc.). From this point of view, if we try to establish a distinction between the two levels of functioning within stage 3, the numerical criterion is the only one available. The reasons arguing against using a criterion of this sort for subdividing stage 2 are much less serious in the case of stage 3, since there seems to be a rather direct link between the number of obliques solved by the child (numerical criterion) and the operational level of his spatial representations (qualitative criterion). It will be remembered also that the use of projective or Euclidian construction techniques, while not always noted by the examiners, is twice as frequent in stage 3B subjects (30 per cent) as in stage 3A (16 per cent). Similarly, referring to Table 28 (p. 155), we observe that 75 per cent of the subjects at stage 3B (86 out of 115) also solve the four easier problems and that 95 per cent (109 out of 115) solve at least three of them, while the corresponding proportions in stage 3A subjects do not exceed 26 per cent (21 out of 81) and 59 per cent (48 out of 81) respectively. It may be that these differences are simply an indication of a greater amount of attention or concentration on the child's part; but they should be recognized as resulting above all from a mastery of operational forms of spatial representation, if we take into account the earlier observation concerning the frequent use of projective or Euclidian procedures. In sum, contrary to what we observed in stage 2, the adoption of a purely numerical criterion to subdivide stage 3 seems to demonstrate the existence of two levels of spatial conceptualization which it would be unwise to ignore.

In conclusion, it may be instructive to examine the extent to which the behavior observed in the *Construction of a projective straight line* test may support or weaken the explanation given earlier (Chapter III), in the analysis of the *Stereognostic recognition of objects and shapes* test, of the earliness of the curvilinear-rectilinear distinction. It will be remembered that this discrimination was undeniably shown to be simpler than that of other Euclidian relations (e.g., dimension of sides and angles, parallelism of sides, etc.) and almost as early as that of topological relations. Lovell (1959) had already observed the same synchronism and had adopted it as a means of rejecting Piaget's hypotheses of the developmental primacy of the topological over the Euclidian in the child's spatial representations. This sort of conclusion does not necessarily follow. As we have tried to show, this synchronism may be due to the fact that the child's primitive discrimination, irrespective of the homeomorphous or heteromorphous character of the figures involved, are more closely related to the qualitative properties of these figures and may be facilitated by partial topological characteristics.

To demonstrate the fairness of such an interpretation, we must ask, following Lovell's own reasoning, whether the curvilinear-rectilinear differentiation is as early as construction of the straight line. Assuming that these two abilities appear simultaneously in the course of development, we could rely on the fact that perfect construction of a straight line requires projective or Euclidian procedures in order to maintain that the curvilinear-rectilinear discrimination itself surpasses the purely topological level and to reject Piaget's hypothesis at the same time. Supposing, on the contrary, that solution of the straight lines is later than the curvilinear-rectilinear differentiation, we could interpret this *décalage* as proof that the curvilinear-rectilinear differentiation is not necessarily Euclidian and that it may be based, as the preceding interpretation supposes, on partial topological characteristics. Comparison of the results obtained in the two tests clearly favors the latter interpretation.

We first observe a span of at least three years between the time when the child no longer confuses curvilinear and rectilinear figures (stage 2B of the *Stereognostic recognition of objects and shapes* test is reached at 4:6 years) and the time when he is able to construct a perfect straight line without having to depend on any perceptual cue (stage 3B in the *Construction of a projective straight line* test is reached at 7:5 years). Also significant is a similar *décalage* between the same curvilinear-rectilinear differentiation and the full stereognostic recognition of the Euclidian properties of geometric shapes (stage 3B of the *Stereognostic recognition of objects and shapes* test is reached at 8:2 years). It is tempting to think that the *décalage* between ability to construct a straight line and ability to differentiate curvilinear from rectilinear does not reflect a structural difference in the spatial relationships underlying these tasks, but simply reflects a difference in difficulty of their respective content. In sum, the *décalage* would be purely horizontal. The curvilinear-rectilinear discrimination and construction of a straight line would both be Euclidian, but the second test would be more difficult than the first because of the simple fact that the Euclidian relations which must be represented would be more complex in the case of the straight line than in the case of stereognostic recognition of curvilinear or rectilinear figures. It is hardly likely that this is the case. Assuming that the child's ability to distinguish the curvilinear from the rectilinear is a Euclidian one and not simply topological, this would mean that the child is able to imagine the straight line—that is, mentally to reproduce or reconstruct it. Yet it is basically this same mental activity of reconstruction which is presupposed in the child's use of the projective or Euclidian procedures necessary to succeed in the *Construction of a projective straight line* test. The considerable *décalage* separating the ability to construct a straight line and the ability to differentiate the curvilinear and the rectilinear thus cannot be explained simply by the fact that the Euclidian relations to be represented are more complex in one case than in the other. It seems, rather, that we are dealing with a real difference in the level of spatial conceptualization. While the curvilinear-rectilinear differentiation depends on partial topological relations whose representation is still at the intuitive or preoperational level, construction of a straight line independent of any perceptual configuration presupposes the use of projective or Euclidian techniques which unquestionably belong to the operational level. It should be noted, however, that in the case of constructing a simple straight line between two points, the required projective operations are still the most elementary. They undoubtedly require the child to be able to choose, from among all possible points of view, the only one which can effectively help his construction; but the coordination which must be established covers only a very limited field. It is limited to arranging a series of similar elements along a single dimension of projective space (before-behind) and in relation to a single viewpoint or a single observer. In this respect, the coordination of perspectives to be studied later (Chapters XIV to XVI) seems much more complex because it deals simultaneously with a group of dissimilar objects which must be arranged along two dimensions at once (before-behind and left-right), according to several successive points of view of the same observer (or several simultaneous viewpoints of different observers).

A second indication that the curvilinear-rectilinear discrimination is not yet an operational procedure concerns the rather direct parallel between the evolution of stereognostic representations and the development of the construction of the straight line. Thus, for example, when the child is able systematically to avoid topological errors and curvilinear-rectilinear confusions (stage 2B reached at 4:6 years in the *Stereognostic recognition of objects and shapes* test), he solves only the straight lines parallel to the rectilinear contours present in his perceptual field (stages 2A and 2B are reached at 3:10 and 4:11 years respectively in the *Construction of a projective straight line* test). This synchronism is easily understood if we accept that there is a functional relationship between the topological successes of the first test and the intuitive successes of the second. The same synchronism continues into the subsequent stage which, in these two tests, marks the progressive mastery of projective or Euclidian operations. On the average, it is around 5:8 years (stage 3A) that, in the stereognosis test, children become capable of the first intracurvilinear and intrarectilinear discriminations, discriminations which are necessarily based on a consideration of certain metric or Euclidian relations; similarly, in constructing a straight line, it is around 5:11 years (stage 3A) that children begin to free themselves of perceptual suggestions and begin to give a good general orientation to their oblique constructions—without always succeeding, however (for lack of sufficient mastery of the projective or Euclidian procedures), in avoiding twists and turns in their lines. And similarly, the progress of stage 3B subjects (about 8:2 years) in stereognostic recognition of more complex geometric shapes (e.g., trapezoids, rhombuses, etc.) compares quite favorably with the ability to construct a straight line as revealed by success with the two obliques (stage 3B, about 7:5 years). This general parallelism is found not only in group comparisons, for even at the level of individual subjects there is a certain interdependence between the two tests, as shown in Table 29. This table divides the subjects with a double dichotomy based on the quality of the solutions to each of the two tests. We clearly see that the great majority of subjects are similarly classified in the two scales. When solutions are of a very primitive or exclusively topological nature in the stereognosis test (stages 0 to 2B inclusively), they are equally primitive or intuitive in the construction of a straight line (stage 0 to 2B); conversely, as soon as stereognostic recognition begins to depend on Euclidian relations (stages 3A and 3B), construction of a straight line itself presupposes at least the partial mastery of projective or Euclidian operations (stages 3A and 3B). The tau correlation of these results is .65.

Table 29

Distribution of subjects* according to their level of functioning on the *Stereognostic recognition of objects and shapes* and *Construction of a projective straight line* tests

	Projective straight line	
Stereognosis	Stages 0 to 2B	Stages 3A to 3B
Stages 0 to 2B	271	38
Stages 3A and 3B	37	127

*The table includes only the 473 subjects who took both tests and were classified on both developmental scales.

In sum, analysis of these various *décalages* and synchronisms clearly seems to confirm the general hypothesis holding that the child's spatial representations are topological before being projective or Euclidian, as well as the specific hypothesis holding that stereognostic discrimination of curvilinear and rectilinear figures is of a partially topological nature. These conclusions, deriving from the same logical reasoning as Lovell's (1959), nevertheless contradict his conclusions. The paradox should be mentioned, particularly when one considers that Lovell's findings are not so very different from the results reported here. In both cases, in fact, it is undeniable that even before the age of four years a number of children manage to construct a perfect straight line, at least when they are lines parallel to the rectilinear sides of the base. Lovell observes 53 per cent perfect solutions in his youngest subjects (3:7 to 4:0 years); on the present scale, comparable behavior is acquired at around the age of 3:10 years (stage 2A). How, then, can we explain the fact that the interpretations are so different despite this basic agreement? We must recall here the influence which the methods of analysis may have on the interpretation of experimental findings (an influence which has already been emphasized in a different context—see Laurendeau and Pinard, 1962). Starting with an individual analysis of the problems used in his test, Lovell was struck by the precociousness of some of the solutions and did not hesitate to interpret them as proof that the very young child is capable of the projective (or Euclidian) representations necessary for constructing a straight line. Having limited the analysis of his results to this single dimension, he felt no need to attach any importance to the relative difficulty of the different problems in his test. Apparently convinced that these differences in difficulty could not refer to different levels of spatial representation, he did not even attempt to explain them. However, in the perspective of a study based on an individual analysis of the subjects, rather than of the problems, these differences assume critical importance and even constitute a first but decisive reason to doubt the equivalence of the intellectual mechanisms at work in each of these problems. In the current experiment, the qualitative analysis of the individual protocols once more confirmed the symptomatic value of such asynchronisms. It demonstrated the intuitive or preoperational character of the child's first linear constructions and showed, particularly, the need to wait until the child can construct a straight line without the perceptual support of rectilinear contours before conceding that he has attained the projective or Euclidian operations. Similarly, if Lovell had tried to explain why a straight line on a circular base was not achieved by his subjects until two years after succeeding with the same straight line on a rectangular base, he might have questioned the projective (or Euclidian) character of the earliest solutions, since projective or Euclidian procedures always presuppose a liberation from perceptual bondage. Unless it is followed by an analysis by subjects, the analysis by problems cannot unequivocally determine the real significance of certain behaviors. Undoubtedly it is this methodological difference which explains the differences between Lovell's conclusions and those reported here.

Chapter VIII

Localization of Topographical Positions: Presentation of the Test

Like the two preceding tests, the *Localization of topographical positions* test seeks to verify the topological character of the child's first spatial representations, but it deals more directly with the particular problem of the extension of topological concepts into projective and Euclidian concepts. The first of three chapters covering this test includes two parts. The first part defines the theoretical context of the test and the second describes its basic structure.

THEORETICAL CONTEXT

As Piaget emphasizes more than once in his work (see especially Piaget and Inhelder, 1948, *passim*), topological concepts consider only the internal spatial relations of a simple object or single configuration. They deal exclusively with the intrinsic relations of neighborhood, continuity, separation, order, etc., which exist among the elements of the object concerned, without trying to locate this object in relation to others. The only relations which topology seeks to establish between two figures concern the structural equivalence or homeomorphism of these figures, taking no account of their respective dimensions, the distance separating them, or their relative positions within a common space. In topological terms, a comparison of these figures requires no more than an analysis of the inherent properties of each and of the conditions which could allow transforming them into one another without changing these properties. It is for this reason that the dimensions of topological space do not conserve straight lines and distances and may all be based on the

166

relations of enclosure (or surrounding) which might be established between the elements of a single object. A topological line, for example, is a unidimensional structure in which each point is located between two others which surround or enclose it, so to speak, in any direction. Similarly, topological surface is derived from the interiority or exteriority of an element in relation to a linear series. Finally, topological volume is defined by the interiority or exteriority of an element in relation to a bidimensional topological surface or structure. Because it is always limited to elements of a single configuration, however complex it may be, topological space could not constitute a global space in which it would be possible to locate several objects in relation to one another according to a general plan which takes objective distances and possible points of view into account. For this reason Piaget conceives of a child's topological space as a mosaic of fragmentary and distinct spaces whose respective borders are fixed by the continuity of a given perceptual field or by the functional unity of each of the child's particular experiential fields.

The child's achievement of spatial structures requires the coordination of these partial spaces into a total space. Such a coordination is not possible without the progressive formation of two distinct and complementary total systems: (a) a *system of axial coordinates,* the source of Euclidian space, in which external objects may be located in relation to one another and placed within a single comprehensive structure which includes the objects as well as the positions themselves; and (b) a *system of perspectives,* the source of projective space, which also assures the coordination of the same objects but this time considers them in relation to the different actual or potential points of view which can be produced by considering them in relation to one another. While distinct, these two systems are rigorously connected and are formed concomitantly in the course of development. Coordination of perspectives, in fact, implies the organization of a stable system of reference around which the projective left-right, before-behind, and above-below dimensions can be established in relation to the successive positions of a single observer (or to the simultaneous positions of several different observers). Conversely, the construction of spatial coordinates requires a differentiation of these various perspectives, without which it is impossible to conceive a reference system which is independent of the temporary point of view or to structure the three basic dimensions of Euclidian space. Analysis of the *Construction of a projective straight line* test has already emphasized this interdependence in pointing to the fact that the projective or Euclidian construction procedures are seen to be contemporary or even simultaneous in children who are able to use them.

Despite this interdependence, it is necessary to specify what these two systems add to the topological concepts. Insofar as *projective* concepts are concerned (these concepts will be more fully discussed in Chapters XI to XVI), we need recall only that they are basically dealing with the relative positions of several distinct objects (or distinct parts of a single object) in relation to a single observer, as well as with the different views of a single object subjected to operations of projecting, sectioning, or surface rotating and unfolding. This intervention of perspective radically transforms the concept of spatial dimension by adding to the internal relations of a single object (or a single configuration) the projective before-behind, left-right, and above-below relations produced by the relative positions of several objects for a single observer. Thus a series of elements arranged so as to hide one another, through the before-behind dimension alone, constitutes the first dimension of projective space and defines the straight line, the basis of all perspective geometry. Similarly, the surface or the projective plane is a result of the addition of the left-right or above-below relations to the before-behind relation, and, finally, it is the simultaneous consideration (or logical multiplication) of these three types of relations which creates volume or three-dimensional projective space. From their very nature, projective concepts ignore the objective distances and real dimensions of objects because they are based on the transformations of apparent size and shape which the diversity of projections and points of view imposes on the objects. Despite this diversity, they conserve the relative position of the objects (or parts of a single object) in relation to the projective plane or the observer's point of view. This is why the development of projective concepts in the child naturally leads to the formation of a general spatial structure whose basic dimensions allow him to place several objects in relation to one another regardless of the point of view involved. This coordination of perspectives, which increases in complexity, flexibility, and stability with development, presupposes in the child a consciousness of the multiplicity of actual or potential points of view and, consequently, a rejection of the distorting egocentrism of the single and momentary viewpoint.

Where *Euclidian* concepts are concerned, we must note particularly the fact that they require the establishment of a stable reference system which allows objects to be located in a homogeneous space including both the objects themselves and their actual or potential positions. This is what basically distinguishes Euclidian space from the topological space to which it is added, and from the projective space with which it is both bound up and contemporaneous. On one hand, in fact, the topological concepts consider only the inherent relations of a single object, with no external reference, and thus must completely ignore the dimensions of the objects and the distances separating them. If the projective concepts, on the other hand, form a comprehensive system which allows the coordination of several distinct objects within a projective plane or in relation to the different possible viewpoints of an external observer, they are directly concerned with the apparent changes in size, distance, or position which a diversity of viewpoints or of projective planes involves and thus do not conserve the real dimensions and distances. Euclidian notions alone imply such a conservation because the general system which they create coordinates the objects as well as their positions. It is the child's discovery of the horizontal and vertical— that is, of the physical equivalence of the three perpendicular geometric pairs of coordinates—which gives him this general system. By virtue of the referent axes which represent as many ordered sequences of potential positions, the objects may be located in relation to one another without undergoing changes in objective sizes and distances. And thus the dimensions of Euclidian space are formed, from the simple straight line, which considers only one of the three axes, to surface and volume which consider two or three at once. It is the progressive coordination of these relations—of which the left-right, before-behind, and above-below concepts form the projective equivalent when an external observer's viewpoint intervenes —which brings the child to the level of his first Euclidian operations and at the same time prepares for the subsequent elaboration of true metrics.

We can see the sort of progress which is covered by this transformation of topological space into a space conceived as a general system of potential positions. In effect, as long as space is limited to localized objects without at the same time including the intervals which separate them, the concepts of distance available to the child can all be reduced to the topological intuitions concerning relations of neighborhood or separation, continuity or discontinuity, etc., which may exist among the elements of a single configuration or the parts of a single object. But as soon as the intervals separating the objects are themselves considered as so many potential positions, space then loses the characteristic of elasticity and inconsistency inherent in topological relations and becomes a rigid and stable structure in which distance and size are conserved and which makes measurement not only possible but necessary. As Piaget notes, this transformation leads the child little by little to remove the objects from space, so to speak, and to consider space more as a homogeneous "container." It thus leads to the establishment of a system of fixed reference points or of referent axes onto which are grafted all the possible directions such as the horizontal and the vertical, whose primary importance and privileged character resulting from everyday perceptual and motor activities should be emphasized. It is due to this network of possible directions that distances can be constructed, objects can be coordinated in space, and the elementary Euclidian concepts of parallelism, slope, similarity, proportion, etc., can be consolidated. As long as he is deprived of these reference frameworks which are external to the objects, the child will be reduced to spatial concepts which are subject to the uncertainty of his visual or tactile explorations, and he will easily confuse two configurations of variously arranged objects (so long as the reciprocal neighborhoods are preserved). This is seen, in one respect, in the fact that the child is often said to be more adept than the adult in recognizing a figure presented in any direction.

For Piaget, then, the establishment of this system of references is one of the most important steps in the development of spatial representations. It is, however, rather slow to develop, and the fact that the child arrives very early at the practical coordinations in relation to his postural and sensorimotor space does not at all exempt him from having again to go through (this time on the representational level) the long steps marking the progressive structuring of his practical space. Thus his first spatial concepts, based solely on the elementary topological relations of order and proximity, are limited to particular configurations or objects without involving any reference point external to these objects. The child then begins to establish relationships between several distinct objects, but these relationships at first cannot develop except as a function of his own body, so that the child himself becomes the only possible reference point without yet being conscious of the relative character of this particular point of view nor of the systematic distortions which it produces. In order that the child's spatial intuitions may shed this distorting egocentrism and become real operational representations, a projective system of perspectives must be formed which coordinates all these possible viewpoints as well as a stable Euclidian representational system, where distance and size are conserved and the many potential directions are articulated.

It is precisely this interdependence of the two systems which the *Localization of topographical positions* test seeks to analyze. The test requires the subject to locate correctly, in a second natural reference framework which has already been structured for him (a miniature landscape), the position of an object which the examiner has placed in a first reference framework identical to the second. The subject must also be able to leave his own point of view because, in the main part of the test, one of the two landscapes is turned 180 degrees from the other. Thus the technique does not explicitly and directly seek to specify the moment when the natural coordinates of Euclidian space (particularly the horizontal and vertical) are constructed by the child, as do others of Piaget's techniques which are specifically designed with this in mind (e.g., sketching the water level in a half-empty and variously tilted jar; actual or graphic planting of miniature trees, houses, or poles on the sides of a miniature mountain; etc.). Success with this task, as simple as it is, nevertheless assumes that the child at least be able to recognize the Euclidian relationships between several objects located in a single pre-existing total structure. It requires at the same time, and perhaps most importantly, the ability to coordinate the projective concepts of left-right and before-behind in relation to the different viewpoints which rotating one of the landscapes entails.

The test is of average difficulty. Insofar as the Euclidian relations to be coordinated are concerned, the task is actually much simpler than another test of the same type (also used by Piaget) where the subject must reproduce the plan of a miniature village either on the same or on a reduced scale. The multiplicity of objects to coordinate in a single frame of reference, especially in the case where the subject must reduce the topographical schema, is evidently much more complex than the present test where he has only one object to locate in a field which is already completely structured beforehand. As for the difficulty of the projective relations to be coordinated, the *Localization of topographical positions* test is, hypothetically, located about midway between the *Construction of a projective straight line* test (see Chapters V to VII), where the subject must line up a series of identical elements along a single dimension (before-behind), and the *Coordination of perspectives* task (Chapters XIV to XVI) where several distinct objects must be coordinated in a bidimensional projective space (left-right and before-behind) according to several different perspectives corresponding to the successive positions of an observer different from the subject himself. In the test analyzed here, it is true that the subject must locate an object in relation to several others, taking account of the left-right and before-behind relationships simultaneously; but, compared to the *Coordination of perspectives* test, the task is relatively simplified because the objects are more concrete and more heterogeneous, because only two perspectives (that of the subject and that of the person opposite him) are effectively used among a multiplicity of possible other perspectives, and especially because the relations to be structured ignore the partial or complete overlaps which an entirely perspective use of the before-behind dimension, in the *Coordination of perspectives* test, might produce. Comparison of these three tests *(Construction of a projective straight line, Localization of topographical positions, and Coordination of perspectives),* then, may help to clarify the problem posed by the delimitation of the steps to projective operations and by the order of succession of these steps.

DESCRIPTION OF THE TEST

The subject is placed before two miniature landscapes which are identical in all respects and are made of thin and smooth rectangular cardboard (35 x 47 cm.), on which a road and railroad tracks are drawn, crossing near the center and dividing the area into four sections of differing shapes and sizes. On each of these landscapes are placed five toy houses which are easily distinguished by their size or color: a red house (base: 7.5 x 2.5 cm.; height: 3.5 cm.), a yellow house (base: 4.5 x 2.5 cm.; height: 3.5 cm.), and three smaller houses (base: 1.5 x 1.0 cm.; height: 2.0 cm.) of different colors (blue, green, and yellow). Figure 14 shows this material.

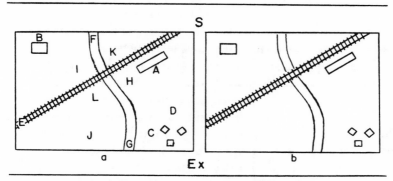

Figure 14. Miniature landscapes of the *Localization of topographical positions* test. The rectangular figures represent the houses; the letters indicated in *a* designate the successive positions which the examiner (Ex) asks the subject (S) to locate in *b*.

The examiner and the subject are seated across from each other, the landscapes being at first placed side by side and in the same direction. The examiner directs the child's attention to the identity of the two landscapes and makes him understand that one of them (on the child's left) belongs to the child and that the other one is his own. He then places a little man made of modeling clay on the roof of the red house, on his own landscape, asking the subject to place a similar man *"at exactly the same place"* on his landscape. He then places the little man on the roof of the yellow house, again asking the subject to do the same. These two examples thus serve to illustrate the instructions and to establish that the child understands (the child is usually quite eager to enter into the game).

Then begins the test proper. Without changing the direction of the landscape, the examiner successively places his little man at 12 different points (see Figure 14) in the order A, B, L, C, F, H, E, D, J, K, G, and I, each time asking the subject to place his man in the corresponding position on his own landscape. This first part of the test completed, the examiner then turns his board 180 degrees, directing the child's attention to this rotation and making him notice that all the elements in the landscape are still in the same places. He then repeats the two examples at the beginning, by way of exercises, and proceeds to the second part. The man is successively placed at the same 12 points as in the first part, but this time in the order B, D, G, A, L, E, K, I, J, H, C, and F. Should the child make a mistake at the first position of this series, the examiner corrects his response by correctly placing the man on the child's landscape; this correction is made only in the case of an error at the first position. Detailed instructions are given in the Appendix.

As the analysis of successes and failures will undoubtedly confirm, the various positions do not all present the same kind of difficulty. They were chosen to emphasize these differences and, more particularly, to verify the topological and still egocentric character of the child's first spatial relations (or prerelations). Thus, with the exception of some purely chance successes, it is impossible to locate exactly the positions in the two parts of the test if one relies simply on a single topological relation of proximity or interiority (e.g., "near the yellow house" could mean anywhere around this house; "on the road" could mean anywhere within the confines of the road; etc.). It is possible, however, for simultaneous consideration of more than one topological relation (e.g., several neighborhoods, etc.) to have some success, particularly for position C which can be located by the topological relations of enclosure or of double neighborhood (i.e., between the road and the blue house, or beside both). But it is rare that an unequivocal definition is possible solely through multiple neighborhood relations. Positions F and G, for example, both located "on" the road and "near" the edge of the cardboard, are topologically identical, as are the I, K, and L positions, all located "near" the intersection of the road and the tracks. At least in the first part of the test, certain topologically similar positions may also be differentiated with the additional intervention of simple perceptual correspondences or of the still quite primitive orientation relations which the child may establish with respect to his own body. Thus, for example, positions F and G are easily distinguishable from each other by their relative distance from the subject (e.g., "near" the subject or "far" from him; "on the side of" the subject or "on the side of" the examiner; etc.). But as soon as one of the landscapes is rotated, resorting to the same prerelations or to the same perceptual correspondences will lead to mistakes and will lead the subject to establish the same egocentric or perceptual relationship between the man and the neighboring object, serving as the main index, as exists between the two elements on the model landscape. Thus position B, for example, located "near" the yellow house and "on the side of" the examiner, will be seen by the subject as being located "near" the yellow house but "on the side of" the railroad tracks on his own landscape. In sum, since he is still not conscious of the relativity of viewpoints, the subject who holds to these prerelations or to perceptual correspondences remains insensitive to the effects of rotating the material.

In principle, only the simultaneous consideration of topological cues and relations of orientation (left-right and before-behind projective relations in an objective reference system) can define the exact location of all positions regardless of what the relative directions of the two landscapes may be. This is not to say, however, that all the problems in the second part are missed as long as the subjects are incapable of the projective operations (coordination of the left-right and before-behind relations) normally required by rotating one of the boards. Numerous factors may in fact contribute to facilitating the solution of some of these problems. Despite the rotation, the correct multiplication of simple topological relations of neighborhood, itself favored by invariant perceptual cues (size, colors, etc.), may at first lead to early success with certain positions, such as position C (neighboring both the road and the small blue house) or position H (neighboring the road and the red house). Furthermore, it should be understood that the child, when he begins to take account of the left-right and before-behind relations, nevertheless does not stop using the topological relations of neighborhood or enclosure. On the contrary, these elementary relations, like the perceptual or egocentric indices, remain the starting point of the child's placements, and the intervention of projective concepts then serves to define the exact location. Rather than having systematically to construct the new relations produced by rotating the landscape (an unnecessarily complicated operation for the child and even for the adult), it is more economical and more natural to rely at first on a simple topological cue (e.g., "near the red house," "on the road," "at the intersection of the road and the railroad," etc.) in order to decide on the position in a general sense, and then to reconstitute the projective relations necessary for the precise localization. This procedure can often exempt the subject from making the normally required double reversal, given that in several problems the previous locating of such a cue object leaves the subject with the sole difficulty of reversing either the before-behind relation (e.g., positions A, B, F, G) or the left-right relation (e.g., position E). In short, only the positions which are difficult to specify unambiguously by means of purely topological cues (e.g., positions I, J, K, L, all located "in a field," "at the intersection of the road and the tracks") require the simultaneous reversal of the left-right and before-behind dimensions and, consequently, presuppose the complete mastery of these projective relations. This is why we must expect the solution of these problems to come much later. It would be unnecessarily lengthy to discuss here the reasons which determined the choice of each position. The several examples we have reported must suffice to show how the diversity of the problems can lend itself to both a quantitative and a qualitative analysis of the solution processes of children at different levels.

Before undertaking this analysis, it is helpful to point out the differences between the method used here and the one used in the original experiment by Piaget and Inhelder (1948) as well as that of Vinh-Bang[1] who is currently working on standardizing the same test. The nature of these differences greatly affects the comparisons to be made between the results obtained in the two types of experiment. Other than those dealing with the number and difficulty of the positions chosen in both cases, the differences are related to four principal sources.

The *first* refers to the importance accorded the problems in which the two landscapes are in the same direction with respect to the subject. In Piaget and Inhelder's experiment, as in Vinh-Bang's, this situation is used exclusively for preliminary examples and demonstrations, and in the test itself one of the landscapes is always rotated 180 degrees. In the present experiment, on the contrary, each situation has an equal number of problems, which makes it easier to identify preoperational behavior—that is, behavior still based exclusively on topological or egocentric indices. When restricting ourselves to the situation in which one landscape is reversed, it is undoubtedly possible to recognize the subjects who are able to coordinate left-right and before-behind relationships; but among those

---

[1] Personal communication.

who cannot do this, it is difficult to distinguish those who still hold to simple topological indices and those who add projective relations to these indices without yet being able simultaneously to coordinate the left-right and before-behind dimensions. In the case of the I, K, and L positions, for example, all three of which are located at the intersection of the road and the railroad tracks, the child who places his clay man near the intersection but in the wrong quadrant may indiscriminately seek to respect only the topological relations of enclosure (e.g., in a field near the intersection but in any random field), to conserve the basis of the egocentric relations of distance or laterality with regard to his own body (e.g., "near me," "far from me," "to my left," etc.), or to reverse the left-right and before-behind relations without completely succeeding. Examination of solutions to other problems may clarify the significance of this ambiguous behavior. But there is nothing to guarantee that the subject uses the same solution processes in these other problems where the more striking topological or perceptual cues limit the number of possible responses (e.g., "beside the yellow house"; "at the end of the road"; etc.) and where, consequently, the projective relations to be coordinated are usually reduced to a single dimension (left-right or before-behind). One or the other of two contrary effects may follow: (1) the correct answers become easier because the subject can establish his relations from a single referent object without having to consider the whole schema; or (2) errors may be favored because the salience of the topological or perceptual indices leads the subject to ignore any other referent activity and keeps him from noticing that more than one position may meet the same conditions of neighborhood or enclosure. For this reason it may be instructive to compare the solutions given to one and the same problem before and after rotating one of the landscape boards. If, even before the rotation, the subject misses the sector for positions I, K, and L, for example, it is probable that his behavior is not yet beyond the elementary topological level; if, on the other hand, the positioning is always correct before, but never after the rotation, analysis of errors made in this second situation may reveal to what extent the relations established by the subject are of a strictly egocentric nature (e.g., the clay man always located in the reverse quadrant or in the same absolute location in relation to the whole area), or of a (still imperfect) projective nature (e.g., the man placed in a quadrant adjacent to the correct position with reversal of only one of the two dimensions).

The *second* difference between this technique and that of Piaget and Inhelder, repeated as is by Vinh-Bang, concerns the constituent elements of the landscape. The two arrangements are fairly comparable in their whole structure, size, and number of objects distributed in them. But it should be noted that Piaget's schema is a relief construction and thus includes some geographical variations (e.g., hills, variations in the ground, etc.) whose presence most certainly increases the number of perceptual or topological indices. The landscape used in the present experiment is a simple, flat piece of cardboard whose character is much less favorable to correct positioning. It is obvious that the number, variety, and arrangement of the constituent elements of a landscape can exert a considerable influence on the difficulty of the task required of the subject. Supposing, for example, that the topographical schema is reduced to a mosaic of topologically similar sections, divided by crossings of the road and identifiable only by their shape and size, the location of the positions would become much more difficult. In this respect, although the arrangement used here is more abstract than Piaget's, the subject's task is still relatively simple since the landscape is divided into only four sectors, and some of these sectors are easily identifiable by the miniature objects which are scattered about them.

A *third* difference which should be pointed out concerns the nature of the task required of the subject. In Vinh-Bang's standardization of Piaget's test, the subject must not only place his man on his landscape at the same place where the examiner has placed his man on the model landscape, but he must also place him so that the clay man's gaze has relatively the same orientation in the two landscapes. The present technique does not include this last specification and the clay man is deliberately deprived of any sign which might identify his face or his eyes. This procedural difference, in opposition to the preceding one, this time has the effect of simplifying the subject's task. Compared to Vinh-Bang's method, the present method should thus give rise to earlier successes.

Finally, the *fourth* difference to be mentioned deals with the spatiotemporal intervals separating the examiner's movement and the subject's response. In his experiment, Piaget places a screen between the two landscapes so that the subject, although he is allowed to re-examine the model landscape when he wants to, is not able to see them both at the same time. In the present experiment, however, the two landscapes are placed side by side, about three centimeters apart, with nothing obstructing the subject's visual field. In principle, Piaget's technique should complicate the task because it requires the intervention of memory and because the simple presence of the screen tends to reduce the number and effectiveness of necessary trials. However, paradoxically enough, the results of a preliminary experiment done with about 15 five-year-old children seemed to indicate rather that the spatiotemporal contiguity conditions, particularly in the part of the test where one of the landscapes is reversed, had the effect of greatly increasing the difficulty of the problems. How can we explain this paradox? First, it is possible that the intervention of a screen requires the subject to concentrate harder so as to construct a more exact and more reliable image of each position which he must locate. But it is also possible that the contiguity of the landscapes creates interferences or new indices whose purely perceptual or topological character easily leads to primitive types of behavior. When the model landscape is left exposed to the subject's view, it is more difficult for him to avoid, for example, the responses dictated by symmetry alone or by the egocentric relationship of the man to his own body.

Be that as it may, despite the risk of increasing the level of difficulty, it seems preferable to avoid using a screen or any other technique designed to prohibit the simultaneous viewing of the two landscapes (e.g., placing one in front of the subject and the other behind him). For one thing, using a screen discourages the youngest subjects, who are intentionally opposed to any instructions which are too confining and who always end up pushing aside or overturning obstacles. Nor would it be a question of using it only with the oldest subjects in the test, because this would favor them to the detriment of the younger ones, and the developmental comparisons would be compromised by this fact. Furthermore, the technique of placing one of the landscapes in front of the subject and the other one behind him also seems inadvisable because it introduces new conditions of spatial orientation into the experiment which would be very difficult to control for. Thus, in order that the landscape behind the subject might seem to be oriented exactly like the one in front of him, one of them must be rotated 180 degrees. Such a rotation may have unforeseeable and ambiguous effects, especially since not all subjects take the trouble to turn themselves completely around but more often turn only their heads toward the model landscape. For this reason it is better to keep to the simplest technique, even if that means introducing further refinements in making comparisons with Piaget's results, who used a technique which is slightly different and which might favor earlier successes.

It is not easy to predict the combined effect of these differences in technique, some of which increase and others of which reduce the difficulty of the task. But the problem has only limited theoretical interest, especially if we recall that horizontal *décalages* are normal at the level of concrete operational thought, which we know to be still dependent on the content or the material on which it operates. But the existence of these frequently observed *décalages* in the replications of many of Piaget's tests is so often a pretext for rejecting either the authenticity or the generality of operational thought that it is worth while to emphasize these differences in experimental technique and material. It is important to be aware of the limits which these differences impose, on the one hand, on the interpretation of results obtained in a particular experimental context and, on the other hand, on the practical application of the norms derived from these results. Yet these possibilities of *décalage* do not compromise the theoretical value of the conclusions concerning the child's spatial representations, since confirmation of the hypotheses subjected to experimentation rests much more on the psychological analysis of the intellectual mechanisms involved in the child's behavior than on the simple chronological ordering of this behavior.

Chapter IX

Localization of Topographical Positions: General Analysis of the Results

Analysis of the results of the *Localization of topographical positions* test includes two parts. The first is a global analysis centering on the relative difficulty of the problems; the second, covered in the following chapter, is an analysis by stages and is based on examination of individual protocols. The present chapter begins with a summary of the criteria used in scoring the problems and discusses the subjects' solutions (successes and errors) to these various problems.

SCORING CRITERIA

The test is basically intended to differentiate two levels of behavior: (a) behavior of a *preoperational* nature—that is, behavior based on egocentric indices, on elementary topological concepts, or on projective and Euclidian intuitions which are not yet fully coordinated; and (b) behavior of an *operational* nature, free of any residue of egocentrism and guided by operations which are clearly projective or Euclidian. It is this basic distinction which the protocol scoring must be able to demonstrate. The subsequent analysis of successes and failures bears directly on it, and the significance of stages describing the development of this behavior will depend on it.

Given that truly correct solutions are possible only by resorting to projective or Euclidian operations, it seems that the surest way to identify this behavior is to be quite strict in evaluating the subjects' responses. It is for this reason that in both parts of the test only the

181

responses where the subject places his clay man in exactly the same place as on the model landscape, or at least in a position which is no more than two or three centimeters from it, are held to be correct. Yet we must not give this margin of error a rigorously geometric definition, as though there were a zone marking a perfect circle with a two- or three-centimeter radius around each position. We recognize the slight modifications which the dimensions of the man and the topographical conditions of each position, may impose. These conditions, in fact, are often such that even a distance of two or three centimeters from a given position may have different effects depending on the dimension involved. As concerns position J, for example, it goes without saying that the tolerable distance must be less in relation to the lower border of the board and the road at the right than in relation to the other two dimensions, because a child's placing of his man too close to this edge or this road may reveal a strong influence of the topological neighborhood cues. The same remark also holds for positions I and L, where the permissible distance is less in relation to the intersection of the road and railroad tracks than in relation to the rest of the sector. Figure 15 illustrates both the strictness which must be observed in evaluating the responses and the relative flexibility of these error zones.

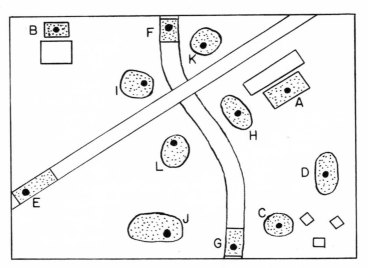

Figure 15. Margin of error accepted in evaluating the responses for each of the positions which must be located in the *Localization of topographical positions* test (see explanations in text).

Despite these requirements, the identification of operational responses is not always possible, especially in the first part of the test where the use of exclusively egocentric or elementary topological cues may often lead to correct solutions. This is the case, for example, with the problems where the positions to be located are at one end of the road; the simultaneous consideration of the relations of enclosure ("on the road"), proximity ("near the edge of the cardboard"), and egocentric orientation ("beside me" or "far from me") may facilitate the localization of these specific positions, if not assure their complete identification. Thus we cannot differentiate these responses from those which might be guided by projective or Euclidian operations (e.g., relating objects to one another according to the subject's viewpoint; considering distances; establishing relationships between objects facing one another, or located in an oblique or parallel direction to each other; etc.) without first knowing whether, in the second part where the model landscape is rotated, the subject is capable of mastering the projective or Euclidian relations and does not restrict himself to still preoperational behavior (e.g., egocentric neglect of the effects of rotation, topological reference to an isolated cue, etc.). However, even in the first part, reducing the tolerable error margin to a minimum may serve to differentiate those responses based on a coordinated and adequate system of topological relations, if not from the Euclidian or metric solutions, at least from the responses based either on isolated (e.g., "on the road") or insufficient (e.g., "on the road and near the edge") topological relations, or on topological relations which are contaminated by elements foreign to the spatial localization itself (e.g., copying the gesture of the examiner who, facing the subject, sometimes must cross the whole landscape to place his man on the subject's side).

The tolerable margin of error is perhaps unnecessarily rigid in the second part where it seems easier, in fact, to distinguish the solutions that derive exclusively from topological or egocentric considerations. Undoubtedly, even when the model landscape has been turned 180 degrees, some special positions may be located through a combination of topological cues (position H, for example, is near both the red house and the intersection). The primitive character of this kind of solution, however, is revealed in the rest of the protocol by a total neglect of the left-right and before-behind relationships.

The subject relies only on the most obvious topological cue (e.g., "near the yellow house," for position B; "on the road," for positions F and G; "in a field," for position H, I, J, K, L); but, while cognizant of this relationship, he will yield to egocentric suggestions and place his man, in the case of position B, for example, somewhere between the yellow house and the railroad tracks—that is, near the yellow house but on the examiner's side of the board. This egocentric attitude might even lead him to ignore the most elementary topological relations. This is the case with the child who, for position A, places his man opposite the red house but on his own side, not hesitating to place it even on the neighboring railroad tracks rather than renounce his egocentric point of view.

The meaning of such responses is easy to understand, since most of the positions chosen by the subject differ appreciably from the model positions. If despite this we require the same precision as in the first part, it is not so much to facilitate uncovering the exclusively topological or egocentric responses as it is an effort better to discriminate the cases where the subject looks for the coordination of projective or Euclidian relations but has not yet fully mastered this coordination. Considering position J, for example, it is possible that in locating the correct sector the subject may take the rotation of the landscape into account rather than rely on simple intuitive or perceptual judgments (e.g., "in the big empty field"); within this sector, however, he will ignore the rotation and place his man near the railroad tracks—that is, on the part of the sector that is closest to him, as in the inverted model. Positions K and L also lend themselves easily to this sort of error. The variations in position resulting from this kind of behavior can be more or less marked; but it would be unwise to neglect them because we would thus risk judging as simple carelessness an imprecision which is actually attributable to a real intellectual difficulty—whence the importance of applying the same rigorousness of scoring to the second part as was applied in the first.

ANALYSIS OF SUCCESSES AND ERRORS

Global analysis of the results provides two complementary kinds of information. Examination of the relative difficulty of the problems first suggests the existence of certain strategies, and the subsequent study of different types of errors then supplies the elements necessary for verifying these inferences. For this reason it is necessary to analyze successes and errors separately.

ANALYSIS OF SUCCESSES

Tables 30 and 31 give the number of successes for each problem in each of the two parts of the test. Comparing the two parts, first, there is no doubt that the first is much easier than the second, since the average percentage of successes obtained by all subjects to the whole group of problems is 80 in the first and only 52.4 in the second. Furthermore, within each of the two parts we note marked differences in difficulty: percentages of successes run between 92.2 and 68.7 in the first and from 69.5 to 37.7 in the second. By the Friedman test,[1] these differences are significant at the .01 level. Expressing this in terms of median ages and ages of accession, these differences in difficulty are not appreciably changed. One will note in particular that, for all problems in the first part, the 50 per cent successes level (age of accession) is achieved before the age of five years, while the same percentage in the second part is found only once before the age of five years and often is not achieved before the age of seven or even eight years.

How should we interpret these differences in difficulty? It is at this point that the study of the content of the problems may serve to determine whether the structure of the test and particularly the choice of positions really demonstrate the complementarity of projective and Euclidian operations, the egocentric character of the first orientation relations available to the child, and the actual influence of topological relations in locating the positions. More precisely, analysis of the results should answer three major questions. The first is whether the topological relations of neighborhood and enclosure which are inherent in the topographical schema play a role in the child's behavior. Assuming that they do intervene, we must then ask whether these relations are adequate to assure the localization of all positions or whether projective and Euclidian relations must be added to them. We wonder, finally, whether they immediately take on an operational character or whether they are first present as intuitive preoperational forms.

[1] Excluded from the first section are the results from subjects aged 8:0 to 12:0 years, where the test is really too easy and loses all discriminative value.

Table 30

Number of successes at each age level and for each position in the first part of the *Localization of topographical positions* test

Age	N						Position						
		A	B	C	D	E	F	G	H	I	J	K	L
12:0	50	50	50	50	50	50	50	50	50	48	49	50	49
11:0	50	50	50	50	50	50	50	50	49	50	49	47	48
10:0	50	50	50	50	48	50	50	50	50	49	49	47	49
9:0	50	50	50	49	49	50	50	50	50	46	50	49	48
8:0	50	50	50	46	46	47	49	50	48	47	46	47	45
7:0	50	50	48	48	43	46	50	49	49	42	44	42	43
6:0	50	49	49	44	41	42	49	49	40	35	38	37	34
5:0	50	47	43	38	42	44	48	48	33	34	36	28	30
4:6	50	46	43	33	27	32	47	46	27	26	27	28	29
4:0	50	43	42	27	25	31	43	42	19	20	26	30	25
3:6	50	38	34	22	18	23	39	33	18	7	17	15	15
3:0	50	30	32	17	19	19	24	25	12	8	15	11	9
Mean		46.1	45.1	39.5	38.2	40.4	45.8	45.2	37.1	34.4	37.2	36.0	35.4
Median age		7:0	7:1	7:8	7:10	7:7	7:0	7:1	8:0	8:3	7:11	8:0	8:1
Age of accession		-	-	3:9	4:1	3:7	3:0	3:0	4:3	4:9	4:1	4:3	4:5

Table 31

Number of successes at each age level and for each position in the second part of the *Localization of topographical positions* test

Age	N	Position											
		A	B	C	D	E	F	G	H	I	J	K	L
12:0	50	47	46	46	46	47	47	49	45	41	39	41	39
11:0	50	45	44	46	47	48	47	45	42	35	41	37	34
10:0	50	47	36	45	42	46	47	43	40	40	36	35	33
9:0	50	43	39	42	41	39	40	34	39	29	27	30	33
8:0	50	41	36	40	41	39	35	33	34	22	32	23	23
7:0	50	33	30	37	43	31	25	25	36	24	18	20	21
6:0	50	33	29	36	37	24	21	20	27	23	19	18	19
5:0	50	21	25	27	38	23	6	6	30	16	7	3	11
4:6	50	24	21	23	35	25	11	3	17	19	8	6	12
4:0	50	24	12	16	20	21	8	4	16	9	4	2	3
3:6	50	16	14	16	15	12	8	3	10	4	5	4	6
3:0	50	16	9	9	12	6	5	4	8	4	4	7	3
Mean		32.5	28.4	31.9	34.8	30.1	25.0	22.4	28.7	22.2	20.0	18.9	19.8
Median age		8:4	8:4	8:2	7:9	8:6	9:4	9:7	8:4	8:11	9:4	9:6	9:2
Age of accession		5:1	5:8	5:0	4:1	5:1	7:0	7:3	5:6	7:8	7:8	8:3	8:4

A. *Importance of topological relations.* As for the first question, analysis of the successes leaves no doubt about the importance of topological relations in the child's behavior. The very unequal difficulty of the problems of the two sections testifies to this. If the child systematically called on the relations of orientation or distance binding the elements of the landscape into a single total structure, we should not understand why the difficulty in constructing these relations would be so different from one position to another. These differences, however, are not at all strange if we assume that the child's behavior is guided either partially or wholly by topological considerations. The first of these two possibilities is that the child begins by relying on neighborhood cues for a first global localization of the position, and then has only to use the relations of orientation and distance in order to ensure accuracy. This use of cue objects limits the variety of possible responses so that the subject may sometimes accomplish his localization without having to coordinate several relations at once. In the case of positions A, B, F, and G, for example, the subject who at first relies on the simple relationship of neighborhood or enclosure has then only a single projective or Euclidian relation (e.g., before-behind, opposite, etc.) to consider in making his choice. The second possibility is to assume that the child uses exclusively topological cues without ever considering the projective or Euclidian relations. But even then the importance of these topological cues would vary with the positions so that the subject's final response, however random it might be, is more likely to be correct in problems where the number of possible responses is quite small (e.g., positions F and G, where only two responses are possible) than in problems where this number is much greater (e.g., positions H, I, J, K, and L, where four responses are possible for each). In sum, the relative difficulty of the problems is easily understood if we admit the preponderant or exclusive intervention of the topological relations of neighborhood or enclosure in the child's behavior.

To this first argument favoring the topological character of the child's first solutions must be added several groups of facts whose interpretation is considerably clarified when they are studied in the light of the same hypothesis. If we compare, for example, positions F and G with position E in the first part of the test (see Table 30), it is not easy to understand why the latter is more difficult than the other two. From the topological point of view, these three positions are equivalent, since each is located at an end of the road or of the railroad tracks. To explain this difference in difficulty, we could emphasize the importance of projective concepts, since the localization of position E presupposes a coordination of left-right relations whereas locating positions F and G assumes coordination of the before-behind relations. Referring to the observations of Piaget and Inhelder (1948, p. 278), we might think that representation of the left-right relations is not available to the child as early as are the before-behind relations. Compared with the latter, the former refer to actions or gestures which are more difficult to coordinate because they are intuitively more homogeneous and thus slower to be freed of the egocentrism which is tied to one's own point of view. But the proof that this factor is not the only one operating is seen in the fact that position E becomes easier than the other two (F and G) in the second part of the test (see Table 31). These results defy analysis so long as we try to explain them exclusively in terms of projective relations; they become very clear if, conceding that projective or even Euclidian representation is more difficult with left-right than with before-behind relations, we assume that the child compensates for this inability by using the simpler relations of symmetry or proximity, whose effect is detrimental in the first section of the test and beneficial in the second. Since the two landscapes are placed side by side, the line separating them either acts as an axis of symmetry or produces additional relations of neighborhood. The subject may thus easily be led to suppose, in the first section, that position E is located at the *outside* end of the railroad tracks in relation to the median axis and as *far* as possible from this axis, which apparently leads to the selection of a position diametrically opposite to the correct position. In the second section, on the contrary, resorting to the same cues of symmetry and neighborhood leads paradoxically to a correct choice because of the rotation of the first board; the subject then supposes that position E is located at the *central* extremity of the railroad tracks in relation to the median axis and as *near* as possible to this dividing line. In sum, if position E is easier to locate than positions F and G in the second section, it is because the former may be identified through a simple composition of topological relations, whereas locating the other two requires an active and conscious reversal of the projective before-behind relations.

The importance of topological indices is also seen in the case of positions A, B, C, and D. In the *first* part of the test, we observe (see Table 30) that positions A and B are much easier to locate than positions C and D. The major difference in difficulty between these two groups of problems is not the number or quality of the orientation relations of each of these groups; it is rather the fact that these various positions are defined by the different topological characteristics by which the subject may first locate a privileged cue object and then establish, around this object, the relations of orientation (egocentric or operational) necessary to locate the position concerned. Positions A and B, for example, are characterized by the immediate neighborhood of a very striking cue object (red or yellow house), and this proximity is so strong that it may guide even the child for whom neighborhood necessarily presupposes contiguity. Positions C and D, on the contrary, are more easily assimilated to any other position located within the same sector, unless the concept of neighborhood retains its cue value despite the lack of contiguity and unless also the child can combine several neighborhoods. For position C in particular, located equidistant from the road and the small blue house, the subject who cannot coordinate several neighborhoods will readily elect to place the man near the small blue house with no concern at all for the symmetrical and equally real proximity of the road and without any intervention of Euclidian considerations of distance. This double progress of coordinating and extending the topological concepts of neighborhood seems adequate to explain the *décalage* observed between the difficulty with positions A and B on one hand and positions C and D on the other. The before-behind orientation relations implied in locating the first two are no less complex than the left-right relations defining the latter two; but the relations of neighborhood are certainly easier to coordinate in the case of positions A and B, where neighborhood is simple and is reduced to pure contiguity, than in the case of positions C and D, where neighborhood is double and must tolerate a certain distance.

The fact that the *décalage* disappears as such in the *second* part of the test, where position B alone is more difficult than the other three (see Table 31), supports this interpretation. In this section, rotating one of the landscapes removes every possibility of success from the child who, as yet unable to master the projective before-behind and left-right relations, cannot achieve a concept of neighborhood that is large enough to go beyond simple contiguity and flexible enough to coordinate the multiple elements which this extension involves. In order to locate positions A, B, C, and D without reversing the projective relations involved, the subject has no choice but better to define, by multiplying them, the relations of neighborhood proper to each of these positions. Position B, for example, is located near both the yellow house and the edge of the board; similarly, position A is near the red house and beside the three small houses; etc. In sum, this multiplication of the topological relations of neighborhood, on which the child may economize in the first section for positions A and B, becomes a minimum condition for success for these two positions as it was already in the first section for positions C and D. This would explain the disappearance of the *décalage* observed in the first section between these two pairs of problems. It is true that locating position B is now more difficult than locating the other three (success percentage of 56.8 versus 63.8 to 69.5); but this difference is easily explained by the fact that position B is the first one that the child must locate after the model landscape is rotated. The solution of the two problems which serve as examples (the man placed successively *on* the yellow house and *on* the red house) is so simple and obvious that the subject can manage it quite well without even being aware of the new difficulties entailed by reversing the orientation relations, which has become a necessity, whereas before he had only to transpose them directly. It is to attract the subject's attention to this new aspect of the situation that he is systematically corrected if he makes a mistake on the first problem (position B). The child's spontaneous remarks (e.g.,*"Oh! I didn't notice, I thought it was the same as before"*) which this correction often stimulates clearly suggest that the greater difficulty with this first problem may be somewhat artificial and due primarily to lack of attention to the change.

Finally, the results on position H also emphasize the importance of topological relations. In topological terms, this position is identical in all respects to the other three positions (I, K, and L) near the intersection of the road and the railroad tracks, with the exception that the relative proximity of the red house may aid in its identification. If the advantage of this topological reference point is not felt in the first part of the test (Table 30), it is because its use presupposes an extension and coordination of the relations of neighborhood; it is possible that these are contemporary with coordination of the egocentric relations of depth and laterality, which is necessary for locating the other three positions. In the second part of the test (Table 31), on the other hand, this advantage is clear, and position H is easier to locate than the other three (percentage of success of 57.3 versus 37.7 to 44.3). It thus becomes equal in difficulty to those (A, B, C, D) whose location, without imposing the simultaneous reversal of the left-right and before-behind relations on the subject, may be more easily assured either by coordinating several neighborhoods or by reversing a single orientation relation from a cue object located in the neighborhood.

In sum, the comparative analysis of the content and level of success of these problems clearly emphasizes the importance of topological relations of neighborhood and enclosure in the subject's behavior.

B. *Inadequacy of topological relations.* We must now ask whether this influence is exclusive or simply auxiliary. In other words, the problem arises whether these topological concepts are enough to guarantee the localization of all positions or whether concepts of another kind must also intervene. In this respect, we need only compare the relative difficulty of the test's two sections (see Tables 30 and 31, pp. 186, 187) to see that the topological concepts are not the only ones operating. The positions to be located are exactly the same in each section, so the *décalage* observed between them must necessarily depend on the fact that, in the second section, one of the landscapes is rotated. Now, supposing that the subject relies exclusively on topological cues—that is, on the neighborhood and enclosure relations inherent in the group of objects constituting the landscape—it would be impossible to understand why the simple fact of rotating the model landscape has such a marked effect on the difficulty of the problems. Once it has been defined in topological terms, any position can be located with equal ease whatever the relative orientation of the two groups which are compared, since topological relations by their very nature are independent of diverse perspectives and points of view. When we define position C, for example, by saying that it is near the road and the group of three small houses, we can change the relative orientation of the two boards without affecting this dual neighborhood relation. To explain the fact that the second part of the test is more difficult than the first, we must then suppose that topological relations are not the only relations at work in locating the positions, but that they are accompanied by other types of relations whose coordination is less difficult in the first part than in the second.

C. *Intuitive character of the first projective or Euclidian concepts.* These additional relations may be of a projective nature (e.g., left-right, before-behind) or of a Euclidian nature (e.g., concept of distance, opposite, etc.). It is even probable, as we shall try to show later, that these two types of relations appear at the same time. Whatever these relations may be, the *décalage* observed between the two parts of the test is much clearer if we assume that the coordination of these relations is not immediately operational in the child, but that it remains for a long time subjected to the limitations which are imposed on it by the egocentrism of intuitive or preoperational thought. If it is true, for example, that the first orientation relations which the child forms are at first linked exclusively to his own point of view and that his first concepts of spatial reference are based on simple perceptual correspondences or symmetries, it is easy to understand that the problems in the first part are solved earlier than those in the second. In fact, as long as the two landscapes are oriented in the same direction, the subject can make his localizations without having to free himself from his own viewpoint and even without having to be aware of the fact that he is using himself as a reference point outside the landscape. On the other hand, as soon as the model landscape is rotated, he must be able to differentiate his own perspective from that of the person facing him, or (which is the same thing) he must be able consistently to locate the observer, who serves as the external reference point, in the same position in relation to the whole landscape. This solution implies a consciousness of the particularly deceptive character of the "false absolutes" which are linked to the exclusiveness of one's own point of view as well as a representation of the transformations produced by the diversity of possible perspectives. In sum, even though most of the problems in the first part can be solved at the level of purely egocentric orientation concepts or purely perceptual correspondences (themselves egocentric by definition), it is not so in the second part where rotation of the model landscape requires continued efforts at objectification and intellectual decentration.

We could, of course, propose a different explanation of this *décalage* between the two parts of the test. Rather than concluding in favor of a prelogical level (intuitive correspondences, egocentric referents, etc.) in the development of projective or Euclidian concepts themselves, it may be that these concepts are immediately operational from the time of their first appearance, and we could then explain the *décalage* with the well-know fact that coordination of projective or Euclidian relations is much easier for the child (and even for the adult) when it can be limited to the operations of direct transposition, as in the first part of the test, without requiring the simple or double reversals of the second. Such an interpretation is both simple and plausible. We know, for example, that the adult himself, already capable of projective and Euclidian operations, shows much less difficulty in a test requiring direct transposition of a spatial whole (e.g., reproducing or simply recognizing a reduced-scale sketch) than in a test requiring him to reverse one or more dimensions of this whole (e.g., mirror drawing or, to mention a less overtly motor task, recognizing the sketch of an object reflected in a mirror). But the basic weakness of this interpretation, despite the attraction of its apparent simplicity, is that it has no real explanatory value. It simply describes the phenomenon—that is, spatial relations are easier to transpose directly than to reverse—without saying why this is so and particularly without saying why the subject can sometimes compensate for his inability to achieve these reversals. In this respect, the interpretation offered earlier certainly goes further. If it is true that projective or Euclidian representations begin by being structured at an intuitive or preoperational level, we can understand that reversing the spatial relations is so difficult for children, in whom the egocentric point of view predominates for a long time, and even for adults, with whom this point of view is still a privileged reference point which they may spontaneously use to avoid having to resort to more complex forms of representation. Before adopting such an explanation, which up to this point has relied on only the comparative analysis of the successes of both sections of the test, we should see whether the analysis of the children's errors confirms the proposed hypothesis and reveals this lack of relativity of viewpoints.

Two major conclusions arise from this first analysis. The first is based on the relative difficulty of the problems of each section and states that the child's first spatial representations are at least partially topological. The second concerns the *décalage* between these two sections and suggests at once the additional appearance of projective or Euclidian concepts, and the initially intuitive or egocentric character of these concepts. It remains to confirm these interpretations by analyzing the errors and the protocols.

Before proceeding to these additional analyses, we must take up the question raised earlier—and left unanswered—concerning the exact nature of the spatial relations which the subject must add to topological relations in order to solve his positioning problems. The question really asks whether these additional relations are exclusively projective, exclusively Euclidian, or whether these two types operate in a concurrent and solidary fashion. Even without making any projections on the results of subsequent analyses, we may suppose that this last possibility is the most plausible. As for the first, it is obvious that even when grafted onto well-defined topological indices, the projective orientation relations (e.g., left-right, before-behind, etc.) are not enough to guarantee accuracy in locating the positions. One and the same topological and projective definition can correspond equally to a number of possible positions which could be differentiated only by Euclidian or metric consid-

erations (e.g., judgment of distances, concepts of opposition, etc.).
A child could try to locate position H, for example, by using various
combinations of topological and projective cues (e.g., to the right
and beside the red house, to the left of the road and to the right of
the red house, etc.); but he could not accomplish this location with
certainty and accuracy without resorting to Euclidian or metric concepts (e.g., opposite the upper right corner of the red house and
equidistant from the red house and the road, etc.). The main reason
for this inadequacy is evidently that projective relations, like topological relations, ignore the conservation of distances and angles.
This is why using Euclidian concepts is necessary for locating the
positions, and this necessity is even more imperative as the topological and projective cues are less numerous and less precise (e.g.,
positions J, K, L). As for the second hypothesis, which holds that
the Euclidian relations are the only ones supporting the topological
relations, we must admit that it is theoretically valuable. Each position may, in fact, be defined by a constellation of topological and
Euclidian indices without the express intervention of any projective
relation. Position A, for example, is located between the red house
and the group of three small houses, but at just so many centimeters
from the red house and just opposite the mid-point of its longest
side; similarly, position E is located on the longer of the two segments of the railroad tracks and at only so many centimeters from
the end; etc. Despite its theoretical plausibility, however, nothing
suggests that we should accept this hypothesis over the third one.
For one thing, the analysis of successes, with which we are at present
dealing, does not support any conclusion about the presence or absence of projective concepts in the subject's behavior. For another,
the analysis of errors, with which we will deal in a moment, should
unequivocally demonstrate the importance which the subject accords the left-right and before-behind projective relations. Attesting
to this is the basic fact that the most commonly observed errors in
the second part of the test, where one of the landscapes is rotated,
consisted of placing the man in a position exactly conforming to the
egocentric left-right and before-behind relations which determine
the same position on the first landscape. Thus, in the case of positions A and B, the subject will immediately respect the neighborhood of the red house (position A) or the yellow house (position B),
but each time will place his man on the wrong side of the house;

similarly, he will systematically reverse positions F and G; etc. In sum, as soon as he begins to be able to establish orientation relations at least with respect to his own body, the subject uses them in his attempts at localization, and this utilization, however egocentric and distorted it may be, is none the less positive and real. Although the intervention of these relations becomes particularly manifest in the subject's errors, we cannot conclude that it is not operant in his successes. It is much more plausible to think that it is omnipresent and to explain the diversity of the responses (successes or failures) by the operational or egocentric quality of the projective concepts available to the child and by the relative complexity of these concepts depending on the nature of the problems.

ANALYSIS OF ERRORS

Analysis of errors is more revealing than that of successes because we can more clearly see there the subject's level of functioning. This analysis is, however, very complex and it is not easy to present its results in a form which is both well organized and complete. The main difficulty comes from the extreme diversity of the observed behaviors, a diversity which depends on several factors, the most important of which should be mentioned here. The first concerns the many strategies which the child may use in attempting to find the positions. When children are still unable to coordinate all the projective or Euclidian relations necessary for an accurate localization, multiple solutions (as unequal as they are varied) abound, which reflect the poorness and diversity of the techniques they use: slavish imitation of the examiner's gesture, simple search for perceptual symmetry, partial or total egocentric deviation, exclusive submission to the topological relations of neighborhood or enclosure, careless or capricious randomness, etc. A second factor concerns the very nature of the problems. Each problem has its own type of difficulty, which contributes largely to diversifying the methods of solution. Thus, when the neighboring area of a cue object is particularly striking because it is immediate or exclusive (e.g., position A), the subject will be much more inclined to focus his localization efforts on considerations of a topological order than if the neighborhood relations were less well defined. Thus, also, when the examiner's gesture of locating his clay man is very long (e.g., position F) or very short (position G), the subject's attention will more willingly focus on this one cue than if the gesture were less salient (e.g., positions located at the center of the landscape). We might mention, finally, as a last source of variability, the fragmentary and limited character of the process of intellectual decentration typical of the intuitive or preoperational level. Intuitive thought is, in effect, defined by focusing attention on the partial and successive aspects of a whole situation without yet being able to engage in the integration and compensation activities necessary for operational objectivity and reversibility. These fluctuations in attention naturally have the effect of varying the strategies from one subject to another for a single problem, and from problem to problem in a single subject. Considering position A, for example, one subject will have noticed particularly the neighborhood of the red house and will neglect all other cues; another will deal exclusively with the relations of enclosure (or surrounding) and will place his man anywhere in the correct sector; another will notice especially, in the second part, that the position is far from the common border of the two landscapes and will choose a symmetrical position on his own board; etc. The same factor of relative centration may also entail considerable intraindividual variations. Thus one and the same subject, after having relied on the topological cues of neighborhood in two or three consecutive problems, may abruptly change his cue in the next problem and focus his attention on the size of the examiner's gesture, which will be his cue until a new aspect of the situation eclipses it, and so on.

For all these reasons, it would be very tedious to present a systematic analysis of all the particular behaviors which each problem might induce. Such an analysis, moreover, would be futile because, even assuming that it were possible, it could hardly serve to identify unequivocally the different strategies used by the subjects. We would certainly be able to formulate certain groups of behaviors which look very homogeneous; but it would be wrong to assume that a single external behavior always reflects a single strategy. Thus, for example, in the case of position B (second part of the test), the response of the subject who places his man near the yellow house but on the wrong side may be just as easily explained by considerations of topological neighborhood alone as by the positive intervention of projective, egocentric, before-behind relations. And, similarly, in the case of positions H, I, K, and L, all located at the intersection of the road and the railroad tracks, the response of placing the man in one of the two meadows adjacent to the correct position may be dictated equally by topological preoccupations of simple neighborhood, by a search for perceptual symmetry, or by an inability simultaneously to reverse both projective dimensions involved (before-behind and left-right). Actually, only a comparison of protocols studied as a whole seems able to differentiate the major strategies which the subjects used. Despite the intraindividual variations just mentioned, the global analysis of a protocol may reveal that most of the subject's responses clearly depend on a single solution principle (e.g., choices which nearly always reflect an egocentric point of view), and this may considerably facilitate the interpretation of the more equivocal responses. Without this minimum of consistency, we will have to give up using an analysis of errors as a source of information and will have to consider this instability as one of the principal characteristics of preoperational behavior.

Recognizing these reservations, however, it may be useful to examine even a rather crude compilation of errors for new indications which could support or weaken the interpretation of the preceding paragraph as to the importance of topological concepts in the child's behavior and as to the egocentric and intuitive character of his first projective or Euclidian representations. The means of doing this compilation consisted in first subdividing the child's board into four main sectors delimited by two reference lines, the first being parallel to the longer sides and the second defined by the side of the road which is closer to the center (see Figure 16). The first line splits the landscape into two equal parts and may, more than the railroad tracks, serve to indicate to what extent the subject manages to coordinate the before-behind relations in locating the positions. The

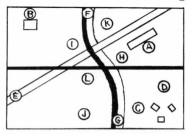

Figure 16. Demarcation of the four sectors of the landscape used in analyzing the errors in the *Localization of topographical positions* test.

second line, chosen over the vertical median line because of the special nature of the road as a reference point, plays a role which is analogous to that of the first insofar as the projective left-right dimension is concerned. Once these four sectors have been delimited, it is easy to assign each incorrect response to one of these sectors, with the exception of cases where the subject simply refused to take the test. In each sector, the classification also has two different categories (E+ and E—) depending on whether or not the subject had respected the elementary relations of enclosure or surrounding (e.g., E+: man placed in the wrong position, but on the railroad tracks, on the road, or in a field like the first man; E—: man placed in the wrong position and on the railroad tracks, for example, when the first man was located in an open field, etc.). The results of this compilation are given in Tables 32 and 33 where, to facilitate comparisons, the designation of the four sectors of the landscape does not correspond to a rigid and predetermined order but always directly refers to the position of the first man in each problem. Examination of these results reveals new elements which may confirm, and even extend, the principal conclusions reported in analyzing successes.

A. Dealing first with the *intervention of topological concepts,* the analysis of successes has already shown and underlined the fact that the subject's difficulty in locating a position is directly tied to the clarity and exclusiveness of the topological characteristics of this position. The analysis of errors now provides more decisive arguments by showing that the subject's responses, even when the location is not accurate, indicate a manifest tendency to respect at least the most elementary topological characteristics of enclosure and neighborhood.

Considering in the first place the relations of *enclosure* (or of surrounding), there is no doubt that the base on which the first man is placed (e.g., on the road, on the railroad tracks, in a field) is a very important factor. Most subjects, even some of the youngest, immediately try to conserve this topological relationship. Some of their spontaneous remarks, although too infrequently recorded to lend themselves to systematic analysis, are quite articulate and quite instructive in this respect (e.g., *"if you put the man in the road, he'll get run over!"*). But Tables 32 and 33 show this clearly since, of all the errors committed in the whole test (both sections combined),

Table 32

Distribution of errors for each position of problem 1 of the *Localization of topographical positions* test, according to the sector in which the responses are located and according to whether the errors respect (+) or ignore (−) the enclosure relations (E)

Sector chosen	E	Position												Total
		A	B	C	D	E	F	G	H	I	J	K	L	
Sector of the correct	+	28	40	65	64	20	14	7	39	79	59	50	42	507
response	−	1	3	3	1	15	7	2	11	2	3	13	2	63
Adjacent sector	+	14	16	44	36	0	0	0	43	53	51	84	30	371
(left-right direction)	−	1	0	0	2	16	11	15	1	10	5	0	2	63
Adjacent sector	+	0	0	6	11	3	17	23	10	25	16	8	30	149
(before-behind direction)	−	1	0	0	6	2	1	4	0	1	0	2	3	20
Opposite sector	+	2	0	6	20	51	0	0	49	12	15	6	54	215
	−	0	0	1	0	8	0	2	1	1	2	0	12	27
Total	+	44	56	121	131	74	31	30	141	169	141	148	156	1,242
	−	3	3	4	9	41	19	23	13	14	10	15	19	173
	+−	47	59	125	140	115	50	53	154	183	151	163	175	1,415

Table 33

Distribution of errors for each position of problem 2 of the *Localization of topographical positions* test, according to the sector in which the responses are located and according to whether the errors respect (+) or ignore (−) the enclosure relations (E)

Sector chosen	E	Position												Total
		A	B	C	D	E	F	G	H	I	J	K	L	
Sector of the correct response	+	163	205	79	131	8	9	2	83	120	47	73	13	933
	−	9	0	1	0	5	6	2	14	2	0	7	0	46
Adjacent sector (left-right direction)	+	15	8	18	7	0	0	0	64	94	43	34	12	295
	−	0	6	0	0	3	2	4	0	0	2	0	2	19
Adjacent sector (before-behind direction)	+	11	21	43	15	5	247	296	22	84	116	57	109	1,026
	−	0	0	6	1	28	4	5	1	3	1	3	2	54
Opposite sector	+	4	8	48	22	162	0	0	51	15	126	187	205	828
	−	0	2	1	0	17	11	13	3	2	11	2	10	72
Total	+	193	242	188	175	175	256	298	220	313	322	351	339	3,082
	−	9	8	8	1	53	23	24	18	7	14	12	14	191
	+ −	202	250	196	176	228	279	322	238	320	346	363	353	3,273

more than 92 per cent involve these elementary enclosure relations
(E+). These relations are even sometimes the only ones which
the subject considers, and he places his man almost anywhere on the
road, on the railroad tracks, etc. Most of the time, however, as we
will see a little later, other localization factors such as neighborhood,
symmetry, egocentric orientation relations, etc., also intervene and
contribute somewhat to the subject's responses. The importance accorded these other factors may even sometimes lead the subject
completely to ignore the enclosure relations. If, all things considered, this happens especially in problems E, F, and G, this is because
these problems are the only ones where the subject is forced to reject
the relations of enclosure when he wants to respect perceptual symmetry (especially in the first part of the test) or when he is still
subjected to as yet egocentric orientation relations (especially in the
second part). For position E, for example, in the first part, the subject who is careful to select a position symmetrical to that of the first
man, in terms of the line separating the two boards, will place his
own man in a field below the three small houses and thus, after some
symptomatic hesitations, will not take account of the fact that the
first man is placed on the railroad tracks.

As for the relations of *neighborhood,* the analysis of errors also
supports the conclusions of the analysis of successes. As we can infer
from the results given in Tables 32 and 33, the subject's incorrect
responses tend to respect the most elementary concepts of neighborhood. Thus, beginning with the *second* part of the test (Table 33),
we note that positions A, B, and D, whose localization is most
clearly favored by the immediate proximity of salient cue objects,
are assigned to the correct sector in 81 per cent of the cases (508 out
of 628)—that is, much more often than in the other three sectors
combined. The corresponding proportion is only 40 per cent (299
out of 754) for positions C, H, and I, where the relations of neighborhood, while not totally missing, are nevertheless more ambiguous: if the presence of cue objects can contribute to identifying the
correct sector in all three cases, the exact localization is complicated
by the multiplicity of neighborhoods (e.g., road and small houses in
C, intersection and red house in H, etc.) and by the relative distance
of these cue objects (e.g., yellow house in I). Finally, for positions
J, K, and L, all three characterized by the absence of any cue object
in their respective sectors, the proportion of responses made in the

correct quadrant is much lower (only 13 per cent): the rest of the responses are concentrated mostly in the sector exactly opposite the correct one, which directly reflects the distorting influence of egocentric orientation relations. In brief, comparing these results shows that the topological cues of neighborhood definitely play a role even in the subject's incorrect responses to problems in the second part of the test. Insofar as they are clearly defined on the model landscape, these cues serve at least to facilitate the general location of the correct sector, and if they are not adequate to assure exact localization, it is because the subject is adhering exclusively to considerations of simple neighborhood, without any concern for relative distance, or because at the most he is adding still-egocentric orientations to them. Analysis of errors in the *first* part of the test (Table 32), which was much easier than the second, also testifies to the importance which the subject gives to concepts of neighborhood. Comparing the different positions, regrouped according to the quality of the neighborhoods which are involved, we observe that the proportion of incorrect responses in the correct sector decreases regularly depending on whether the positions have simple and obvious neighborhood relations (positions C, H, and I: 43 per cent) or nearly nonexistent ones (positions J, K, and L: 33 per cent). These proportions are thus distributed as in the second part, but the differences are much less marked here for the simple reason that the factors of gesture imitation and especially of perceptual symmetry work against choosing the correct sector in the first part, whereas they favor it in the second because of the rotation of the model landscape. The importance of these last factors, often irreconcilable with elementary neighborhoods, varies from problem to problem and from subject to subject, but always has the effect of turning the subject from the correct sector and favoring the other three. The search for symmetry, for example, is betrayed in most problems by the relative frequency of responses situated in the sector adjacent to the correct one on the left-right plane. If the choice of this sector is not at all favored in problems H and L, where the responses also run into the other sector adjacent to the correct one and even into the opposite sector, this is because these two positions are located very near the intersection of the two lines dividing the landscape into quadrants, so that the slightest imprecision on the subject's part makes the four sectors equally probable. Imitation of the examiner's movement, furthermore, may also lead the subject to bypass the correct sector for the one which, on the before-behind plane, is adjacent to it, as is the case in problems I, D, and J. In these last two problems (D and J), imitation of the gesture may even combine with the pursuit of symmetry to favor the choice of the sector opposite to the correct one.

B. Dealing now with the *intervention of projective orientation relations* in the subject's behavior, and especially with the still-egocentric character of these first projective concepts, the analysis of successes can only indirectly prove this by relying on the observed difference in difficulty between the two parts of the test. Indeed, this *décalage* assumes a very clear significance if we recognize that coordination of the projective relations is necessary only to the solution of problems in the second part, and if we accept Piaget's position on the anteriority of egocentric concepts in comparison with operational concepts. In this respect, however, analyzing the failures is more directly instructive, as is seen in Table 33 where we note that the great majority of errors committed in the second part reveal a partial or total inability objectively to coordinate the projective orientation relations. The phenomenon is especially strong in problems E, F, and G. Examination of the protocols reveals that 82 per cent of the 829 errors in these problems consist of placing the man at one end of the road or of the railroad tracks, as in the model landscape, but of systematically selecting the wrong end, which amounts to exactly reproducing the egocentric perspective offered by the model. In problems A, B, and D, where the simplicity of the neighborhoods immediately leads to the choice of the correct sector, the same phenomenon is seen differently but no less clearly. At least in problems A and B, in fact, examination of the protocols indicates that 96 per cent of the 377 responses in the correct sector consist of placing the man very near the cue house but on the side which is exactly opposite the correct position. If this same egocentric obedience is not seen in problem D, it is undoubtedly because the three small cue houses in this case are too close to the edge of the board for the same reversal of the before-behind dimension to be possible for the subject. As for positions J, K, and L, where the neighborhood relations are the least differentiated, the importance of egocentric relations is revealed especially in the preponderant choice of the sector just opposite the correct one. It is also indirectly revealed, particularly in problems J and L, by the relative frequency of responses located in the sector adjacent to the correct one on the before-behind plane. Choice of this sector may be dictated by considerations of perceptual symmetry, but rotating the model landscape has the effect of making responses based on symmetry concurrent with those based on egocentric relations. Finally, in problems C, H, and I, the results are less characteristic. The choice of the correct sector is favored by the presence of cue objects in this sector; but the ambiguity of these neighborhoods often leads the subject to choose various sectors depending on whether he relies on totally egocentric relations (e.g., the sector opposite the correct one, in C and H), on neighborhood cues considered in a clearly egocentric fashion (e.g., the sector adjacent to the correct one on the left-right plane, in I and H—that is, to the left or right of the intersection in relation to the subject), or finally on considerations based on symmetry (e.g., the sector adjacent to the correct one on the before-behind plane, in I).

C. It remains to emphasize more specifically the importance of two kinds of strategies, mentioned earlier on more than one occasion, which the subject sometimes uses in one or the other of the sections of the test and which are likely to be demonstrated especially by analyzing errors in the first section. The first of these strategies is *copying the examiner's movement.* The two landscapes are placed side by side between the examiner and the subject, who face each other, so that the examiner's motions in placing his man on the first board are directly perceived by the subject. Since the instructions require the subject to do the same thing the examiner does—that is, to place his man similarly on the other landscape, in the same place, etc.—it is possible that the very length of the examiner's gesture serves the subject as a cue in the same way as do neighborhoods, enclosures, and projective or Euclidian relations. In other words, the subject may just as easily pay attention to the subjective or dynamic elements as to the objective or static elements of the situation. The influence of this factor is seen only in the first part of the test where it is reflected in the inappropriate reversals (or pseudo reversals) which will have, in the second part, all the appearances of the real reversals typical of the operational level. Analysis of errors with certain problems in the first part (Table 32) is very revealing in this respect. In the case of positions F and G, for example, where the examiner's gesture is particularly full or restricted, the subject's errors are more often on the wrong than on the right end of the road (39 per cent versus 20 per cent of all errors). In other words, the subject is strongly influenced inappropriately to reverse the before-behind dimensions of the landscape, a reversal which can be explained by the concern with copying the size of the examiner's gesture. In problem E, where errors are concentrated in the sector opposite the correct one (44 per cent versus 17 per cent), this interpretation may be nearly the same, except that the tendency to copy the examiner's gesture is reinforced here by a concern for symmetry leading the subject to select the end of the railroad tracks which is farthest from the line dividing the two landscapes. The subject does not merely copy the length of the examiner's gesture, but also copies other features of this movement and, particularly, what we could call the route which he follows. To place his man on B, for example, the examiner's gesture must visibly pass over the yellow house. The subject who wants to copy this particular aspect of the gesture will place his man beyond the yellow house on his own board, which involves an unnecessary and inaccurate reversal of the before-behind relations linking the man to the yellow house. Returning to the protocols we see that, in this problem, 35 of the 43 (81 per cent) incorrect responses in the correct sector (Table 32) are errors of just this sort. If this imitation of gesture does not seem to intervene consistently in the other problems, it is probably because the examiner's gesture is not unique in its length (e.g., positions I, H, L) or in its route (e.g., positions A, C, J, K), or because exactly copying the movement would require the subject to go beyond the border of the landscape (e.g., position D). The subject's attention is thus focused on other aspects of the situation, such as the topological relations or the egocentric orientation relations already pointed out.

The *search for symmetry* is the last strategy to be discussed. We make only brief mention of it here because the preceding analyses have already shown more than once that using this procedure can have a positive or negative influence on the efficacy of other procedures. This search for symmetry which the subject may spontaneously adopt is suggested to him by the natural axis of the line separating the two boards placed side by side before him. Depending on whether the man in the model is close to or far from this symmetrical axis, the subject places his man at a corresponding position on his board, doing so at the risk of ignoring the most elementary relations of neighborhood or enclosure. In problem A, for example, he will often select a position located beside the yellow house (rather than the red house) and rather toward the interior of the board—that is, a position closely corresponding to that of the first man in terms of his relation to the dividing line. An equivalent phenomenon occurs in problem B, where the subject will place his man beside the red house and toward the exterior of the board. Examination of the protocols indicates that, of the 106 errors committed in these two problems (Table 32), at least 24 per cent are of this type. It is in problem E, however, that this tendency toward symmetry is most manifest. The subject cannot resist the temptation to put his man either at the end of the railroad tracks which is farthest from the line separating the two boards, or near the three small houses and opposite the first man without any concern for the railroad tracks, or, finally, somewhere near the red house (which is an acceptable compromise for the subject who wants both to respect the symmetry relations and to imitate the size of the examiner's gesture). Returning to the protocols, we see that these three types of behavior account for 54 per cent of the 115 errors committed on this problem (Table 32). This search for symmetry is less marked in the other problems, but not absent, as preceding analyses have shown. It is especially revealed in nearly all responses where the relations of neighborhoods or enclosure are ignored. In the case of position G, for example, located at the end of the road which is off-center with respect to the whole board, we note that 65 per cent of the 23 responses located outside the road (the "E—" in Table 32) are assigned to the sector adjacent to the correct one, on the left-right plane, and tend to be concentrated around a position symmetrical to that of the first man, with respect to the dividing line.

Comparing the two strategies, however, it seems that the search for symmetry is not easily dissociated from gesture imitation. It is not impossible, first of all, that responses supposedly due to symmetry are themselves derived from a concern with imitating the lateral (left-right) direction of the examiner's gesture in relation to to the central vertical axis dividing the two landscapes. It is nonetheless true that this vertical axis, which is clearly delimited in the visual field, might be used as a cue by the subject even if he is not able to see the examiner's gesture. On the other hand, it is hard to

understand that the static aspects of the situation alone may suffice
to explain the responses which earlier were attributed either to
copying the path followed by the examiner's gesture (e.g., before-
behind reversal in relation to the house, in A and B) or simply to
copying the length of this movement (e.g., before-behind reversal in
positions F and G). At the most, we could assume—still dealing only
with these two cases—that the false reversals are due to considerations of symmetry which this time are in relation to an imaginary
horizontal axis across the middle of the two boards. In sum, the false
before-behind reversals may more probably be interpreted in terms
of gesture imitation than in terms of a search for symmetry, because
the experimental situation offers the possibility of seeing the examiner's gesture and includes no overt horizontal axis in the perceptual field. Errors made on the lateral plane, on the other hand, may
as easily be due to preoccupations with symmetry as to gesture imitation (or even to both at once), because the vertical axis separating
the two boards and the left-right direction of the examiner's movement are both directly visible to the child.

The functional relationship which seems to link the search for
symmetry with gesture imitation is perhaps more radically tied to
the fact that these two strategies are subjected to similar egocentric
limitations. On the one hand, perception of symmetry as it is considered here is closely linked to a particular position of the subject in
relation to the line separating the two boards, but this transposition
does not at all imply a coordination of the man's position with the
other elements of the landscape within a single total structure. Gesture imitation, on the other hand, amounts to a simple accommoda-
tion of the subject's action to the most superficial and most easily
perceptible aspects of the examiner's motion, without consideration
of any of the objective relations defining the man's position in the
whole structure. It is easy to see that these two strategies both have
the more general characteristics of intuitive or preoperational egocentric thought. The search for symmetry is clear if we accept that
intuitive thought, lacking mobility in its decentrations, cannot
freely coordinate its activities of analysis and synthesis, and that for
a long time it is dominated by considerations of an elementary
topological nature. Rather than trying to establish the spatial correspondence between two distinct and complementary landscapes, the
subject at the intuitive level finds it easier to consider them both as

a single perceptual whole and to coordinate, around the vertical axis dividing this totality, the elementary topological relations of order or succession which constitute the basis of perceptual symmetry. Similarly, gesture imitation, when it is restricted solely to the subjective aspects of the examiner's movement and is blocked by even the most elementary compensations—which demand, for example, that a model's brief gesture be equivalent to a long gesture of an imitator sitting across from him—illustrates the inadequacies of intuitive thought which is characterized by a lack of differentiation of different viewpoints, a distorting influence of perceptual effects, and a lack of coordination of successive states within a single transformation.

In a control experiment done in our laboratory, Royer (1964) gave a single group of 50 subjects (average age of four years) the test discussed here, as well as a modified form of it, designed to eliminate the factor of gesture imitation (the subject closes his eyes or turns his head while the examiner positions the first man) and to reduce considerably the role of symmetry (the two landscapes are separated by two meters and the subject is thus unable to maintain the same central position in relation to the line dividing them). The results supported the role played in the original form of the test by gesture imitation and symmetry, and produced an additional strategy of searching for horizontal linearity (the subject sometimes trying to line up his man along the horizontal line of the first man's position). Royer correctly sees in these three strategies the still-clumsy attempts to use projective relations whose intervention may sometimes involve very primitive topological errors. The modified version of the test, by working against the use of these primitive strategies, significantly raised the subjects' level of functioning.

In sum, preceding analyses support the main point of the predictions made at the beginning. In the first place, the importance of the *topological concepts* of neighborhood and enclosure appears not only in the analysis of successes, where the relative difficulty of the problems is closely tied to the clarity and simplicity of these relations, but also in the analysis of errors, where the subject's choice shows a preference for positions which respect at least these basic relations. In the second place, the intervention of *projective concepts* is seen especially, and rather paradoxically, in the egocentric behavior where the subject shows himself to be unable to make the reversals required by the rotation of the first board and where, taking account of the most elementary neighborhood and enclosure relations, he systematically elects to put his man in positions which from his own point of view conserve the same left-right and before-behind relations as the corresponding positions on the first board. Finally, concerning *Euclidian* (or metric) *concepts,* we still cannot evaluate their real importance, but there is little danger in inferring that they do intervene, at least in many of the correct responses, since the level of accuracy demanded by the scoring criteria would not very often be reached if topological or even projective cues alone were used.

Chapter X

Localization of Topographical Positions: Analysis by Stages

In a developmental study of this sort, analysis of the protocols furnishes a necessary complement to the individual analysis of the problems. If we wish to identify and define the successive steps leading to mastery of the intellectual task considered here, it is most instructive to examine how children at different age levels respond to the test. This examination is made in the light of the conclusions of the preceding analyses concerning the different strategies which the subjects use and leads directly to the establishment of a developmental scale. The distribution of subjects on the scale determines the age at which each stage is reached, and the content of the protocols reveals the degree of consistency which the subjects show in their solutions.

This analysis is in three parts. The first summarizes the criteria used in constructing the developmental scale and the second gives the distribution of the subjects on this scale. The last part, the most elaborate, is a detailed description of the stages and gives examples illustrating the solutions proper to each.

ESTABLISHING A DEVELOPMENTAL SCALE

The criterion adopted to establish the stages is the number of successes attained by the subjects with the different types of problems. It might have been useful to choose a more refined criterion, more closely tied to the quality of the intellectual processes of the subjects' behavior; but the unequal difficulty of the problems and their very multiplicity, the diversity of possible strategies, and the

211

infrequency of children's spontaneous remarks which might have revealed their level of conceptualization are factors arguing against a method of analysis by stages based solely on qualitative criteria. Without abandoning the attempt to identify the mechanisms underlying the subject's behavior—as the following discussion will show—it is better to adhere to a simple criterion which is directly observable and easily accessible to anyone who may wish to use the same test for diagnostic purposes.

The results obtained on the relative difficulty of the two sections of the test (see Tables 30 and 31: Chapter IX, pp. 186, 187) immediately suggest two general levels in the scale. The problems of the first section may be solved by still-egocentric (or preoperational) procedures, while those of the second section require a minimum of intellectual decentration or objectification of spatial relations. Furthermore, in each section the positions A to G are distinguished from positions H to L by the fact that location of the former, which are more clearly delimited by neighborhood and enclosure relations than are the latter, does not require that the subject be able to coordinate projective or Euclidian relations. For reasons deriving from both statistical results and the internal analysis of the problems, the scale must then include at least four levels of difficulty. Referring now to Table 34, which regroups, by level, the average frequencies of success per problem given earlier in Tables 30 and 31, we note immediately that although the differences in difficulty are significant from

Table 34

Redistribution of the mean successes (reported in Tables 30 and 31) on each position of the four levels of difficulty in the *Localization of topographical positions* test

Level of difficulty							
1		2		3		4	
Position	Mean	Position	Mean	Position	Mean	Position	Mean
1-A	46.1	1-J	37.2	2-D	34.8	2-H	28.7
1-F	45.8	1-H	37.1	2-A	32.5	2-I	22.2
1-G	45.2	1-K	36.0	2-C	31.9	2-J	20.0
1-B	45.1	1-L	35.4	2-E	30.1	2-L	19.8
1-E	40.4	1-I	34.4	2-B	28.4	2-K	18.9
1-C	39.5			2-F	25.0		
1-D	38.2			2-G	22.4		

(a) Within-group differences are all significant (Friedman test: .05 level), except for group 2.
(b) Between-group differences are all significant (Mann-Whitney U test: .01 level).

one group to another (Mann-Whitney U test, .01 level), the problems assigned to one level are not always equally difficult (the difference being significant at the .05 level in three out of four groups, by the Friedman test), and that there is even a slight overlap between levels. The problem is then one of whether we should confine ourselves to these four levels and then, considering all successes at a single level as equivalent, require the subject to satisfy a rather rigorous numerical criterion (e.g., four out of five) in order to be assigned to this level. Or, on the other hand, would it be better to try to establish a more refined scale and combine only problems of equivalent difficulty? Such a solution, which gives more weight to statistical considerations than to the test's internal structure, and amounts to multiplying the number of levels on the scale (at most, we may conceive of as many levels as there are problems), undoubtedly rests on a laudable concern with constructing as transitive a scale as possible—that is, a classification wherein success with problems at a given level automatically implies solution of all problems at lower levels. But multiplying the levels of the scale would, on the contrary, result in further compromising the transitivity of the classification, since we cannot assume that a scale of difficulty established from results obtained on the whole sample is applicable on the level of individual solutions. It is quite obvious that this absolute transitivity could exist neither in fact nor in principle, and for several reasons. The multiplicity and variety of strategies available to the preoperational child have effects which are unpredictable from one subject to another, or even from one moment to another in a single subject, and may be reflected in apparent successes (or pseudo successes) which are impossible to uncover with any certainty. We also know that intuitive or preoperational thought, by its very nature, is not at all systematic; depending on fluctuations in attention, it may attach itself in turn to different aspects of a single situation, so that a subject may at a given moment adopt a strategy that allows him to solve easily a problem which had been judged difficult and consequently missed by most of the subjects. In brief, the heterogeneity of strategies and the vicissitudes of intuitive thought itself prohibit any search for absolute transitivity in the series of problems.

Does this mean that we must simply use the techniques adopted by most of the common psychometric tests and construct a homogeneous scale solely from the total scores of the subjects, without considering the difficulty of the problems? Such a technique would hardly be any more promising since it is based on equally tenuous postulates. Unless the difficulty of the problems is similarly distributed for each individual in the group, the protocols assigned to each level by simple total scores could not be homogeneous enough to define actual levels of development. This condition presumes perfect transitivity of the scale, and we have just shown that this is neither true nor possible. Thus it is better to reject this method because, should we decide to adopt it in spite of everything, we would miss the possibilities of other methods which allow the delimitation of successive developmental levels without requiring that the difficulty scale of the problems be completely transitive.

In relation to the two preceding techniques, the technique which we adopted is a compromise solution. It retains the most valuable elements of these two techniques (e.g., importance given to the relative difficulty of the problems and to the number of successes in a protocol), but avoids their excessive rigorousness both by recognizing the fact that the transitivity of the scale can only be imperfect and by tempering the limiting effects of a rigid application of pure statistical seriation with considerations of a qualitative nature (e.g., importance given to an internal analysis of the problems, to natural fluctuations in attention, to the possibility of pseudo successes, etc.). Thus the scale which we propose includes two main levels according to whether the successes are located in the first or the second part of the test. Each part has itself two levels of difficulty depending on whether the subject solves only problems A to G (levels 1 and 3), or also solves problems H to L (levels 2 and 4). The criteria that determine the correctness of each response have already been reported in detail in the first part of the preceding chapter. Each of the four levels of difficulty thus refers to a group of five or seven problems which are considered to be equivalent. For a level to be attained, the subject must solve four out of five or five out of seven (depending on the case) of the problems at this level. We needed a criterion strict enough to weed out the pseudo successes produced by basically inadequate but accidentally effective strategies, and at the same time lenient enough to avoid overly penalizing temporary distractions.

The developmental scale derives directly from these levels of difficulty. It includes, besides the usual stage defined by total incomprehension of the task (stage 0), three general stages of development, the last two each being divided into two substages. Stage 1 includes subjects who miss both parts of the test. Their strategies rely solely on the elementary neighborhood or enclosure cues, the search for symmetry, or copying the examiner's gesture. These procedures may lead accidentally to correct solutions, but subjects at this stage do not even meet the criterion required for mastery of the first of the four levels of difficulty just defined. At stage 2, the very first considerations of a projective or Euclidian order (egocentric orientation relations, extension of neighborhoods, primitive intuitions of distance, etc.) are added to the topological concepts and guarantee the partial or total solution of the problems in the first part. As primitive as they are, these first coordinations are slow to develop. They are barely evident in the first substage (substage 2A) where only the positions most clearly defined by salient topological relations (positions A to G) are located, and appear more strongly (substage 2B) in locating the more difficult and more ambiguous positions (H to L). When the model landscape is rotated (second part of the test), however, the egocentrism inherent in the child's first projective or Euclidian concepts causes him systematically to miss all the problems in the second part, with the exception of some isolated and purely chance solutions. Finally, stage 3 marks the progressive appearance of operational projective and Euclidian representations. In substage 3A the subject solves only problems A to G, whose solution, because of some very obvious neighborhood and enclosure cues, does not necessarily presuppose the double left-right and before-behind reversals entailed by rotating the model, but may be limited to the simple reversal of one or the other of these two dimensions. It is only at substage 3B that the subject achieves the decentration and logical coordination of projective and Euclidian relations, which are necessary for the exact location of the positions least clearly identifiable by topological indices (H to L).

DISTRIBUTION OF SUBJECTS ON THE DEVELOPMENTAL SCALE

Table 35 distributes the subjects on the developmental scale just defined. The median age for each stage increases regularly and consistently from stage 0 to stage 3B. There is no exception to this progression, and the distances from one stage to another are marked

Localization of Topographical Positions

Table 35

Distribution of subjects by age and by stage in the *Localization of topographical positions* test

Age	N	Unclassified	Stage										
			Frequencies						Cumulated percentages				
			0	1	2A	2B	3A	3B	1	2A	2B	3A	3⟩
12:0	50	1				3	11	35			100	94	7⟩
11:0	50				1	1	16	32			98	96	6⟨
10:0	50	1				4	17	28			100	92	5⟨
9:0	50	1				11	16	21			100	76	4⟨
8:0	50	7			1	12	17	13		100	98	70	3⟨
7:0	50	3		1	6	16	13	11		98	85	51	2⟨
6:0	50	11		1	13	13	6	6		98	64	31	1⟨
5:0	50	1		5	21	19	2	2		90	47	8	44
4:6	50	4		10	24	10	1	1		78	26	4	⟨
4:0	50	2		17	22	7	2		100	65	19	4	
3:6	50	2	3	23	18	3	1		94	46	8	2	
3:0	50	1	5	31	14				90	29			
Total	700	34	8	88	120	99	102	149					
Median age*			3:2	3:7	4:5	6:4	8:11	10:2					
Age of accession									−	3:7	5:4	7:2	9:

*See footnote to Table 16.

enough (by the Kolmogorov-Smirnov test, all differences are significant at the .01 level) for us to accept the general transitivity of the scale and go on with the cumulative percentages which determine the age of accession to each stage. We note that stage 1 is already passed by three years. Stage 2A is reached at 3:7 years, stage 2B at 5:4 years, stage 3A at 7:2 years, and stage 3B is not reached before 9:8 years. Differences between boys and girls are not significant at any point (Kolmogorov-Smirnov test, .01 level).

The same table indicates that 34 protocols are not classified on this scale because they do not satisfy the criteria adopted in establishing the stages. Some of these subjects solve the problems of the second level (positions H to L in the first part) after having missed those of the first level (positions A to G of the same part); others solve problems of the first and third levels (positions A to G in both parts) without solving those of the second; etc. But the fact that the proportion of consistent protocols is 94.3 per cent (566 out of 600) or 90.3 per cent (323 out of 357), depending on whether or not we include subjects who solve or miss all four groups of problems, shows that the classification as a whole is highly transitive. However, we should point out two facts arising from the analysis of these 34 protocols.

We observe first that these cases are not randomly distributed in the age sequence but are concentrated particularly at 6:0 and 8:0 years, where they represent 22 per cent and 14 per cent of the subjects respectively. We also note that this group of protocols includes two specific types. The first, seen in 14 of the 34 nonclassified subjects, is especially frequent at the age of 6:0 years (seven subjects out of 11) and consists of solving the problems at the first and third levels of difficulty (positions A to G in each part) and missing those at the second and fourth (positions H to L in each part). The second type is no less frequent than the first (15 subjects out of 34) and is seen especially at the age of 8:0 years (six subjects out of seven). It consists of solving the problems in three of the four levels of difficulty and missing those of the second (six subjects) or the third (nine subjects). It is not easy to give these facts a better than purely conjectural or *ad hoc* explanation. The first of these two types of aberrant protocols may be explained by the fact that certain subjects, already capable of the first projective coordinations that appear toward the age of six years, are still too dependent on the elementary neighborhood or enclosure cues to be able to locate, even in the first part, the positions less clearly defined by these cues. As for the second type, it is possible to suppose that after having used very simple procedures (immediate vicinity or egocentric projective relations) which were adequate at first but soon became inadequate (whence failures at level 2 or 3), the subject is then led to use more effective procedures which he may already be capable of at the age of 8:0 years.

Whatever the value of these explanations of the unclassified protocols, the great majority of subjects could immediately be classified on the proposed developmental scale. We might have expected much more consistency, especially since some very primitive strategies—such as copying the examiner's movement or trying to assure symmetry—may favor a number of apparent successes (or pseudo successes) in the second part of the test. If the influence of this factor were shown to be essential, it would have been preferable to abandon this classification scheme in favor of a method based more directly on the structure and quality of the strategies used by the subjects. But in fact the solutions inspired by a concern with symmetry and with imitating the examiner's gesture did not have a prejudicial effect on the scale's consistency. As the detailed analysis of the stages will show in a moment, this is not to say that these primitive strategies occur only accidentally or sporadically in the protocols, or that it was not necessary to accord them as much importance as the strategies based on topological cues. Rather, of all the strategies available to the child, gesture imitation and the search for symmetry are the only ones which could produce failure with the easy problems and success with the more difficult ones. The inconsistency which may ensue from this is, however, greatly reduced by the stringency of the criteria defining success in each of the four groups of problems (four solutions out of five and five out of seven). It is further reduced by the infrequency of subjects who exclusively and systematically use these two strategies, given that (1) the positions located in the center of the board, or defined by obvious neighborhoods, lend themselves to this sort of solution much less than the others, and (2) intuitive or preoperational thought, by its very nature, is concerned only with partial and always different aspects of a single situation and consequently relies on varying strategies depending on the problems and on chance fluctuations in attention.

All things considered, although it is based simply on the number and type of problems solved by the subjects, the proposed classification seems to satisfy the minimum requirements of a developmental scale. Detailed description of these stages will show that the protocols assigned to each stage are highly homogeneous in terms of the strategies which the subjects used.

DETAILED DESCRIPTION OF THE STAGES

Description of the stages is the last step in the analysis. It is this description which may best demonstrate the quality of strategies typical of each stage and the progressive structuring of the child's spatial operations.

STAGE 0: REFUSAL, OR INCOMPREHENSION OF THE INSTRUCTIONS

The infrequency of subjects classified at stage 0 (only eight) is easily explained. First of all, the youngest children taking this test are at least three years old, while the two preceding tests were administered to two-year-olds as well. Furthermore, the task required of the subject is extremely easy to understand, especially the first part. Verbal instructions are reduced to a minimum *("put your man in the same place as mine in your landscape"),* and the very concrete examples at the beginning allow the child to assimilate this task to the numerous imitative activities with which he is already familiar. Finally, the test in its present form does not require the child to justify his behavior, and it thus becomes accessible to even the youngest children, who naturally have more difficulty with verbal expression or are more reluctant to use it.

This is probably why not a single subject at stage 0 flatly refused to take at least part of the test. Most of the solutions, however, are incorrect, and even if we can sometimes recognize procedures typical of the following stage (e.g., search for symmetry, gesture imitation, etc.), subjects at stage 0 do not understand the task well enough to apply themselves to it systematically and consistently. After several conscientious but rather fruitless attempts, some of them obstinately refuse to do such a monotonous exercise and, despite all the subterfuges the examiner employs to maintain interest, they often do not even complete the first part of the test. Following is an example.

43 (3:0): *First section.* For *position A* (near the red house) the subject selects the wrong side of the board—the upper right corner rather than the lower left—which amounts to copying exactly the examiner's movement (long motion crossing the whole board). For *position B* (near the yellow house), he places his man *on* the roof of the yellow house and consequently ignores the most elementary of the enclosure relations. A response of this sort is not explainable even by a concern with satisfying other relations which are irreconcilable with this one and may be considered as a first manifestation of refusal to follow instructions. By the third problem, the subject flatly refuses to go on with the test.

Other subjects are more patient and resign themselves, with no great enthusiasm, to going on with the test a little longer. Most of the solutions offered, however, unequivocally show that this apparent docility and good nature hardly make up for lack of ability or incomprehension. The refusal to follow instructions thus reveals itself in several ways: frequent neglect of the most obvious indices of neighborhood and even of enclosure, choices overtly motivated by considerations which are totally foreign to the task (e.g., *"it's prettier here," "it's fun to put it here,"* etc.), attitudes of perseveration leading the subject to choose a single position several times in a row (e.g., beside the red house, on the roof of a house, etc.), treating the experiment as a game in which the subject may play with the material or decide on a location only after having run his man along numerous paths, etc. The following example is a good illustration of this sort of behavior.

41 (3:6): *First section.* In *problem A,* the subject places his man beside the yellow house and across from the railroad tracks (search for symmetry). *Problem B* is solved, but the subject again places his man in position B for *problem L* following. For *position C* (between the road and the group of three houses), he places his man against the shorter outside edge of the red house (short motion like the examiner's). After having placed his man near the three small houses in response to *problem F,* he leaves him in the same place for *problem H* following, despite the examiner's comments on the change in the model's position. For *position E* (end of the railroad tracks), he halts the man near the middle of the tracks, but only after having run him along a long trip over the landscape. *Problem D* entails a response of pure symmetry: the subject places his man near the tracks and opposite the first man. Barely moving him in the following *problem J,* he places him on the tracks and then solves *problem K* correctly, against all expectations. But in the *next two* problems *(G and J),* the man each time is placed *on* the roof of the red house, which marks the beginning of an obstinate sort of behavior that is followed without exception until the sixth problem of the *second section:* the subject systematically places his man on the red house or just beside it, despite the examiner's constantly reminding him of the instructions; the examiner then decides to terminate the examination.

This example shows in a particularly striking manner the lack of comprehension and the stubbornness of stage 0 subjects. The following protocol is less inconsistent. It shows manifest signs of incomprehension and stubbornness, but nevertheless reveals a more genuine intellectual effort.

17 (3:0): *First section.* The subject immediately solves *problem A.* He misses *problem B,* however, placing his man near the yellow house but on the wrong side (facing the tracks), probably in imitation of the examiner's gesture which consists of passing over the yellow house. He also misses *position L,* which is more difficult to locate because of the lack of cue objects near it: contrary to all expectation, the subject puts his man in the middle of the road rather than in the neighboring field to the right, which reveals the beginning of impatience and stubbornness. However, the *next four problems (C, F, H, and E)* are immediately solved despite a certain imprecision in the case of position C, which he locates closer to the road than to the three houses, and in position H which he brings too close to the intersection of the road and the tracks. He then fails *problem D* by placing his man inside rather than outside the group of three houses (undifferentiated neighborhood or imitation

of the route traced by the examiner's movement). The greater difficulty of *position J* discourages the subject, who refuses to place his man anywhere and he maintains the same negative attitude through the *last three problems (K, G, I)* of the first section.

Second section. Rotating the model landscape attracts the child's attention and he agrees to start the test again; but he systematically misses the first nine problems, solves the tenth *(position H)* probably without even knowing it, and suddenly refuses to do the last two problems.

This subject's behavior presages that of subjects in the following stage. The protocol includes some successes and the solutions may be compared, as a whole, with those of stage 1 children: imitation of the examiner's motion, importance of elementary topological relations, search for symmetry, etc. The subject is classified at stage 0 rather than at the following stage because he still shows, despite some real effort, too many overt signs of incomprehension and stubbornness: refusal to complete even the first section, neglect of the most primitive relations of neighborhood and enclosure, etc.

STAGE 1: TOPOLOGICAL SOLUTIONS, SEARCH FOR
SYMMETRY, AND GESTURE IMITATION

Subjects at stage 1 understand the nature of the task and apply themselves to it rather willingly without resorting to the evasions typical of stage 0 (e.g., complete refusal, perseveration, playful attitudes, etc.). The examiner does not need to over-insist in order to sustain the child's interest, for the child always finishes the first part and usually even the second without prodding by the examiner. The solutions are still very primitive, however, and ignore the most elementary projective and Euclidian concepts.

The protocols are studded with isolated successes, but these successes are still very infrequent and never reach the minimum number (four out of five or five out of seven) required at each of the four levels of difficulty of the sequence of stages. Even in the first part, which is always easier, only six (7 per cent) of the 88 subjects classified in stage 1 managed to solve four out of seven of the problems of the first level (A to G) and three out of five of the problems of the second (H to L), an achievement which is still below the minimum criterion.

If errors are so numerous among subjects at this level, even with the easiest problems, this is clearly because the subjects are trying to locate the positions without taking into account the projective and Euclidian relations uniting the objects which are already placed in a single structure and uniting the man even to those elements closest to him. The relations of neighborhood are certainly considered, as are the relations of enclosure, but they are never accompanied by spatial relations which could assure the correctness of the localizations. From this fact stems the behavior of placing the second man *beside* (or *on*) the same object as the first man, but a little carelessly within this restricted sector and without the precision which only the simultaneous consideration of directions and distances could guarantee. If it happens that the subject wishes to expand or modify these localization strategies, it is then the search for symmetry or gesture imitation which is substituted for the as yet inaccessible projective or Euclidian concepts and which often lead him, unpredictably, to ignore the most elementary neighborhood and enclosure cues. The following three protocols, which for the sake of conciseness include only the portions that concern the first section of the test, clearly illustrate the procedures typical of stage 1.

13 (3:0): *First section.* In *problem A* the subject places his man near the yellow house, on the side of the railroad tracks and just opposite the first man (symmetry response). In *problem B* he begins by again choosing a symmetrical position (near the red house and toward the outside of the landscape), but immediately changes his mind and, without abandoning the red house, places his man in front of it (toward the interior of the landscape), perhaps through a concern with copying the examiner's gesture which had to pass over the yellow house. *Problem L* is solved, though it is impossible to determine the influence of symmetry (and gesture imitation) in this solution. For *position C* (located between the road and the three small houses), the subject places his man midway between the road and the yellow house and thus perfectly imitates the size and direction of the examiner's gesture (short movement toward the interior of the landscape). *Problem F* is immediately solved but *problem H* is not: the man is placed at the intersection of the road and the railroad tracks, but in the sector exactly opposite the correct one (symmetrical to the first man's position in terms of its relation to the line separating the two boards). Success again in *problem E and D;* in the latter case, however, the subject begins by placing the man between the yellow house and the edge of the landscape (perfect imitation of the examiner's gesture, in length and direction), then immediately changes his mind before this unexpected and incorrect neighborhood. In *problem J* the search for sym-

metry overrules the elementary relations of enclosure; rather than place the man in a field, the subject places him on the road and opposite the first man, so that the two men are nearly equidistant from the dividing line. The same thing occurs in *problem K,* where the man is again placed on the road and opposite the model. But gesture imitation regains the upper hand in *problem G,* where the subject places his man on the wrong end of the road. Finally, in *problem I,* the subject selects a location close to position L and thus conforms to the cues of neighborhood (near the intersection) and enclosure (in a field), but does not consider the other elements in the landscape at all.

27 (4:0): *First section.* After having immediately solved *problems A and B,* the subject misses *problem L,* placing the man first in the correct sector but near the end of the railroad tracks, then lower between the yellow house and the tracks, and finally again in the correct sector but still too far from the correct position. *Position C* first produces a purely symmetrical response (opposite the first man and toward the middle of the empty field); then, probably bothered by the absence of the anticipated neighborhoods, the subject brings the man closer to the road while leaving him in the wrong sector. *Problem F* is solved without hesitation, but *problem H* is not, for the subject places the man against the red house rather than midway between this house and the road. He also misses *problems E and D,* both for reasons of symmetry: in the former (E) he places the man just below the three small houses and, in the latter (D), near the outside of the tracks in the yellow house's sector. For *problem J,* the subject identifies the correct sector but places his man too near the road. Failure with *problem K* is again due to the concern with symmetry (the subject placing the man beside the yellow house). For *position I* the subject begins by placing his man exactly on the intersection of the road and the railroad tracks, then carries him into the empty field nearly opposite the yellow house and finally selects, in the same sector, the angle formed by the road and the railroad tracks (more or less equivalent to position L).

20 (5:0): *First section.* The first response *(problem A)* is one of pure symmetry, the subject placing his man near the yellow house and beside the tracks. *Problem B* is correctly solved. In *problem L* the subject identifies the correct sector but places the man much too far away (opposite the yellow house). In *problem C* the search for symmetry leads the subject to place his man in the large empty field just opposite the first man. He then solves *problem F;* but in *problems H and E* it is again symmetry which dictates the choice of a position located between the yellow house and the railroad tracks in the first case (H), and a position located at the wrong end of the tracks in the second (E). For *position D* the man is placed opposite the model but in the large empty field and very close to the road, a little as though the neighborhood of the road had been as-

simulated to that of the board's edge, near which the first man is standing. The following two problems are also missed for reasons of symmetry:
in *problem J* the man is placed between the road and the three small
houses (a solution exactly opposite to the one given in problem C) and,
in *problem K,* the man is placed between the road and the yellow house.
The subject then solves *problem G* but misses *problem I* by placing the
man against the yellow house and on the side of the railroad tracks.

There is no need to provide many more examples. The three
protocols reported above are quite sufficient to demonstrate the
primitive character of the various strategies which stage 1 children
must use since they are still unable to depend on projective or
Euclidian considerations. Reading these examples, however, brings
out two facts which should be discussed because they concern not
only these three particular cases but all protocols classified at the
same level.

The first of these facts concerns the causes of the errors. Contrary to what we observe in stage 0, where errors are quite inconsistent since they are due mostly to incomprehension of the task
or to refusal to follow instructions, the errors of children at the
present stage are much more homogeneous and may include certain
dominant types of solutions, which could pass undetected in a superficial examination but which a more subtle analysis should bring to
light. Truly the real significance of each response, considered individually, is difficult to determine, and reading the examples given
above may create the impression that the interpretations we have
given reflect the examiner's system of thinking more than the subject's. There is, in fact, some danger of artificially introducing rigorousness into thought whose main characteristic may be precisely a
lack of consistency and organization. However, when each response
is seen in the context of the whole protocol, we soon notice that
many isolated responses are mutually clarified and may be similarly
interpreted. The phenomenon clearly occurs in the examples cited
above, particularly concerning responses that result from a search
for symmetry. In sum, the analysis of these typical stage 1 protocols
reveals not that children ignore all spatial relations in their attempts
at localization, but that the relations which they consider are too
elementary (e.g., neighborhood, enclosure, symmetry, etc.) and too
poorly coordinated to insure accuracy. In other words, even when
it results in repeated failures, the behavior proper to this level may

serve to define a genuine level of development, however primitive it may be. This is precisely what distinguishes it from the behavior at stage 0, where randomness and rigid perseveration are the rule and where fantasy or purely subjective reasons (e.g., *"I like that one better"; "that one is so pretty";* etc.) are more influential than even the most elementary considerations of a strictly spatial nature.

The second fact to be mentioned concerns the inordinate importance which the stage 1 child accords symmetry and gesture imitation. Many errors are probably explainable by the child's inability to coordinate the multiple relations of neighborhood or enclosure and especially to complete them by estimating distances and directions; but most of the errors still seem to be due to gesture imitation, a search for symmetry, or even both procedures at once. The fact is even more surprising in that it was neither predicted nor predictable at the start. We know that Piaget always attributes the children's most primitive responses to this test (or to similar tests) to factors of neighborhood or enclosure (surrounding). Thus it is legitimate to ask first why the children he examined seem never to have resorted to procedures of symmetry or gesture imitation, and then to ask whether the frequency of this behavior in the children studied here does not refute the general conclusions concerning the exclusively topological character of the child's first spatial representations. In replying to the first question we must recall that in the experimental situation designed by Piaget the model landscape is rotated from the very beginning, and that the two boards are placed in the same direction only to make the child understand the task before the experiment itself begins. It is only in this last situation (first part of the present test) that the intervention of symmetry and gesture imitation can be apparent, since rotating the model landscape, which requires mentally reversing the projective relations, has the effect of transforming responses based exclusively on symmetry and gesture imitation into pseudo successes. As for the second question, it seems that the use of these new strategies by the youngest children does not at all contradict Piaget's basic hypothesis because they themselves may be reduced to concepts deriving either from elementary topology or from spatial coordination activities which are much closer to perceptual or sensorimotor schemata than to strictly representational schemata. The search for symmetry, in fact, may directly reflect a concern with order or neighborhood. Just as the child may often try to place his man beside the road, the red house, etc., he may just as well wish to place him like the first man, *beside* the line dividing the two boards, between this line and some cue object, etc., or again to place him such that this line is *between* the first man and his own. The search for symmetry may also depend simply on mechanisms of perceptual activity which are still quite primitive. If the child perceives the two landscapes as a single global configuration rather than as two distinct and juxtaposed systems which must be related to one another, it is quite natural for the laws governing the perceptual organization of good forms, among which symmetry is crucial, to determine at least partially the child's behavior and reduce the role attributable to representational activity as such. Similarly, copying the examiner's gesture is directly assimilable to ordinary imitative behavior, whose simplest forms are known to be already available to the child at the sensorimotor level. The experimental situation facilitates this imitative behavior in that the child's responses can follow the examiner's gesture without any delay. The instructions themselves invite the child to do this by making him notice the perfect identity of the two landscapes and by requiring him always to do *"the same thing"* as the examiner, to place his man *"in the same place,"* *"at the same position,"* etc., as the examiner's. Thus there is nothing surprising in the fact that the youngest children, still unable to objectify their spatial representations, are inclined to reproduce only the most overt and most subjective aspects of the examiner's action. In sum, in order to understand the mechanisms underlying the search for symmetry and the imitation of movement, it may be necessary to go beyond the limits of an interpretation based solely on topology: but nothing requires the intervention of higher spatial relations which derive from projective or Euclidian geometry. It is sufficient to recall that these very primitive strategies rely directly on the perceptual or sensorimotor schemata which have already been structured by the child who has achieved his first spatial representations and may, when the situation is ripe, make up for the inadequacies and imperfections of intuitive or preoperational thought. When they are limited to the rudimentary forms observed in children at the present stage, the search for symmetry and gesture imitation are no more highly evolved than the most elementary topological concepts. Even assuming that they go beyond the level of purely perceptual or sensorimotor activity, they are still basically intuitive, in source as well as in function; and, as we have already tried to point out (Chapter IX), both of them reflect the egocentrism of preoperational thought.

STAGE 2: PROGRESSIVE, BUT STILL EGOCENTRIC, USE OF PROJECTIVE RELATIONS (LEFT-RIGHT AND BEFORE-BEHIND)

Stage 2 is characterized by gradual success with the first part of the test, since the child is now able to establish spatial orientation relations with respect to his own body. These new egocentric relations of laterality and depth are gradually substituted for the search for symmetry and gesture imitation. They are grafted onto the topological relations of neighborhood and enclosure and may thus lead to the exact localization of the easiest positions (first section of the test). Use of these new relations, as imperfect and rigid as it still is, nevertheless represents considerable progress over the behavior of the preceding level. The child establishes a fixed reference point outside the landscape, and this first victory marks the beginning of an intellectual construction which will progressively become more objective, but which will not be fully realized until real projective and Euclidian operations appear. The efficacy of these first egocentric concepts is, however, still quite limited. It is seen only in the special situation where both landscapes are oriented in the same direction; as soon as one of them is rotated (second section of the test), the egocentric character of these first orientation relations is openly revealed by the fact that the child continues to place his man in positions corresponding to his own perspective, as though the first board had not been turned at all. If the child does notice the unexpected neighborhoods which his egocentric attitude produces, he can only turn to more primitive behavior, dictated by the purely topological considerations of neighborhood (and surrounding). In sum, subjects classified at stage 2 completely fail the second section of the test but succeed with at least part of the first. They are distributed into two substages, depending on whether the successes in the first part are limited to problems A to G (substage 2A) or extend to problems H to L (substage 2B).

A. *Substage 2A*

At substage 2A, only the problems at the first level of difficulty (positions A to G in the first section) are solved in a large enough number to satisfy the established criterion. All subjects classified at this substage solve at least five of the seven problems at this level, but none of them manage to solve more than three of the problems of the second level (positions H to L in the first section), more than four of the seven in the third level (positions A to G in the second section), or more than three of the five problems in the fourth level (positions H to L in the second section).

Thus it is obvious that the spatial representations of the substage 2A child are still quite fragile. Although the projective left-right and before-behind relations begin to operate somewhat systematically at this level, they are none the less exclusively egocentric, as seen in the generalized failure with the problems in the second section where the subject takes no account of the rotation of the model landscape and remains a captive of his own perspective. What distinguishes the present substage from the following one is particularly the fact that, even in the first part, these egocentric orientation relations are still only slightly structured and but poorly coordinated. The child may, without too much difficulty, succeed in locating positions A to G because the relations of neighborhood or enclosure are so obvious in these positions that he is not required simultaneously to consider (that is, to coordinate or to multiply) the left-right and before-behind dimensions in order to locate them. Once he has recognized, for example, that position A is located beside the red house, the child has only to deal with the before-behind dimension. Similarly, for position E, when he notes that the man is placed at the end of the railroad tracks, he need only choose between left and right. On the other hand, when the relations of neighborhood and enclosure are more equivocal, as with positions H, I, K, and L, which are identically definable in topological terms (e.g., in a field and beside the intersection), the child is unable to make his localizations with any certainty because he is still unable to take into account the left-right and before-behind dimensions simultaneously. When possible, he will sometimes use a more distant reference object to identify at least the correct sector (e.g., position H is to be located in the sector with the red house); but he most often reverts to more primitive solution procedures based only on topological cues, symmetry, or gesture imitation. The following two protocols, given in detail, are among the most typical of this substage.[1]

39 (3:0): *First section. Problems A to G* are solved, with the exception of *problem F* where the subject places his man on the wrong side of the road, probably in order to copy the examiner's movement. In *problem H,* he places the man between the road and the group of three houses, which partially respects the neighborhoods and reproduces the examiner's gesture. In *problem I,* the subject places the man between the house and the intersection (symmetry response). *Problem J* is solved but not *problem K,* where the subject, by placing his man near the road in the largest open sector, performs a pseudo reversal which is again attributable to imitative behavior. Finally, in *problem L,* the subject selects a position (in the red house's sector) which is exactly symmetrical to the first man's position.

Second section. In *problem A* the subject places the man near the red house but away from the center of the landscape (same egocentric before-behind relations as on the model landscape). In *problem B,* the position chosen (near the short side of the red house toward the center of the board) conforms to the left-right egocentric relations and to the length of the examiner's gesture. In *problem C* the subject is careful to conserve the neighborhood of the three small houses, but he places his man on the wrong side (facing the red house). *Problem D* has a purely symmetrical response, the subject placing his man very close to the large side of the red house toward the interior of the landscape. In *problems E, F, and G* the responses are all egocentric, the man being placed each time on the wrong end of the road or of the railroad tracks. The same thing happens in *problem H,* where the subject takes no account of the reversal and places the man in the larger of the two open fields at the same height as the first man. In *problem I* the man is placed on the tracks, opposite the red house, for no apparent reason. Egocentrism is evident in *problem J,* where the subject puts his man in the small open field in precisely the place which would be correct were the board not rotated. *Problem K* is solved. In *problem L,* finally, the subject places the little man in K with no concern for the rotation.

6 (4:0): *First section.* Of the seven *problems A to G, problem D* alone is incorrect: rather than placing the man beside the three small houses, the subject places him in front of the yellow house and not far from the line dividing the two boards (symmetry and gesture imitation). In *problem H,* the subject first chooses a position located in the small open

[1] From now on, description of the protocols will follow the alphabetical order of the problems—which is closer to their order of difficulty—rather than their order of presentation during the test.

sector, next to the middle of the road segment bordering this sector, then changes his mind and places the man near the yellow house in the position already described in problem D. In *problem I,* the man is placed near the intersection of the road and the tracks but in an incorrect sector (small open field). *Problem J* is solved, but not *problem K,* where the subject first gives a symmetry response (between the yellow house and the road), then places the man on the railroad tracks beside the red house. *Problem L* is solved.

Second section. Problem A is solved. In *problem B* the subject respects the proximity of the yellow house but ignores the before-behind reversal: he places his man beside the yellow house, but facing the tracks. He also fails at *problem C:* the subject conserves the proximity of the three small houses but incorrectly places his man on the side facing the red house. He solves *problem D* but misses *problem E, F, and G* by choosing the wrong end of the road or the tracks each time as though the first board had not been rotated. In *problem H* the man is first placed in the small open field and then brought next to the smaller side of the red house inside the landscape, a little as though the subject had successively noticed the different topological relations of neighborhood and enclosure (e.g., in a field, near the intersection, beside the red house) without managing to reconcile all of them. In *problem H* the subject places his man to the right of the yellow house in the lower corner of the board and thus conserves, between the man and the yellow house, the same egocentric relation in the two landscapes. His egocentrism is even more obvious in *problem J,* where the subject decides to place the man in the small open sector. Symmetry, on the other hand, dictates the response to *problem K,* the subject placing his man between the road and the group of three houses opposite the first man. Finally, in *problem L,* the subject totally ignores the rotation of the board and places the man in K (the perfect egocentric counterpart to position L).

This sort of protocol is typical, and it would be superfluous to cite others. They are remarkably homogeneous, more in the quality than in the number of errors made. Especially in the second part, the responses of substage 2A children to *problems A, B, E, F, and G* are nearly all of the same type. In fact, 81 per cent of the errors observed with *problems A and B* consist of placing the man very near the cue house but on the side opposite the correct position, with no concern for the before-behind reversal; similarly, 89 per cent of the errors in *problems E, F, and G* consist of placing the man on the wrong end of the road or the tracks without taking account of the left-right or before-behind reversals. The systematic nature of these errors shows without any doubt that the child at this level, in trying to locate the positions, is interested in projective relations but that he is interested in them only in relation to his own body, disregarding the changes produced by rotating the first board. These early projective concepts thus do not have the objectivity and relativity required in real projective operations of which they are both the foundation and the outline. They are adequate for solving the problems at the first level of difficulty (problems A to G of the first part), where the simplicity of the neighborhoods and surroundings spares the subject from having to consider more than one projective dimension at once and greatly reduces the difficulty of estimating distances. The weakness of these first spatial orientation concepts, however, is reflected in the failure with the problems of the second group where, for lack of an equally effective topological basis, simultaneous consideration of the two projective dimensions is necessary in locating the positions. It is then that the more primitive behavior of the preceding stage reappears, as with the children in the examples: exclusive attention to topological relations, gesture imitation, concern with symmetry, and randomness.

However, it sometimes happens that the errors at this level are less rudimentary than this. This is the case with certain children who continually identify the correct sector but place their man at any position within this sector and quite far from the correct position. The following is an example.

37 (4:0): *First section.* Success with *problems A to G.* Failure with *problem H,* where the subject places the man in the correct sector but much closer to the road than to the red house. In *problem I* the subject begins by placing his man at the correct position, then changes his mind and puts him first in the corner of the landscape near the yellow house, and finally puts him across from the railroad tracks without abandoning the proximity of the yellow house. *Problems J and K* are solved. *Problem L* is as well, although the man is then placed a little bit too far from the intersection.

Second section. Problem A is solved but not *problem B,* where the subject places the man on the wrong side of the yellow house. Success with *problem C.* In *problem D* the man is placed against one of the three small houses, probably simply through consideration of proximity. The subject succeeds with *problem E,* then misses *problems F and G* by selecting the wrong end of the road both times. Success with *problem H.* In *problem I,* the man is placed first in the larger open sector near the intersection, then brought to different positions around the yellow house and finally located very close to position B. *Problems J, K, and L* are all missed, the subject choosing positions which exactly correspond to the egocentric perspective of the first board.

We might ask why this sort of protocol is classified at the same level as others of substage 2A in which the errors in the first part seem to derive from much more primitive strategies. The fact that these children are able to locate at least the correct sector seems to show that unlike the others, they know how to coordinate the two left-right and before-behind projective dimensions and that their lack of precision is due only to the imperfection of their Euclidian or metric concepts (e.g., correct estimation of distances, conservation of angles, coordination of opposites, etc.). But this is not necessarily the case. In problems where the correct sector is identifiable by obvious cue objects, the child may rely on these cues without concern for any other spatial relation, and it is then this exclusive concern with partial aspects of the situation which explains the inaccuracy of the response. On the other hand, when these cues are ambiguous or even nonexistent, the response of the child who chooses the correct sector without finding the exact position lends itself to two interpretations. The first assumes that selecting the correct sector derives from an attempt at coordinating the egocentric orientation relations, but that the ambiguity of these cues of proximity or surrounding keeps the subject from giving this effort the precision necessary for an exact localization. The second interpretation simply attributes the child's selecting the correct sector to the effects of chance (one out of four, or even one out of two when dealing with the empty sectors alone), with the chances of finding the correct position within this sector then being much slimmer. It is appropriate to note that of the 120 subjects classified at substage 2A, only 11 (9.2 per cent) show errors which are uniquely of this sort (choosing the correct sector but an incorrect position within it); in all other cases, the mistake is more than once, if not always, in the sector itself. It is logical to assume, when a given subject chooses an incorrect sector several times, that his isolated successes are purely chance occurrences. Be that as it may, given the infrequency of subjects who make this type of error and the difficulty posed by the interpretation of this behavior, it is better not to create a distinct category within the substage.

B. *Substage 2B*

Substage 2B is hardly different from the preceding one except as concerns the problems at the second level of difficulty (positions H to L in the first section), which from this point onward are correctly solved (at least four out of five). In sum, children classified at this level are able to overcome nearly all the difficulties posed by the problems in the first section and thus show their ability to deal with the left-right and before-behind orientation relations, at least on the egocentric level. The egocentric character of these first projective notions is also evident in the errors made in the second section. As in the preceding substage—but perhaps even more systematically— we find in this substage the same indifference to the rotation of the first board and the same coordination behavior based solely on the subject's own perspective. Two examples will suffice to illustrate the solutions typical of this level. The protocols belong to children of 5:0 and 6:0 years of age, but even those of children from 10:0 to 12:0 years classified at this substage do not differ significantly from them in the quality or frequency of successes and failures.

38 (5:0): *First section.* The subject solves all the *problems A to G,* with the exception of *problem E* where he places the man on the wrong side of the railroad tracks (symmetry response). He also solves *problems H to K,* but misses *problem L* by placing his man near the intersection of the road and the railroad tracks, but in the sector containing the red house.

Second section. Success with *problems A and B.* In *problem C* the subject places his man between the group of three houses and the border of the landscape, thus ignoring the left-right reversal necessitated by the rotation of the first board. In *problem D* he probably notes only the proximity of the three houses and places his man between the two houses inside the landscape. Egocentric perspective is obvious in *problems E, F, and G,* where the subject chooses the wrong end of the road or the tracks each time. Finally, in *problems H to L,* which are all missed, the position he chooses always corresponds exactly to the egocentric perspective suggested by the first board: the subject places his man in L in *problem H,* in H in *problem I,* in K in *problem J,* in J in *problem K,* and in H in *problem L.*

36 (6:0): *First section.* Only *problems C and K* are missed. In *problem C* the man is placed against the small house closest to the road but on the side facing the red house. In *problem K,* the subject chooses the cor-

rect sector but places his man too near the road (toward the middle of
the segment delimiting this sector).

Second section. In *problem A,* the man is placed on the wrong side
of the red house, first on this side of the tracks and then between the
house and the tracks. In *problem B,* the subject begins by choosing
position A, then moves his man near the red house but on the wrong
side, still forgetting the before-behind reversal. In *problem C,* he ignores
even the neighborhood of the three small houses in order to conserve the
egocentric perspective of the first board, placing his man between the
yellow house and the road. The same egocentrism is apparent in *problem
D,* where the subject respects the proximity of the three small houses this
time but places his man first between the two innermost houses and then
in the corner of the board adjacent to the three houses. The same egocentric attitude is seen in *problem E,* where the man is placed on the
wrong side of the tracks. *Problem F* is solved, against all expectations,
but not *problem G,* where the subject chooses the wrong end of the road.
In *problem H,* also missed, the subject seems to rely on the presence of
the red house in identifying the correct sector, but then places the man
too near the house in relation to the intersection. In *problem I* the man
is placed in H with no concern for the left-right reversal. *Problem J* is
doubly missed, if that is possible: the subject first places the man on the
road, nearly opposite the yellow house, and thus conserves the egocentric
perspective suggested by the model; finding himself in an unexpected
setting, the subject suddenly moves the man toward the left and puts
him at almost the same height in the smaller empty sector; but then, not
satisfied with this new location, which he seems to think is too far off-
center in relation to the model, he puts him back on the road in the
first position he had chosen. The response to *problem K* is still egocentric, the man being placed near the intersection but in the large
empty sector. Finally, in *problem L,* the subject places his man near the
intersection, first in the sector containing the red house and then in the
smaller empty sector, each time a victim of his egocentric attitude.

The way these children use the egocentric left-right and before-
behind orientation relations is at once disconcerting and instructive.
It is disconcerting because it sometimes leads to ignoring the topological relations of neighborhood and enclosure, which we know to
be more basic and more primitive than the orientation relations
themselves. The phenomenon is not a new one, since even by stage
1 the search for symmetry and gesture imitation could also cause
the subject to ignore neighborhoods and surroundings. What is perhaps surprising here is the fact that consideration of the elementary
topological relations, hypothetically mastered during the first stage,
may sometimes give way to the new acquisitions typical of the second

stage rather than integrating themselves into them. It is true that this phenomenon is far from being generalized and that the child usually manages to reconcile the topological and the egocentric orientation relations, as the two protocols reported above clearly show. Although the phenomenon occurs especially in certain cases where these two types of relations are shown to be incompatible (see especially the responses given problems C and J in the second section by the last subject), it is nonetheless instructive. In any case, it shows that the application of a new instrument of thought may somewhat eclipse the effectiveness of previously mastered instruments. The conflict will continue until the child's intellectual centrations, which have become more mobile while submitted to an increasingly flexible regulatory system, both allow him to recognize the absurdities to which a too-exclusive attachment to partial aspects of the situation will lead, and guide him along a new intellectual progression which in this particular case is marked by the gradual discovery of the relativity of projective dimensions. The hesitations and gropings of some substage 2B children already mark the beginning of this intellectual progress, which will be confirmed in the next stage, but which at this stage is paralyzed by persistent egocentric bondage. The following protocol illustrates these first efforts toward decentration.

25 (8:0): *First section.* All problems are solved.
Second section. In *problem A* the man is first placed between the red house and the railroad tracks (egocentric response), then moved to the correct position. Same treatment in *problem B:* the first response is egocentric (man placed on the wrong side of the yellow house) and then spontaneous correction remedies it. In *problem C* the subject first places his man between the two innermost small houses, then moves him to the larger empty sector near position J (that is, "to the right" of the road as on the model). The response to *problem D* is dictated exclusively by considerations of neighborhood: the man is placed between the two small houses facing the red house. *Problem E* is solved, but only after correcting an initial egocentric response (wrong end of the tracks). *Problem F* is not solved (wrong end of the road), and then *problem G* is immediately solved. In *problem H* the man is first placed close to the correct position, but this effort toward decentration cannot resist the egocentric suggestions which keep the subject from recognizing the value of the response: he moves the man to place him rather "to the left" of the red house, as on the first board, then to place him back on the correct side but too close to the house in relation to the

road. He also misses *problem I,* the man being placed in the large open sector nearly opposite the three small houses (search for symmetry or reversal limited to the left-right dimension). The two successive responses given *problem J* again reveal the same inability to coordinate the two necessary dimensions: the subject first places his man between the road and the yellow house (left-right reversal only or simply an attempt at symmetry), then moves him between the road and the group of three houses (before-behind reversal only). In *problem K,* the position chosen by the subject (between the road and the group of three houses) is again guided by considerations of symmetry or by an effort at decentration limited to the left-right dimension. Finally, in *problem L,* the subject places his man in the sector containing the red house, first at some centimeters and then right beside the intersection, and thus in both cases remains faithful to his own point of view.

We could not emphasize better the importance accorded the left-right and before-behind relations by children at this substage. Although the frequency and nature of the errors in the second section indicate that the child's budding projective representations are still very egocentric, there is no doubt that consideration of orientation relations systematically intervenes in the child's behavior and greatly contributes to solving the problems in the first section. We may not, however, infer that the use of these egocentric projective concepts presupposes the conscious, explicit, and deliberate representation of a whole system organized along multiple dimensions of projective space and constructed around the child himself as a center of reference. We cannot count on verbal indications (e.g., justification of responses, description of positions, etc.) which might clarify the nature of the intellectual mechanisms underlying the child's behavior;[2] therefore, it is wiser simply to point out that, at least at the behavioral level or at the level of enactive thought, the egocentric projective relations assume a primary importance in the child's localizations. We know full well that external action is not necessarily accompanied by consciousness of the intellectual processes on which it is based. We know particularly that egocentric thought, by definition, does not distinguish between the subjective viewpoint and other possible viewpoints, and that the subject at this level is not even able to see that his spatial representations are centered ex-

---

[2] In this respect, it will be most instructive, in a later analysis, to compare the results of the present test with those of another test, administered to the same children, covering the concepts of left and right.

clusively on his own perspective. For this reason we should expect that only the discovery of the multiplicity of possible points of view —a discovery which is reserved for a later stage—can make the child aware of the limits which have long been imposed on his action by the egocentric nature of his first spatial representations.

STAGE 3: OPERATIONAL COORDINATION OF PROJECTIVE RELATIONS

The reduction of egocentrism, already begun in some stage 2B subjects, is generalized in the third stage and is reflected in the second section of the test by an increasing ability to reverse the left-right and before-behind dimensions. This progress occurs in two principal steps. In a first step (substage 3A), the child still cannot perfectly coordinate the left-right and before-behind dimensions and thus can locate only those positions characterized by limiting neighborhoods or surroundings (problems A to G). In the second step (substage 3B), the coordination of the two projective dimensions assures the double reversal necessary for locating the positions less well defined by topological cues (positions H to L).

A. *Substage 3A*

In substage 3A, the first section of the test is no longer difficult. All children classified at this level solve at least five of the seven problems A to G and at least four of the five problems H to L. In the second section, on the other hand, the localizations become much more difficult. If the child can reach the minimum criterion of five solutions out of seven in problems A to G, it is because the evidence of the topological cues allows him to hold to a simple projective reversal. Once the cue object has been located (e.g., beside the red house, at the end of the railroad tracks, etc.), the child no longer has to pay attention to the whole landscape in order to decide whether to place the man in front of or behind the house, at the left or right end of the railroad tracks, etc. On the other hand, the minimum criterion of four solutions out of five is never reached in problems H to L where the ambiguity of the topological cues, especially in problems J, K, and L, requires the child to coordinate—that is, to consider simultaneously—several projective reversals. The tenuousness of these first coordinations is seen in the numerous errors, most of which consist of systematically ignoring at least one of the two reversals necessitated by rotating the first board.

The existence of this first level within stage 3 shows that the transformation of egocentric orientation relations into real projective operations is slow to mature and goes through a long period during which the projective left-right and before-behind relations are first considered separately before being coordinated into a single system in the next substage. Analysis of the protocols is particularly instructive in this respect. It reveals that the acquisitions proper to this stage, however limited they may be, are evident not only in an apparent dichotomy of successes and failures (problems A to G versus problems H to L); they also include a partial change in the type of failures, especially in the notable decrease in the number of localizations based entirely on the subject's egocentric perspective. In order to base this assertion on complete numerical results, we would have to give each error an individual interpretation. For lack of such a systematic analysis, it is at least possible to refer to clear examples. In problem K, specifically, the responses based entirely on egocentric concerns are rather easy to recognize. Given the absence of salient neighborhood cues, they are generally identifiable when the subject places the man in the sector which is exactly opposite the correct one. The proportion of these errors, which reached 72 per cent of all the errors with this problem in substage 2B, is exactly half that in the present stage. This reduction is compensated for by the appearance or increase of two different types of errors. The first consists of placing the man in the sector adjacent to the correct one (that is, between the road and the yellow house, or between the road and the group of three houses), and it may be explained by the fact that the child recognizes the need for the reversals without managing to execute more than one of them. The second type of error consists of identifying the correct sector but choosing an incorrect position within this sector. Thus the double reversal appears to have been made, but the inaccuracy of the localization indicates that the child is unable to carry his projective coordinations to their conclusion. Either he again becomes a victim of his egocentrism and, without abandoning the correct sector, places his man in a position which corresponds to the position occupied by the first man in relation to himself (e.g., on the child's board, it is the angle formed by the railroad tracks and the edge of the board which is the egocentric equivalent of position K of the inverted landscape). Or he may try to accomplish the localization by allowing metric or Euclidian considerations to intervene (e.g., estimation of distances, directions, angles, etc.), but without achieving this because the coordination of even the most elementary metric relations itself is hindered by projective difficulties due to the rotation of the first board.

As in any analysis by stages, examination of the whole protocol can best determine the interpretation which should be given to separate responses. The following two examples are typical of the great majority of children classified at substage 3A. They clearly emphasize the particular difficulty which these children have, in the second part of the test, in leaving their egocentric perspectives when locating the positions requires that they consider several dimensions at once.

17 (7:0): *First section.* All problems are immediately solved.

Second section. In *problem A,* the subject first gives an egocentric response (wrong side of the red house), spontaneously corrects it, and then finally reverts to his first error. The response to *problem B* (which opens the second section of the test) is clearly egocentric (wrong side of the yellow house). *Problems C, D, E, F, and G* are solved with no hesitation. In *problem H* the subject places his man in the small empty sector (correct left-right reversal in relation to the road, but incorrect before-behind reversal in relation to the railroad tracks). In *problem I,* the man is finally placed between the yellow house and the edge of the board, but to the right of the house just as is the first man with respect to the subject, after having first been incorrectly placed to the left of the yellow house and still between this house and the edge of the landscape. In *problem J,* the position selected (between the road and the group of three houses) respects the before-behind reversal but ignores the left-right. The response to *problem K* is clearly egocentric, the subject placing the man beyond the red house and somewhat to the left, as on the model landscape. Finally, in *problem L,* the subject places the man to the left of the road (opposite the first man), as on the rotated board.

27 (8:0): *First section.* All problems are solved except *problems C and D,* where the subject brings the man a little too close to the three small houses, and *problem L,* where the man is too close to the road in relation to the railroad tracks.

Second section. Problems A to G are all immediately solved. In *problem H,* the subject places the man in the large empty sector opposite the first man (before-behind reversal without the left-right reversal). *Problem I* first gets a correct response, but it is quickly abandoned by the subject, who places his man in L (left-right reversal without the before-behind reversal) then in H (no reversals), and again nearly in L (but closer to the road than to the tracks). *Problem J* is narrowly missed, the subject placing his man a little too far from the road. In *problem K,* only the left-right reversal is achieved, the man being placed between the road and the group of three houses. Finally, in *problem L,* the subject first places the man near the intersection, in the sector with the yellow house (left-right reversal without the before-behind reversal), then carries him into the small open sector (no reversals), still near the intersection, and finally returns to his first partially egocentric choice.

As we can see in these two examples, which were selected from among several quite similar ones, rotating the first board involves localization difficulties which substage 3A children are able to overcome in problems A to G, where the cue objects favor at least identifying the correct sector, but which are still insurmountable in problems H to L, where the ambiguity of the cue objects requires the child to coordinate more than one reversal. Analysis of the errors committed with these last problems is quite revealing in this respect. In Table 36 we note that the choice of an incorrect sector is at least twice as frequent as the choice of the correct sector (70 per cent

Table 36

Analysis of errors made by substage 3A subjects in problems H to L of the second section of the *Localization of topographical positions* test

Type of error	Sector chosen		Total
	Incorrect	Correct	
Egocentric	171	56	227 (83%)
Other	19	28	47 (17%)
Total	190 (70%)	84 (30%)	274 (100%)

versus 30 per cent),[3] and particularly that errors overtly attributable to difficulties of an egocentric origin are nearly five times as numerous as the others (83 per cent versus 17 per cent). In the two protocols just presented, the errors are almost always of this main type: the child ignores one of the two necessary reversals and selects an incorrect quadrant.

The other type of error (choosing an incorrect position within the correct sector) is much less frequent: it should be mentioned, however, because it demonstrates the particular forms which ego-

---

[3] The difference becomes much greater (81 per cent versus 11 per cent) when problems H and I are not considered—in these problems the identification of the correct sector is much easier than in problems J, K, and L because of the presence of the cue houses.

centric thought may assume while becoming objectified. The following two examples are chosen from among the several rare subjects all of whose errors were located in the correct sector.

17 (8:0): *First section.* Success with all problems.

Second section. In *problem A* the man is first placed on the wrong side of the red house, then brought back to the correct position. *Problem B* is missed, the subject placing his man on the wrong side of the yellow house with no concern for reversal. *Problem C* is immediately solved. In *problem D* the subject begins by placing his man in the correct position, then puts him in the middle of the three small houses, and finally brings him back to the correct position. *Problems E and F* are immediately solved, but not *problem G*, where the subject chooses the wrong end of the road. In *problem H* the man is placed right against the red house, facing the landscape, but too far from the intersection. In *problem I* too the correct sector is identified; but the man is first placed midway between the yellow house and the railroad tracks, then close to the yellow house and still opposite the tracks. *Problem J* first has a purely egocentric response (in the center of the small open sector); the subject soon changes his mind and places the man in the correct sector, but several centimeters from the middle of the track segment which borders this quadrant. In *problem K* the choice of the correct sector is immediate, but the position within this sector (the angle formed by the tracks and the edge of the board) is basically egocentric; the subject quickly grabs the man, looks for a more satisfactory position (in the same sector) and, after a brief hesitation, simply puts him back in the first position he chose. Finally, in *problem L* he places his man in three successive positions, but always near the intersection of the road and the railroad tracks: first in the small open quadrant, then in the sector containing the red house, and finally in the correct position.

37 (10:0): *First section.* All problems are solved.

Second section. Problems *A to G* are all solved. In *problem H* the man is placed in the correct quadrant but too close to the intersection. *Problem I* is solved. In *problem J* the subject identifies the correct sector, but places his man between the correct position and the railroad tracks. Similarly, in *problems K and L,* the correct sector is identified each time but the man is placed too near (in H) and too far (in L) from the intersection of the road and the tracks.

There is no doubt that these two subjects have already partially mastered the projective reversals required by the rotation of the first board, as is demonstrated by the frequency of solutions to the easiest problems (A to G) and the systematic choice of the correct sector even in the most difficult problems (H to L). It is no less obvious that these acquisitions are still quite unstable. In the first of these subjects, residual egocentrism is openly betrayed not only by a massive failure with the most difficult problems, but again by the primitive character of the responses to some easy problems (e.g., B and G), and particularly by the numerous gropings and hesitations which precede the final (correct or incorrect) choice. In the second subject, the rotation of the first board also produces an almost total failure with problems H to L, but the instability of the spatial representations, rather than manifesting itself in openly egocentric errors or hesitations as did most of the preceding subject's responses, here produces errors with flaws in distance estimation only. However, it would not be correct to imagine a systematic opposition between these two types of errors, nor especially to assume that coordination of Euclidian or metric relations is slower to develop than the coordination of projective relations. In fact, it is unusual for a protocol to include only metric errors, without any sign of projective egocentrism. The last subject cited above is an extreme example; in most cases, however, both types of error appear in a single protocol. Nor does anything suggest that metric errors persist longer than projective ones because, even at this substage, these are much more numerous than metric errors and because solution of the first section itself, while long since mastered, requires a minimum ability to estimate distances correctly. Thus it would be purely arbitrary to dissociate the projective aspects from the Euclidian or metric aspects in the operational construction of space. If we accept rather that, in line with the hypotheses made at the beginning, these aspects are both different and inseparable from each other and develop concomitantly in the child, it is logical to suppose that the difficulties met by coordinating the projective relations may hinder the coordination of metric relations. Thus both types of relations are more difficult to coordinate in the second section of the test because the rotation of the first board requires the subject to disregard his own point of view and complicates the estimation of distances, directions, angles, etc., which are necessary for accurate location of the positions. Thus also, even within the second section, positions H to L are more difficult to locate than the others because the ambiguity of the cue objects requires the subject to coordinate several projective reversals at once and accordingly compromises the efficacy of his efforts at accuracy.

In sum, although the present test deals directly with the projective aspects of spatial representations, by implication it touches the Euclidian and metric aspects as well. In most of the errors made at substage 3A this influence is seen in the choice of an incorrect sector or of an egocentric position within the correct sector. In the much more infrequent cases where the error located within the correct sector is not openly egocentric, the rest of the protocol generally indicates that these isolated responses reflect in a different form the same inability to coordinate projective concepts in any detail.

B. *Substage 3B*

Substage 3B marks the end of this long process of gradual decentration and operational construction which we have traced through the preceding stages. The child finally becomes capable of the necessary coordinations and reversals, and the minimum criteria of success (five out of seven in problems A to G and four out of five in problems H to L) are met in both sections.

This is not to say that the children classified at this level have no further difficulty in achieving their localizations. On the contrary, we have found a large number of subjects who, in problems of the second section, spontaneously begin by choosing an overtly egocentric position before going on—either immediately or by successive movements—to the reversals necessitated by the rotated board. In this respect, the behavior observed at this level is very simliar to that of the preceding substage, with the difference that the child's efforts more often succeed because they are more systematic. The gropings which he still yields to, rather than being guided by purely empirical considerations (e.g., to see *"what would happen if I put it there"*), are henceforth guided by activities of anticipation and compensation proper to operational thought. The sequence of gropings is sometimes so ordered and so constant that we may trace the route which the child travels in locating the positions. The following protocol gives some clear example of this type of behavior, which is systematic in some children, consisting of placing the man at an egocentric position and then going by successive steps to the necessary two reversals.

118 (12:0): *First section.* Complete success.
Second section. Problems *A to G* are solved with no hesitation, except in problem G where the man is first placed on the wrong end of the

road and then brought back to the correct position. *Problems H and I* are immediately solved. In *problem J,* the man is first placed in the small open quadrant (totally egocentric response), then brought to between the road and the group of three houses (first reversal) and finally to the correct position (second reversal). The same thing occurs in *problem K:* the subject first places his man in the large open sector and opposite the group of three houses (egocentric response), then places him between the yellow house and the road (first reversal), and finally puts him in the correct position in the small sector (second reversal). In *problem L* the man is placed near the intersection of the road and the railroad tracks, but in the sector containing the yellow house (correct reversal in relation to the road but incorrect in relation to the tracks).

It is obvious that the solutions which the child gives are still quite laborious. The fact that they are generally correct, despite numerous hesitations, shows that the gropings observed at the present stage mark a fundamental advance over those of the preceding stages. Undoubtedly these indecisive responses of multiple trials followed by errors or partial solutions were already scattered among the protocols classified in the most primitive stages. If the first man, for example, had been located to the left and at the base of the rotated landscape in relation to the subject, the second man could have been placed first to the left and at the base of the rotated landscape, then higher but still to the left, and then to the right but at the base, etc., without any real progress and with no functional connection between these successive movements. In the present stage, however, as we can see in the protocol just cited (see, for example, the solution given *problem J*), the child's gropings become systematic and consist of integrating or coordinating the successive partial reversals. The successive reversals are not, in fact, independent of each other. Rather than seeing them as a succession or a simple substitution of isolated reasonings, as though the child forgot the results of the first reversal when he attempted the second, we should see them instead as two distinct and complementary moments of a single deduction process which leads the child slowly but surely toward the correct solution.

It would be superfluous to give other examples of this sort. The protocols assigned to this last substage are strikingly homogeneous. Success is the rule, and when it is not immediate, it is preceded with hesitations and gropings which are distinctly more highly evolved in children of this level than in those of preceding levels, as we have just seen. As for the errors to which the subjects at this last stage sometimes fall victim, suffice it to point out that they are almost always (in 86 per cent of the cases) clearly attributable to egocentric difficulties (absence of double reversal or choice of an incorrect sector), as they were in the preceding substage.

In sum, the description of the multiple steps leading to the operational coordinations necessary for the solution of these problems once more indicates that the child's spatial representations begin by relying on elementary topological aspects (relations of neighborhood, surrounding, or enclosure, etc.) before projective or Euclidian considerations are added, however primitive they may be at the time. Thus the solutions typical of the first stage, already reached before the age of three years, take no account of the projective or Euclidian relations (coordination of the left-right or the before-behind dimensions, elementary estimation of distances, etc.); they rely solely on the topological cues furnished by elements of the first landscape (e.g., beside the red house, on the road, etc.), or again on cues related simply to symmetry or gesture imitation, which we have seen to be as primitive as the topological relations themselves. During the second stage, the child begins to recognize the projective dimensions, and comes to coordinate them more or less easily depending on whether the concomitant topological cues are clear (stage 2A: 3:7 years) or ambiguous (stage 2B: 5:4 years); but these first coordinations remain basically egocentric, as witnessed in the child's complete inability to make the reversals required in the second part of the test. It is only at the third stage that the child can finally free himself from his own point of view in order to accomplish first (substage 3A: 7:2 years) the simple reversals for solving the easiest problems, and finally (substage 3B: 9:8 years) the double reversal necessary for locating the positions which are the most difficult because they are the least well defined by topological cues.

Chapter XI

Concepts of Left and Right:
Presentation of the Test

The next three chapters deal with the *Concepts of left and right* test. The first of these three chapters will present the experiment, placing it within its theoretical context and, as in preceding sections, will be followed by two chapters covering the analysis of the results.

THEORETICAL CONTEXT

Before going on to the description of the test itself, it is important to define its scope and significance and to point out the major findings of numerous works which the question of the left-right discrimination has generated in the past.

SCOPE OF THE TEST

The concepts of left and right are integral parts of the projective representations of space. They are included in the group of relationships which constitute projective space, a space which Piaget's theory asserts is not the first to develop in the child. In this respect, suffice it to mention briefly here the considerations raised in the preceding chapters (see especially Chapter I) concerning the chronological *décalages* observed by Piaget in the evolution of the child's first topological, projective, and Euclidian representations. We should recall particularly that the first projective concepts, whose structuring would be both contemporary and solidary with that of the first Euclidian concepts, are nevertheless consecutive to the first topological concepts, and that this primacy of the topological over the projective (and Euclidian) has, according to Piaget, a logical as well as a chronological meaning. The projective adds to the topological a new element or a basic factor whose intervention has the effect of externalizing, so to speak, the spatial relations inherent in an object (simple or complex) and of changing the significance of the dimensions affecting the space occupied by this object. Thus, in effect, in projective space the different elements of a single object are no longer considered solely in terms of the multiple relations between these elements, as is the case with purely topological space; they are also considered in relation to an external observer whose infinitely variable perspective produces a network of new relations (e.g., projective transformations, multiplication of perspectives, etc.) between the observer and the object, or between the parts of the object themselves in relation to the observer. For this reason, the very dimensions of space are radically transformed when they are considered in projective rather than topological terms. The relations of interiority and exteriority (or enclosure), which form the three dimensions of topological space, are henceforth changed into relations of perspective, deriving precisely from the subordination of objects to the observer. Thus an object placed *between* two others (and thus inside a line) may be equally and successfully considered as to the left or to the right (width), below or above (height), or in front of or behind (depth) the other two, depending on the external observer's perspective. If the same object becomes external to the line formed by the other two, it is then defined by two out of the three dimensions (left-right and before-behind, left-right and above-below, or before-behind and above-below), still depending on the observer's point of view. And a novel object, outside the plane formed by the other three objects, may be defined by all three dimensions of projective space created by the observer's perspective. In sum, projective space implies an expansion or an enrichment of the closed system of topological relations, adding to it an external reference point which entails both a revision of the dimensions proper to topological space and the creation of a new system of relations between the external observer and the object.

This brief summary of the characteristics of the first projective concepts of space should be enough to define the scope of the *Concepts of left and right* test which we consider in this chapter. This test is intended to explore a very particular aspect—one of the most elementary, in fact—of projective space. The test does not deal with the more complex representations or operations covering the transformation of projections, the construction of perspectives, etc.; it deals only with the development of the most basic concepts of projective space in an effort to understand the child's construction and progressive coordination of the major dimensions of this space. We should further point out that even at this elementary level, the present test covers only a very fragmentary aspect of space since only the left-right dimension is directly treated. Thus the test is different from the other three tests (*Construction of a projective straight line, Coordination of perspectives,* and *Localization of topographical positions*) which also study certain aspects of the child's projective representations. Without presuming anything about the relative difficulty or the interdependence of these different tests, it seems immediately obvious that each concerns a particular aspect of projective operations. *Construction of a projective straight line,* for example, studies only the child's ability to accomplish the projective operations of aiming—that is, to construct the before-behind relations (depth) linking a certain number of elements together in a concrete situation which does not at all require coordinating the other two directions (width and height) of projective space. On the other hand, the *Coordination of perspectives,* which will be considered later (Chapters XIV to XVI), requires the simultaneous coordination of the two left-right and before-behind relations, by a logical multiplication which conditions the child's recognition of the arrangement exactly reproducing the perspective of an observer who is variously located around a block of miniature mountains. *Localization of topographical positions,* also studied above, requires a logical multiplication of this sort, implying the coordination of two projective dimensions, particularly in the second part where one board is rotated. The difference between these last two tests will be discussed later (Chapter XIV). Suffice it to emphasize here particularly the fact that, in the last test mentioned (*Localization of topographical positions*), the projective concepts depend directly on topological concepts and are naturally accompanied by Euclidian concepts.

The *Concepts of left and right* test is thus not without similarities to the other tests we have mentioned. Although the obvious relationship of these various tests suggests a strong developmental synchronism, it is still useful to see how each may serve to clear up some aspects of the development of projective concepts and to see especially, in a context which is as simplified as possible, how the child develops the basic concepts of left and right. Piaget (1924) offers a systematic analysis of the development of these concepts in a book published during a period when his operational theory of space had not yet been explicitly worked out and when the emphasis was mainly on the progressive disappearance of the child's egocentrism. Piaget's analysis, inspired by Binet's earlier systematic observations, has since been the object of much replication and control, to a much greater extent than the other aspects of spatial representations previously analyzed. For this reason it could be helpful to present a brief résumé of the major works covering this problem before we go on to describe the test.

EARLY WORKS

Binet and Simon's (1908) very first scale included an item, located at the age of six years, on left-right discrimination (designation of one's own right hand, and then the left ear). The first revision of the same scale (Binet, 1911) retained this item but placed it at the age of seven years, the age at which 75 per cent of the children solved it. Terman's (1916) American adaptation of the same test increased the number of items on left-right discrimination (always on the child's own body) to three or six (depending on whether the child succeeded with the first three); this test was solved by most of the six-year-old children. In addition, Terman observed that the mentally deficient, at whatever age, never really managed to make this distinction. Thus it is not easy to understand why the 1937 revision (Terman and Merrill, 1937) dropped this test despite its great diagnostic value, and we should probably assume that this omission was due to the use of other more discriminating tests.

Piaget's systematic replication of Binet's test, from 1924, covered fundamentally different interests. While Binet saw the test mainly as an excellent diagnostic instrument, Piaget was more interested in demonstrating what this test might illustrate about the child's ability to deal with the logic of relations and progressively to free himself from the basic egocentrism which keeps him from differentiating his own point of view from the point of view of others. The experimental technique designed by Piaget was directed toward this objective. It did not simply require the child to designate a few parts of his own body, but also some on the examiner standing opposite him. The investigation also dealt with the relativity of left and right in relation to two or three objects which were visible to the child or which were first exposed in front of him and then hidden after 30 seconds (e.g., *"is the pencil to the left or to the right?"* for two objects, or again *"is the pencil to the left or to the right of the key? and of the penny?"* for three objects) in order to demonstrate the child's ability to distinguish the as yet absolute character (e.g., *"is the pencil to the left or to the right?"*) from the purely relative character of concepts of left and right (e.g., *"is the pencil to the left of the key, to the right of the penny?,"* etc.). The test was administered to about 240 subjects, aged from four to twelve years, from a middle-class urban population. Considering that a task is solved at a given age when at least 75 per cent of the children at that age give it the correct response, Piaget observed that the ability to designate parts of one's own body was acquired at five years; but the purely absolute character of this differentiation—left and right still being no more than names assigned to one part or another—was obvious in that before the age of eight years the child could neither correctly point out the left and right parts of the examiner facing opposite, nor correctly recognize that an object was in the examiner's right or left hand when he was facing the subject. Finally, it is significant to note that, although the child of seven years (if not six) could correctly locate two objects placed to the right and left of him, we should not conclude that he could already completely objectify his concepts of left and right or make the distinction between the absolute terms "to the left" or "to the right" and the completely relative terms "to the left of" or "to the right of." Piaget's findings indicate that this last form of relativity, which is necessary for solving the problems where three objects are lined up in front of the child, was not achieved before eleven or twelve years (depending on whether or not the objects remained in the subject's view). We note in particular that the child was frequently led to reply that it is (in the case of the center object) "in the middle" without being able to locate it either to the right or to the left of either of the other two. In sum, the development of the concepts of left and right would occur in three successive stages following a process of decentration going from pure egocentrism to complete relativity. During a first stage, which runs from about five to eight years, the child relies solely on his own point of view in distinguishing left from right and is thus enslaved in an egocentrism of which he is entirely unaware. The second stage (from eight to eleven years) corresponds to an initial form of relativity (socialization or reciprocity of viewpoints) in which the child becomes able to put himself in another's point of view and thus to recognize the left and right of a person opposite. Finally, the last stage (around eleven or twelve years) is defined by complete objectification and reciprocity, as seen in the ability of the child who is then able to consider concepts of left and right from the point of view of the objects themselves. It is this particular aspect of Piaget's conclusions about the child's first projective representations which we must reconsider here, using the same basic technique but including some differences in details, particularly concerning the number of questions asked and the scoring criteria. Before giving the specifics of this technique, it may be instructive to recall briefly the findings of works more recent than Piaget's in this area.

In his comparative study of mental development, Werner (1948) analyzed the child's first spatial concepts and showed that construction of space is the result of a progressive differentiation of the ego from the external world, beginning with practical concepts which are centered mainly on physical action and related to one's own body. Using numerous examples (or anecdotes) as illustrations, he insisted in particular that this lack of objectification and the realistic character of the child's first spatial intuitions are not unanalogous to certain forms of primitive behavior, or even to certain adult forms of psychopathological representation of space. As concerns especially the concepts of left and right, however, Werner was happy to adopt Piaget's three classic stages, showing that these three stages derive from a more primitive type of practical space, whose characteristics are similar to sensorimotor space as described by Piaget (1936, 1937).

We might also mention here the work done in the U.S.S.R., as summarized by Shemyakin (1959), on some aspects of left-right discrimination. Even though the fact that it is only a summary (and a translated summary at that) requires the usual reservations, it is interesting to point out certain aspects of these works which are more directly related to the concepts of left and right. The experiments of Shemyakin himself and others whom he mentions suggest that the child's ability to differentiate the basic directions of his own body (left-right, up-down, before-behind) becomes sharper in the first year of life, but that this differentiation has only a practical and visuotactile character until the advent of language. He insists especially on the role of vertical posture and walking in structuring the basic spatial concepts. Here he cites the elegant work of Voronova on the differentiation of spatial directions by children (number and age unspecified by the author) who had been forced to stay in bed for long periods of time due to poliomyelitis or early paralysis (preschool children, age unspecified) and who still had chronic disturbances of their motor apparatus. Everything seemed to indicate that (a) conditioning of the vascular reflex in these children was more difficult to establish in the case of the up-down differentiation than with the left-right (probably, as the author points out, as a result of the persistence of left-right cues, even in a horizontal position); (b) the intermediate or combined differentiations (e.g., upperleft) were more difficult than the simple ones; (c) conditioning in the direction labeled "to the right" was the easiest to establish, while conditioning in the direction labeled "down" was the most difficult; and, finally, (d) these results were the same when conditioned verbal stimuli (e.g., "up," "down," etc.) were substituted for conditioned direct stimuli (e.g., four lights arranged in the shape of a cross). Furthermore, Shemyakin reports some of Kolodnaya's longitudinal studies, done over a period of two years in two children who were 2:1 and 4:11 years old respectively at the beginning of the experiments (and in five control subjects aged from two to seven years). It seems that the differentiation of the left and right hands, even though it appeared near the end of the first year, continued to develop during a good part of the preschool period. The consistent preference for the right hand for some activities was spontaneously established around three or four years of age, but any connection between the word and the corresponding hand was still lacking. Analysis of the reactions of one of these subjects was quite revealing in this respect. When he was asked to identify his right hand and his left hand, this child always moved his right hand slightly before responding, and did not like to have to respond quickly because he "had to think" each time about which hand he used for drawing. In general, he was quicker to recognize his right hand than his left. If, however, he managed to differentiate up and down, such as the top and bottom of an object, he nevertheless failed to name the left and right sides of an object placed in front of him as well as to point out the left and right of a person opposite him without first having learned that "the right" was the hand which that person used in greeting him. Finally, even at the age of seven years, as everyone knows and as Kladnitskaya's observations confirmed (again reported by Shemyakin), verbal differentiations of the left and right hands and the corresponding spatial directions were shown to be quite difficult: some normal children still made mistakes when they were asked, during physical education exercises, to raise the right (or left) hand; about 30 per cent turned the wrong way when they were asked to turn to the left (or to the right); etc. Kladnitskaya observed, however, that children managed to associate the hand and the direction more easily in the case of the right side than of the left and that all normal children at this age unerringly made the before-behind and up-down discriminations.

In another perspective, the development of concepts of left and right has generated some normative studies which need be only briefly mentioned here. Benton and his collaborators (see Benton, 1959) systematically approached this problem by giving 158 children from six to nine years of age (about 20 boys and 20 girls at each of four age levels) a rather long test containing five categories of problems: (a) pointing out parts of the subject's own body with his eyes open; (b) executing simple commands requiring the designation of contralateral members (e.g., *"touch your left foot with your right hand"*) while the subject has his eyes open; (c) same situation as in (a) but with the subject's eyes closed; (d) same as in (b) but with the eyes closed; (e) designating parts of the body of a person (front view on a graphic sketch). Benton's rather crude analysis compared only the mean number of items solved or the percentage of correct responses observed at each age level, first in categories (a) and (b) combined, then in categories (c) and (d) combined, and finally in category (e). Following a line of reasoning which seems to be justified, as we will see later, Benton judged responses which systematically reversed left and right as correct. The results naturally revealed an increase with age in the means and percentages of each of the three sections. Benton noted, however, that the difference between the last two sections was not significant, so that removing the visual clues had no critical effect. The third section, on the other hand, which required the subject to reverse his own point of view, was clearly more difficult than the others, and successes seemed to be largely by chance, especially in the first of the four age levels (on four items the mean was 2.08 at six years, 2.24 at seven years, 2.76 at eight years, and 3.23 at nine years). Benton has not failed to point out the agreement of these findings with Piaget's findings, as to the difficulty of section 3 in particular; but he did not adopt the Piagetian interpretation in terms of egocentrism. Following a line of reasoning which seems to lie somewhere between subtlety and a vicious circle, he noted that the particular difficulty with such a reversal, rather than deriving from the egocentric attitudes which Piaget refers to, could have been due to the fact that the task pre-supposed the intervention of certain intellectual characteristics such as abstract reasoning, visual imagery, and symbolic formulation. Be that as it may, a method of analysis of this sort cannot be conclusive as long as it is based only on mean scores and percentages of correct responses, whose real significance is greatly obscured by the effect of chance responses.

In this respect, Galifret-Granjon's less ambitious experiment (1960) is less ambiguous. The author used two tests. The first consisted of three problems borrowed from Piaget's (1924) test: (a) left-right recognition on oneself; (b) left-right recognition on an opposite; (c) recognition of the relative position of three objects lined up in front of the child, who must respond with his arms crossed. The test was administered to children at seven age levels (from six to fourteen years), the last two levels including two ages each and the number of subjects being about 40 in each level (slightly more boys than girls), except at six years where there are 22, and at the last two levels where there are 66 and 63 respectively. Considering only the analysis by test (no errors permitted), the results indicated that the first one was immediately solved by 86 per cent of the six-year-olds, the second had a 48 per cent success with children of seven years (80 per cent at eight years), and the third had 49 per cent success with ten-year-old children (62 per cent at eleven to twelve years and 66 per cent at thirteen to fourteen years). The left-handed children, especially at the lowest age levels, seemed slightly disadvantaged in relation to the right-handed subjects. The author's report states, although no detailed figures on this are provided, that there was no difference between boys and girls. The second test which Galifret-Granjon used was a reduced form of the classic test developed by Head (1926) to study certain aspects of symbolic thought and spatial orientation, especially in patients with aphasia or other language disorders. Galifret-Granjon used only three of Head's tests: (a) imitation of movements of an observer facing the subject; (b) execution of movements on oral command alone; (c) imitation of the movements of schematic drawings. The subject population was the same as in the preceding test. Analysis by test reveals that the first one was solved by 53 per cent of the nine-year-old subjects (58 per cent at ten years and 70 per cent at thirteen to fourteen years), the second by 55 per cent of the subjects at seven years (82 per cent at eight years), and the third by 55 per cent of the subjects at ten years (68 per cent at thirteen to fourteen years). Right-handed subjects seemed slightly better in the second test only. In regard to the differences between boys and girls, the author reports the respective median percentages at each age level but fails to say anything about the significance of the differences (although the results seem to suggest a slight superiority of girls). In sum, even though comparisons between these tests are almost meaningless because of considerable differences in technique and number of items, the two tests are complementary to one another and it is still possible to integrate them into a single instrument of psychological diagnosis.

The same normative interests led Elkind (1961d) to replicate Piaget's experiment on a larger scale, introducing some differences particularly in the nature of the problems. His test included six categories of items: (a) designating parts of the subject's own body; (b) designating those of the examiner, seen from the front; (c) identifying the relative positions of two objects placed on the table, with the subject facing the examiner; (d) same situation as in (c) but with the subject sitting beside the examiner; (e) identifying the relative positions of three objects lined up on the table with the subject facing the examiner; and (f) same situation as in (e) but with the subject sitting beside the examiner. As we can see, only categories (d) and (f) are new to Piaget's tests, and we should recall that Piaget had already suggested the possibility of such variations. The test was administered to 210 subjects (sex not specified by the author), 30 per age level from five to eleven years inclusive, randomly selected from a population which was ethnically quite homogeneous though coming from a very heterogeneous large urban center. Using Piaget's criterion (passing age for a category of items set at the age where at

least 75 per cent of the subjects can solve every item in the category)
—a criterion which may be applied here in spite of its theoretical
ambiguity—Elkind obtained results which are quite comparable to
Piaget's. The age differences between the two series of results for
each of the four comparable categories was never more than one
year. Elkind also found, as has Piaget, a tendency for the younger
children to attach an absolute meaning to the concepts of left and
right, particularly in categories (e) and (f) where the child will
transform more relative terms such as "to the left of" or "to the
right of" used in the questions into "to the left" or "to the right."
The same tendency was strikingly revealed, for example, in the behavior of the child who incorrectly gave category (d) the same responses which had already been given (correctly) to category (c), explaining that *"it's easy, I remember where they were just then"* (i.e.,
before he himself changed sides). Elkind again points out that a
number of children (only after nine years) responded incorrectly to
the items in categories (c) and (e) because, as they themselves asserted
during the test, they spontaneously adopted the examiner's point of
view, a procedure which beautifully reveals the older child's ability
to understand the relativity of viewpoints. Elkind's discussion of
Piaget's interpretation, however, seems to raise more problems than
it solves. Piaget's interpretation is based on the progressive socialization of child thought, and Elkind reproaches it for its lack of formal
rigor and especially for its purely descriptive nature. The criticism
is less valid if we are careful, as is Piaget in concluding his very
early work, to place the egocentric manifestations of the concepts of
left and right within the general context of child logic, and if we are
aware of the major role which this egocentrism plays in the progressive structuring of projective space. In any case, the more explicit
formulation which Elkind proposes hardly goes beyond the purely
descriptive level itself. Concerning the first stage, for example, is it
really helpful to replace Piaget's concept of pure egocentrism, which
is meant to describe the child's inability to differentiate his own
point of view from another's, with Elkind's concept of nondifferentiation, which he proposes to designate the same basic indissociation?
Moreover, the nondifferentiation which Elkind refers to would be
defined by a paradoxical mixture of underdifferentiation (the child
not distinguishing his own point of view from that of another) and
overdifferentiation (the child distinguishing the left and right on his

own body but not with objects); the most we can say about it is that it is ambiguous, particularly if we remember that the egocentrism of child thought precludes consciousness of his own point of view, which a hypothetical overdifferentiation would imply. Similarly, to characterize the second-stage child's ability to distinguish another person's point of view, Elkind suggests replacing the concept of socialization or reciprocity of viewpoint with a concept of "concrete differentiation," referring to the fact that the child's differentiation requires a "perceptual" clue or support at this level (e.g., another person or a change in position). The objectification and complete relativity that Piaget speaks of in describing the extension of concepts of left and right to relations existing between the objects themselves would then be replaced with a concept of "abstract differentiation," to emphasize the fact that this differentiation is hereafter independent of any perceptual clue related to particular contents. It does not seem that the substitution which Elkind proposes is unequivocal enough (e.g., a specific meaning must be given the terms "concrete" and "abstract," the "perceptual" clues which are presumably present in stage 2 and absent in stage 3 must be defined, etc.) to be an appreciable advance over the lack of rigor and explanatory value of Piaget's interpretation. Be that as it may, it seems that in order to judge Piaget's interpretation we should put it back into the more general context, not so much of what Elkind calls Piaget's "biological" theoretical model, as of Piaget's operational theory on the development of projective space in the child.

To conclude this brief review, we might refer to Benton's (1959) extensive study, previously cited. In this study, Benton presents a mass of other works dealing with the left-right differentiation which are less directly related to the experiment described here (e.g., relationships with digital agnosia, mental deficiency, cerebral lesions, learning difficulties, etc.). Because of the current opinions touching certain aspects of this problem, it may be useful to point out that the ability to distinguish left from right does not appear to be closely related to motor left-handedness or right-handedness. Benton and Menefee (1957), for example, tested children from 4:11 to 8:5 years (mental age of 4:11 to 10:9 years) in different aspects of lateralization (degree of left-sidedness or right-sidedness) and left-right discrimination (with a group of tests which were described above) and obtained only a weak correlation (.24) between the two functions. According to Benton, the left-right differentiation in the child could be only slightly related to the degree of lateralization and in any case would be conditioned more by mental age (r=.74 with mental age). We should even add that mental age itself is not the only factor at work, as shown in Benton's 1955 systematic study (see Benton, 1959) of a group of 100 mental defectives (intelligence quotient of 53, mental age ranging from six to nine, with a mean of 7:4), divided into three groups according to the type of mental deficiency diagnosed (brain injured, "familial," and of unknown etiology). Compared to normal children of equivalent mental age, the mental defectives' results were significantly lower at each of the four age levels (except at six years), although there was no difference as a function of type of deficiency. From all appearances, the level of intelligence as measured by I.Q. is a crucial factor in itself.

Another controversial problem concerns the relationships between reading difficulties and difficulties in spatial orientation dealing with the left-right discrimination. Benton (1959) discusses, for example, the findings of Harris's (1957) study in which slow readers were shown to be less able than normal children of the same age to make the left-right discrimination on their own bodies; but the deficiency here was only provisional since the difference observed at seven years had already disappeared by nine. Among the slow readers, however, Benton makes a clear distinction between cases of basic left-right confusion and cases of systematic reversal. His own research in this area seems to show that this second form of mistake is more common than the first, although he still finds it impossible to provide the actual proportions. Meanwhile Coleman and Deutsch's (1964) more recent study seems to support Harris's earlier conclusions. They gave tests of lateral dominance (Harris's tests, 1957) and left-right discrimination (Benton's test) to children from a lower socioeconomic level (boys and girls from 9:5 to 12:3 years, and almost all Negro), some of whom were classified as normal readers and others as retarded readers. The results indicated no significant difference between the groups in lateral dominance, in left-right discrimination of a person facing opposite, or in left-right discrimination of parts of their own bodies. On the other hand, Coleman and Deutsch's results do not support Benton's observations as to the frequency of systematic reversals, since they observed no significant difference between the good and poor readers on this point. Results obtained by Lovell, Shapton, and Warren (1964) on children younger than those studied by Coleman and Deutsch (9:8 on the average) revealed that the poor readers differed significantly from the better ones only in the left-right discrimination of their own bodies, this discrimination on a person facing opposite them probably being too difficult for children of this age range.

We might draw some conclusions from the group of works outlined in this brief (and incomplete) survey. In the first place, the projective concepts of left and right evolve progressively from an initial state of confusion, variously conceived as a form of egocentrism or undifferentiation, to a final state of decentration or differentiation. In the second place, it seems that the inherent difficulty in this development, referring only to the conceptual or representational plane, appears on at least two levels, if not three: the child begins by distinguishing his own left and right, and extends this discrimination to the left and right of an observer facing him before finally being able to distinguish the relations of left and right which could exist between objects themselves in relation to an observer. The ages at which these different levels of development are reached, in the various studies discussed above, vary according to examination techniques, scoring criteria, subject population, etc.; but in spite of this it should be instructive, when we analyze the results of the test considered here, to point out the major points of convergence on this particular aspect of the problem between the various studies. Thirdly, particularly in Werner's observations and in the studies summarized by Shemyakin, we must emphasize the influence which the clues derived from the child's physical and external action on the left-right discrimination, not only at the most primitive levels preceding the appearance of language and other symbolic functions —that is, during this period which Piaget refers to as the development of sensorimotor intelligence—but also at the more highly evolved levels of the first intuitions deriving from the beginnings of mental representation. And, finally, it seems that the mastery of concepts of left and right is rather directly related to differences in mental age and I.Q. It appears not to be affected by the child's degree of left-handedness or right-handedness, with which it is usually associated; but it is often accompanied, at least at the beginning, by difficulties in learning to read, even though Benton's distinction between the cases of basic confusion of left and right and the less primitive cases of systematic reversal of left and right (which are presumably observed in dyslexia) should probably be recognized. We shall return later to this last form of deficiency, for it may have repercussions for the scoring criteria of the tests.

Adoption of this test of the concepts of left and right in studying the development of space in the child serves two major purposes. The first consists of verifying the existence of the three stages of development as proposed by Piaget, by applying a basically similar technique (except for certain variations in details such as the number of questions and the scoring criteria) to a population which is larger and more diversified: in this we shall attempt to see to what extent the ages of accession to the different stages conform to the ages observed in Piaget's and subsequent works. The second objective is to clarify some problems which are still inadequately covered in the earlier works. First among these is the problem raised by the child's systematic reversals. Rather than considering these reversals simply as errors, we should try to integrate them into the developmental scale by determining whether this behavior constitutes a particular level of development or whether it should not be accepted as correct at all stages (as Benton interprets it) because it is foreign to the basic left-right confusion, while noting that this behavior decreases progressively with development. Furthermore, the fact that this test is part of a group of tests administered to a single population of children should throw some light on the significance of the concepts of left and right in the child's total spatial representations: dependence relationships with the dimensions covered in other tests and a possible homology of the stages revealed in the different tests; interpretation of concepts of left and right in the more general and more recent context of the operational theory of space, which Piaget had only partially worked out at the time of his first studies on the logic of the relations; eventual rapprochement (regarding the conventional or arbitrary—and unstable—character of the expressions "left" and "right") between the systematic reversals and the simple topological relations of internal opposition (left and right then being arbitrary, lacking any reference to an external observer as such) which operate in tests like *Localization of topographical positions, Construction of a projective straight line,* etc.

Finally, let us emphasize the fact that the *Concepts of left and right* test considers only the left-right dimension. Representation of the other two projective dimensions (before-behind and up-down) has not been the subject of such systematic investigations, especially if we speak of the child's ability progressively to shed egocentric attitudes which, as in the case of left-right relations, should in principle work against the socialization and objectification of the before-behind or up-down relations (e.g., the subject and the examiner are side by side but in such a way that the child faces the window, for example, and the examiner faces the door, asking him: *"Is the window in front of you or behind you? in front of me or behind me?,"* etc.). Tests such as *Coordination of perspectives* and *Localization of topographical positions,* in which the child must be able to coordinate two out of three projective dimensions, will undoubtedly allow certain comparisons. Piaget notes, for example (Piaget and Inhelder, 1948, p. 278), that the before-behind relations seem easier to handle (perspective transformations) than the left-right relations, and he explains these findings by the child's greater ease in recognizing his own point of view (and thus in being able to disregard it) in the case of the before-behind relations, since before and behind are not, as are left and right, equally accessible to the child's immediate action. But with the possible exception of Shemyakin's (1959) observations on children suffering from motor disturbances, discussed earlier, it seems that no one has systematically tried to ascertain whether the before-behind and up-down relations still require a certain amount of time to free themselves from the initial egocentric bondage, despite the important chronological *décalages* suggested by the very strong and differentiated kinesthetic and visual clues.

DESCRIPTION OF THE TEST

The *Concepts of left and right* test is divided into three sections, each designed to reach one of the three principal phases in the progressive structuring of these concepts, which Piaget recognized earlier (1924) and which have been confirmed by most of the authors dealing with the same problem. Details of the test are given in the Appendix.

In the *first* section the child must designate parts of his own body. He is seated beside the examiner to whom he must point out, in turn—and in this order—his right hand, left leg, right ear, left hand, right leg, and left ear. In the *second* section, the examiner and the child are standing facing each other and the child must then designate, in a different order and this time on the examiner, the same parts of the body as in the first section. Finally, the *third* section includes two series of questions which require the child to describe the relative position of three objects placed before him on the table. For the first series, the examiner and the child are seated side by side in front of a table on which the examiner places three objects in a horizontal row (a block on the left, a miniature plate in the middle, and a pencil on the right). The three objects are exposed to the subject's view while the examiner asks him six questions on the position of the objects in relation to each other (e.g., *"Is the pencil to the left or to the right of the plate? is the plate to the left or to the right of the block?"*). In the second series, the examiner first replaces the objects with three analogous ones (a miniature cow at the left, a little lamppost in the center, and a small boat on the right) and then asks the subject to look at them carefully so he can remember their exact positions after they are hidden by a screen. Allowing the child to look at them for 15 seconds, the examiner then inserts the screen and asks the child the same six questions on the relative position of the three objects.

As a whole, the test is quite similar to all those since Binet and Simon (1908), and especially after Piaget (1924), which clinical and developmental psychology use in exploring the degree of difficulty or the level of achievement of left-right differentiation. It differs from them, however, in certain minor respects which might be mentioned here, in view of the consequences which they could have on comparisons with results obtained on various populations. We should point out first that the test described here includes only three types of difficulty, each of which refers, as in Piaget's technique, to a crucial moment in the progressive apprehension of the relativity of left and right (pure egocentrism, socialization, objectification). We could have introduced a greater variety of questions or problems into each of these three types of difficulty. For example, we might have asked the child (as has Benton, 1959) to designate parts of his own body first with his eyes open and then with his eyes closed, when certain potential reference points would thus have disappeared. Similarly, for subjects already able correctly to identify their own body parts as well as those of an examiner facing them, we could have complicated the situation by asking them to perform some movements which would include both their own body parts and those of a person facing them (e.g., *"Point to my left hand with your right hand,"* etc.) (see, for example, Benton, 1959; Galifret-Granjon, 1960; Head, 1926). Following Head's (1926) very old technique which was recently replicated by Galifret-Granjon (1960), we might also have used certain situations of gesture imitation of static models (e.g., graphic images) or living models (e.g., the examiner himself), presented front view or sideways to the subject. Finally, in order to see to what extent the child is aware of the relativity of points of view, it would have been easy to replicate (as did Elkind, 1961d) one of Piaget's procedures requiring the child to judge the relative position of two or three objects placed on a table, but requiring him to be at two successive observation points. These various techniques all have their merits. Some, however, seem more directly concerned with the flexibility and capacity for attention which the subject demonstrates in handling the left-right concepts than in the comprehension of the essentially relative character of these capacities, which in our opinion is the more basic question. Others, on the other hand, deal instead with the learning aspect of left-right discrimination (for which they also provide the opportunity) but in a much too limited and restricted context to allow a meaningful control and especially a real explanation of this particular aspect of the problem of left-right discrimination. It seemed that we had to avoid introducing elements which might obscure the real course of normal development of this differentiation and to stick to situations which are at once the most basic, the simplest, and the most common. The only exception to this principle seems to be the part of the third section where an element of memorization intervenes, the subject having to close his eyes to resolve a difficulty he had already attempted with his eyes open. But, as we shall soon see, this variation does not appreciably change the difficulty of the task; under the guise of a modification in the experimental situation, repeating the same questions is a convenient way of partially controlling for the effect of chance in the response to questions similar to those in the first part of the same section.

A second point which distinguishes the present test from most similar tests concerns the number of questions asked in each section. In studying the child's ability to distinguish left from right, on himself or on someone else, often a very limited number of questions is considered sufficient. As Table 37 indicates, the tests used by most authors usually contain no more than four questions. If a particular experiment goes as high as six, these questions are not necessarily asked of all subjects; this is the case with Terman (1916), for example, where only the subjects who have missed one of the three principal questions are asked the supplementary questions. In every case, the number of questions seems too limited to be able to distinguish chance successes, which are very much favored in this sort

Table 37

Number of questions used by some authors in evaluating the various aspects covered in the *Concepts of left and right* test

Author	Number of questions asked			
	Own body	Another person	Three objects visible	hidden
Binet-Simon (1908)	2			
Binet (1911)	2			
Terman (1916)	3 (6)*			
Piaget (1924)	4	4	6	6
Benton (1959)	6	4		
Galifret-Granjon (1960)	2	2	6	
Elkind (1961d)	4	4	6	
Vernon (1965)		1	6	

*The same three questions may be used in a second trial.

of problem, from successes which are clearly based on an understanding of the spatial concepts involved. We could of course reduce the danger of confusion by increasing the stringency of the scoring criteria (which almost always exclude any partial errors), but the efficacy of this means is proportional to the number of questions asked. Also, in order to guarantee a minimum of reliability, it seemed preferable to include six questions per section. This number was a compromise solution: a shorter test would not allow us to distinguish the chance successes and a longer one would not avoid monotony (which is a source of error attributable to simple, temporary, shifts in attention).

A third and last point that should be mentioned concerns the order of presentation of the questions. Alternating the questions deals not only with the left-right dimension itself but also with the part of the body involved, so that the subject never has to identify the same part (left, then right) twice in a row. This is probably a minor point, but it should be raised, however trivial it may seem, because using such precautions in the order of the questions was not always considered possible or necessary in many other tests of the same sort. It seems advisable, however, to favor as much as possible the independence of the child's responses to each question and thus to reduce the (fortunate or unfortunate) effects of chance. Is it necessary, in fact, to specify that a child does not necessarily have to know how to distinguish left from right in order to be able to raise his hands one at a time when he is asked to raise his right and his left hands successively? He needs only a minimum effort of internal consistency for his first choice, even a purely chance one, to imply *ipso facto* two consecutive successes or failures. The spacing of questions covering the same part of the body helps at least to reduce the frequency and especially the efficacy of this kind of procedure, which is based more on chance than on understanding.

Chapter XII

Concepts of Left and Right:
General Analysis of the Results

The results of the *Concepts of left and right* test were submitted first to a global analysis, consisting mainly of studying the relative difficulty of the problems. This global analysis provides the elements necessary for the analysis by stages which is presented in the next chapter. The first part of this chapter gives the criteria used in scoring the problems and the second part gives the results obtained from these different problems.

SCORING CRITERIA

Scoring a test such as this one does not at first seem to raise any particular difficulties. There is only one correct response to each question, and any given response clearly constitutes either a success or an error. We could, as numerous authors have done (e.g., Galifret-Granjon, 1960; Benton, 1959; etc.), count the number of successes observed in each protocol, arriving at a single numerical result which would serve both to demonstrate the primitive behavior based purely on chance (equal number of successes and errors) and perhaps to delimit the principal steps leading to the mastery of the concepts of left and right (by assessing the difference between the subject's actual score and the score obtainable purely by chance). Although it is current in psychometrics, the only advantage to this sort of procedure is its extreme simplicity. Its drawbacks are too well-known to merit discussion here and too numerous to be worth facing, even for comparative purposes. Simply because it assigns equivalent values to all successes and to all failures, whatever the difficulty of the problems, this technique can be of no use in an analysis whose main objective is to recognize the natural sequence of the steps marking the development of an ability. In order to remove the drawbacks of such a technique, it would not be enough to assign the successes a score proportional to the difficulty of the problems. Even if these problems are given different numerical scores, combining the points into one total score amounts to giving each problem the same value, since it is always possible for success with difficult problems to make up for failures with easier problems.

In order to provide indices with real developmental significance, then, the scoring must deal separately with each section of the test. This is the only possible way to test the initial hypotheses concerning the complexity of the three types of tasks required of the subject. Within each type of problem, on the other hand, it is crucial that the subject's responses be evaluated as a whole, since the objective is not so much to determine whether the subject can, for example, identify his right hand or his left leg, but rather to know to what extent the concepts of left and right correspond to a stable and specific ordering in the subject's body image. The way to increase certainty on this point is to require the subject to point out his left limbs and his right limbs several times in succession without error. If he makes even a single mistake in the course of six consecutive trials, the concepts of left and right have not yet acquired, in his mind, the stability required for each level of structuring. In fact, whether they are still subject to exclusively egocentric representations or whether they arise from a complete relativity, the concepts of left and right must always conserve, in relation to the point of view adopted at the start, a constant definition without which they would lose all meaning. This is why it is necessary in each section of the test to require that the subject answer each of the six questions correctly before we can claim that the difficulty of any given section has really been mastered.

At first glance, the severity of these requirements seems exaggerated. Adoption of this sort of absolute criterion raises the danger of attributing to flaws in spatial representation errors which may be due simply to passing distractions or to fatigue. But it is clear—as various attempts at reducing the stringency of the scoring have in fact shown—that the danger is more apparent than real; in any case it is much less serious than the opposite danger of overestimating the capacities of a subject who makes only one or two errors. In fact, any other classification scheme based on less strict scoring criteria would produce a much greater number of unclassifiable protocols (that is, protocols characterized by a combination of success with difficult problems and failures with easier ones), because this sort of indulgence would probably remove the necessary control for the effects of chance.

To this scoring method, which does not permit a single error out of the six questions of each section, only one exception is made: it takes account of systematic reversals of left and right (allowing no errors within this category itself) which a limited number of subjects (especially the youngest) are guilty of in the first problem (only 24 out of the 400 subjects studied fall into this category). It is obvious that these children are not responding randomly, and the protocol of a single subject may frequently show a consistent reversal of this type. In the second problem, for example, when the subject must locate the left and right of the examiner who is facing him, the responses often either retain this systematic reversal or conform more consistently to reality, the subject in this latter case remaining faithful to his egocentric point of view with no concern for the change required by the new situation. Benton (1959) notes that these cases of systematic reversal are observed, though in a limited number, in experiments done on any population of any importance. He reports the findings of a study especially designed to examine the possible relationships between this particular phenomenon and various other psychometric—or purely psychological—dimensions of behavior. He found that, contrary to common beliefs, this systematic reversal seems to be related neither to left-handedness nor to digital agnosia, nor to any particular deficiency in mathematical ability, as Cénac and Hécaen (1943), for example, noted long ago in a more general interpretation based on specific disturbances of the body image. The only significant deficiency which Benton was able to demonstrate in subjects who showed these systematic reversals concerned the development of linguistic abilities, as measured by standardized tests of reading, spelling, punctuation, grammar, etc. Furthermore, he observed in the same children an almost complete inability to reverse the left-right relations on an opposite: only one of the nine (11 per cent) cases of systematic confusion that he examined managed to make this discrimination, as against 46 out of 72 control subjects (64 per cent) who did not show this confusion but who were comparable to the others on all other points. From all evidence, then, it seems that this sort of consistent reversal should not be evaluated by the same criteria that are applied to the usual errors and confusions. Although we must avoid any superficial interpretation of the role of language in structuring the concepts of left and right, it is still true that the test is not intended to determine whether the subject has properly mastered the conventional linguistic terms designating left and right; it is designed to demonstrate whether he can give a specific meaning to these concepts and above all grasp their essentially relative character. It is easy to understand that a child may poorly use the words that he has learned; but if he introduces the rigor and consistency of the conventional system into his own system, his concepts may attain the same degree of structure as those of children who had adopted the usual terminology from the beginning. The terms "left" and "right" may be a special example of cases where the accepted convention is slow to develop or difficult to retain—even some adults have difficulty in this area—and this is why evaluation of the protocols which include these systematic reversals must be based on a principle of internal consistency rather than on external conformity to the established usage. As soon as the responses in the first section are systematically reversed, these responses are considered as a complete success with the problem, and this initial reversal then serves to interpret the rest of the protocol. For example, the child who in the first problem systematically reverses all the left-right relations with respect to his own body and who, in the second problem, designates the real left and right of the examiner, is scored as succeeding with the first problem and failing with the second.

Does the previously mentioned fact that these systematic reversals are found especially in the youngest children challenge the basis of such a scoring criterion, in which some categories of failures are held as successes (and vice versa)? Perhaps, because of their very precociousness, it is preferable to regard these behaviors as basically primitive and, without grouping them with the real failures which reflect a genuine confusion, reserve them for a specific intermediate level between the time when the child still cannot attribute a stable spatial localization to the terms "left" and "right" and the time when this localization becomes coherent and conforms to reality. To dispel doubt arising from the earliness of systematic reversals, we need only point out—to anticipate the results to be discussed in a moment—that the children who make these consistent reversals are exactly the same average age as those whose protocols are of an equivalent level but without this sort of reversal. What is probably even more decisive is the common-sense argument that it is completely normal for the mastery of linguistic conventions to strengthen with age, since the child has more and more occasion to use the concepts of left and right and, consequently, to be corrected when he uses the terms incorrectly. It goes without saying that the younger the child, the more likely he is to reverse the terms without these reversals necessarily keeping him from grasping the relativity of the relationships.

RELATIVE DIFFICULTY OF THE PROBLEMS

The main objective of the global analysis of the results is to examine the relative difficulty of the problems of the test. This study should allow us to determine whether the order of difficulty which was predicted in constructing the test is confirmed by the facts. For each problem, the index of difficulty derives simply from the number of subjects in each age group who replied consistently (with or without systematic reversals) to the six questions of the problem. Table 38 gives the result of this count for the four problems in the three sections. The last column of the table combines the results of

Table 38

Distribution of subjects by age level and by success on each of the problems of the *Concepts of left and right* test

Age	N	1. Own body	2. Another person	Three objects 3a. visible	Three objects 3b. hidden	Three objects (3a + 3b)
12:0	50	49	42	36	40	33
11:0	50	47	40	29	30	26
10:0	50	49	40	28	27	22
9:0	50	49	37	21	17	16
8:0	50	47	26	15	15	10
7:0	50	42	19	8	10	7
6:0	50	32	7	4	5	2
5:0	50	24	10	3		
Total	400	339	221	144	144	116
Median age		9:0	9:9	10:3	10:5	10:7
Age of accession		5:1	7:10	9:9	9:9	10:8

the last two problems (third section), the criterion for success being then 12 correct responses out of 12.

Comparing the number of successes, the median ages, and the ages of accession (criterion of 50 per cent of successes), the table suggests that the test includes three distinct levels of difficulty: the lowest level corresponds to problem 1 (location of left and right on the subject's own body), the intermediate level to problem 2 (location of left and right on a person facing him), and the highest level to problems 3a and 3b (left-right relations in a group of three objects), which have exactly the same degree of difficulty. However, when we submit these differences to the Kolmogorov-Smirnov test to determine whether the developmental curves differ significantly, we find that problem 1 is really easier than all the others (at the .05 level, one-tailed test), but that problems 2, 3a, and 3b are equivalent. On the other hand, if we combine problems 3a and 3b of the last section (see the last column of Table 38), requiring that the subject solve all 12 questions on the left-right relations in a row of three objects, the difficulty of the task then increases considerably and becomes significantly different from the level of difficulty of problem 2 (.05 level, one-tailed test). Thus the test may be divided into three levels progressively achieved by the child: the first is the ability to designate correctly the left and right of his own body six times in a row; the second is the ability to designate, again six times in a row without error, the left and right of a person facing him; the third is the ability to respond correctly to two groups of six questions on the left-right relationships inherent in a series of three objects.

It remains to justify regrouping problems 3a and 3b into a single problem defining the highest level of difficulty. We could in fact suppose that support for the initial hypotheses concerning this three-level hierarchy derives simply from this regrouping, the greater difficulty of the third level being artificially due to the fact that the scoring criterion is more stringent at this level (12 out of 12) than at the preceding two levels (six out of six). The *décalage* that was observed then would not necessarily reflect the nature of the problem but only the degree of perfection achieved in mastering two basically similar types of difficulty. However, if we compute the total number of responses given to each of the six questions in each problem (see Table 39), we see at once that the criterion imposed by

Table 39

Total number of successes with each question of the four problems in the *Concepts of left and right* test (N=400)

Problem	Question					
	1	2	3	4	5	6
1. Own body	355	344	354	352	349	348
2. Another person	285	284	281	278	278	282
3a. Three visible objects	323	254	199	324	226	294
3b. Three hidden objects	305	223	303	298	260	306

regrouping problems 3a and 3b (12 consecutive successes) still does not achieve the stringency imposed in problems 1 and 2. The main obstacle to be overcome by the subject in problems 3a and 3b is locating the central object in relation to the other two, this central object both to the left of one of the end objects and to the right of the other. Locating the end objects is much simpler because these objects are always to the left or always to the right, whatever the second term of the relationship; nor should we be surprised to discover that the subject rather easily manages to apply the terms "left" and "right" to these end objects even though, in designating the position of the middle object, the as yet absolute nature of these terms leaves him no other choice than to use such expressions as "between them," "in the middle of them," etc. In sum, as the results given in Table 39 clearly show, the only really difficult questions in problems 3a and 3b are the two questions (2 and 5 in both cases) concerning the position of the central objects in relation to the end objects. The other questions are at least as easy as those of problem 2 and, if they are shown to be more difficult than those of problem 1, that is perhaps partially because they include thornier questions on the central objects. Whatever the case, it seems to be the central objects in problem 3a and 3b that the children stumble over when they are still unable to grasp the basic relativity of the concepts of left and right. Even regrouping problems 3a and 3b, the number of these crucial questions is no more than four; this is hardly enough to control for the effects of chance and is less than the number of questions which serve in the first two problems to distinguish the chance successes from authentic ones. Thus, far from being a statistical artifact designed to increase the difficulty of the third level of the proposed scale, regrouping problems 3a and 3b helps—in an important though barely adequate way—to establish the real difficulty of the task of identifying the relative positions of objects in a single group.

This much established, it is now possible to compare the results described here with those of the major studies of other authors. In most cases, the comparisons show a remarkable agreement. Two types of differences, however, should be mentioned. The first concerns the age difference which Piaget (1924) observed between success with questions dealing with three visible objects (eleven years) and success with questions bearing on three hidden objects (twelve years). The results reported here do not support this sort of *décalage* at all. On the contrary, problems 3a and 3b are of nearly equal difficulty at all age levels (see Table 38) and we also note that solving problem 3a without solving problem 3b is just as frequent as the converse case (28 times in both cases). Even if we decided, in order to facilitate the comparison, provisionally to adopt Piaget's criterion of 75 per cent to determine the relative difficulty of the problems, the *décalage* still would not appear. Assuming that we should still admit very minimal differences, we would even have to ask whether the order of difficulty is not rather the reverse, since at the age of twelve years problem 3b is already solved by 80 per cent of the subjects and problem 3a is not yet solved by more than 72 per cent (see Table 38). But, in fact, the difference observed between the present results and Piaget's has scarcely any theoretical consequences, even though it invites a re-examination of Piaget's explanation of the supposed *décalage* between solving these two types of problems. As he explains it (1924), as long as the child can rely on perception, he will be content with perceiving the relations; but when he is required to act simply on memory, he must also recall the items and resort to a topographical memory—that is, he has to imagine the relationships rather than simply perceive them. The lack of *décalage* here requires us either to reject this interpretation without further ado, or to change it by introducing an additional condition. We may in fact choose to reject Piaget's explanation by refusing to believe either in the existence of this so-called topographical memory, or in the need for it to intervene in solving the last problem of the test (hidden objects). In either case, the child would limit himself to recording the total image of the three objects in his mind and thus simply memorize the items, and would neither construct nor analyze the relationships except as the questionnaire leads him along this route, just as he must do when the objects are still visible. If such a form of memorization exists, it would perhaps be more fragile than when it is rooted in the relationships themselves and would probably not withstand the test of time; but the memory of items which it would record might be strong enough to last for the short period of questioning in the experiment. Should we prefer to retain Piaget's explanation, changing it somewhat, we should rather affirm the role of a topographical memory, even adding that this is probably the sort of spatial memorization which predominates in the child whatever his level of development, since memorization is basically an active reconstruction of reality. But then, because memory can reflect only the exactness of the relations which served to construct it, we should observe no difference in the child's structuring process, whether it is bearing on actually perceived or on memorized items. This is why, to return to the particular case concerned here, as soon as the child is able to grasp the left-right relationships uniting the objects exposed to his view (problem 3a), he relies on these very same relations in order to memorize the spatial arrangement of the objects (problem 3b). In sum, according to this interpretation, the only situations which could favor the appearance of a *décalage* between reasoning on currently perceived objects and reasoning on simple memory representations would have to consist of tasks which are complicated enough to surpass the subject's capacities for simultaneous apprehension. If, for example, we ask a child (or even an adult) to memorize the spatial arrangement of a row of 12, 10, or even only eight objects in order then to question him on the left-right relations existing between these different objects, we should expect numerous errors—more, in any case, than if the subject's perceptual activity allowed him to determine the position of the elements at any time during the questioning. But the extreme simplicity of the tasks included in the present test precludes any intervention of this additional factor of complex understanding, so that the basic equivalence of the two situations represented by problems 3a and 3b becomes obvious. In order to choose between these two types of explanation, we would have to rely on more complete data. Besides, this particular problem is part of the larger and still unresolved question of the relationship between image and thought.

The second point on which the present results differ from those obtained by other authors concerns the age at which success with

each problem is normally observed. If, in order better to compare
the results, we rigidly adopt the traditional criterion according to
which a problem is considered as solved when for the first time in
the sequence of age levels at least 75 per cent of the children reply
correctly to all questions in the problem, we observe (see Table 38)
that this age is around seven years for problem 1, ten years for
problem 2, twelve years for problem 3b, and more than twelve years
for problem 3a. Compared to ages obtained in earlier studies
(Piaget, 1924; Galifret-Granjon, 1960; Elkind, 1961d) using the
same type of analysis, Montreal children generally show a delay of
at least one year (see Table 40), and even two to three years for the

Table 40

Comparison of the ages at which some authors situate normal success with the questions
covered in the *Concepts of left and right* test

Author	Criterion	Normal age of success			
		1. Own body	2. Another person	3a. Three visible objects	3b. Three hidden objects
Piaget (1924)	75%	5:0	8:0	11:0	12:0
Galifret-Granjon (1960)	75%	6:0	8:0	11:0-12:0*	
Elkind (1961d)	75%	5:0	7:0	10:0	

*At this age, the percentage obtained is still below criterion (it is only 60, and does not
exceed 66 even at 13:0-14:0 years).

easiest problems. The fact that this delay is more marked in the first
two problems—that is, precisely in the problem that includes a
greater number of questions than the corresponding studies with
which we compare them—might lead us to attribute the delay solely
to these methodological differences. However, it is easy to show that
this factor hardly changes things. If we score only the first two or the
first four questions in each problem in order to compare these distributions to the distributions resulting from scoring all six, we at
once note (see Table 41) that 75 per cent success is achieved at an
earlier age only in the case where the first two questions alone are
considered—and it is still a difference of only one year. This is
largely explained by the fact that the smaller number of questions
favors chance successes. In any case, this early success does not make
up for the two or three years' delay in the first two problems. The
significance of these comparisons is not changed even when, rather

Table 41

Percentage of success at each age level, according to whether the scoring concerns the first two questions only, the first four, or all six questions in each of the first two problems of the *Concepts of left and right* test (N=50 per age level)

Age	1. Own body			2. Another person		
	2	4	6	2	4	6
12:0	98	98	98	86	84	84
11:0	98	98	94	86	80	80
10:0	100	98	98	88	84	80
9:0	100	100	98	78	74	74
8:0	94	94	94	62	56	52
7:0	90	86	84	56	40	38
6:0	80	68	64	30	20	14
5:0	66	52	48	26	22	20

than covering the first two or four questions in each problem, the scoring deals only with the questions whose content is the same as that of the questions asked in earlier works. In sum, if the results show that it may not have been necessary to include more than four questions per problem in order to control for the effect of chance, they show above all that the delay discussed here is surely not due to the difference in the difficulty of the problems on one side or the other. It seems rather to arise from differences in sampling techniques, which do not have the same rigorousness and scope in every case and do not always guarantee a correct representation of all levels of ability.

Thus, despite these differences from the earlier studies, differences which do not have real theoretical consequences, the relative difficulty of the problems generally confirms the initial hypotheses of the three principal stages leading to mastery of the concepts of left and right. This kind of analysis, however necessary and instructive it may be, is still a very crude one and can only indirectly shed light on the nature of the difficulties the child encounters in forming these concepts. For example, the variable difficulty of the problems may suffice to show that the child begins by being able to locate left and right on his own body before recognizing the same dimensions on a person facing him. We might even interpret these findings in egocentric terms and say that before becoming aware of the multiplicity of possible viewpoints, the child begins by grafting his concepts of left and right onto the referent elements entering his own perspective; this perspective is the only one he knows (though he does not yet recognize it as such) and he accords it a universal and absolute character. But, in actuality, an interpretation such as this, which is formulated in terms of egocentrism, goes beyond the information provided by the preceding analysis. In fact, it is not limited to asserting that a certain number of children cannot always correctly locate left and right on an opposite after having done so on themselves; it also states that these errors reflect the flaw in perspective which is inherent in egocentrism. This appeal to egocentrism would be more legitimate were there many cases of systematic errors in designating left and right on the examiner, since this type of error is the very proof that the subject's behavior is not random but instead reflects a clearly definable system of representation, however imperfect it may still be. But the qualitative study of the protocols, based on successes as well as on failures, is precisely the analysis by stages which we now take up and which may, better than any other analysis, demonstrate the intellectual mechanisms operating in the progressive development of the concepts of left and right.

Chapter XIII

Concepts of Left and Right:
Analysis by Stages

The detailed description of the stages, with which most of this chapter is concerned, is preceded by two brief sections. The first is a general view of the developmental scale established by the preceding analysis, and the second gives the distribution of subjects in this scale.

ESTABLISHMENT OF A DEVELOPMENTAL SCALE

The development of the concepts of left and right includes three levels which directly reflect the different levels of difficulty recognized in the preceding analysis. As usual, this scale is preceded by a stage which includes various forms of incompetence and incomprehension. This incompetence is here reflected in a massive failure with all problems, where the child never arrives at any systematic type of distinction between left and right in the six questions of each of these problems. Stage 1, on the other hand, defines the first structuring of these concepts. From now on, the child gives them a meaning which is stable enough, but which still lacks any real relativity: although he manages to recognize the opposition inherent in the concepts of left and right, he still makes mistakes in the actual localization of these two dimensions. Thus, in designating his own body parts, the stage 1 child's responses may be entirely correct or consistently wrong. However, because the concepts of left and right still have absolute value in his eyes and are unconsciously but exclusively tied to his own point of view, it will never occur to the child of this level to reverse the relations in order to point out the

278

left and right of the examiner facing him; though holding them in opposition to each other, he will continue to judge the two dimensions according to his own perspective. When he is then required to describe the relative positions of three objects lined up before him on the table, he may—if he does not revert to an "anythingness" provoked by an impression of the problem's excessive difficulty— succeed in conserving a remarkable coherence in locating the two end objects and will almost always be in accord with his previous judgments. But he will inevitably fail with the question concerning the middle object in the row, and the nature of his failure often directly reflects the still-absolute character of his concepts of left and right. The relation of opposition, which is the whole definition of the "left-right" dichotomy during stage 1, is not, however, immediately asserted by the child's intelligence; the child begins simply by feeling the need for this relation before being able to state it with certainty. It is to distinguish these two moments within a single general level that stage 1 includes two substages. During substage 1A, the child's convictions are still uncertain, and the left-right opposition is respected only occasionally, often only in the first problem or sometimes only in the second, and his other responses reflect instead the inconsistency typical of stage 0. Substage 1B, on the other hand, marks a real advance in that the left-right opposition is respected in the first two problems or is replaced, in the second, by very hesitant attempts at decentration.

In the course of stage 2, the child becomes aware of the role played by his own point of view in his representation of the left-right dimensions, and at the same time discovers the multiplicity of potential viewpoints. Consequently, careful always to make his conceptions of left and right correspond to the temporary perspective through which he sees reality, he will easily succeed (second problem) in reversing the relations established on his own body in order to adapt them to the specific viewpoint of an opposite person. These commendable efforts to coordinate objects with the observer's viewpoint surely contribute to investing the concepts of left and right with a certain relativity, but it is a relativity which is still too unstable to allow the child to understand that a single object, placed in the middle of a row of three, may be considered as at the left or at the right without this verbal change requiring that the observer shift positions. In order to admit this possibility, as well as to grasp the full and complete meaning of the expressions "to the left of" and "to the right of," the child must add relations that link the objects to each other to the relations that link the objects to various viewpoints. This dual relativity, which alone is capable of guaranteeing success with all questions on the three objects (problems 3a and 3b), does not become available to the child before stage 3. Until the last stage, the concepts of left and right include both the relative and the absolute, and they remain, so to speak, absolutes relative to the different viewpoints of a mobile observer. In other words, the expressions "to the left" and "to the right," while consistently adapted to the perspective of the observer in question, for a long time remain the only expressions admitted and understood and are not differentiated from the more objective expressions "to the left of" and "to the right of."

DISTRIBUTION OF SUBJECTS ON THE DEVELOPMENTAL SCALE

Table 42 distributes the subjects on the developmental scale outlined above and gives the various statistical indices which characterize the distribution. The general progression of median ages clearly reflects the transitivity of the stages. Two categories of exceptions, however, should be mentioned even though they are certainly not enough to affect the general classification. The first

Table 42

Distribution of subjects by age and by stage in the *Concepts of left and right* test

| Age | N | Unclassi-fied | Stage | | | | | | | | |
| | | | Frequencies | | | | | Cumulative percentages | | | |
			0	1A	1B	2	3	1A	1B	2	3
12:0	50	2	1	3	2	11	31	98	92	88	65
11:0	50	2	2	2	5	15	24	96	92	81	50
10:0	50	3	1	1	5	21	19	98	96	85	40
9:0	50	3	1	1	8	24	13	98	96	79	28
8:0	50	3	2	3	16	19	7	96	89	55	15
7:0	50	3	3	10	17	13	4	94	73	36	9
6:0	50	1	11	11	22	4	1	78	55	10	2
5:0	50		20	14	10	6		60	32	12	
Total	400	17	41	45	85	113	99				
Median age*			5:7	5:10	7:2	0:1	10:9				
Age of accession								(4:6)	5:8	7:9	10:11

*See footnote to Table 16.

category of exceptions consists of the unclassified protocols (17 of the 400 subjects tested, or 4.3 per cent)—that is, subjects who were excluded from the general classification for not having produced a pattern of errors and successes which conforms to the order of difficulty of the problems. These subjects will, for example, solve the last two problems after having failed with the first two (two subjects out of 17), or will miss only the second problem (15 out of 17) for failing to make either some (eight out of 15) or all (seven out of 15) of the reversals necessary for the correct designation of the parts of the examiner opposite. The rather high frequency of this second type of protocol might suggest that it is much less a question of cases of accident than it is of cases reflecting a real mode of structuring the concepts of left and right. We rejected this possibility after considering, first, the insignificant proportion of these aberrant protocols in the whole sample and, second, the homogeneous distribution of these same protocols in the age sequence (a fact which clearly seems to preclude a precise relationship with any given developmental level). In all probability these exceptional behaviors, like the other infrequent behaviors which were not classifiable, are instead simply the expression of fluctuations in interest and attention. In this perspective, we might even have put these protocols back into the general classification, using the highest level of difficulty attained by each subject as the criterion for classifying them into levels. In fact, it is primarily a concern with preserving the homogeneity of the substages which explains the exclusion of these few inconsistent protocols.

The second category of exceptions to the rule of transitivity of the stages concerns the substage 1A subjects, whose age distribution is not significantly different from that of subjects in the two adjacent levels (.05 level, Kolmogorov-Smirnov test), while all other distributions, compared in pairs, are significantly different from each other. Substage 1A is basically a transitional level between stages 0 and 1B, dependent on both of them in the sense that the very first (left-right) distinctions made by the subject at this level are always accomplished through response sequences which are overtly inconsistent. But the transitional nature of substage 1A behavior is surely not a sufficient justification for retaining this stage, when the characteristics of this behavior do not really differ from behavior observed at one or the other of the two neighboring levels. Whether it is defined by elements borrowed from adjacent stages or by proper and *sui generis* elements, any true stage of mental development must at least lend itself to a proper psychological (and chronological) definition; without this there is a great risk of introducing artificial nuances into the description of the facts. If substage 1A is retained in the classification, it is precisely because the statistical indications concerning chronological age were not thought to be sufficient to justify eliminating it. In fact, because of the age limits involved, the distributions obtained in stages 0 and 1A are abruptly interrupted at the age of 5:0 years and thus can give only a very approximate idea of the relative frequencies of the behaviors proper to these levels in the youngest subjects. If the distributions were not truncated like this, it is quite probable that the differences would be much more marked. On the other hand, the *décalage* observed between substages 1A and 1B is more pronounced, and suggests that the smallest addition of lower age levels would perhaps be enough to uncover the presumed divergence. Be that as it may, the absence of such a statistical confirmation leaves only three possibilities: we might combine the substage 1A subjects with those of substage 1B, assuming that they are all basically at the same level of reasoning; or we might instead combine substage 1A and stage 0, this time presuming that the strategies of children assigned to substage 1A require a still too-fragile and too-hesitant comprehension of a rather simple opposition relation; or, finally, we might maintain the proposed distinction in order to throw light on the nature of these behaviors and turn to purely logical considerations in justifying the decision. For diagnostic reasons as well as for reasons of theoretical analysis, it seems advantageous to consider these highly unstable cases as distinct from those which reflect the steadiness and consistency proper to substage 1B. The second solution hardly seems feasible since it amounts to holding as equivalent the inconsistent responses of stage 0 and the responses of substage 1A, which reflect a clear effort toward coherence. In sum, despite some reservations, it seems preferable to admit that substage 1A corresponds to a genuine level in the development of the concepts of left and right and to leave the appropriate regroupings to any investigator who wishes to contest the legitimacy of this distinction.

This much accomplished, returning to the results in Table 42 should show how slow the concepts of left and right are to develop and how regular the development is. The age of accession to sub-stage 1A cannot be determined since it is below 5:0 years, the lower limit of the subjects tested; but the general distribution suggests that this accession is located around 4:6 years, or about one year before accession to substage 1B. The size of the differences that separate the following stages (from two to three years) clearly indicates that we are dealing with three transformations which are clearly distin-guishable and distinct despite their interdependence. Thus the child is not aware of the important role of his own viewpoint in the defi-nition of left and right until after a certain period of productive exercise. Similarly, assuming that we could assimilate it to the view-point of a second observer, the viewpoint of objects could be clear only to children who are already used to coordinating the concepts of left and right with the various possible perspectives of a single observer. Despite this interdependence, each successive transforma-tion is unique and generally rather abruptly apparent in the course of development, as the detailed analysis of the stages will show by pointing out the remarkable homogeneity of the protocols at each level and the relative rarity of transitional stages and even of transi-tional cases.

Finally, before going on to the detailed description of the stages, we should point out that the differences between boys and girls were never significant (.05 level: Kolmogorov-Smirnov test).

DETAILED DESCRIPTION OF THE STAGES

STAGE 0: TOTAL INCOMPREHENSION

The 41 subjects who completely ignored even the most elemen-tary concepts of left and right are classified at stage 0. Very rare, however, are subjects who refused to respond to the questionnaire at all. This is probably because the terms used were already familiar to the children, although still not corresponding to any well-defined concepts. Only one subject adopted a flatly negative attitude from the start and resisted all of the examiner's attempts to get him to respond; another child refused to continue the test after the second problem. In all other instances, the children responded to all the questions and often did so with a disconcerting aplomb which can be explained only as a deep lack of awareness of the difficulties raised by the questionnaire. This assurance notwithstanding, the result is a generalized failure on all problems, since the left-right opposition is never systematically respected. Despite their highly fantastic nature—that is, in spite of having no real connection with the concepts of left and right—the responses are never based entirely on chance but almost always reflect the particular strategy adopted by the child.

Thus, in the *first problem,* some children (five in all) correctly identified their own body parts (hands, ears, legs) but always pointed to either the right side or the left side. This perseveration sometimes permits one exception (for example, the child beginning by showing his left hand and then consistently selecting the right side), but this exception is not enough to mislead us concerning the subject's general strategy. In other children (also five cases), the perseveration consists of always designating the same side, not for all of the parts to be identified but for each of these parts individually: for example, they designate first their right hand (correct), then their left ear (correct) and their left leg (incorrect), but repeat exactly the same behavior in the following three questions where they are required to point out, in the same order, the same three parts but on the opposite sides. A third type of reaction is seen in some children (again five cases) who apparently did not dare designate the same part twice and, still unable to assign a real meaning to the terms "left" and "right," chose to locate the parts first always on the right and then always on the left (or vice versa). Other children (six cases) combined the preceding two types of behavior: because the examiner alternately uses the terms "left" and "right," terms which they vaguely suspect to refer to the two sides of the body, these children refused to point out the same part twice or to designate the same side of the body several times in a row. Unable to locate the real left and right, they made arbitrary choices which they probably forgot as they went on—whence the inconsistency of these protocols, an inconsistency which is tempered only by this element of internal coherence wherein a localization error in the first three questions entails a complementary error in the last three.

Besides these clearly characterized strategies, we observe two more types of behavior which, in order to minimize the errors in interpretation, we might be tempted simply to combine with the more general class of chance behavior without even distinguishing them. In both cases, in effect, the strategy apparently adopted by the subject is not retained in all six questions, and the response sequence can really be no more than the effect of chance, despite striking similarities with more systematic sequences. Nevertheless, it seems useful to classify these behaviors into two principal types, if only to make the descriptions clearer. The first type is the behavior which most closely resembles the behavior of stage 1: the 11 subjects of this type make so many or so few errors (five successes or five failures out of six questions) that they actually seem to be trying, without completely succeeding, to oppose the terms "left" and "right." The behavior of the second type, observed in eight subjects, is closer to what was just described, notably to simple perseveration and to the pseudo decentration which, for example, leads the subject first to designate all his right-hand parts, then all his left-hand parts. But because not all the responses of a single subject derive from a single strategy, it is not really possible to determine unequivocally the dominance of one or another solution, nor even to state that the effects of chance or of pure fantasy are not adequate to explain the response sequence. Thus, when a child, in responding to the six questions, designates first his right side twice, then his left side twice, and finally his right side three times, the sequence of his responses may indiscriminately be the effect of chance, of fantasy, of perseveration, or of a pseudo alternation. And it would be both unwise and futile to try to settle the question, since all these explanations are basically equivalent and they presume, in the child, the same ignorance of the relations of opposition which are indispensable to any definition of the concepts of left and right, however primitive it may be.

The *second* problem of the test again leads to exactly the same strategies in almost the same proportions: consistent designation of the same side of the body at least five times out of six (six subjects); uniform designation of the same side for each part (two subjects); successive designation of three parts, first on one side and then on the other (seven subjects); one or two errors in the first three questions and complementary errors in the last three (seven subjects); a single error or success (eight subjects); and, finally, response sequences with no overt relationship to any particular strategy (10 subjects). Rather rare, however, are subjects who adopted the same strategy in the first and second problems (only eight out of 40, or 20 per cent). This relative rarity clearly shows the basic equivalence of the various strategies described and at the same time explains the absence of any significant relationship between the children's age and the strategy employed. In fact, the child may decide on a moment's whim to proceed in any fashion whatever and will not be at all systematic. Any effort toward coherence has little importance for him anyway, since in any case the task required of him surpasses his level of comprehension. The strategy which he adopts, rather than being inspired by an effort to adapt himself to the nature of the problems, serves only to disguise an ignorance which the examiner's insistence or a laudable concern for cooperation keeps him from admitting.

Children of stage 0 are even more disoriented in the *last two* problems, as seen in the considerable increase in responses of pure perseveration (36 per cent of all responses to these problems) and purely chance responses (46 per cent), the latter almost all provoked by a whim or fantasy of the moment. The rest of the responses (18 per cent) include errors similar to those observed in later stages and break down into categories which are so diversified (the same type of error is almost never found in two subjects) and so unsystematic (the same subject never makes the same type of error in two problems) that they can probably be explained by purely fortuitous factors.

STAGE 1: RELATION OF INTERNAL OPPOSITION ONLY

The main characteristic of stage 1 children is the understanding that the terms "left" and "right" are names or labels which do not relate to objects in a purely arbitrary and unstable fashion, but instead constitute spatial localization factors with a stable and regular reference. The child discovers, in effect, that these two terms refer to body parts which are each placed on the same side, or to external objects which are considered as to the left or to the right depending on whether they are placed to the left or the right of the salient reference point which is the body itself. In his responses to the questions, then, he introduces a consistency which reflects this law of regularity, and the consistency of the responses often precedes even the knowledge of what left and right really are. It is clear that this principle of stability or regularity already reflects the child's grasp of a relationship of opposition between left and right. But because this relationship, though it is the simplest of those which underlie these concepts, is still the only one which gives them meaning, the child will unduly exploit the principle of stability of spatial localizations deriving from it and will spontaneously connect this stability to his own point of view without being aware of the role of such a limited perspective in the definition of left and right. Everything located on one side of him will be judged as to the left, for example, and everything on the other side will be considered to the right. Despite this understanding of the opposition relations expressed by these terms and also despite this constant coordination of objects with his own perspective, left and right remain essentially absolute terms that describe objects located in two contiguous and nonoverlapping spaces. Because the borders defining these spaces are determined with reference to a viewpoint which is unaware of itself, the child perceives neither their extreme mobility nor their continual fluctuation.

Thus the behavior typical of stage 1 subjects is very easy to predict. In the *first* problem, these subjects can easily designate their left and right parts, or will completely reverse these relations and thus demonstrate that they have established the relation of opposition between the terms "left" and "right." Once they have decided (rightly or wrongly) that "right" corresponds to a particular side of the body, it is precisely the discovery of opposition which leads them always to locate the "right" parts on the same side and the "left" parts on the opposite side out of a concern for coherence or internal consistency. These children maintain the same attitude in the *second* problem. They continue to oppose the terms "left" and "right" as well as always to judge them with respect to their own viewpoint, so that the questions are all missed if they responded correctly to the first problem or, on the contrary, they are all correctly solved if they have reversed the relations at the beginning. Finally, confronted with the row of three objects of the *last two* problems (3a and 3b), the stage 1 subject will easily apply the terms "left" and "right" to the two end objects; but he often hesitates, and sometimes even completely refuses, to apply the same terms to the central object because this object implicitly serves as the demarcation point between the left side and the right; unable to fit into either one, then, the object has no attribute other than being located "in the middle."

This typical behavior, directly attributable to total egocentrism, is probably not the only behavior characteristic of the first stage; but it is frequent enough, as we shall soon see, amply to justify the interpretation that this first stage is dominated above all by ego-centrism. Even when a protocol does not exactly conform to the above description, it always reflects an absolute ignorance or un-awareness of the relativity of left and right. This is what the more detailed analysis of the protocols assigned to stage 1 will now try to describe. In order to make this analysis more precise, we must first present the distinction between substage 1A and substage 1B within this first stage.

A. *Substage 1A*

The main characteristic of subjects at stage 1 is not so much knowing how to locate actual left and right as understanding that each of these terms refers to one of the two opposite sides of their bodies; therefore we could, in principle, reserve stage 1 for subjects who succeed (or fail through systematic reversals) on all the questions of the first problem (where they are required to locate left and right on their own bodies), without solving any of the subsequent problems. Such a procedure, as simple as it is, nevertheless ignores two categories of facts and thus risks not doing justice to some subjects. It ignores first the various types of failure, types which are as useful in evaluating the levels of functioning as is consideration of the successes alone. In the second problem particularly, it is essential to distinguish the failures resulting from a regression to primitive strategies typical of stage 0 from, on the other hand, failures resulting from either a still too-absolute definition of the concepts of left and right or an effort at decentration which is still too unstable to guarantee the child's ability unerringly to consider the viewpoint of another viewer. In the first case, in fact, the failure is explained by the very unstable and still undeveloped character of the coordinations intervening in the concepts of left and right: the child is unable to transpose into a second situation, or simply to conserve, the strategy which produced success with the first problem. In the other two cases, however, the definition of the terms "left" and "right," as incomplete and limited as it still is, is structured strongly enough to be generalized (even too much) to various situations requiring the use of these concepts. It is this difference between two levels of structuring that the distinction between substage 1A and substage 1B attempts to illustrate.

If level 1A must include the subjects in whom comprehension of the first concepts of left and right is very weak and unstable, it naturally includes a second group of subjects to whom we would not do justice with a cruder classification using successes on the first problem and failure on the others as a criterion. This is the case with subjects whose errors in the first problem are analogous to those of subjects in stage 0 (perseveration, pseudo alternation, etc.), but whose responses to the second problem are no longer inconsistent and are systematically right or wrong, apparently including an intentional application of the relation of opposition inherent in the left-right dichotomy. As different as they are in appearance from the protocols of subjects who consistently oppose the terms "left" and "right" in the first problem and then revert to more primitive strategies, this sort of protocol reflects basically the same instability and the same imperfection in structuring the concepts of left and right. In fact, we need not think that the first problem must favor an understanding of the relation of opposition of left and right any more than the second one, because as long as this relation is the only element in the definition of these concepts, the nature of the task imposed on the subject does not essentially differ from the first to the second problem.

In sum, substage 1A is seen clearly as a transitional stage. It combines the subjects who can establish a stable opposition between the concepts of left and right in one of the first two problems, but who, probably because they are unable to see this opposition as an express and necessary condition for the definition of these concepts, ignore it at another time and revert to strategies which are completely unrelated to the projective relations concerned. This substage includes 45 subjects; examination of the responses to the first two problems allows us to divide them into four different groups (see Table 43). The first group (group A) is made up of the 18 subjects who un-

Table 43

Types of behavior observed in substage 1A subjects in the first two problems of the *Concepts of left and right* test (N=45)

		Problem	
Type	N	1	2
A	18	Systematic successes	Chance responses
B	9	Systematic errors	Chance responses
C	10	Chance responses	Systematic successes
D	8	Chance responses	Systematic errors

erringly succeeded in pointing out their right and their left parts (problem 1) but, when asked to designate parts of the examiner's body (problem 2), adopted one or another of the strategies typical of stage 0 or simply resorted to chance. A second group (group B: nine subjects) systematically reversed left and right on their own bodies and then were also satisfied with primitive or purely chance responses. The third group (group C) includes the 10 subjects who proceeded like the stage 0 children in the first problem, but who then managed unerringly to locate the left and right parts of the examiner. Finally, the last group (group D: eight subjects) systematically reversed the left and right of the examiner after having given primitive responses to the first problem. The fact that these four groups do not differ appreciably in chronological age indicates that it is a question of behaviors which are basically equivalent in terms of the level of functioning of the underlying intellectual mechanisms. In the last two problems, the protocols all become much more homogeneous and are already easier to characterize than those of stage 0, although the increased difficulty confuses a number of subjects and frequently causes them to seek solutions on a very whimsical basis. Of the 90 responses given these two problems by the 45 subjects of this substage, 37 seem to reflect pure fantasy. We also find responses of a very primitive level: simple alternation between left and right (twice); responses of perseveration (14 times) almost always consisting of locating the objects on the same side, and preferring the right side (11 times out of the 14 cases), which the last term of the alternatives offered in the question regularly suggests; etc. But several times the localization of the end objects is consistently right (16 times) or wrong (21 times): the errors or inconsistencies then exclusively concern the central objects, whose localization is either combined with that of the objects with which they are compared or simply determined in an absolute manner as though the subject had decided that the row was made up of two objects to the left and one to the right (or vice versa). Despite appearances, these responses do not surpass the degree of accuracy presumed to be available to subjects assigned to such a low stage. At most they imply the grasp of some sort of opposition between the terms "left" and "right," an opposition which the substage 1A child, as indicated by his responses to the first two problems, is already able to respect, although still only globally and uncertainly. This instability is again revealed here in the form of two complementary and interdependent symptoms. The first is the fact that only a minority of subjects (11 out of 45) manage to conserve the left-right opposition in the two successive problems of three objects. The second symptom concerns the fact that in these two problems the number of purely chance responses or, rather, of responses which are impossible to relate to any specific strategy, is exactly the same as the number of responses resulting from this principle of opposition (37 in both cases). These facts suggest that if the relation of opposition necessary for even the very rudimentary definition of the concepts of left and right is already sensed by the substage 1A child, it is still so undeveloped and implicit that it is as likely to be ignored as it is to be respected.

We should point out one last detail whose omission might suggest that there is an error in classification. The reader will recall (see Table 43) that among the four different types of protocols assigned to stage 1A, the third (group C) includes subjects capable not only of demonstrating consistency in their responses to the second problem but also of unerringly pointing out the real left and right of the examiner. Since this success is preceded by a failure with the first problem, we might be led to judge these protocols as unclassifiable and thus to exclude them, as we did the protocols containing failure on the first two problems and success on the last two. At first glance, such a procedure may seem, if not the only sensible one, at least the one most likely to reduce the risks of errors of classification. But, all things considered, this procedure is based on a judgment which is much more unwise than that on which the allocation of these subjects to substage 1A is based. In order to declare them unclassifiable, we would in effect have to assign an absolute value to their success with the second problem and, consequently, consider that this success does not result simply from a coherent application of the principle of left-right opposition (grafted onto an initial arbitrary choice), but rather derives from a real coordination of viewpoints and from an intentional and specific reversal of left-right relations. If we accepted such an interpretation, we would first have to explain the fact that substage 1A subjects, able to locate the left and right of the examiner without error (group C), are in fact neither more numerous nor older than subjects of the same substage who consistently make mistakes in this task (group D). Furthermore, in order to exclude from substage 1A the protocols which include success with the second problem, we could base the argument only on one or the other of two opposite and equally unacceptable suppositions. Either we would have to admit, against all logic and all evidence, that the mere opposition of the terms "left" and "right" by the child, beginning with an initial arbitrary choice, could indiscriminately produce either success or systematic failure in the first problem (group A or B), while it could lead only to systematic failure in the second problem (group D only). Or we would have to assume that the errors in the second problem are never due to the arbitrariness of the child's initial choice in his opposition of left and right, but that they imply a genuine ability to locate the actual left and right on his own body, the errors then arising from an inability to make the necessary reversals. This second assumption has no foundation, neither at substage 1A, where even the subjects who can already surpass the behavior typical of stage 0 still make numerous errors on the real left and right of their own bodies (see group B), nor at substage 1B, where we observe a large proportion of subjects still making mistakes in locating their own body parts. Thus it is hardly likely that such knowledge can immediately assert itself in the second problem in children of the present substage who, in the first problem, still act like stage 0 subjects. It is much safer to assign a completely relative value to the successes and systematic errors observed in one of the two problems and to admit that the nearly equal frequency of these two types of responses in the second problem confirms the highly arbitrary character of the subject's initial choice (left or right) in the first question.

B. *Substage 1B*

In substage 1B the relation of opposition which gives the concepts of left and right their first meaning is asserted and stabilized. These concepts assume, therefore, a first level of relativity in that they become basically dependent on each other both in definition and in the space to which each of them refers. This relativity, however, is only a weak reflection of the relativity that characterizes the various dimensions of a projective space, in which the terms that refer to these dimensions must retain a constant meaning while referring to realities which are constantly changing with the points of view involved. This second sort of relativity completely escapes the substage 1B subjects. The concepts of left and right, at this level, refer to areas whose only mobility is that of the subject's own point of view. In this sense, then, we can say that the subject at this level refers to a viewpoint (his own) in the definition of the terms "left" and "right"; but, unable to recognize it as such, he is still unaware of the basic role which this viewpoint plays. When he becomes aware of it, he will also be able to stop considering it as an exclusive reference point and to integrate it into the group of perspectives which may variously affect left-right relations. Before this time, however, and for a remarkably long period (about two years separate substage 1B from stage 2), left and right are absolutes defined only by his own point of view. In substage 1B children, this sort of egocentrism produces two rather clearly defined types of symptoms. One group arises from the comparative analysis of the behavior observed in the first two problems and the other from examination of the responses to the last two problems, and particularly to questions concerning the middle object in the row.

Beginning with the analysis of the *responses to the first two problems* (Table 44), we note that most subjects at this substage

Table 44

Types of behavior observed in substage 1B children in the first two problems of the *Concepts of left and right* test (N=85)

Type	N	Problem 1	Problem 2
A	44	Systematic successes	Systematic errors
B	7	Systematic errors	Systematic successes
C	31	Systematic successes	Partial successes
D	3	Systematic errors	Partial successes

(groups A and B: 51 out of 85, or 60 per cent) do not differentiate the left or right of the examiner (seen from the front) from their own left and right. In other words, when the child designates his real left and right in the first problem, he consistently misses the second problem (44 subjects); when, on the other hand, he misses the left-right relations on his own body from the very beginning, he solves all the questions of the second problem (seven subjects). It is interesting to note that the proportion of subjects who are really able to locate their own left and right increases considerably here in relation to what it was in the preceding stage. If, in fact, in order to make allowance for purely fortuitous successes, we attempt to reduce the number of systematic successes observed in problem 1 by a number equal to that of the systematic errors in the same problem, we may then estimate (see Table 44) the proportion of subjects who no longer make arbitrary choices to be about 76 per cent [or (44+31)–(7+3) out of 85], while the corresponding proportion in the preceding substage (see Table 43) is only about 33 per cent (or 18–9 out of 27). It seems, however, that this progress is not the cause but simply the reflection of the new intellectual needs of the child who after this point is careful systematically to oppose the terms "left" and "right." If it were in fact the cause, it would be difficult to explain how some children can also manage to introduce the same consistency into a series of erroneous responses. It is easier to understand that such an advancement is rather the consequence of a search for coherence, a search which sooner or later leads the child to want to assign to these terms a stable and definitive meaning.

In addition to these subjects who do not seem to suspect the need to reverse the left-right relations on an observer seen from the front, substage 1B also includes other subjects (groups C and D of Table 44) who discover this error in perspective but are still unable to avoid it. After a correct designation (31 subjects) or a systematic reversal (three subjects) of their right or left body parts in the first problem, these subjects attempt to make the transpositions required by the difference in the observer's orientation; but this effort is still so costly for them that sooner or later they return to their own point of view. Without having the coherence of the responses given by subjects of the same substage who are still total victims of this egocentrism (groups A and B), these responses nevertheless have their own characteristics which clearly distinguish them from the behavior typical of stages 0 or 1A. The response sequence, in fact, most often includes a single success (14 cases) or a single error (12 cases); when it includes more than one (two successes in five subjects; two errors in three subjects), these exceptions in the sequence are concentrated at the very beginning or at the very end of the series and also reflect a type of irregularity which, despite everything else, is different from the behavior dictated by fantasy or whimsy. The hesitations seen in subjects of groups C and D, assuming that they are due to a real— and still very rudimentary—recognition of the relativity of viewpoints, could in principle justify creating an intermediate level between substage 1B (which would then be reserved for children characterized by total egocentrism) and stage 2, when the egocentrism loses its strength and the simple reversal of left-right relations becomes possible. But the statistical results do not at all justify this addition. If the age of the subjects who are still clearly egocentric (groups A and B) seems slightly lower than that of other subjects of substage 1B (groups C and D), the differences are nevertheless not significant (.05 level, by the Kolmogorov-Smirnov test), even when the comparison includes opposing the presumably most precocious subjects (four or five successes out of six items) to all the other subjects. Therefore, because there is no reason to think that this lack of difference is due to accidental factors (e.g., truncated distributions, etc.), it seems that we must attribute the partial success of groups C and D to a first effort toward decentration, and admit also that a simple temporary recognition of the relativity of viewpoints is not an appreciable advancement over overt egocentrism.

Let us now consider the *responses to the last two problems* by subjects of the same substage 1B. Examination of these responses reveals in two ways the lack of relativity which still characterizes the concepts of left and right at this level. In the first place, subjects of this substage do not often understand the exact meaning of the question requiring them to place two objects in a reciprocal relation rather than to attribute an absolute value to them. Thus the expressions "to the left of" and "to the right of" are not understood as such but are interpreted or transformed so that they acquire the absolute meaning of "to the left" or "to the right." Some subjects even spontaneously try to describe the second object mentioned in the question, as though this question required locating the objects individually rather than in relation to each other.

5 (6:0): *Problem 3b* (from left to right: a cow, a lamppost, a boat). "Is the light to the left or to the right of the boat?—*To the right, and the boat is to the left.*"

In other children, this same difficulty in understanding the relationships to be established between the objects may be seen in the different but no less symptomatic reactions consisting, for example, of refusing to establish the left-right relations between the two nonadjacent objects, or trying always to locate the second object mentioned in the question rather than the one with which the question is actually dealing, etc.

In truth, however, the main obstacle for subjects of level 1B concerns the object located in the middle of the row of three. It is significant to point out that 92 per cent (or 78 out of 85) of the subjects at this stage committed at least one error of localization out of four questions relating to the middle object and that, of all the responses given to problems 3a and 3b, 44 per cent (or 75 out of 170) involved errors dealing exclusively with these central objects. These statements are not at all surprising if we accept that the terms "left" and "right" are still seen as absolutes at this level. The two end objects, then, each belong to a different space, and the central object either defines the border separating these two spaces or may belong equally to one or the other without any clue or rule deciding it. The obstacle created by the presence of this central object may sometimes be expressed directly and naïvely, as in this child:

29 (8:0): *Problem 3b* (left to right: a cow, a lamppost, a boat). "Is the boat to the left or to the right of the cow?—[Before replying] *And the light, does it count?*"

But it is the responses to the questions bearing directly on the central objects which best show the subjects' hesitation and their persistence in thinking in absolute terms. Some say, for example, that the objects are placed neither to the right nor to the left but *"right in the middle."* Others will place both of them generally to the right or to the left, as though they had chosen easily to avoid the difficulty by deciding once and for all that the border of the two contiguous spaces is at the left or at the right of the central object. Finally, others will locate the central object on the left side or the right side depending on the side chosen for the end object with which this middle object is compared in the question and will thus give consistently wrong responses. And often, in this last case, the child gives the impression that he is reversing the terms of the question without being aware of doing so, so that a question such as this one: *"Is the light to the left or to the right of the boat?"* easily becomes: *"Is the boat to the left or to the right of the light?,"* or even simpler: *"Is the boat to the left or the right?"* Finally, there are some other behaviors which are more difficult to define because the various elements described above may be mixed in various proportions;

but this diversity always allows the uncommon difficulty with the questions concerning the central object to appear. The following protocol excerpt is particularly remarkable for the way this difficulty is presented.

22 (8:0): *Problem 3b* (left to right: a cow, a lamppost, a boat). "Is the cow to the left or to the right of the light?—*To the left.*—Is the light to the left or to the right of the boat?—*To the left of the cow.* [!]— Listen to me carefully. I am asking you, Is the light to the left or to the right of the boat?—*To the right of the boat.*—Is the boat to the left or to the right of the light?—*To the right of the light.*—Is the cow to the left or to the right of the boat?—*To the left.*—Is the light to the left or to the right of the cow?—*To the right of the boat.* [!]—Listen to me very carefully. Is the light to the left or to the right of the cow?—*To the left of the cow.*—Is the boat to the left or to the right of the cow?—*To the left . . . no . . . to the right.*"

The inconsistency which this protocol seems to reflect at first glance is fairly well resolved if we understand that, for this child, the middle object is a sort of border between a left-hand space occupied by the cow and a right-hand space occupied by the boat. So, when we question him directly about the middle object, we should perhaps see his complementary errors (*"to the left of the cow"* and *"to the right of the boat"*) as a very unskillful way of eluding the question on the middle object and of simply expressing that the cow is on the left side and the boat is on the right.

In sum, it seems fairly clear that the substage 1B child does not at all grasp the meaning of the questions in the last two problems because they require a form of relativity as yet unsuspected by him. This incomprehension is reflected in various types of errors (see Table 45). As we have just seen, the most characteristic errors (type F), which we note in 48 per cent of the subjects in problem 3a and 40 per cent in problem 3b (or 44 per cent on the average), concern the position of the middle object. The child adopts one of three types of behavior, none of which is really more frequent than the other two: he may decide once and for all to locate the middle object to the left or to the right in an absolute way, he may attribute it to the same side as the object with which it is compared each time, or, finally, he may simply state that the object is "in the middle" without seeing the possibility of speaking of left or right in such a case. Regarding this type of error, it is helpful to remark also that the

Table 45

Distribution of substage 1B subjects according to the six behavior types (A to F)* observed
in problems 3a and 3b of the *Concepts of left and right* test

Problem 3a	Problem 3b						Total
	A	B	C	D	E	F	
A			1				1
B		6				2	8
C		7	8	1	2	2	20
D	1			1	1	2	5
E		1	4	3		2	10
F	1	2	7	3	2	26	41
Total	2	16	20	8	5	34	85

*A=systematic alternation
B=perseveration
C=chance responses
D=solution of all six questions of one of the two problems
E=error consisting in locating only the second object mentioned
F=error concerning only the central object

questions bearing on the central object are the only ones which can
reveal the subject's inability to understand the sort of relativity required in using the expressions "to the left of" and "to the right of."
Even when the child always succeeds with the questions concerning
the end objects, there is still no proof that the left-right object relationship is grasped as such. The child who correctly chooses the
right, for example, in replying to the first question of problem 3a
(*"Is the pencil to the left or to the right of the plate?"*) may be quite
satisfied with thinking in absolute terms, as if the question did not
include a second term (*"Is the pencil to the left or to the right?"*).
Whether or not the second object mentioned in the question is repeated in the subject's response, the problem remains entirely one of
whether the subject distinguishes between the expressions "to the
right" and "to the right of." He may, in fact, find it enough to leave
the second term understood since the question mentions it explicitly,
or he may just as easily mention it simply as a more or less mechanical repetition or slavish imitation of the examiner's terms—whence
the crucial nature of the two questions directly concerning the middle object, as a means of revealing the subject's ability to understand
the form of objective relativity implied in the last two questions.

A second type of error (type E of Table 45: 12 per cent of the
subjects in problem 3a and 6 per cent in problem 3b, or an average
of 9 per cent) reveals the child's lack of understanding even more

overtly. These errors consist of responding with the position of the second of the two objects compared in the question, rather than trying to locate the first one as the question requires, and adopting one or the other of the above three types of behavior when the second term of the relationship is the middle object. In problem 3a, for example, which has from left to right a block, a plate, and a pencil, the child may choose the "right" for the third and fifth questions (*"Is the block to the left or to the right of the pencil?"* and *"Is the plate to the left or to the right of the block?"*), and the left for the second and fourth (*"Is the plate to the left or to the right of the block?"* and *"Is the pencil to the left or to the right of the block?"*); but he will just as easily choose the left or the right for the other two questions (*"Is the pencil to the left or to the right of the plate?"* and *"Is the block to the left or to the right of the plate?"*) depending on the type of error which he makes in the problem concerning the central object.

The other response types (still referring to Table 45) which we note in the last two problems are much less typical of substage 1B and are more similar to the preceding stages. Some of these errors consist of simply reverting to very primitive behaviors which are based, particularly, on a simple alternation principle (type A: 2 per cent on the average), or on overt perseveration (type B: 14 per cent), when they are not purely chance repsonses (type C: 23 per cent). Besides these three response types which clearly reveal the child's inability or lack of interest, we sometimes observe a last type of behavior (type D: 8 per cent) consisting of responding correctly to all the questions in one of the last two problems, including the two questions on the middle object, but without ever being able to respond correctly to the other problem. Such behavior may be classified as failure, because we cannot discard the possibility of one chance success in a series of six questions of which only two pose any real difficulty.

STAGE 2: RELATION OF EXTERNAL OPPOSITION, BUT SUBJECTIVE ONLY

The perhaps overextensive analysis of the behavior observed in subjects at the first stage should help to reduce the amount of description in the second. Suffice it to emphasize here that the main difference between the two stages is in the disappearance of certain

categories of errors, the remaining errors being of the same nature
and probably of the same origin as in the preceding stage. The
essential advancement—and, as a matter of fact, the only advancement—concerns the questions on the localization of the left and
right of the examiner seen from the front (problem 2). Success with
these questions by stage 2 children is added to success with the
questions concerning left and right on their own bodies. In both
cases, however, it is important to note that the child's success does
not imply the ability to point out true left and right, but only the
ability to oppose the terms "left" and "right" in a consistent manner and to make, in the second problem, the reversals required in a
situation of two persons facing each other. Thus, when they are
correctly designated in the first problem (or in 96 per cent of the 113
subjects at this stage), left and right are also correct in the second
and, reciprocally, they are systematically reversed in the second
when they have been reversed in the first (or in 4 per cent of the
subjects). As we can see, as the structuring of the concepts of left and
right becomes stronger, these cases of systematic reversal become
rarer and rarer: excluding here a number of successes equal to the
number of failures in order to account for the effects of chance, the
proportion of subjects able to point out correctly their true left and
right is about 92 per cent (or 96 per cent–4 per cent), while this
proportion was 76 per cent at substage 1B and only 33 per cent at
substage 1A. Of course, the synchronism between the structuring of
the concepts of left and right on one hand and the knowledge of
real right and left on the other does not justify any conclusions about
the reciprocal dependence of these two aspects of a single general
problem; however, because the structure attained may in certain
cases still be independent of the real left and right, it is not out of
the question to suppose that the former genetically precedes the
latter and, consequently, that it may be one of its determining causes
or conditions.

In any event, considering now the more important question of
structuring, stage 2 marks a considerable advancement in the meaning of the concepts of left and right. These concepts assume, in
effect, a second type of relativity whereby they no longer depend
only on each other but also on the point of view of the person who
is considering them. The child notices, in sum, that the border
delimited by these terms is constantly changing as a function of his

own displacements and that his personal viewpoint always plays a crucial role in establishing this border. This new awareness leads him *ipso facto* to assign a completely relative value to all the potential perspectives which he discovers at the same time. Thus he understands that with an examiner seen from the front—that is, placed at a position corresponding to a complete rotation of his own body—the left and right sides become reversed with respect to his own viewpoint, and he then proceeds systematically to carry out this reversal in the second problem.

As mobile as the border separating left and right in space may be, varying constantly with the actual or imagined displacements of one's own body, it nonetheless retains a singular steadiness or rigidity. At each point of view, in effect, there is still only one possible dichotomy, so that the terms "left" and "right" retain their absolute value. Once the border separating the left and right spaces has been determined for a given perspective, the objects can be located only in one or the other of these spaces—or in neither one, when they are exactly on the border; but these objects can never be considered as located to the left of one object and to the right of another at the same time (that is, from one and the same perspective). It is precisely the relationship implied in the expressions "to the left of" and "to the right of" which is overlooked by the stage 2 child. In order to understand this relation clearly, the child would have to be able to coordinate the objects not only with the imaginary viewpoints of an observer but also with themselves. This double coordination will mark the culmination of a process of decentration of which the present stage is only the first step. In sum, in certain respects the stage 2 child is hardly different from the stage 1 child. Both exclusively adopt an observer's viewpoint in judging left and right; but, because the stage 1 child is still not at all conscious of the role played by perspective in his judgments, he depends spontaneously and exclusively on his own perspective. In stage 2, on the other hand, the child gradually becomes aware of the role which he himself plays as an observer, in his definition of left and right, and he becomes increasingly able to integrate his own point of view with other potential viewpoints. In both stages, however, the observer's viewpoint serves exclusively to define a fixed border between two complementary areas of the same global space, two areas which are so opposed to each other that the child shows no less reluctance in claiming that a single object can be to the left and to the right at the same time than he would show, for example, in thinking that an animal could be both a dog and a cat.

Thus it is this persistence in thinking in absolute terms that explains the stage 2 subject's failure with the last two problems. Because this failure is explained in the same way as was that of the stage 1 subjects (and particularly substage 1B), we find the same types of errors and in nearly the same proportions (see Table 46).

Table 46

Distribution of stage 2 subjects according to the six behavior types (A to F)* observed in problems 3a and 3b of the *Concepts of left and right* test

Problem 3a	Problem 3b						Total
	A	B	C	D	E	F	
A						3	3
B			1	6		1	8
C			5	1	1	9	16
D	1	2	5	5		7	20
E				1	2		3
F			11	9	2	41	63
Total	1	2	22	22	5	61	113

*See footnote to Table 45.

Thus, in 55 per cent of the subjects on the average (63 subjects out of 113, or 56 per cent, in problem 3a, and 61 out of 113, or 54 per cent, in problem 3b), only the middle objects are poorly located (type F): either they are grouped with the end object with which they are compared (44 per cent of the cases) or they are simply located in the middle, the subject not seeing the possibility of being more accurate (10 per cent of the cases). In order to estimate better the difference in difficulty between these questions and those which deal with the end objects—a difference which appears to be both the distinctive characteristic of behavior at this level and the key to its interpretation—we would have to add, to the first group of cases mentioned, the subjects who manage to reply correctly to all six questions of one of the problems (type D: 20 subjects out of 113 in problem 3a, and 22 out of 113 in problem 3b, or an average of 19 per cent); success with the question on the middle object would then be seen as purely fortuitous or still unstable enough to be combined with one of the types of failures already described. In sum, in nearly three quarters of the subjects (55 per cent plus 19 per cent), the errors focus on the central objects. This should be enough to show that the main difficulty met by stage 2 subjects is the coordination or synthesis of the subject-object and object-object relationships: while the former are already mastered at this level, the latter are still completely ignored, and for these subjects, left and right remain largely absolute concepts. Because the expressions "to the left of" and "to the right of" have no precise meaning, some subjects (three out of 113 in problem 3a, and five out of 113 in 3b, or an average of 4 per cent) even try to locate the second object mentioned in the question rather than the first (type E), a confusion which unequivocally reflects the real incomprehension of the relationship to be established. Finally, stage 2 also includes a certain number of perseveration or simple alternation behaviors (types A and B: 11 subjects in problem 3a, and three subjects in problem 3b, or an average of 6 per cent), as well as apparently chance responses (type C: 17 per cent of the subjects, on the average) where the errors bear equally on the end and on the middle objects. These various behaviors could not better reflect the inability of these subjects to understand the task required of them, while the concepts of left and right are nevertheless correctly used by them each time these concepts are included in a context where they could have an absolute meaning.

STAGE 3: EXTERNAL AND OBJECTIVE OPPOSITION RELATION

In the course of stages 1 and 2, the concepts of left and right have assumed two successive and distinct meanings, the second being a refinement and completion of the first. We may state that these two meanings reflect two analogous types of relativity. At first (stage 1) different from each other simply because they are based only on a relation of internal opposition, the terms "left" and "right" next (stage 2) acquire a second form of relativity which requires the intervention of the variable viewpoint of the person who is using them. Now—in the same analogical language—we may characterize stage 3 by the appearance of a last form of relativity whose main contribution is to integrate into a single system the viewpoint of the subject observer and the point of view of the objects themselves, a little as though these objects constituted a second observer whose constantly changing viewpoint had to be reconciled with the first.

In sum, at stage 3, the child for the first time becomes capable of a genuine coordination of viewpoints, the term "coordination" assuming here the strictest meaning of "co-ordination" and thus denoting a combination or synthesis of two distinct groups of relations. Despite some very misleading appearances, the second problem does not at all require this coordination of perspectives, if coordination means unification or integration of two sets of independent relations. Far from being independent of each other, the two perspectives in the second problem (that of the child and that of the examiner) belong, on the contrary, to the same family of relationships, since the partner facing opposite represents only one of the potential positions of the child himself, a position which does not change the internal spatial relations of the objects (parts of the body) to be identified. The solution thus rests only on the discovery of the type of transformation (reversal) inherent in the transition from one state (the child's position) to another (partner's position) and, more specifically, on a coordination of two potential positions or perspectives of a single observer. On the other hand, when the decision must concern the relative positions of a group of objects in a row, to be compared in pairs, the problem is quite a different one because the internal relations of the series do not have the stability of those existing between the left and right parts of the body. For each object of a series (with the obvious exception of the two end objects), the left-right relation varies constantly with the second term of the comparison—that is, with the temporary perspective attributed to the object. As long as the internal relations linking the objects refer to a fixed dichotomy (e.g., parts located on both sides of the body; two objects placed side by side on the table; etc.), the child does not necessarily need to include them in his reasoning in order to derive correct solutions. But as soon as a precise coordination is necessary each time to determine the internal relationships and as soon as this coordination differs from the one which links the object to any one of the subject's viewpoints, the child cannot correctly identify the position of each object without integrating, through a new type of operation, the spatial relations resulting from these two conditions. Thus it is by using this new operation that stage 3 subjects can correctly respond to the last two problems of the test.

Let us make clear, however, that the "new operation" just mentioned must be given only a very relative meaning. It is new in the particular context of this test on the concepts of left and right; but it is already quite familiar to the child, since it amounts to a simple multiplication of relations, an operation which is analogous, for example, to arranging leaves according to both size and gradations in color (e.g., Inhelder and Piaget, 1959), or bowls according to height and diameter, with the difference being that these asymmetrical multivalent relations—to use Piaget's terminology (1949, p. 138)—are replaced here by asymmetrical bivalent, or rather trivalent, relations. We know that for Piaget (e.g., 1941), multiplicative operations of this sort are, in principle, contemporary with additive operations. In other words, as soon as he is able to arrange a group of elements along a particular dimension (e.g., hue), the child can also achieve a more complex seriation by introducing a second dimension (e.g., size), then a third, etc., and can create a whole structure of two, three, or n dimensions. There are numerous experiments showing that these multiplicative operations form a part of the first manifestations of concrete operational thought. Conservation of continuous or discontinuous quantities, for example, is acquired by the age of seven to eight years and often, at this age, is justified by a compensation principle derived from a logical multiplication (e.g., *"It's shorter, but it's wider"*). Nearly all domains of thought include analogous examples.

But then, if the form of the operation has already been familiar to the child since the advent of concrete operational thought, it is difficult to understand why we must wait until about eleven years (or 10:11, to be exact) to see this operation being applied to the particular content represented by the projective concepts of left and right. It might be necessary to think that the coordination of viewpoints, which gives these concepts their highest form of relativity, does not really come from concrete multiplicative operations but rather from operations which have already reached the formal level. Besides the fact that in terms of chronological age it coincides with the appearance of the first signs of formal thought, this coordination of viewpoints is not unanalogous to certain coordinations and operations observed at the formal level. In the concepts of relative time, speed, and movement, for example, and also in the simple comprehension of proportions, the relativity can in fact be seen only in the coordination or fusion of two or several isolated relations into a single general system. But such a fusion—and this is what distinguishes it from multiplicative coordinations—belongs to a higher level of integration, where all the constituent elements of several systems of relations are considered simultaneously. Adopting Piaget's classical expressions, these are operations of the second power in which intellectual reflection does not bear directly on the relations between objects, but rather on the relationship between relations themselves. The coordination to be established in the present test does not reach this level of formalization. It is confined to relations of the first power (relationships between objects) to be connected with one another in the form of a simple logical intersection. If it thus proves so difficult—and, consequently, so late—to coordinate the relations linked to the observer's perspective and the relations inherent in the objects themselves, it is not that the operation in question is a formal-level operation, but merely that the existence of relations between objects is itself very slow to strike the child's attention. In fact, it can reveal itself only by virtue of a second decentration, following the first decentration which was marked by the integration of the temporary viewpoint into the group of all possible viewpoints. It is this new decentration which leads the child to consider the objects as so many virtual observers each of whom can have a right and left side. It goes without saying that the child cannot coordinate these relations with others before discovering them, and it is likely that this coordination follows very closely upon the discovery itself. Perhaps we should see here a new example of the horizontal *décalages* which are the rule at the level of concrete operations, where the particular dimensions of reality directly determine the rhythm of the appearance of various types of operations.

Thus it is the accession to this last form of relativity which characterizes stage 3. The subject at this level is then able to succeed, without error, with all the questions constituting problems 3a and 3b of the test. This essential advancement over the behavior of the preceding two stages marks the achievement (complete objectification) of the projective concepts of left and right.

The slowness which characterizes the structuring of the concepts of left and right is not surprising in itself, since it has already been demonstrated in numerous works (Piaget, 1924; Benton, 1959; Galifret-Granjon, 1960; Elkind, 1961d; etc.), to which we are only adding further confirmation. But the fact that this slowness is seen in children who already use the terms "left" and "right," or who seem to understand their meaning by the age of six or seven, raises a delicate problem. This is a fact which in any case seems quite difficult to reconcile with the hypotheses of certain theoreticians (e.g., Bruner, 1964, 1966) who seem to accord a primordial role to linguistic instruments in the origins of the corresponding operational structures. The problem of the relationship between language and operational thought is still being vehemently debated (see Sinclair, 1967, for example) and this is not the place to bring it up. However, at least in the limited and very particular case considered here, it seems clear that knowledge of the terms "left" and "right" is not very dynamic in this respect and does not strikingly influence the rhythm of development of the corresponding concepts. Rather, this rhythm seems to obey conditions which regulate the intellectual transformations implied in the normal course of development. The empirical data concerning the difficult problem of the developmental synchronisms between various operations are still rather inconclusive (see Pinard and Laurendeau, 1969), and it is probably better to reserve judgment on such a long-debated issue. It will be fruitful to touch on it later (Chapter XVII) when we present a global analysis of our results, an analysis which is centered mainly on a search for synchronisms.

Meanwhile, in conclusion, it is important to emphasize the direct and instructive relationship between the results provided by the *Concepts of left and right* test on one hand and the *Localization of topographical positions* test on the other. In the second part of the latter test (rotation of the model landscape), the constant involvement of the left-right as well as of the before-behind dimensions first produces egocentric errors before giving rise to the correct location of the various positions. If we exclude the most primitive levels (0, 1, and 2A), where the topological cues are almost the only ones guiding the subject, the last three levels (2B, 3A, and 3B) of the scale describing the development of the child's topographical representations are directly comparable to the three stages included in the development of the concepts of left and right. At the first of these three levels (substage 2B), egocentrism is so limiting that it causes the child to place the man at the same absolute position as on the model landscape (e.g., on the right side if it is on the right side on the model), in defiance even of the topological neighborhood and enclosure cues which are nevertheless quite obvious and used immediately by the youngest subjects. It is unquestionably the same egocentric attitude which keeps some children, at substage 1B in the *Concepts of left and right* test, from understanding the need to reverse the relations first established on their own bodies when they are asked to designate the parts of the partner facing them. Following this is a period of partial decentration, or simple decentration lacking coordination. This includes substage 3A of the *Localization of topographical positions* test, where the child succeeds in taking account of the landscape's rotation when topological neighborhoods and surroundings allow him to ignore one of the two projective dimensions (left-right or before-behind) and in effect spare him the necessity of coordinating two systems of projective relations. Similarly, in stage 2 of the *Concepts of left and right* test, the child achieves only the simple reversal required to locate the left and right of a person facing him. Finally, the last level in each test is characterized by the coordination of two systems of relations: coordination of the projective left-right and before-behind dimensions in the *Localization of topographical positions* test, and coordination of the left-right relations concerning both the observer's viewpoint and that of the objects themselves in the *Concepts of left and right* test. This psychological parallelism itself is accompanied—and it is here that it becomes even more instructive—by a remarkable chronological parallelism, clearly indicated in Table 47, which presents the ages of accession to the three corresponding levels of the two tests. The synchronism is not perfect, however, and includes a slight *décalage* in which each of the levels considered is consistently achieved several months earlier in the *Concepts of left and right* test than in the *Localization of topographic positions* test. This *décalage*, which increases from level to level, is obviously due to the relative difficulty of the two tests. At the third level, especially, where the *décalage* is fifteen months, it seems that the difference concerns neither the form

Table 47

Ages of accession to the three corresponding levels of the *Localization of topographical positions* and *Concepts of left and right* tests

Test	Pure egocentrism	Partial decentration	Complete decentration
Localization of topographical positions	5:4	7:2	9:8
Concepts of left and right	5:8	7:9	10:11

nor the nature of the coordinations to be established, but rather the elements involved in these coordinations. In the *Localization of topographical positions* test, in fact, the elements to be coordinated are the left-right and the before-behind relations—that is, two groups of relations which are about equally familiar to the child. On the other hand, in the *Concepts of left and right* test, not all the elements to be coordinated are accessible to the child at the same time: the first, or the left-right relations of his own perspective, have been familiar to the child at least since he has been aware of the role of the observer in using the terms "left" and "right" (stage 2), while the second relations, those inherent in the objects themselves, have not yet been discovered by the child and thus cannot be immediately coordinated with the others without a previous new effort at decentration. Thus it is particularly because this second discovery is later, and not because the synthesis of these different relations is in itself more difficult to achieve, that the ability to coordinate the two systems of relations in question seems later in the *Concepts of left and right* test than in the other. Despite this *décalage* between the two tests, the synchronism of the acquisitions is still striking and may serve to confirm the interpretations and comparisons made above, particularly as concerns the behavior reflecting egocentric attitudes. During the first stage, for example, which covers a period of twenty-two months in one of the tests *(Localization of topographical positions)* and twenty-five months in the other *(Concepts of left and right),* there is an overlap of no less than eighteen months when the behavior (successes and errors) is basically the same in both tests, as we have seen. It appears that we should see this overlap as a new confirmation of the interpretation already given to the behavior of children at these two levels. It is this interpretation, holding that the child's knowledge of reality is for a long time distorted by egocentric attitudes, which is still not accepted by those who would explain the immaturity of child thought by merely negative characteristics such as ignorance, inconsistency, chance, etc.—characteristics whose only function is to emphasize that the child is not yet an adult (see, for example, Benton, 1959). The indications provided by analysis of these last two tests are already turning out to be significant: the child's errors are not by chance and are always, at some period of development, based on an apprehension of reality which is centered exclusively on his own point of view.

Chapter XIV

Coordination of Perspectives: Presentation of the Test

The *Coordination of perspectives* test is the last to be discussed. As with the preceding tests, the first of three chapters dedicated to it is reserved for describing the experiment, and the subsequent two chapters present the analysis of the results. The presentation of the experiment begins with a brief section describing the theoretical context within which it is located; the second section consists of a detailed description of the test itself.

THEORETICAL CONTEXT

The *Coordination of perspectives* test studies the development of projective concepts. We know that, according to Piaget (see Piaget and Inhelder, 1948, *passim*), these projective concepts are slower to develop than are the topological concepts. Piaget attributes this *décalage* to the fact that in projective space, a given object is no longer considered only in itself but always in relation to an external observer, with whom it establishes perspective relationships, or to other objects with which it constitutes a complex system of relative viewpoints, each being in a projective relationship with the others and with the observer himself. Thus, in the *Coordination of perspectives* test, the subject's task obviously is not limited to observing a succession of partial perspectives, each one limited to the point of view established by one or another partial perception; it necessarily implies an integration of these partial perspectives in a general system which includes simultaneously all the relationships existing between the observer and each of the objects as well as between the objects themselves.

310

Thus the test is not unanalogous to the *Localization of topographical positions* test (see Chapters VII to X), which also goes beyond elementary topology by requiring the subject to complete the topological concepts of neighborhood with concepts of a Euclidian nature (e.g., distance, angles, etc.) and projective concepts (e.g., coordination of the before-behind and left-right dimensions when the model landscape is rotated 180 degrees). The two tests, however, do not overlap: while the *Coordination of perspectives* test is directly interested in projective space, the *Localization of topographical positions* test seeks rather to explore the relationships between the projective and the Euclidian. In effect, it requires the subject to integrate his system of perspectives and his system of coordinates into a single unit, with each of these systems depending on the other, in order to coordinate successfully the relations of order and distance, despite the reversal in perspective entailed by rotating the model landscape.

What characterizes the *Coordination of. perspectives* test is that it is designed specifically to determine the principal steps marking the progressive development of projective space. Thus it is very closely related to the *Concepts of left and right* test which has been shown (see Chapters XI to XIII) to explore the subject's ability to distinguish and objectify the left and right relations—an ability which is related to one of the most fundamental aspects of projective space. But it differs from this test especially in that it requires the subject to manipulate two dimensions at once (left-right and before-behind) by a logical multiplication which is even more direct and obvious than in the coordination of perspectives necessary for the objectification of left and right. Similarly, the *Coordination of perspectives* is related to the *Construction of a projective straight line,* the analysis of which occupied three earlier chapters (Chapters V to VII), as well as to various tests (not replicated here) designed by Piaget and Inhelder (1948) to study the child's ability to imagine an object in perspective (e.g., projection of shadows, development of volumes, etc.). Despite these obvious similarities, however, these other tests differ from the present one in that they require only simple representation or coordination activities concerning a single object successively placed in various positions with respect to a single observer. The *Coordination of perspectives* test, on the contrary, requires coordinating several objects in relation to a single observer occupying several successive positions, or to several observers placed in different locations. It requires him also to coordinate the relative positions of several objects among themselves and of each of these objects in relation to a mobile observer (or several immobile, but variously located, observers). As Piaget notes in describing his test, this difference implies systematizing the projective left-right, before-behind, etc., relations with respect to an observer without the randomness which characterizes the use of such concepts in purely topological contexts as, for example, when it is a question of differentiating the two directions of a linear sequence. Furthermore, this difference requires that a general system be constructed to include the numerous possible viewpoints, precisely because the coordinations to be made concern several objects and several imaginary observers simultaneously.

However, if we refer to the results obtained by Piaget, who has expressly noted their apparent contradiction, success with tests that require the coordination of perspectives seems to appear no later than success with tests of simple representation of the various perspectives or projections inherent in a single object. We might ask why the child has so much difficulty in imagining or reconstructing the perspective of an isolated object placed in front of him, when the difficulty of a test that requires him to coordinate the projective relations linking several objects arises precisely from the fact that the child cannot disengage himself from his immediate egocentric perspective. The apparent contradiction would, according to Piaget, be explained by the child's inability to recognize the many possible points of view in the two situations. This lack of differentiation would be just as distorting in the case of an isolated object to be imagined in perspective or in projection as in the case of numerous objects to be coordinated with a mobile observer. According to Piaget, true representation is not a process of simply stating an empirical or perceptual finding; it includes an activity of anticipation or of mental reconstruction. Thus the representation of a simple or complex perspective would not be a phenomenon of purely perceptual centration, always related to a particular point of view; it would necessarily require an awareness of one's own point of view and, consequently, of the other potential viewpoints—which is the same as saying that the representation of any perspective, whatever it may be, implies creating a general system which coordinates all perspectives.

It is this complexity which also explains why, in the domain of perspective or projection as in many other areas, the concept or representation is much slower to develop than is the corresponding perception. Piaget mentions more than once the paradox of the child being very late in mastering the rudimentary concepts of perspective while, on the other hand, the perceptual egocentrism where perspective intervenes very early and always follows the subject's own point of view does not seem to favor the advent of the first concepts of perspective or of projection, which themselves are egocentric. This paradox would be due to the fact that perceptual or conceptual egocentrism presumes, by definition, a lack of differentiation of viewpoints. It presumes also that any awareness of one's own point of view presupposes the simultaneous awareness of different points of view. This requires the development of a total system where all possible viewpoints are coordinated, a total system which is inaccessible to perceptual activity and to egocentric concepts.

DESCRIPTION OF THE TEST

The experimental apparatus (Figure 17) consists of a plain green cardboard square (52 cm. on a side), on which three colored paper cones representing a group of mountains (or a group of tents, etc.) are placed. The square base is made of four smaller pieces of equal size (26 cm. on a side) bound together by strips of canvas, and the cross formed by these two lines can serve as a reference point for the subject wishing to estimate the degree of overlap of the mountains. The three paper cones are different in color and size and are placed at fixed positions on the board. The largest, a red cone, has a 20 cm. base diameter and is 11.5 cm. high; the middle-sized cone is blue and has a 14 cm. base diameter and a height of 7.5 cm.; finally, the smallest cone, colored yellow, has a base diameter of 9 cm. and is 5 cm. high. The material also includes (see Figure 18) a set of nine sketched scenes (18 x 14 cm. each) which reproduce nine different perspectives in miniature; two of these, however (pictures H and I), are in fact impossible, given the actual positions of the mountains.

At the beginning of the test, the subject faces the examiner so that he can see the blue mountain at his left and the yellow mountain at

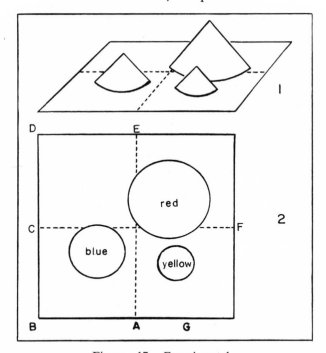

Figure 17. Experimental material used in the *Coordination of perspectives* test. The three cones are seen from the front in 1 and from above in 2. The letters indicate the positions at which the little man is successively placed (F, C, B) and the various perspectives corresponding to pictures A, B, C, D, E, F, G reproduced in Figure 18.

his right in front of the red mountain (see Figure 17, position A). The examiner shows the subject a toy man (about 3 cm. high) and explains that this man is going for a walk around the three mountains and is going to stop at various places to take pictures. The examiner then explains that the subject's task is to recognize, among several pictures representing various views of the setup, the one which corresponds to the man's view each time. As an example, he places the man on position A, directly in front of the subject, and

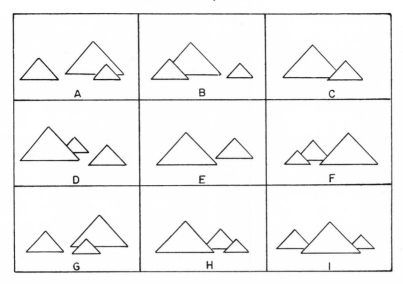

Figure 18. The set of nine pictures, showing various perspectives, which the subject chooses from in the *Coordination of perspectives* test.

asks him to choose which of the two pictures A and D corresponds to the photographer's view. The subject is usually able to identify the correct picture because, in this example, his own point of view and that of the man happen to coincide. But whether the response is correct or incorrect, the examiner does not go on to the test itself before first explaining to the subject why picture A should be chosen and picture D rejected. He emphasizes the fact that only picture A, and not picture D, conserves the same left-right and before-behind relations, with respect to the little man, as on the board itself, which encourages the subject who is able to do so to use the same terms when he justifies his choices during the test. The detailed instructions are given in the Appendix. The test itself includes two parts.

FIRST PART

In the first part, the examiner places the little man successively at positions F, C, and B (see Figure 17) and the subject's task is to find, from among five different alternative pictures, the one which seems to correspond exactly to the little man's perspective. The subject must then justify his choice and also explain why he rejected each of the other pictures. The number of explanations required of him may appear to be excessive and may discourage some children; but we can hardly reduce it since evaluation of the responses must consider not only the accuracy or inaccuracy of the child's choice, but also (and particularly) the nature and diversity of the projective relations on which his choice was based. For this reason it is helpful repeatedly to give the subject the chance to use the many relations defining the particular perspective represented by each picture. Thus, the reasons alleged to justify the rejection of some pictures are just as instructive as those on which the subject bases his initial choice.

In this first part, the relative difficulty of the problems and the precision of the observations permitted by the experiment depend equally on the variety of pictures offered for the subject's choice and on the particular position occupied by the little man. For this reason, in each of the three problems in this section, the five alternative pictures represent variously attractive perspectives depending on the level of intellectual decentration attained by the subject. In *problem F,* for example, two of the pictures presented with the correct picture (F) give an egocentric view of the layout: picture A exactly reproduces the point of view of the subject (stationed at A) and picture G is still basically egocentric since it represents the view seen by the subject when, forgetful of the strict instructions, he leans slightly toward the little man (at F) in order to try to see the same thing as he does. On the other hand, in order to locate the cases where the subject's intellectual decentration is still limited to certain partial aspects of the man's view, the examiner also suggests picture H, in which the blue mountain is behind and between the other two, as in the correct picture (F), but with the difference that the yellow mountain is to the right and the red mountain is to the left. Thus picture H does not correspond to any possible perspective, but the fact that it is essentially the mirror image of picture F may easily confuse the subject whose attention is focused only on the projective before-behind relations. Finally, picture D completes the choices offered to the child. It presents a perspective which is possible but which is doubly incorrect with respect to picture F, since it contradicts both its left-right and its before-behind relations. The subject who chooses picture D thus gives clear proof of total incomprehension (or of randomness), and the subject who rejects it, on the contrary, is naturally led to mention expressly all the projective relations which have determined his choice. Similarly, in the second problem (*problem C*), the choice offered to the subject includes two pictures (A and B) of an egocentric nature, one picture (E) where only the before-behind relations are reversed, and finally a picture (F) where all the projective relations are reversed and where, consequently, the yellow mountain itself is visible.

Before presenting the third problem (*problem B*), the examiner asks the subject, stationed at A up to this point, to move to E and to bend down so that he can see the same view as the little man (*"Make yourself very small like the little man and tell me what you see,"* etc.). Thus the subject can see, if he has not already grasped it, that the possible viewpoints can differ radically and that a small mountain can even disappear completely behind a larger one. The examiner refrains from any verbal commentary, regardless of the subject's remarks, and then presents him with problem B. This change in perspective is intended to test the resistance of the child's egocentric attitudes. Thus two of the alternative pictures (pictures E and D) present perspectives which are egocentric, but which differ from each other depending on whether the subject remains totally immobile in the position assigned to him or leans slightly toward the little man. Picture A is also retained because it reproduces the subject's earlier egocentric perspective, a perspective which some subjects may continue to see as the only correct one. Finally, with the correct picture (B), picture I completes the choices offered to the subject. The composition of this last picture (red mountain in the foreground as in E, blue mountain to the left and yellow mountain to the right as in A) may thus induce simultaneously the two egocentric viewpoints which correspond to the two positions successively occupied by the subject.

Probably it would have been possible to make further use of this multiple-choice method. In the first problem, for example, picture H reverses the left-right relations without touching the before-behind relations; but none of the pictures shows the converse (e.g., blue mountain in the foreground with the red mountain to the right and the yellow mountain to the left). Similarly, in the second problem, picture E conserves the left-right relations by reversing only the before-behind relations, but the converse is not suggested to the subject (e.g., blue mountain to the left in the foreground). Finally, in the last problem the four incorrect alternative pictures include a predominant element of egocentrism, so that the inter-mediate reactions between absolute egocentrism and complete de-centration can scarcely appear. Moreover, success with this last problem may be partially explained by factors foreign to intellectual decentration itself. Picture B in effect gives the perspective seen from a position next to the one occupied by the subject during the pre-ceding two problems and, among the five pictures suggested, it is the only one which does not include a gross egocentric error. For this reason the selection of the correct picture in this problem may be facilitated by the subject's remembering a previously perceived arrangement, or it may be the result of a simple process of elimina-tion available to the subject who has begun to free himself from his egocentrism. In sum, although the errors with this problem unequiv-ocally reflect a genuinely egocentric attitude, we should not see success with it as positive proof of the child's ability to reconstruct by anticipation or to imagine objectively all of the projective rela-tions seen by the little man.

Thus the method adopted in this first part of the test is a com-promise. By reducing the number of problems and of alternative pictures (absurd or possible), we are probably losing some additional information which might be useful; but we are also reducing the length of a test which has already been judged to be too long and too monotonous by the youngest subjects and, by the same token, we discourage responses induced by chance or randomness in subjects whose field of attention is naturally quite limited. This is why, rather than trying to determine the importance given by the child in each problem to the two projective dimensions which he is to coordinate, it is more profitable to use the problems to analyze the objectification of the left-right relations (problem 1) and before-behind relations (problem 2), and to reserve the last problem for the more intensive examination of egocentric resistances.

SECOND PART

In the second part of the test, the subject's task is essentially the same as in the first; but, rather than having to recognize the picture showing the view from one or another of the little man's positions, the subject must instead select the position which the man would have to occupy in order to see each of the views which the examiner presents. As in the first part, he must justify his response each time.

This part of the test includes five problems.[1] The subject is first returned to his original position at A and the examiner shows him successively pictures C, F, B, E, and I, asking him each time to place the man in the position that corresponds to the perspective illustrated in the picture. The first four pictures give actual views whereas the last one is an impossibility, the red mountain being shown in the foreground with the blue mountain to the left and the yellow mountain to the right. This insoluble problem, presented immediately after four ordinary problems, is probably enough to discourage the subject; but it is very useful in that it permits us to determine whether the subject really considers and coordinates all the necessary projective relations. The problems of this second part were chosen to control for the quality of the responses in the first part. This is why the first three pictures (C, F, and B) presented to the subject correspond exactly to the three positions occupied by the man in the preceding section. The fourth picture (E) gives a point of view which had already been perceived earlier by the subject. Finally, the fifth picture (I), which does not correspond to any possible perspective, is meant to single out the cleverest subjects, who are able to see its absurdity and thus are able to consider the projective left-right and before-behind relations simultaneously.

As a whole, then, the test replicates the main point of the one designed by Piaget and Inhelder. The material used here is obviously much simpler and more schematized. The dimensions of the apparatus are reduced by half and the composition of the miniature group of mountains is spare and simple, in contrast to the complexity of the model used by Piaget and Inhelder. Their three mountains were distinguished from each other not only by color and height (10 to 30 cm.), but also by their variety of shapes and by a set of geographical reference points (e.g., river, path, snow-capped peak, house, cross, etc.) whose presence could sometimes facilitate the solutions. In this respect, the arrangement described here is

[1] In fact, the test used in the experiment included a sixth problem which we had to exclude from the analysis. The picture presented to the subject was intended to reproduce the three mountains seen from a point located somewhere between position E and the corner closest to the red mountain. Several subjects questioned the possibility of such a perspective, claiming (not without some reason) that the size and proximity of the red mountain would have to hide at least one of the two other smaller mountains from the little man.

much more similar to that of Vinh-Bang[2] in his standardization, which uses three simple miniature objects (a tower, a tree, and a house) selected so that their appearance does not vary appreciably regardless of where they are viewed from.

As concerns the questioning itself, only the first two of the three techniques used by Piaget and Inhelder were retained. In the third, the subject had to reconstruct effectively the man's perspective using cardboard cut in the shape of mountains and given to him for this task. After some preliminary tests, it was decided to discard this third technique, which was too difficult for the children, which they very soon lost interest in, and whose results lend themselves to objective scoring only with great difficulty.

[2] Personal communication.

Chapter XV

Coordination of Perspectives: General Analysis of the Results

The analysis of the results of the *Coordination of perspectives* test covers two chapters. The first is devoted to the comparative study of the problems, with no systematic reference to the individual protocols. The second chapter is an analysis by stages, derived from the earlier analysis, and distributes the protocols into a series of stages describing the gradual objectification of the child's projective representations.

As in the *Localization of topographical positions* test, with which the *Coordination of perspectives* test is naturally compared, the general analysis of the problems includes two parts dealing with successes and errors respectively.

ANALYSIS OF SUCCESSES

In the first section of the test, a problem is solved when the subject selects the picture corresponding to the little man's perspective and rejects all the others. In the second section, the first four problems are all considered solved when the subject locates the man at the position exactly corresponding to the perspective reproduced in the picture given to him, or at least places him at a position which is close enough to the correct position so that the man's perspective does not differ appreciably from that represented in the picture. In the fifth problem, the solution is obviously the discovery of the impossibility of locating the man at a position that corresponds to the perspective presented in the picture.

Table 48 gives the number of successes by problem and by age

Table 48

Number of successes at each age level and for each problem in the two sections of the *Coordination of perspectives* test

Age	N	Section 1			Section 2				
		F	C	B	C	F	B	E	I
12:0	50	35	25	32	34	39	28	13	13
11:0	50	26	24	26	28	34	32	33	7
10:0	50	24	11	19	23	31	23	25	4
9:0	50	19	15	18	23	22	17	17	4
8:0	50	12	4	10	13	21	11	21	1
7:0	50	10	5	10	7	16	14	16	0
6:0	50	3	2	5	10	10	2	13	0
5:0	48	4	4	5	5	3	2	1	0
4:6	50	1	3	4	4	3	1	4	0
Total	448	134	93	129	147	179	130	161	29

level. Table 49 gives the results of the McNemar test applied to the differences in difficulty between all the problems compared two at a time. We see from these results that in the first section positions F and B are equally difficult, but that both are significantly easier than position C. The problems of the second section increase from easiest to most difficult in the order F, E, C, B, I. In this series, if we exclude problem I, which is more difficult than the others, we note that not one of the problems differs significantly from its immediate neighbor but that all other differences are significant. And comparing the two sections, we note first that problem I is clearly more difficult than the others but that the second section is generally

Table 49

Results of the McNemar test (X^2 values) applied to the differences between each of the problems of the *Coordination of perspectives* test (N=448)

	Section 1			Section 2				
	F	C	B	C	F	B	E	I
Section 1								
F		16.84*	0.17	1.11	18.43*	0.07	3.58	97.44*
C			10.81*	24.64*	57.34*	11.26*	27.56*	47.25*
B				1.60	20.00*	0.00	4.92*	86.20*
Section 2								
C					7.75*	2.04	0.49	105.48*
F						17.58*	3.15	142.31*
B							4.53*	90.09*
E								116.87*
I								

*Significant at least at the .05 level.

easier than the first. We note in particular that problems F and C are significantly more difficult in the first section than in the second, that problem B is equally difficult in both sections and that problem C of the first section is significantly more difficult than all the problems of the second section (obviously excluding problem I). Finally, the correlations (Table 50) between the problems are all positive and significant. We see that it is problem I, by far the most difficult in the whole test, which naturally yields the highest correlations. The weakest correlations, on the other hand, concern problem E, the only problem in which the correct response requires selecting a

Table 50

Phi coefficients between problems in the *Coordination of perspectives* test (N=448)

	Section 1			Section 2				
	F	C	B	C	F	B	E	I
Section 1								
F		.588	.516	.352	.627	.398	.351	.814
C	.588		.478	.516	.628	.405	.341	.569
B	.516	.478		.422	.541	.423	.280	.633
Section 2								
C	.352	.516	.422		.470	.385	.190	.646
F	.627	.628	.541	.470		.471	.374	.880
B	.398	.405	.423	.385	.471		.263	.745
E	.351	.341	.280	.190	.374	.263		.716
I	.814	.569	.633	.646	.880	.745	.716	

position which has already been occupied by the subject himself.

The most interesting fact among all the results concerns the *décalage* in the difficulty of the two sections of the test. This *décalage* appears especially clearly when, in order to objectify the comparisons, we consider the particular case of problems F, C, and B, which are repeated in both sections. We have just seen that while problem B is equally difficult in both sections, both problems F and C are more often solved in the second section than in the first. In order to explain the relative ease of the second section, we could suggest first a learning or habituation factor. There is no doubt that the first part of the test gives the subject the chance to familiarize himself with the task or the material, and that this experience may to a certain extent facilitate the solution of the second part. In particular, the fact that the subject must shift his own position in the last problem of the first part certainly helps to warn him of the diversity of possible viewpoints. It is also interesting that it is precisely in this last problem that we find no *décalage* in difficulty between the two parts. From the time the subject is given the chance to change his position, he may force himself to adopt a more objective attitude and to conserve it during the rest of the examination.

The learning factor, however, is not the only nor the most important one. The relative ease of the second section may also be related to the fact that choosing the position that corresponds to the picture is possible for the subject who is satisfied with considering only certain partial or dominant aspects of the projective relations concerned. In order to find the position that corresponds to picture F, for example, the subject must be aware only of the fact that the blue mountain must be located behind the other two. In the first section, on the contrary, identification of the correct picture requires (in principle) the simultaneous consideration of the left-right and before-behind relations since, among the alternative pictures, he can always find two that have the same partial dominant characteristics. Thus the solution of the same problem F requires, in the first section, the elimination of picture H in which the blue mountain is located behind the other two mountains, exactly as in picture F. The subject who relies solely on this partial characteristic will indiscriminately choose picture H or picture F, or he may expressly state that the two are equivalent.

In support of this interpretation, we can first point out that the last problem of the second section (problem I) was shown to be the most difficult of all and was solved by only 6 per cent of the subjects (29 out of 448). This massive failure is undoubtedly the result of the specious nature of the problem. Not only does the picture present a concretely impossible perspective, but it is placed at the end of a series of ordinary problems, and the subject has not been warned in any way that the pictures presented to him may not correspond to any actual perspective. This traplike aspect surely exerts a considerable influence, but we must still try to determine its scope. In any case, it is hardly likely that the subject who is careful each time to determine all of the projective relations concerned would be led, by simple perseveration or submission to the instructions, to designate a position which (hypothetically) he knows to correspond only partially to the picture presented to him. On the other hand, the subject who is used to considering only part of the relations implied in each new perspective may very well persist in this same attitude when he is presented with picture I, whose very absurdity precludes any possibility of selecting the correct position by the subject who considers all the relations. In sum, assuming that at any moment during the investigation the subject turns to certain dominant relations in order to solve the problems, we can easily explain the special difficulty of the last problem of the second section: partial consideration of the projective relations may be enough for the solution of the other problems of this section, but it can lead only to a wrong choice in response to picture I.

This interpretation, holding that the greater ease of the second section is due to the still partial nature of the decentrations effected by the subject, is further supported when we make the same comparison between the two sections but this time add, to the successes of the first section, all the responses in which the picture accepted by the child is more or less consistent with a dominant partial relation (e.g., left-right, before-behind). This is the case with pictures H, E, and A for problems F, C, and B respectively. The comparison of the results obtained with these problems, after this extension of the successes of the first section (Table 51), shows that the difference

Table 51

Relationship between successes and errors in the two sections of the *Coordination of perspectives* test when the criterion for success in the first section is extended*

Section 1	Section 2					
	Position F		Position C		Position B	
	+	−	+	−	+	−
+	117	47	101	66	91	104
−	62	222	46	235	39	214

*So that even at least partially decentrated responses are considered as successes.

in difficulty between the two sections is not significant in the case of problems F and C (McNemar test: .01 level) and that, on the contrary, it becomes significant in the case of problem B, which is now easier in the first than in the second section. We see also that the correlation between the two sections remains high and significant, since the phi coefficients calculated from these new results are .523 for problem F, .501 for problem C, and .470 for problem B. In the first part, then, judging all responses that reflect at least a partial decentration of the subject's own perspective to be correct is enough to cause the differences in difficulty between the two sections to disappear, at least with respect to problems F and C. These results are easily understood if we admit that the identification of positions corresponding to the perspective reproduced in these two pictures (the task in the second section) requires no more than one partial decentration, while the correct identification of the pictures giving the perspective of the man placed in these same positions (task in the first section) requires, in principle, that the multiple relations defining each perspective be considered simultaneously. And it is not impossible—as we may see in the examination of the individual protocols giving the subjects' justifications for accepting or rejecting the different pictures—that some subjects may arrive at the correct solution by relying on only partial relations; these successes, however, can be no more than chance occurrences.

If this explanation seems reasonable in the case of positions F and C, how then can we interpret the fact that problem B is equally difficult in both sections (29 per cent of the successes: Table 48) and becomes appreciably easier in the first than in the second (44 per cent versus 29 per cent: Table 51) as soon as we add the responses consisting of choosing picture A, whose composition does not radically differ from that of picture B, to the correct responses of the first section? This apparent contradiction vanishes as soon as we examine the position of the subject when this particular problem is given to him. We know that the subject is moved from A to E for this last problem of the first section. Now, among the five pictures open to his choice (pictures A, B, E, D, and I), three include a dominant characteristic overtly conforming to the subject's new egocentric perspective (i.e., pictures E, D, and I in which the red mountain is in the foreground). These pictures are quickly eliminated when the subject is capable of a minimum of decentration. Of the two remaining pictures (A and B), picture A itself is easily rejected by the subject who is able to remember the view which he had when he was sitting at A. In effect, picture B alone is appropriate for the subject who wishes to avoid choosing a picture representing a perspective which is at present or was previously egocentric. This is why problem B is equally difficult in both sections when the correct solution, in the first section, is limited to the choice of the correct picture. While the same limitation, in problems F and C, removes a part of the responses based on still-partial decentrations, it is not so in problem B, where any decentration, total or partial, can naturally produce the correct response, as in the second section. This is also why problem B becomes easier in the first than in the second section when we add the responses of selecting picture A to the correct responses of the first section, under the assumption that this picture is easily assimilable to picture B for a subject who depends on partial and dominant relations. This addition in fact facilitates the problem; but there is no proof that the choice of picture A reflects an authentic partial decentration comparable to the one which, in problems F and C, could cause subjects to select the pictures that reproduce only some of the dominant partial relations. Since the subject has already been stationed at A, the choice of this picture could in fact derive from a sort of pseudo decentration or a decentration a posteriori, whereby the subject relies much more on a memory reconstruction or on the recognition of a previously perceived perspective than on a real anticipation of a perspective which has been unknown to him until now. It is even possible that the choice of this picture results from a still more primitive and overtly egocentric attitude, according to which some subjects would be led to think that this perspective, already seen from the position occupied earlier, is the only perspective which is visible from whatever position the man occupies. In brief, the *décalage* observed between the two sections in the difficulty of problem B would reflect only the heterogeneity of the children's strategies.

In conclusion, the relative ease of the second section would be due above all to the quality of the intellectual processes engaged in the solution of each of these two types of problems. This interpretation relies mainly on the two groups of facts just discussed: the first concerns the relatively great difficulty of the last problem of the second section (problem I), and the second relates to the leveling of the difficulties following the extension of the criteria applied to the evaluation of responses in the first section. The learning or habituation factors, also used in explaining the same phenomenon, could have only a secondary effect. In fact, it is difficult to see how, in such a short and homogeneous test, the intervention of these factors could entail such a marked general *décalage* between the two sections without similarly affecting some specific problems such as problems B and I.

ANALYSIS OF ERRORS

The analysis of errors gives further confirmation to the preceding interpretations. Such an analysis, however, must be limited to the errors committed in the first three problems of the first section of the test. The diversity of the responses given to each of the problems in the second part is so great that it is impossible to classify them in any really useful manner—that is, to create a limited number of behavioral categories which are homogeneous enough to guarantee the identity of the corresponding strategies. In spite of these limitations, it is still very instructive to determine, for each of the three problems of the first section, the frequency with which the different alternative pictures are selected by subjects at each age level.

PROBLEM C

Beginning with the second problem (position C), in which the results seem to be clearest (see Table 52, first section), we note that the median ages that correspond to the distribution of each response group progress in an order which entirely confirms the above interpretations. The choice of the correct picture (column C), which in principle requires the consideration of all the necessary projective relations, is preferred by the oldest subjects. The following level (column E/CE), in which the chronological distribution differs significantly from that of the preceding level (at the .01 level: Kolmogorov-Smirnov test), includes the subjects who are led by a still-partial decentration either to choose picture E, in which only part of the projective relations to be considered are reproduced, or to judge pictures C and E to be equivalent since the relation which they consider essential (i.e., the disappearance of the yellow house) is respected in both cases. After this comes the group of typically egocentric responses (column A/B/AB) which are reflected either in choosing a picture that reproduces the subject's own view (picture A or picture B, depending on whether the subject scrupulously stays at the position assigned to him or whether he leans slightly toward the little man in order to see the same thing), or in judging the two pictures to be equivalent. The difference between this level and the preceding one is significant (at the .025 level). Finally, the last level ("Others" column) combines the behaviors consisting either of making incoherent choices (e.g., choosing two or three pictures which

Table 52

Distribution by age level of all responses* to the second problem (position C) of the first section of the *Coordination of perspectives* test

Age	N	Original data					First readjustment					Second readjustment — Justified response				Second readjustment — Unjustified response			
		C	E/CE	F	A/B/AB	Others	C_c	C_p/E/CE	F	A/B/AB	Others	C_c	C_p/E/CE	F	A/B/AB	C_p/E/CE	F	A/B/AB	Others
12:0	50	25	11	1	13		24	12	1	13		24	12	1	12			1	
11:0	50	24	9		16	1	20	13		16	1	20	13	1	16				1
10:0	50	11	13	1	25		10	14	1	25		10	14		25				
9:0	50	15	13	1	21		12	16	1	21		12	15	1	20	1		1	
8:0	50	4	3	4	34	5	2	5	4	34	5	2	5	4	31			3	5
7:0	50	5	10	1	31	3	2	13	1	31	3	2	10	1	29	3		2	3
6:0	50	2	6	3	19	20		8	3	19	20		4		17	4	3	2	20
5:0	48	4	5	2	11	26		9	2	11	26		4		4	5	2	7	26
4:0	50	3	4	3	10	30		7	3	10	30		3		1	4	3	9	30
Total 448		93	74	16	180	85	70	97	16	180	85	70	80	8	155	17	8	25	85
Median age		10:7	9:2 (6:6)	8:1	5:0		10:11	8:11 (6:6)	8:1	5:0		10:11	9:5 (8:3)	8:4	8:4	(5:5)	(5:0)	(5:10)	5:0

*The responses are identified by the usual letters (the / indicates *or*) designating the pictures chosen by the subject: e.g., A/B/AB means that the subject chose picture A, or B, or A and B indiscriminately. C_c=choice of picture C while mentioning the complete relations; C_p=choice of picture C while mentioning only the partial relations.

really have nothing in common), or of categorically refusing to make a choice. The fifth response group (exclusive choice of picture F) is really too thinly scattered to make it possible to give some meaning to the median age of the corresponding distribution. This same infrequency is reassuring as to the authenticity of the other response groups, since picture F, giving a perspective which is diametrically opposed to that of the correct picture, was intended to serve precisely as a control by helping us to recognize purely random responses. If we combine the two columns F and "Others" into a single distribution in order to compare it to the distribution of the preceding level, the difference is clearly significant (at the .01 level).

The responses to problem C are thus divided into four very distinct types which we can consider as four levels of development. There is no doubt about the existence of behavior based on partial decentration activities (choice of picture E), and the evidence indicates that these responses come earlier than the correct responses. It would probably be unfair to conclude, on one hand, that the choice of the correct picture invariably reflects the effect of complete decentration or, on the other hand, that the choice of picture E is the only one to reveal the inadequacy of this decentration. If it is in fact possible for some children to be led to select picture E because they recognize in it the presence of a dominant partial relation, it is quite probable that other children may choose the correct picture for the same reason. In fact, examination of the protocols indicates that of the 93 subjects who chose picture C (correct response), 23 could be classified with the 74 subjects at the intermediate level, since eight of these 23 subjects did not justify their responses at all and the other 15 did not justify them adequately, merely mentioning the disappearance of the yellow mountain. All of the other subjects also referred to the partial overlap of the red mountain by the blue one and saw this as an indication of relative distance. The second section of Table 52 gives the results of this readjustment by distinguishing the cases where the justification mentions the complete relations (C_c) from cases where it mentions at most the partial relations (C_p). The median ages of the first two groups of subjects are slightly modified by this readjustment. The sequence of the levels is not upset, but the difference between columns $C_p/E/CE$ and $A/B/AB$ ceases to be significant. Finally, the third section of the same table gives the results of a second readjustment which excludes from every level the subjects who did not justify their choices. The ages reported in the first part of this third section show that the responses based on complete decentration are given by the oldest subjects (10:11 years), the egocentric responses by the youngest (8:4 years), and the intermediate-level responses by the subjects of intermediate age (9:5 years). The differences between these three distributions are significant (at the .01 level between columns C_c and $C_p/E/CE$ and at the .025 level between columns $C_p/E/CE$ and $A/B/AB$).

The only question worth discussing at the moment concerns the quality of the responses given by subjects of intermediate age. In principle, we should expect pictures C and E to be about equally attractive to the subjects at this level, unless we could show that these subjects' choices are systematically influenced by certain characteristics of these pictures. Examination of the protocols indicates that of the 80 subjects at this level who justified their choices, 17 considered pictures C and E to be equivalent, 48 chose picture E, and only 15 chose picture C. According to these results, it seems obvious that the intermediate-level children have a marked preference for picture E. The main reason for this preference was expressly given by 39 of these 48 subjects and, against all expectations, this reason depends precisely on the fact that in picture E, as in the little man's perspective, the blue and the red mountains do not overlap. As paradoxical as that may be, the absence of overlap seems justified to them because, in their eyes, *"the man is supposed to see the whole red mountain where he is standing,"* or because *"on the board, there is a space between the red mountain and the blue one, so there must be one in the picture, too."* At first glance, these preoccupations may appear to be legitimate, especially when they emphasize the man's need to see the red mountain in its entirety. The actual overlap is in fact not very great and depends mainly on the examiner's accuracy in placing the little man on the board. In at least some cases, therefore, the child's response may conform to reality. It is nevertheless true that all these children ignore the projective before-behind relation, symbolized in picture C by the very overlap whose accuracy they question, and that they accept the perspective in picture E, where the red mountain, contrary to the actual situation, is in the foreground. This, it seems, amply justifies placing these subjects at the intermediate level. But there is more to say. If some verbal expressions suggest a vague concern with accuracy, there are even more which indicate more clearly that in fact the real interest is in finding in the picture the equivalent of the distance perceived between the red and the blue mountains on the board (this is the case with 26 of the 39 subjects who expressly opposed the overlap of the mountains). The following two cases are clear examples.

48 (11:0): *"They* [i.e., the red and blue mountains] *are stuck together and, here* [pointing to the space between the two mountains on the board], *there is a little space."*

49 (9:0): *"The line is clear in the middle* [i.e., the area between the two mountains on the board is open] *and, here in the picture, the blue one 'enters' the red one a little."*

These children consider the partial overlap of the two mountains as an index of undue proximity, because it is contrary to their own perspective. Thus we see how the subject's real efforts toward decentration may be countered by persistent egocentric attitudes, attitudes which clearly characterize intermediate-level behavior.

In summary, in order to outline the most important points of the preceding discussion, we can divide all 150 subjects who chose pictures C or E (column C_c and column $C_p/E/CE$ of Table 52, third section) into two main groups depending on the justifications which they offered. The first group (41 subjects) includes those whose attention is focused exclusively on the most striking of the projective relations in these two pictures (the absence of the yellow mountain, or rather its disappearance behind the blue one). Within this group, however, the subjects show no specific preference for either of these two pictures because the group includes not only the 17 subjects who expressly stated the equivalence of pictures C and E, but also 15 subjects who chose picture C and nine who chose picture E. The second group (109 subjects) includes the subjects who not only rely on the disappearance of the yellow mountain, but also emphasize the major difference between the two pictures (the presence or absence of overlap of the blue mountain over the red one). However, within this latter group, two consistent tendencies appear in the interpretations which the subjects give to this overlap. The 70 subjects who chose picture C rightly saw in it an indication of the relative distance separating the two mountains from the observer.

Conversely, all 39 subjects of this same group who selected picture E ignored this essential aspect and rejected picture C precisely because of this overlap, claiming that such an overlap either suggests that the mountains are too close to each other or involves an unacceptable limitation of the view which the observer is supposed to have of the mountain. In other words, the preference accorded picture E by these latter subjects unquestionably reflects egocentric preoccupations. As for the problem of whether we should attribute these egocentric attitudes to an incomprehension of graphic symbolism or whether we should, on the contrary, see this incomprehension as the result of egocentric attitudes, the question remains open, and it would seem rather presumptuous to attempt to untangle this inextricable web in which causes and effects are in constant interaction.

PROBLEM F

The analysis of the results of problem F (see Table 53) leads to nearly the same conclusions. Beginning with the raw data (first section of the table), we note that the median age of the subjects who choose the correct pictures (column F), when this identification presumably requires a total decentration of the projective relations concerned, is higher (significant difference at the .01 level: Kolmogorov-Smirnov test) than that of subjects for whom the choice is still influenced by egocentric considerations (choosing picture A or G or both indiscriminately), and these latter subjects are much older (significant difference at the .01 level) than those whose responses ("Others" column) correspond to incoherent and purely chance choices or who consistently reject all the pictures presented to them. Thus the different response levels in problem F can be arranged in a sequence similar to that of problem C, with the exception that the category of responses which had been considered as intermediate between total decentration and pure egocentrism (column H/FH) is not located at an intermediate age between the two extreme categories in problem F, as was the corresponding category (column E/CE of Table 52) in problem C. We find, in fact, that the median age of subjects who chose picture H, or who considered pictures F and H to be equivalent, is slightly lower than that of subjects whose responses are clearly egocentric, even though the difference between the two is not significant. Must we then reject the earlier interpretations stating that the choice of picture H is dictated by a partial

Table 53

Distribution by age level of all responses* to the first problem (position F) of the first section of the *Coordination of perspectives* test

Age	Original data						First readjustment					Second readjustment							
												Justified response				Unjustified response			
	N	F	H/FH	D	A/G/AG	Others	Fc	Fp/H/FH	D	A/G/AG	Others	Fc	Fp/H/FH	D	A/G/AG	Fp/H/FH	D	A/G/AG	Others
12:0	50	35	1		14		27	9		14		27	9		12			2	
11:0	50	26	1		22	1	22	5		22	1	22	5		22				1
10:0	50	24	2		24		22	4		24		22	4		24				
9:0	50	19	5		25	1	14	10		25	1	14	10		23			2	1
8:0	50	12	4	1	28	5	10	6	1	28	5	10	6		26		1	2	5
7:0	50	10	8	1	28	3	4	14	1	28	3	4	10		26	4	1	2	3
6:0	50	3	3		26	18	1	5		26	18	1	4		16	1		10	18
5:0	48	4	3		16	25		7		16	25		2		8	5		8	25
4:6	50	1	3	4	13	29		4	4	13	29		1	1	2	3	3	11	29
Total	448	134	30	6	196	82	100	64	6	196	82	100	51	1	159	13	5	37	82
Median age		10:3	(7:3)	(–)	8:0	5:0	10:5	8:4	(–)	8:0	5:0	10:5	8:10	(–)	8:7	(5:2)	(4:8)	5:5	5:0

*Same note as to Table 52, *mutatis mutandis.*

decentration effort which leads the child to consider only the dominant before-behind relation (blue mountain in the background)? Or should we admit, contrary to all the laws of logic, that this effort at decentration does not mark any real progress over egocentric behavior? The problem merits some discussion.

We should note first of all that these so-called intermediate responses (column H/FH) are very infrequent (only 30 out of 448). Because of this infrequency, the responses dictated purely by chance may considerably affect the distribution and, since these "anything-ness" attitudes are naturally more frequent in the youngest subjects, the median age of this group may be lowered accordingly. Even assuming that this could be the case, the question is still entirely one of knowing why these so-called intermediate-level responses are less numerous in problem F than in problem C. We could always refer to a simple difference in the difficulty of the two problems, a difference which is likely to make the shift from pure egocentrism to complete decentration faster in problem F than in C. But this would only translate the same findings into a new language without at all explaining why complete decentration occurs so much more easily in F than in C.

In order really to answer this question, it is first worth noting that the responses that consist of choosing picture H, or of considering pictures F and H to be equivalent, are not necessarily the only ones to imply an inadequacy of decentration. Just as in problem C, it is in fact probable that the choice of the correct picture is sometimes based on a simple partial relation and that these responses are not really superior to those of the intermediate level. Analysis of the protocols allows us to readjust these first results (see the second section of Table 53) and shows that of the 134 subjects who chose the correct picture, 34 did not give a single reason which could justify their preferring picture F to picture H. When we add to these 34 subjects the 30 who chose picture H (or who judged pictures F and H to be equivalent), the median age of this larger group increases from 7:3 to 8:4 years. This increase partially re-establishes the balance, since the age of children at the egocentric level (8:0) is then four months lower than that of children at the intermediate level; but the difference is not significant (even at the .05 level), and the responses of this supposedly intermediate level should not really be judged to be more highly developed than those of the egocentric level. It is not easy, however, to understand how a certain type of response which is unquestionably characterized by a beginning of decentration may not mark any real progress, when the tested results prove (see the significant *décalages* between the median ages of the group of egocentric subjects and that of decentrated subjects) that development proceeds from absolute egocentrism to absolute decentration, or decentration at least adequate for the coordination of multiple projective relations. Besides, a closer examination of the protocols (see the third section of Table 53) indicates that even when all subjects whose responses could have been dictated purely by chance (e.g., lack of verbal justification, purely fantastic justifications, etc.) are excluded from the comparisons, the difference between the median age of subjects at the so-called intermediate level (8:10) and the median age of egocentric subjects (8:7) is not significant. However, the same treatment applied to the corresponding groups of problem C (see Table 52, p. 329) reveals a significant difference (at the .025 level) between the median age of intermediate-level subjects (9:5) and that of egocentric subjects (8:4). This comparison of problem C with problem F is all the more instructive because the intellectual mechanisms implicit in the responses of corresponding levels are basically the same in both cases. If the difference is significant in problem C without being so in problem F, it is less advisable to question the reality of the psychological progress which these supposedly intermediate responses reflect as a rule than to look for the factors which might minimize this progress in a particular case. In other words, when there is reason to assume that the distance separating two successive steps in a single evolutionary process is unduly short, we should ask first whether this rapprochement marks an overpersistence of a lower-level behavior or an early appearance of a higher-level behavior, and then look for the causes of this possible acceleration or delay.

The results just reported show that if the distance that separates the responses of the intermediate level from the responses of the egocentric level is shorter in problem F than in problem C, it is not because the egocentric responses are slower to disappear in problem F than in C (the absolute number and median age of egocentric subjects are very much the same in both cases), but because the intermediate-level behavior lasts longer in C than in F. In sum, the shift from absolute egocentrism to complete decentration is more abrupt and faster in F than in C. Several factors may explain this phenomenon. We may note first of all that the necessary effort toward decentration may encounter fewer obstacles in F than in C because the perspective of the little man and that of the subject have more elements in common in the former case. The large red mountain, in particular, which the subjects adopted as the dominant reference point, is in fact located to the right of the little man (at F) and also to the right of the subject (at A). Between pictures F and H, which the subject at first retains in order to conform at least to the dominant relation (blue mountain in the background), the subject decides to reject picture H in which the red mountain is presented to the left, contrary to the situation in the little man's perspective as well as in his own. Furthermore, the distinction to be made between the two critical pictures offered in problem F (pictures F and H) concerns the projective left-right distinction, while the analogous distinction between the two critical pictures in problem C (pictures C and E) concerns the before-behind dimension. It is quite possible that in the construction of projective space, the coordination of the left-right relations is quicker to develop than the coordination of the before-behind relations, especially when the experimental context (as in the present experiment) includes a condition of graphic symbolism, where any difficulties in comprehension can concern only the before-behind dimension. Finally, of all the factors likely to influence the relative difficulty of the two problems, perhaps the most decisive concerns the more or less obvious character of the details that distinguish the critical pictures in each instance. In problem F, the left-right reversal of the red and yellow mountains, in fact, makes picture H visibly quite distinguishable from picture F while, in problem C, the slight overlap of the blue mountain over the red one and the slight difference in height between the two mountains (graphic translation of depth) leave picture C fairly indistinguishable from picture E. This is probably why examination of the protocols reveals that the judgments of equivalence between the two critical pictures are much more frequent in problem C than in problem F (21 versus five). It is also instructive to note that nearly half (10 out of 21) of the subjects who chose pictures C and E equally in problem C expressly stated the identity of these pictures (e.g., *"those two pictures are alike," "the man sees that one, too, because it's the same thing as the other,"* etc.). On the other hand, this explanation is never given in problem F: the few subjects who chose both pictures F and H either did not make any real comparison between them and merely judged them both to be correct (e.g., *"the man could also see that one"*), or they were aware of the different position of the two mountains (e.g., *"that one is possible, too: it is like the other one, but the mountains are not arranged the same way"*), but did not attach any real importance to it, as though it were unnecessary or impossible to choose between them.

Assuming that the influence of this factor is a real one, it remains to ask how this influence can in one case (problem F) favor the decentration necessary for the correct solution and in another case (problem C) entail the persistence of intermediate-level responses, whose distinctive characteristic is basically a still-insufficient decentration of the projective relations to be coordinated. The answer is quite simple. In each of these problems, the subject begins by trying to find the dominant relation which is the most striking and the most necessary to the little man's perspective, and, each time, he finds two pictures that involve this dominant relation (e.g., disappearance of the yellow mountain in C, blue mountain in the background in F). If he does not notice that the two pictures he has selected differ from each other with respect to other dimensions, he judges them to be equivalent or identical. On the other hand, if he is aware of these differences—and he will be aware of them much more easily when the concrete situation is likely to accentuate them —he will continue his search into a second phase that consists of analyzing these differences, identifying their meaning (correctly or not), and returning to the little man's perspective in order to determine the various elements in relation to the new projective relation(s) considered. In sum, because he is still unfamiliar with the concerns and requirements of operational thought, the child is not spontaneously inclined, or is simply not able, to consider all the relations which he would have to coordinate each time. When the circumstances force this requirement on him, he will often submit to it successfully, but the instability of his reasoning will be betrayed precisely by his overdependence on the peculiarities of each concrete situation.

PROBLEM B

The results obtained in problem B generally agree with those of the preceding two problems. We find first (Table 54, first section) the same three major levels. The first (column B) corresponds to the choice of the correct picture, whose identification does not, however, require complete decentration, since picture B becomes the only choice possible for the subject who is able to surpass at least the primitive egocentrism inherent in the other four pictures presented to him. The second level (column D/D/DE) combines the responses which consist of choosing one or the other of pictures E and D (or both indiscriminately), visible from the position occupied by the subject, and which thus reflect the purest egocentrism. The last level ("Others" column) is reserved as usual for the incoherent responses or the various forms of rejection of this task. The differences in median ages between these three levels are clearly significant (at the .01 level: Kolmogorov-Smirnov test).

The other two response categories raise problems of interpretation. The first of these categories (column I) consists of selecting picture I, a picture in which some of the elements proper to both perspectives (A and E) successively offered to the child are reproduced. The infrequency of subjects opting for this picture (21 out of 448) gives only slight value to the corresponding median age; but there is no doubt that the large majority of these subjects are found at ages where egocentric behavior predominates in all areas. The choice of a concretely impossible view, picture I, probably reflects the as yet very primitive and undifferentiated egocentric preoccupations of the child: either the subject emphasizes the proximity of the red mountain with respect to his own temporary perspective and ignores the arrangement of the other two mountains, or he emphasizes the arrangement of these two mountains in relation to the little man's perspective (which itself is the same one he had had at the beginning of the test) and completely ignores the relative position of the red mountain. It may be the particular character of this form of still very unarticulated egocentrism which explains its instability and, consequently, its infrequency.

The last category to be mentioned (column A/AB) covers many more subjects. This type of response (choosing picture A, or picture A or B indiscriminately) is explained either by an attitude of recur-

Table 54

Distribution by age level of all responses* to the third problem (position B) of the first section of the *Coordination of perspectives test*

Age	N	Original data					First readjustment					Second readjustment							
												Justified response				Unjustified response			
		B	A/AB	I	D/E/DE	Others	B_c	B_p/A/AB	I	D/E/DE	Others	B_c	B_p/A/AB	I	D/E-DE	B_p/A/AB	I	D/E/DE	Others
12:0	50	32	6		12		26	12		12		26	12		10			2	
11:0	50	26	7		16	1	22	11		16	1	22	11		16				1
10:0	50	19	9	2	18	2	17	11	2	18	2	17	11	2	18				2
9:0	50	18	9	4	17	2	15	12	4	17	2	15	12	3	16		1	1	2
8:0	50	10	8	2	23	7	7	11	2	23	7	7	11	2	21			2	7
7:0	50	10	7	7	20	6	7	10	7	20	6	7	8	5	17	2	2	3	6
6:0	50	5	10	3	14	18	1	14	3	14	18	1	8	1	12	6	2	2	18
5:0	48	5	7	1	3	32		12	1	3	32		6		3	6	1		32
4:6	50	4	5	2	4	35		9	2	4	35		1		2	8	2	2	35
Total	448	129	68	21	127	103	95	102	21	127	103	95	80	13	115	22	8	12	103
Median age		10:2	8:2	(7:2)	8:6	5:0	10:6	8:1	(7:2)	8:6	5:0	10:6	9:0	(7:5)	8:8	(5:0)	(6:3)	(7:0)	5:0

*Same note as to Table 52, *mutatis mutandis*.

rent egocentrism (choosing the pictures that correspond to the subject's perspective in the first two problems), or by a partial decentration process (choosing the pictures that respect at least the major left-right and before-behind relations). It was also predicted that the median age of subjects in this group would fall somewhere between that of the strictly egocentric subjects (choice of picture D or E) and that of the subjects most capable of complete decentration (choice of picture B). In fact, the median age obtained is not only lower (significant difference at the .025 level) than that of subjects at the first level (column B), but it is even lower than that of the purely egocentric subjects (column D/E/DE), although the difference in the latter case is not significant (even at the .05 level). These results are not appreciably different when subjected to the readjustment (see the second section of the table) which was already applied to the corresponding results in problems C and F—that is, when we add to this pseudointermediate level the 34 subjects who were classified in the first group but whose choice of the correct picture was not defended in such a way as to eliminate picture A *ipso facto*. The second readjustment (see the third section of the table), in which the choices are distinguished according to whether or not they were defended, involves greater changes in the distributions, but it does not make the difference in median age between the egocentric and the supposedly intermediate subjects a significant one. In sum, the original predictions concerning the meaning to be attributed to these responses do not seem to be confirmed by the facts.

How can we explain, then, the paradoxical fact that two groups of subjects of the same median age give two different types of responses, some of which (choice of picture D or E) undeniably reflect a very primitive egocentrism, but others of which (choice of picture A or B) might indicate the beginning of a no less undeniable decentration? It is possible that this last category of supposedly intermediate responses may in fact be much less homogeneous than the other, a hypothesis which only the examination of the protocols themselves could verify. The reference to the protocols—to be kept to a minimum in the present chapter—shows once again how inadequate the analysis of behavior can be when it is limited to the choice-rejection dichotomy in relation to a particular picture. It shows in fact that the 102 subjects (column B_p/A/AB of the second section) who selected either picture B (without fully defending their choice) or picture A, or both at once, may be divided into two distinct groups. The first combines the 45 subjects whose choice of the pictures visible from position B seems to have been dictated by a genuine effort toward decentration: either the subject expressly saw the difference between his own point of view and that of the little man (e.g., he rejects picture D, saying that *"the man can't see that one because I'm the one who sees it"*), or his response, while not explicitly guided in that way, was at least preceded by analogous responses where the effort at decentration is clearly expressed. The second category includes the 57 subjects who almost always chose the pictures visible from A regardless of the man's position (C, F, or B), while nothing in the protocols indicates a real effort at decentration. It is obvious that this behavior reflects either the egocentric mind's natural imperviousness to experience (as well as the importance accorded its first impressions), or a deep-seated incomprehension of the task required of him, an incomprehension which spontaneously causes the subject to prefer the pictures he had been induced by the examiner to accept as correct in the examples at the beginning of the test.

Table 55 gives the result of this regrouping by dividing the 102 subjects by age level. The age *décalage* between the two types of behavior is quite marked. Although all the subjects chose the same

Table 55

Distribution by age level of the two different types of error in response $B_p/A/AB$ in the third problem of the *Coordination of perspectives* test

Type of error*	Chronological age									Total
	4:6	5:0	6:0	7:0	8:0	9:0	10:0	11:0	12:0	
Type 1	1	2	2	5	5	8	6	6	10	45
Type 2	8	10	12	5	6	4	5	5	2	57
Total	9	12	14	10	11	12	11	11	12	102

*See description in text.

pictures, the median age (9:5) of those whose behavior reflects some decentration is higher than that (6:5 years) of the subjects of the second group (the difference is significant at least at the .01 level: Kolmogorov-Smirnov test). A closer analysis of the protocols would permit us to see whether the early appearance of this last category reflects an extremely primitive form of egocentrism or whether it reflects instead the combined influence of egocentric attitudes and incomprehension. But this is not the place to undertake such an analysis; the results reported above are more than adequate to show both that referring to the protocols is much more instructive than examining the subjects' choices alone and that a single category of apparently identical responses may in fact include basically dissimilar types of behavior.

Chapter XVI

Coordination of Perspectives: Analysis by Stages

The analysis by stages, presented in this chapter, provides a complement to the preceding analyses by illustrating with concrete examples the different steps in the child's progressive construction of a system of perspectives. Most of the chapter is dedicated to a description of the stages. Before proceeding with this description, however, we must briefly describe the general structure of the developmental scale and give the distribution of the subjects on this scale.

ESTABLISHMENT OF A DEVELOPMENTAL SCALE

The construction of the developmental scale for the *Coordination of perspectives* test depends exclusively on the subject's responses to the three problems constituting the first section of the test. We must recall that in the second part the subject's task consisted of placing the man in a position corresponding to the picture presented by the examiner and verbally justifying each choice. The reasons for excluding this entire second part are of two kinds.

In the first place, scoring the responses to problems in the second section has been shown to be very difficult, for two reasons. First, the identification of the strategies employed by the child is very unreliable when it is based on the peculiarities of the positions which were chosen. Even when the response is correct, it is impossible to know whether the child considered all the necessary projective relations, whether he allowed himself to be guided by partial and dominant characteristics, or whether this response is simply the effect of a happy coincidence, favored by the fact that the subject may wish to

344

hold consistently only to the three positions used by the examiner himself in the first section. When the response is incorrect, on the other hand, the number of possible interpretations is even greater, as we can well imagine, ranging from simple inaccuracy to pure randomness. We should add that the identification of the subject's strategies is hardly facilitated by examining their verbal explanations, which too often consist of merely describing the picture without establishing any real link between the arrangement described and the position of each mountain in relation to the little man. The examiner thus receives a perfect description of the view which the little man must actually have, but this description does not at all correspond to the point of view which is actually visible to the man from the position assigned him by the child.

Certainly we could have tried, by different means, to reduce the difficulties raised by the interpretation of responses to the second part of the test. More than an individual analysis of each response could have done, simultaneous consideration of a single child's responses to these five problems could have, for example, revealed his strategies and facilitated the establishment of some criteria for classification. For a second reason which is even more basic than the first, it did not seem necessary to use new methods of analysis: the result of such analyses, already compromised by the instability and uncertainty of the initial data, could add nothing substantial to the information provided by the first part of the test. The study of successes and errors, reported in the preceding chapter, shows in fact that the problems of the second section as a whole are easier than those of the first, especially since consideration of isolated projective relations is usually enough to locate the positions in the second section, whereas the child cannot respond correctly to the questions in the first section without considering more than one projective relation at a time. The partial equivalence of the two parts of the test does not seem to be in doubt, since we note a correlation of .67 (Kendall tau) between the classification of subjects according to the stage attained in the first part, on one hand, and their classification according to the number of problems solved in the second part, on the other hand. If we eliminate the subjects classified at stage 0, the correlation drops from .67 to .58, but it remains highly significant. The meaning of this correlation becomes especially clear when we regroup the results of the two sections into two dichotomies: in the

first section, the subjects who are completely incapable of intellectual decentration are opposed to those who manage it at least partially, and in the second section, the subjects whose success is nil or
almost nil (no success or one isolated and probably chance success)
are opposed to those who succeed with at least two of the five problems. The result of this rearrangement (Table 56) clearly shows

Table 56

Distribution of subjects* according to their response level in both sections of the *Coordination of perspectives* test

Section 1	Section 2: number of problems solved			
	Including stage 0		Excluding stage 0	
	0-1	2-5	0-1	2-5
No decentration	202	34	88	28
At least partial decentration	49	152	49	152

N=437 (13 subjects having been judged unclassifiable in section 1) or 317 depending on whether or not the 120 subjects at stage 0 are included.

that success with the problems of the second section begins to be a
little systematic just when the child becomes capable, in the first, of
considering at least some of the projective relations involved. In
sum, the uncertainty, inaccuracy, and paucity of this additional information, as well as certain practical considerations (e.g., the
length of the examination), seem amply to justify basing the analysis
by stages solely on the results of the first section, despite the theoretical interest of the observations in the second section.

The proposed developmental scale includes three successive
stages plus an initial stage (stage 0) during which even the meaning
of the questions and the nature of the task are totally beyond the
subject's ability. The *first* stage is that of full egocentrism. It is divided into two substages according to whether the subject's egocentric attitudes are still accompanied by signs or overt admissions of
incomprehension (substage 1A), or whether these egocentric attitudes are consistently reflected in the choice of the picture corresponding to the subject's own perspective (substage 1B). The *second*
stage is a transitional stage. The protocols of this level are characterized either by a variously proportioned mixture of pure egocentrism, partial decentration, and even complete decentration, by a
mixture limited to only two of these three components, or, finally,

by a more homogeneous group of responses which are all partially decentrated. The stage is divided into two substages depending on whether the number of responses which are completely decentrated is lower than (substage 2A) or equal to (substage 2B) two out of three. Finally, the *third* stage includes the protocols in which every trace of egocentrism has completely disappeared.

DISTRIBUTION OF THE SUBJECTS ON THE DEVELOPMENTAL SCALE

Table 57 distributes all the subjects into this developmental scale, excluding the 13 subjects who were not classified because they were inconsistent or aberrant (e.g., mixture of partial or complete decentrations and randomness). The progression of median ages increases regularly from 5:0 to 11:0 years without a single inversion. What is especially striking in this table is the difficulty of the test:

Table 57

Distribution of subjects by age and by stage in the *Coordination of perspectives* test

			Stage										
		Unclassi-	Frequencies						Cumulative percentages				
Age	N	fied	0	1A	1B	2A	2B	3	1A	1B	2A	2B	3
12:0	50		1	1	3	19	12	14	98	96	90	52	28
11:0	50		1		10	16	12	11	98	98	78	46	22
10:0	50			1	15	15	13	6	100	98	68	38	12
9:0	50	1	2	1	12	20	7	7	96	94	69	28	14
8:0	50	2	3	5	17	18	4	1	94	83	48	10	2
7:0	50	2	8	6	18	12	3	1	83	70	33	8	2
6:0	50	1	26	7	10	5	1		47	33	12	2	
5:0	50	5	34	4	4	2	1		25	16	7	2	
4:6	50	2	45	2		1			6	2	2		
Total	450	13	120	27	89	108	53	40					
Median age*			5:0	6:7	8:2	9:3	10:4	11:0					
Age of accession									6:0	6:6	8:5	11:8	—

*See footnote to Table 16.

nearly 30 per cent of the subjects (120 out of 450) are assigned to stage 0, and the percentage of subjects of 12:0 years located at the last stage is hardly more than 25 and does not appreciably differ from the corresponding percentage at the preceding level (substage 2B). Because these last two distributions are strongly truncated, the meaning of statistical comparisons is quite problematical. In fact, the differences are significant between stages 0 and 1A (at the .01 level: Kolmogorov-Smirnov test) and between substages 1A and 1B (at the .025 level); but the level of significance between stages 1B and 2A is only .05, is similar between substages 2A and 2B, and does not even reach this strict minimum between stages 2B and 3. Thus, it is with great reservation—and assuming that results from older subjects would confirm the transitivity of the scale—that the frequencies are cumulated and the ages of accession to these different levels are calculated. Examination of these ages of accession reveals even more directly the difficulty of this test. Even at 6:6 years (substage 1B), the subjects are completely oblivious to any decentration (even partial decentration), and we must wait more than five years (since 2B is achieved at 11:8 years) before the subjects are able to coordinate the left-right and before-behind relations in at least two of the three problems. Finally, barely one quarter of the subjects of 12:0 years manage to resolve perfectly all three problems of the test. The results are nearly the same for boys and girls at all ages, except at 12:0 years where the difference reaches the .05 level of significance, favoring the boys.

DETAILED DESCRIPTION OF THE STAGES

To illustrate better the particular difficulties of this test, and especially to define concretely the characteristics of each level of the proposed scale, nothing can replace an analysis of the protocols. The detailed description of each of the stages will include a liberal sampling of protocol excerpts.

STAGE 0: INCOMPREHENSION OR REFUSAL

Stage 0 combines the 120 subjects who were unable to grasp the nature of the task. This lack of comprehension is most often obvious beginning with the example at the start of the test proper. There are, in fact, numerous children who saw the different pictures only as new mountains which the little man can look at and photograph, or near which they themselves can locate the little man, rather than as various views of the three mountains arranged before them. Other children seemed to grasp the difference between the real objects and their reproduction more easily, but did not understand why only one of the two pictures could correspond to the man's view. The child was satisfied when a picture contained three mountains or at least the mountain near which the man was standing and, without thinking to determine the relative position of the mountains, he listened more with submission than with interest and intelligence to the examiner's explanations. And many children, apparently able to understand the initial example, nevertheless refused to take the test after the first or second question of the first section, claiming that the examiner was always asking the same question, that the task was too difficult, that the questions were boring or too numerous, etc. One subject even openly protested, demanding that he be given a task better adapted to his age!

To these often categorical and somewhat hasty refusals are added the numerous more or less overt indications of incomprehension observed during the test itself. Several children, perhaps influenced by the explanation in the initial example, began by choosing only one of the five alternative pictures; but, when the examiner pressed them to defend their rejection of the other four pictures, they readily admitted that the other pictures, or even all five, were equally possible. Furthermore, contrary to what is observed in the protocols assigned to the later stages, it frequently happened that the picture(s) was (were) chosen with no relation whatever to the child's egocentric perspective or to that of the observer. Thus, in problem 1 (man located at F), the choice of picture D almost invariably reveals the child's lack of comprehension, because the choices observed at later stages are made consistently on picture A or G, or on picture F or H, depending on whether the subject is still a victim of his egocentric perspective or whether he is capable of partial or total decentration. Even when he chooses pictures obviously related to his own perspective or to that of the little man, the stage 0 child invokes reasons which are completely foreign to these considerations. Thus the preference accorded picture A, particularly in the first problem (position F), arises not so much from egocentric attitudes as from a concern with slavish imitation of the examiner's solution in the immediately preceding example. Similarly, in the second problem (position C), the child who chooses picture C or E has not necessarily understood that the man can no longer see the yellow mountain; he may simply be struck by the absence of the yellow mountain, an absence which makes these pictures simpler and more easily distinguishable from the others. Finally, in more than one case, the choice of one or another picture depends solely on secondary preoccupations: for example, the child chooses the picture closest to the man on the table, a picture located within the man's field of vision, etc.

The following three protocol excerpts very clearly illustrate some of the manifestations of incomprehension described above.

5 (4:6): *Problem 1* (position F). Chooses card D. "Explain to me why you say it's that one that the man can see.—*Because it's that one.*—And this one [card A], can he see this one?—*No.*—Why can't he see it?— *Both of them* . . . —And this one [card G], can he see this one?—*No.*— Why can't he see it?—*Because there is only one that he can see.*—And this one [card F], are you sure that he isn't seeing this one?—*Yes.*—Explain to me why he can't see it.—*Because it's too far* [card F is actually, along with card H, one of the cards which is farthest away from the little man on the table.]—And that one [card H], are you sure that that's not the one he sees?—*Yes.*—Why can't he see it?—*Because it's too far.*"

Problem 2 (position C). Points to card C, saying spontaneously, "*The yellow one is hidden.*—Explain to me why you say that it's that one that the man sees.—*Because* . . . —And this one [card E], you are sure that this isn't the one he sees?—*Yes.*—Explain it to me.—*Because the blue one is in the front* [impossible to know whether this remark refers to the picture or to the board].—And that one [card A] . . . ?—*He can see it.*—Explain it to me . . . —*Because he can.*—And that one [card F] . . . ?—*Yes, he can.* —And that one [card B] . . . ?—*Yes, he can.*—Explain it to me. . . . —*Because it's not too far from him.*" In sum, the child rejects only card E, the one which is farthest from the little man.

Problem 3 (subject at E, man at B). Chooses card D, explaining, "*Because he sees the blue point, the red and then the yellow one.*—And that one [card B]?—*He can see it, too.*—Which one is better?—*That one* [card D.]—Then why can't he see this one [card B]?—*Because he is too far* [card B is in fact the farthest from the man].—And that one [card I] . . . ? —*Yes, he can.*—Which is the better of the two [D or I]?—*That one* [card I].—Explain it to me. . . . —*Because he turns to the left.*—And that one [card A], is that the one he sees?—*No.*—Tell me why. . . .—*Because it's there* [showing card A which, in the group of cards, is found at the end closet to the little man but 'behind' him, if we agree that his face is turned toward the mountains, on the board].—And that one [card E] . . . ? —*No.*—Explain it to me. . . . —*Yes, he could see it.*"

39 (5:0): *Problem 1* (position F). Chooses cards A and G. "Which is the best of all?—*That one* [card A].—Tell me why. . . .—*Because there are two good ones: that one* [card A] *and that one* [card G].—Then why are both of them good ones?—*Because that one is there, that one is there, and that one is there* [indicating the three mountains on card A one by

one].—*And that card there* [G]?—*Because that one is there, that one is there, and that one is there* [thus designating each mountain on the card]. —*And that one* [card D], *does he see that one?—No.*—Tell me why.— *Because that one is there, that one is there, and that one is there* [same as previously]." He then rejects cards F and H, still in the same manner, without going beyond pure description.

Problem 2 (position C). Chooses card A "*because the mountain was there* [without the examiner knowing which mountain he is referring to]. —*And that one* [card E], *are you sure he doesn't see that one?—Yes.*—Explain it to me.—*Because the blue one is there and the red one is there* [concomitant gestures].—*And that one* [card C], *you are sure that he doesn't see that one?—Yes.*—Explain it to me. . . . —*Because it is like the other one* [i.e., like card E].—*And that one* [card F], *are you sure . . . ? —Yes.*—Explain it to me. . . .—*Because the yellow one is there, the blue one is there, and the red one is there.*—And that one [card B], are you sure . . . ?—*Yes.*—Explain to me. . . .—*Because it's arranged like that* [pointing to the three mountains on the card]."

Problem 3 (subject at E, man at B). Chooses card E "*because the little man sees like that.*" Then rejects cards B, I, and D in turn, pointing to the three mountains each time. Finally declares card A to be correct, but returns to his usual pattern of simple description for all justifications.

33 (7:0): *Problem 1* (position F). Chooses card A, saying: "*The blue one.*—Only the blue one?—*No, the red and the blue ones.*—He doesn't see the yellow one?—*No.*—Then explain to me why you say that it's that one that he sees.—*See, my finger it's a man, he is here* [placing his finger on the left side of card A]. *He sees the mountains.*—And that one there [card G], does he see that?—*Yes, that one and that one* [i.e., the red mountain and the blue mountain on card G].—Explain it to me.—*It* [pointing to the red mountain on the card] *is near it. We can say that here* [middle of the left side of card G] *is the man: he can't see the yellow one.*—And that one [card D], does he see that?—*No.*—Tell me why. . . ."—Then tries to make the examiner understand something incomprehensible to him, using gestures rather than words and showing all the cards at the same time. Finishes by saying: "*The man is here* [middle of the right side of card D] *and he is looking at the red one and the blue one.*—And that one [card F] . . . ?—*No.*—Explain it to me. . . .—*He sees that one* [red mountain on the card] *and that one* [blue mountain on the card], *he doesn't see the yellow one.*" In sum, the child seems to be saying that the little man sees only the red and blue mountains on any card.

Problem 2 (position C). Chooses card A and explains himself: "*Look, he is here* [i.e., middle of the right side of card A] *beside the blue mountain. He sees the blue one, the red one, and not the yellow one.*—And that one [card B], does he see that?—*No, it's that one* [card A].—Explain it to me. . . .—*Look, we can say that* [finds a stick on the table and puts it on the right side of card A] *this is a man. He sees the blue one and the red one.*—And that one [card F] . . . ?—*No.*—Explain it to me. . . .—*Be-cause he is too far.*—And that one [card C] . . . ?—*The red one, yes, he sees it.*—And that one [card E] . . . ?—*No.*—Explain it to me. . . .—*Yes, yes he sees it* [placing his stick on card E]."

Problem 3 (subject at E, man at B). Chooses card I and, to explain himself, again places the stick on the left side of card I, saying: "*See, here, near the blue one, he sees the red one and the yellow one.*—And that one [card A] . . . ?—*No, he sees the blue one and the yellow one.*—And that one [card D] . . . ?—*No.*—Explain it to me.—*Because he is here* [right side of card D], *near the blue one.*—And that one there [card E] . . . ?—*Yes.*—Explain it to me. . . .—*He can't see the red one, he sees the blue one here.*—And that one [card B] . . . ?—*No.*—Explain it to me. . . .—*He sees the blue one, then the yellow one there.*"

As we can see in these examples, it is the explanation given by the child, much more than the nature of his choices, which reveal his strategies and his level of understanding. This is also the reason why stage 0 includes all the children who completely refused to de-fend their choices and their rejections, all those who resorted to reasons which are fantastic or irrelevant to the task (e.g., *"because I want it," "because it's the prettiest picture," "because it's forbid-den,"* etc.), and finally all those who, in explanation, were satisfied with describing the arrangement of the mountains on the board or on the cards without ever emphasizing the concordances or dis-cordances underlying their choices and their rejections. In sum, although stage 0 children may select the same pictures as children at later stages, these choices are considered to be arbitrary as long as we cannot prove that the subject's or the little man's perspective effec-tively influences them.

It remains to ask whether it is legitimate to consider as equiva-lent a type of behavior in which the subject's incomprehension is indirectly reflected in the apparent aimlessness of his choices (or even by the undifferentiated acceptances of all the alternative pic-tures) and a type of behavior in which this incomprehension leads the child instead to select, for example, only the pictures located in the little man's field of vision. This last kind of behavior shows un-questionably that the child does not even understand the representa-tional value of the pictures, while the first two behavior types are more equivocal. They could in fact reflect a total egocentrism where-by a lack of awareness of the possible points of view leads the child to think that anything may be visible from anywhere and, consequently, that any picture may represent the man's perspective (or that all the alternative pictures are equally accurate).

The question is all the more pertinent as, contrary to what we observed in other tests and despite the fact that the present test was not given to children younger than 4:6 years, the number of subjects assigned to stage 0 (120) is more than a quarter of all the subjects. Attaching too much importance to the consistency of the choices and to the type of explanations offered, in interpreting the protocols, may result in relegating to stage 0 the most primitive egocentric attitudes, based on the implicit postulate that everything is visible from everywhere, or attitudes which are still too unconscious to be verbalized. However, before condemning this kind of procedure, we must ask two questions. The first is the question of how we might distinguish primitive egocentrism from total incomprehension, especially if we accept that this incomprehension will naturally result in randomness. Lacking verbal justification, it hardly seems possible to test whether the subject's choice is inspired somehow by his own perspective or by that of the little man. Similarly, in the case where the subject accepts all or nearly all of the pictures, the only way to dissociate true egocentrism from temporary fantasy is to recognize at least the consistency shown by subjects at later stages, choosing only the pictures representing an equal number of elements—that is, two or three mountains, according to whether the subject himself can see two or three or whether he grants the possibility of seeing two or three of them to the little man.

Even assuming that such a differentiation between primitive egocentrism and real incomprehension were possible, the basic question would still be whether this differentiation is desirable and necessary or whether all incomprehension, whatever its particular expression, is not based on a very primitive form of egocentrism. In order to understand the nature of the problem presented to him, the child must be aware of the fact that any displacement around an object (simple or complex) entails changes in his view of this object. This very understanding already presupposes a minimum of intellectual decentration—a certain awareness, however fleeting it may still be, of the many possible points of view and thus a certain liberation from his own temporary point of view. This first decentration does not *ipso facto* guarantee the correct anticipation of the various perspectives presented to the child, since all stage 1 subjects can understand the instructions and are still irresistibly inclined to choose the pictures that correspond to their own perspectives. This first awareness, however, does represent a fragile but genuine progress over the primitive egocentrism of the beginning, which is so unaware of itself that the child is unable to understand even the meaning of the problem. It is probably this state of elementary egocentrism which is observed in seemingly different but basically equivalent forms in all stage 0 children. In principle, then, this radical egocentrism would constitute a real and positive level of development despite the fact that stage 0, in its present form, is negatively defined by the child's inability to understand the task because he is still not even vaguely aware of the multiplicity of possible viewpoints. The number of subjects assigned to this level testifies to the primitive nature of this first awareness.

STAGE 1: COMPLETE EGOCENTRISM

Stage 1 subjects have a consistently egocentric attitude. This egocentrism may be revealed in various ways. It particularly takes the most obvious form of choosing egocentric pictures, but it is sometimes concealed under appearances of decentration whose illusory nature is most instructive (e.g., choosing the picture that corresponds to the perspective seen by the subject just before his change in position; choosing the egocentric picture and rejecting all the others while pointing to the place where the man would have to be in order to see them; choosing the egocentric picture with an accurate description of the man's view; etc.). Table 58 shows how the 116 subjects of this level are divided according to the number of problems in which they give proof of clear egocentrism or of pseudo decentration. We note immediately that these two types of egocentrism are found

Table 58

Distribution of stage 1 subjects in the *Coordination of perspectives* test according to the number of problems yielding overtly egocentric behavior and pseudo decentrations

Overt egocentrism	Pseudo decentration				Total
	0	1	2	3	
0		2	0	4	6
1	17	1	13		31
2	7	37			44
3	35				35
Total	59	40	13	4	116

simultaneously, in varying proportions, in nearly half the subjects (51 out of 116, or 44 per cent), but that pure egocentrism strongly predominates over pseudo decentration (37 versus 13). The other protocols (65 out of 116, or 56 per cent) are more homogeneous in this respect since we find only one or the other of these two types of egocentrism; but we note that pure egocentrism still predominates here (59 versus six subjects).

This distinction between substages 1A and 1B, to be discussed more fully later on, is based solely on the presence or absence of incomprehension (defined as in stage 0) in any one of the three problems.[1] Thus the distinction does not at all affect the description of the different types of egocentrism observed in stage 1 and to which we now turn.

A. *Overt Egocentrism*

Beginning with the most obvious cases, the typical and most frequent behavior consists of selecting the picture that represents the mountains as they appear from the position occupied by the child. However, depending on whether he stays strictly in the position assigned to him or whether he leans slightly toward the man in order to see the same thing he does, the child will choose picture A or G in the first problem (position F), picture A or B in the second problem (position C), and picture E or D in the last problem (subject at E, man at B). Many subjects could not even distinguish between the two pictures in each of these pairs. Regardless of their specific content, the explanations invariably amount to asserting that, in the picture selected, the mountains are arranged in the order in which the subject himself perceives them, while this order is not respected in the rejected pictures. A rather frequent behavior is fairly revealing in this respect: the subject chooses the egocentric picture and, in order to justify rejecting the others, he systematically rearranges the three mountains as he sees them in each of the pictures to be rejected, without according the least importance to the little man. More or less explicit, depending on the case, these references to the subject's own point of view, however, never assume a restrictive or

[1] The same Table 58 implicitly distinguishes the subjects assigned to one or the other of these two substages: the nonitalicized numbers represent the 27 subjects of substage 1A, since the number of problems on which the classification of these subjects in the table is based is never more than two out of three; the others (89 subjects) are classed in substage 1B.

relative meaning: on the contrary, his own perspective constitutes a kind of absolute norm and represents the only possible view of the set of mountains, regardless of the point from which they are seen. Following are some examples.

22 (9:0): *Problem 1* (position F). Chooses card A and explains: *"Because the yellow one is to the right, the blue one is to the left . . . —*Explain to me why he can't see that one [card G].—*Because the yellow one is on the left like that* [i.e., too much to the left with respect to the red one].—Tell me why he can't see that one [card F].—*Because the yellow one is on the left.*—Explain to me why he can't see that one [card D].— *Because the yellow one is in back and the red is on the left . . . —*Explain to me why he can't see that one [card H].—*Because the red one is on the left and the blue one* [!] *is on the right . . ."*
Problem 2 (position C). Chooses card A again and defends his choice thus: *"Because the blue one is on the left and the red one on the right.—* Explain to me why he can't see that one [card E].—*Because we don't see the yellow one.*—Explain to me why he can't see that one [card C].—*Because we don't see the yellow one.*—Tell me why he can't see that one [card F].—*Because the yellow one is on the left and the red one is on the right.*—Tell me why he can't see this one [card B].—*Because the yellow one doesn't 'hit' the red one* [i.e., does not cover part of the red one]."
Problem 3 (position E, man at B). Chooses card E, saying: *"Because the yellow one can't be seen."* Then rejects one by one cards B, I, D, and A, claiming each time: *"because we can see the yellow one."*

35 (9:0): *Problem 1* (position F). Chooses card G *"because the red one is on that side* [i.e., on the right], *the yellow one is here* [i.e., in front], *and the blue one is there* [i.e., on the left].—Explain to me why he can't see that one [card A].—*Because the yellow one is more down there* [i.e., too much to the right].—Explain why he can't see that one [card D].— *Because the red one is on the wrong side, the blue one is, too, and then the yellow one is, too.*—Explain why he can't see that one [card F].—*Because the blue one is in the rear and the yellow one is here* [i.e., on the left].—Explain to me why he can't see that one [card H].—*Because the red one is on the wrong side and the blue one is between the two."*
Problem 2 (position C). Chooses card A and again explains that the mountains are correctly arranged (with respect to himself). Then rejects cards E and C, saying each time that *"the red one and the blue one are on the wrong side and there is no yellow one."* Card F is rejected because *"the blue one is in the middle and the yellow one is on the wrong side."* For card B, also rejected, he simply describes the arrangement of the picture.
Problem 3 (subject at E, man at B). Chooses card D, saying: *"The blue one is there* [i.e., on the right], *the red one is here* [i.e., on the left]

and the yellow one is in the back." Then rejects cards B and I, saying for each one that *"the blue one is on the wrong side, and the yellow one is, too, and the red one is in the middle."* Justifies the rejection of card E by the fact that *"there is no yellow one, and the red and blue ones are on the wrong side."* Finally, card A is rejected because it does not agree with the child's present view.

22 (7:0): *Problem 1* (position F). Chooses card A *"because the yellow mountain is beside the blue one and the red one is in the back.*—Explain to me why he can't see that one [card G].—*It's that one there, because the red one is in the back* [which is true of card A as well!].—Then, that one there [card A], you are sure that he doesn't see that one?—[. . . .]—Explain to me why he can't see it.—*I don't know* . . . —Explain to me why he can't see this one [card D].—*Because the yellow one is in the back.*—Explain to me why he can't see that one [card F].—*The yellow one is there* [i.e., on the right on the board] *and the red one is behind the yellow one* [on the board].—Explain to me why he can't see that one [card H].—*I don't know."*

Problem 2 (position C). Chooses card A, again emphasizing its conformity with his own point of view, as in the preceding problem. Then rejects cards E and C *"because the yellow one isn't there."* Also rejects card F, alleging that *"the yellow one isn't in the right place."* Finally rejects card B, but cannot defend his rejection.

Problem 3 (subject at E, man at B). Chooses card D, again justifying himself by the agreement of the picture with his own point of view. Rejects all the other cards *"because the mountains aren't arranged the same way* [i.e., as they are in front of him]."

42 (7:0): *Problem 1* (position F). Chooses card A *"because the yellow one is in front, the red one is behind and the blue one is on the side.*—Explain to me why he can't see that one [card G].—*The yellow one is in the back . . . No, that one is good, too, it is like this one* [card A].—Explain to me why he can't see that one [card D].—*The yellow one is in the back.*—And that one [card F]?—*Because the blue one is behind.*—And that one [card H] . . . ?—*Because the blue one is behind."*

Problems 2 and 3. Chooses pictures A and D respectively, justifying his choices and rejections in the same way as the other subjects already cited.

17 (8:0): *Problem 1* (position F). Chooses card A *"because the little man is supposed to be here* [toward the right of card A].—Explain to me why he can't see that card [card G].—*That can't be the one because the yellow mountain would have to be there* [pushes the yellow mountain toward the left, but nearer the red one than before so that the blue one is slightly hidden].—And that one [card F] . . . ?—*Because the yellow one is here* [far left of the card] *and the blue one is there* [behind the red one].—And that one [card D] . . . ?" In reply, he rearranges the moun-

tains so as exactly to reproduce card D seen from his own perspective. Same thing for card H following.

Problem 2 (position C) and *problem 3* (subject at E, man at B). Chooses picture A in problem 2 and E in problem 3 and systematically rearranges the mountains so as to reproduce each of the rejected pictures.

These protocol excerpts beautifully describe the range of typically egocentric behavior. The first of these subjects consistently chooses the picture that corresponds to the position he occupies during the test. The second selects instead the picture which he himself can see when he leans slightly toward the little man. The third resembles the first, but rather unconvincingly rejects the pictures that correspond to the positions neighboring his own. Finally, the fourth subject, in at least one problem (position F), sees the pictures that correspond to his own position (A) and to the immediately neighboring one (G) as equivalent. The reasons invoked by the four subjects as a basis for their choices and rejections are strikingly homogeneous and always amount to either asserting or denying, depending on the case, the agreement of the picture with their own temporary perspective. The fifth and last subject cited in the example is particularly related to the first in that he always chooses, without hesitation, the only egocentric picture; but the absolute nature of this egocentrism is especially clear in the subject's tendency constantly to rearrange the elements on the board so as to form a succession of viewpoints which are different but consistently egocentric and independent of the little man.

The determination of these children always to refer to their own perspective raises the question whether these behaviors really express an egocentric attitude or whether they derive instead from a simple misunderstanding of the task. This misunderstanding could derive from the example (given before the test proper) in which the man is placed directly in front of the subject. The explanation then given by the examiner to demonstrate the correctness of picture A might encourage the child to continue looking for the picture that corresponds to his own position with respect to the board. The danger inherent in this example was already anticipated in some preliminary experiments. But, for one thing, we had to use an example to explain the relations to be established between the elements on the board and their graphic representation. For another thing, it was not possible to use an example other than picture A, since any other position would have required a decentration which is hypothetically still inaccessible to the youngest subjects. This is why the instructions were designed to reduce, from the very first problem, the possibilities of misunderstanding the task: the examiner directs the child's attention to the little man's position and at the same time insists, by word and gesture, on the necessity for selecting the picture which is visible from the man's new position.

It is difficult to determine, in each particular case, the level of comprehension of the instructions; but several indications suggest that this exclusive attachment to one's own viewpoint comes from a genuine egocentrism in most of the subjects assigned to stage 1. Almost without exception, they understand that they are to locate the man's perspective and not their own; if they fail at this task and systematically revert to their egocentric perspective, we must attribute this either to their ignorance of the effects produced by changes in position on changes in viewpoints, or to their inability to anticipate the transformations that follow these changes in position. Among these indications, we should mention first the children's many attempts (which the examiners must continually curb) to change position and to place themselves behind the man in order to see the new arrangement of the mountains. Also worth noting, in at least half of the protocols classified at this level (58 out of 116), are the explicit references to the man's perspective or to his various positions. The following protocol excerpts, for example, cannot really be interpreted as a lack of comprehension of the instructions.

5 (10:0): *Problem 1* (position F). Choice of picture G *"because the yellow mountain is closer to the red mountain.*—And that one [card H], are you sure he doesn't see that one?—*Yes.*—Explain to me why . . . — *Because the man is not on the correct side; he would have to be there* [i.e., in E].—And that one [card A] . . . ?—*He can't see it because, where he is, he can't see all of the blue one. He sees only part of it."* Etc.

Problem 2 (position C). Chooses picture A *"because, from that side, he first sees the blue one; after that he sees the red one, and after that, the yellow one.*—And that one [card C] . . . ?—*It's not that one, because the man sees the yellow one."* Etc.

46 (8:0): *Problem 2* (position C). Chooses picture A *"because he* [the man] *sees the blue one, the red one and the yellow one.*—And that one there [card E] . . . ?—*No . . . because there is no yellow one.*—And that one [card C] . . . ?—*No . . . because there is no yellow one.*—And that one

[card F] . . . ?—*No . . . because the yellow one is there* [indicates that it is on the left in the picture] *on the card and, here, it is there* [i.e., on the right on the board].—And that one [card B] . . . ?—*No . . . I don't know. Those two are almost the same* [i.e., A and B]. *It's hard. It seems to me that it's that one* [card B].—Why do you think it's that one?—*I don't know. When you look at them the way the little man looks at them, I think it's that one.*" Etc.

13 (7:0): *Problem 3* (subject at E, man at B). Chooses picture E *"because he is at the end, he can't see the yellow one.*—And that one [card A] . . . ?—*No, not that one, because where he is, he sees just the blue one and the red one.*" Etc.

We could not see egocentric thought any more clearly than this. It would be unfair to use these occasional references to the man's position as a reason for questioning the authenticity of other responses where these references do not appear. In fact, the characteristic lack of differentiation of perspectives in egocentric thought may be such that the subject's temporary point of view is a kind of norm which he may refer to even when he is trying to describe the viewpoint of someone else (see especially the very last example reported). It is quite natural, then, to expect that the normative character of this egocentric viewpoint is often reflected in verbal expressions having no reference to the man, deriving from just this normative and absolute character (e.g., *"the red mountain has to be in back," "that picture isn't good because it doesn't have a yellow mountain,"* etc.).

Another argument against the hypothesis of the children's incomprehension of the instructions at this stage is the consistency they show in the two parts of the questionnaire. We know that the second part requires the subjects to identify the positions corresponding to each of five pictures. Assuming that the subject has not understood the task in the first part and consequently has forgotten or ignored the man's presence, the possibility of a similar oversight disappears completely in the second part, since the instructions ask the subject himself to assume the responsibility for the man's displacements. Now, at the qualitative as well as at the quantitative level, the results observed in this second part only corroborate those of the first. We see, for example, that the number of correct localizations is relatively small: in fact, of the 116 children assigned to stage 1, 40 (or 34 per cent) cannot locate any of the positions, 48 (or 41 per cent) succeed with only one, 23 (or 20 per cent) succeed with two, three (or 3 per cent) with three, and two (or 2 per cent) with four out of five. In sum, only among the last five subjects is the *décalage* between the two parts of the test marked enough to suggest an initial misunderstanding of the task. In all others, the successes are scattered and based on chance, and they are generally related, accidentally, to some strategy where egocentric bondage is always present. Thus, some children placed the man in the very center of the group—that is, between the three mountains—and always selected the same position regardless of which picture was presented to them, as though varying the positions was useless since all the pictures are, in principle, visible from any point. Other children still held to positions located inside the landscape but chose a different one each time and placed the man near the mountain which seemed to dominate the picture (e.g., *"he should be able to see the red one best"*). In spite of the favor enjoyed by the interior positions, most of the subjects still placed the man on the edge of the landscape. Such behavior seems more highly developed; but apparently we must see it more as a concern with imitating the examiner's gestures in the first part of the test than as a real beginning of understanding projective concepts. Witness the subject's simple alternations between several preferred positions, the successive and ordered choice of each corner or each side of the board, the preference accorded the two positions (A and E) occupied by the subject during the first part, the absence of any recognizable system, etc.: these indications confirm the earlier diagnosis of an absolute ignorance of the relativity of viewpoints. If we add to all these reasons the fact that by this stage (and consequently also at the following stage) the choice of the picture reproducing the subject's own perspective is frequently accompanied, in a single protocol, by more or less timid efforts at decentration, there is hardly any doubt that this type of behavior results from genuinely egocentric attitudes rather than from a simple incomprehension of the instructions.

A second type of behavior, less frequent than the preceding type, is also found in subjects at the first stage. It consists of choosing all the pictures in which the mountains visible to the subject are included, as though the relative position of these mountains were not important in itself. Below are some examples.

49 (7:0): *Problem 2* (position C). Chooses picture A *"because it has a blue mountain, and then a yellow one and then a red one.*—And that one [card B], are you sure that's not the one he sees?—No . . . He sees it that way, too.—Explain to me why he sees it that way, too.—There is a blue one, a red one, a yellow one.*—And that one there [card E], you are sure he doesn't see that one?—Yes.—Tell me why.—A mountain is missing, the yellow one is missing.*—And that one [card C] . . . ?—Yes.— Explain it to me . . . —There is still a mountain missing, the yellow one. —And that one [card F] . . . ?—No, it's like that, too.*—Explain it to me . . . —There is a yellow one, a blue one, a red one."*

34 (8:0): *Problem 3* (subject at E, man at B). Chooses card D *"because he sees the blue one, the red one, and the yellow one.*—And that one [card B] . . . ?—He can see it.*—Explain it to me . . . —He sees all three mountains.*—And that one [card I] . . . ?—He can see it.*—Explain . . . — He sees all three mountains.*—And that one [card E] . . . ?—No, he can't see it.*—Explain it to me . . . —There isn't a yellow mountain.*—And that one [card A] . . . ?—He can see it.*—Explain it to me . . . —He sees all three mountains."*

Piaget and Inhelder (1948, pp. 219ff.) observed the same type of behavior; their analysis of it showed that the subjects yielded in a different way to the same egocentric illusion as the subjects of the preceding type. There is no doubt that systematically selecting the picture corresponding to one's own perspective overtly ignores the multiplicity of possible points of view and crystallizes the group of projective relations into one rigid and immobile structure; but, in fact, indiscriminately selecting several pictures with the sole condition that all elements visible to the subject be present in each one is not proof of decentration, since it really amounts to both completely forgetting the projective relations linking the elements to different possible observers, and implicitly admitting that any picture is visible from any point and that all perspectives are equivalent.

In order to confirm both the difference and the equivalence of these two types of behavior, it would be absolutely necessary for the second type to be quite frequent throughout the protocols. The only clue which we can mention in favor of this equivalence concerns the fact that not one subject adopted the second type of behavior without also having adopted the first, in at least one of the three problems. This sort of coincidence suggests that these two types of reaction are of comparable difficulty and reflect a single intellectual attitude. But, then, how can we explain the fact that one is so much more widespread than the other? We should perhaps see this as the effect of the particular conditions in which the test takes places. With the very example used as an introduction, the examiner's explanations suggest that the subject must choose only one picture. Besides, in the test itself, the child who spontaneously chooses more than one picture is urged to state which one he thinks best and is thus further dissuaded from a plurality of choices. Finally, the pictures suggested to the child do not always present the variety necessary to produce this plurality. Thus, for example, none of the five pictures presented in problem 1 eliminates any of the mountains, and the child whose spontaneous reaction would be indiscriminately to accept all those containing the three mountains visible from his own positions will not easily yield to such a suggestion, especially when he has been dissuaded from it in the preceding example. In the same way, the third problem offers four pictures in which the three mountains are included, the fifth showing only two of them: since the child occupies a position (E) from which he can see all the mountains (or only two, depending on his angle of vision), he will easily be led to select the only picture that represents two of the three mountains (first type of reaction) rather than indiscriminately selecting the other four (a choice which he would find excessive, considering the nature of the instructions). These conditions favor the first type of reaction at the expense of the second even though, in principle, both are equally probable and basically equivalent.

B. *Pseudo Decentration*

Along with these rather overtly egocentric behaviors, the present stage includes some other even more puzzling types of reactions which we may call pseudo decentrations because, under the cover of partial decentration, they conceal a radical undifferentiation of the possible points of view and a complete primacy of the subject's own viewpoint. The first of these types of behavior consists of selecting the same egocentric pictures in the third problem (subject at E) that had already been chosen in the first two problems. In sum, rather than choosing picture E or D, yielding to the egocentric illusion of their temporary positions, these children opt instead for picture A, or for pictures A and B considered as equivalent. Would we be justified in concluding that these children are capable of decentration and that their choice of pictures A and B arises from an awareness of the fact that the man is in the position they have just left? This possibility is not precluded; but it seems wiser to see it as a disguised form of egocentrism whereby these children implicitly accept the postulate that the pictures visible from their previous position (of which they have quite a vivid memory) are the only ones visible to the man, regardless of his position. This interpretation is based not only on the fact that these children give no evidence of decentration during the first two problems; we must further note that the median age of children who choose these pictures A or B (8:4 years) is about the same as that of children (8:2 years) who immediately select the overtly egocentric pictures (E or D). It is also symptomatic that the selection of picture B, when it occurs, always leads to the same type of explanation as that of picture A and never precludes it. Finally, some children prefer instead to designate picture I—that is, the one among the five alternatives which somehow constitutes a compromise between the two perspectives successively visible to the subject during the test: in picture I, in fact, the yellow and blue mountains are to the left and right of the red mountain, respectively, as in the view visible from A, but the red mountain is in front of the other two, as in the view visible from E. Below are several examples of these responses given in the third problem by children who otherwise belong at stage 1.

31 (11:0): *Problem 3* (subject at E, man at B). Chooses picture A *"because the blue one is there, the red one is there, and the yellow one is just in front.*—Explain to me why he can't see this one [card B].—*The yellow one is not beside the red one, it's right in front . . .* —And that one [card I] . . . ?—*Because we see the whole yellow one* [on the board] *and it is supposed to be in front.*—And that one [card E] . . . ?—*Because he sees the yellow one.*—And that one [card D] . . . ?—*Because the red one is not supposed to be there."*

43 (9:0): *Problem 3* (subject at E, man at B). Chooses card B *"because the blue one is there, the red one there, and the yellow one there* [each time designating the corresponding mountains on the card].—Explain to me why he can't see that [card I].—*The red one isn't on the correct side.*—And that one [card E] . . . ?—*There is no yellow one.*—And that one [card D] . . . ?—*The red one isn't on the correct side.*—And that one [card A] . . . ?—*That one is correct. The red one is there, the blue one there, and the yellow one there* [designating the mountains on the card in turn]."

43 (10:0): *Problem 3* (subject at E, man at B). Chooses card D *"because the red one hides the yellow one a little bit, and then the blue one is on the other side.*—Explain to me why he can't see that one [card E] . . . ?—*The yellow one is missing.*—And that one [card I] . . . ?—*The yellow one would have to be in the blue one's place and the blue one in the yellow one's place.*—And that one [card B] . . . ?—*The yellow one would have to be in the blue one's place and the blue one in the yellow one's place.*—And that one [card A] . . . ?—*I think that one's right.*—Explain to me why you think this is the right one.—*I don't know . . . I'm all mixed up."*

49 (7:0): *Problem 3* (subject at E, man at B). Chooses card A *"because there is a blue one, then a yellow one, then a red one.*—And that one [card E], why can't he see that one?—*Because the yellow one is hidden.*—And that one [card I] . . . ?—*No, it's that one.*—Explain to me . . . —*He sees a blue one, then a yellow one, and then a red one* [same description as for card A].—And that one [card D], why can't he see it?—*Because he doesn't see the red one in front.*—And that one [card B] . . . ?—*Because the red one is hidden a little bit* [by the yellow one, on the board, in position A]."

40 (10:0): *Problem 3* (subject at E, man at B). Chooses card I *"because the blue one is there* [i.e., on the left on the card], *the red one is there* [i.e., in front], *and we can't see the yellow one very much.*—Explain to me why he can't see this one [card B].—*Because the blue mountain is not in front of the red one* [on the board] *and the yellow mountain isn't there* [i.e., to the right of the other two].—And that one [card E] . . . ?—*We are supposed to see the yellow one and we don't see it* [on card E]. —And that one [card D] . . . ?—*Because the red one is there* [i.e., on the left on the card] *and it's the blue one that's supposed to be there, and the yellow one is there* [i.e., in the center].—And that one [card A] . . . ? —*Because the yellow one is not in its place, and the blue one is in its place and so is the red one."*

In sum, with all these children we might seem to be dealing with a beginning of decentration because they do not consistently adopt the pictures corresponding to their perspective at the time (E or D); but this interpretation does not stand up to a more meticulous analysis of the protocols. The first subject chooses picture A, but his reason for rejecting picture B *("because the yellow one is not beside the red one but is right in front of it")* clearly shows the futility of this so-called beginning of decentration. The second subject first chooses picture B, but his very vague justification of this choice and his subsequent acceptance of picture A, which he sees as equivalent by giving the very same reason, rather clearly indicate that his initial choice arises much less from the man's present perspective than from his own previous perspective. The confusion to which the following subject is victim, and which he spontaneously admits, could not better reveal the egocentric hold exerted on him by his present (choice of picture D) and his previous perspectives (choice of picture A). The fourth subject is hardly more sure of himself, since he first accepts picture A and then picture I almost immediately, justifying this dual choice in exactly the same terms; his rejection of picture B *("because the red one is hidden a little bit"),* on the other hand, is directly due to the perspective proper to picture A. Finally, the last subject included in the example adopts a similar compromise: he chooses picture I and rejects picture B for reasons pertaining to his egocentric perspective at the time, clearly showing that the subsequent rejection of pictures D and A is not a real effort at decentration but simply expresses the fact that both pictures, each in its own way, contradict the compromise picture (I) chosen by the subject. Certainly nothing guarantees that these children are capable of the minimum decentration necessary for the mental construction of an as yet unexplored perspective. It seems wiser to see this behavior as a persistent undifferentiation between two viewpoints successively perceived by the subject, or (which amounts to the same thing) a simple recognition or memory reconstruction of a viewpoint already perceived a moment before and consistently held to be the only correct one from the beginning of the test. This is why, in the third problem, only the responses where picture B is chosen to the exclusion of all the others should be classed among the truly decentrated responses. This choice, of course, is not always based on all the projective relations implied in the perspective to be identified and may even be easier than that of pictures F and C of the preceding two problems, solely because the subject himself was already able to observe the set of mountains from the position where the man is at present located. But, in order to distinguish between pictures A and B, both corresponding to viewpoints familiar to the subject, and in order to be able to choose picture B to the exclusion of picture A, it seems necessary to apply to a reconstruction, if not an anticipation, of the elements inherent in the man's perspective.

A second type of pseudo decentration observed in stage 1 children consists of choosing the pictures that correspond to their own perspective at the time while indicating the place where the man should stand in order to see one or another of the rejected pictures, or (which is the same thing) emphasizing the need to rotate the board in order to make the rejected pictures visible. Below are two excerpts of protocols in which this type of pseudo decentration sometimes appears.

32 (12:0): *Problem 1* (position F). Chooses cards A and G, saying: *"I'm sure it's one of these two.—Which* do you think is better?—*That one* [card A].—Explain to me why . . . —*Because I would have said that one* [card G], *but the yellow mountain would have to be more toward the center here* [pushing the yellow mountain toward the blue mountain on the board].—Yes, but why did you choose this card [card A]?—*Because it couldn't be that one* [card G].—You are sure that he doesn't see that one [card G]?—*Yes.*—Explain . . . —*Because the yellow mountain is here* [i.e., near the center, on the card] *and there* [board] *it is over there* [i.e., toward the outside].—And that one [card D] . . . ?—*Oh no!*—Explain . . . —*Because it isn't placed in the same way. It would have to be turned sideways* [i.e., the board].—And that one [card F] . . . ?—*Because the yellow one is not on that side.*—And that one [card H] . . . ?—*Because they aren't arranged like that* [i.e., as in A].—What isn't arranged the same way?—*Everything."*

Problem 2 (position C). Points to cards A and B. "Which is better?—*They're almost the same. It's hard! Ah! here* [card B], *the red one and the blue one are stuck together, it's not that one. This one is the right one* [card A].—Explain to me why . . . —*It can't be the others because this one* [card A] *is arranged the same way, like that* [i.e., the board].—And that one [card E], why can't he see that one?—*Because there aren't two, there are three.*—And that one [card C] . . . ?—*Well, there is no yellow one either, it can't be the right one.*—And that one [card F] . . . ? —*He could, but not from that position.*—Explain it to me . . . —*Because we would have to change the mountains: the yellow one there* [i.e., in the place occupied by the blue one on the board] *and the blue one right in the middle* [i.e., as in card F].—And that one [card B] . . . ?—*I'm afraid I made a wrong choice at first!* . . . [reflection] . . . *No, not that one, because it isn't the same way* . . . —What isn't the same way?—*The red one."* Etc.

5 (10:0): *Problem 1* (position F). Chooses card G *"because the yellow one is closer to the red mountain.*—And that one [card H], why can't he see that one?—*Because the man isn't on the right side; he would have to be there* [points to position E].—And that one [card A] . . . ?—*Because, where he is, he can't see all of the blue one, he only sees part of it* [without noticing that the blue one is not at all hidden on card G which he has chosen].—And that one [card D] . . . ?—*Because the yellow one is*

behind the red one.—And that one [card F] . . . ?—*Yes, he can see it.*—
Then, which is the best one?—*That one* [card G]."

Problem 2 (position C). Chooses card A *"because, from this side, he
sees the blue one first. Then, he sees the red one and, then, the yellow
one.*—And that one [card C], tell me why he can't see that one.—*Because
the man sees the yellow one.*—And that one [card F] . . . ?—*Because he
sees the blue one in front. He would have to be here* [points to position
F!].—And that one [card E] . . . ?—*Because there isn't a yellow one in
the pictures.*—And that one [card B] . . . ?—*Because we would have to
put him here* [designating the corner of the board between F and G]."
Etc.

As we might notice in reading these two excerpts, the behavior
which we are discussing here never appears in an isolated way in a
single protocol, but is always mixed with behavior belonging to
other types of egocentrism or pseudo decentration. The first of these
subjects, in rejecting the pictures, twice mentioned the need to move
either the man or the board (problem 1: card D, and problem 2:
card F). But we note first the vagueness of the first intervention and
the specific nature of the second, which is very closely related to the
overtly egocentric behavior already described, consisting of rearrang-
ing the elements on the board so as directly to reproduce the perspective of the rejected card. We note especially that the subject persists
in selecting the most egocentric card in both problems and that the
whole protocol is filled with extremely primitive egocentric attitudes. The second subject included in the example is perhaps a bit
more advanced. In three instances he is careful to designate the position where the man would have to be in order to see the rejected
pictures (problem 1: card H, and problem 2: cards F and B); but
these positions are incorrect in two cases (cards H and B) and, if it
happens that the third (card F) is correct, it is important to remember that position F corresponds to the position occupied by the man
in the preceding problem when, despite some hesitation, the subject
chose a clearly egocentric picture (G). Consequently it is not surprising to note that the rest of the protocol is saturated with overt
egocentrism, as seen generally in the persistent return to the pictures
corresponding to the subject's own perspective (A and G), and particularly in the repeated allusion to the absence of the yellow mountain in rejecting pictures C and E of problem 2. This second subject's protocol also includes (e.g., problem 1: card A) some reactions
of another type of pseudo decentration to be discussed in a moment.

In summary, we need not accept the authenticity of the decentration attempts described above. At most, this behavior reflects the subject's understanding of the fact that no picture is visible from just any position (or that a change in position entails a change in perspective). There is nothing new in this, since understanding the instructions already presupposes this elementary awareness and is accessible to all stage 1 children. It is for this reason that the express use of this type of argument by some children need not indicate their ability to anticipate the perspective visible from a particular position, not even from the position which they themselves designate; basically, they are more interested in locating a position different from their own (and from that of the man) than in positively locating the one actually corresponding to the picture involved.

It remains to describe briefly a third and last type of pseudo decentration, perhaps the most embarrassing of all because it seems partially to satisfy the criterion used up to now in recognizing true intellectual decentration—that is, the ability to imagine or to anticipate the perspective of a group of objects visible from a position not yet occupied by the subject himself. Although they still consistently choose the typically egocentric pictures, some children are able to describe (sometimes with a great deal of accuracy) the picture that corresponds to the man's perspective when justifying their choices and rejections. This paradoxical behavior, clearly illustrated in the last protocol cited above (problem 1: card A), is even more obvious in the following protocol excerpts.

33 (9:0): *Problem 1* (position F). Chooses picture A. "Explain to me why you say that the man can see that one.—*The red mountain is at his right, and the blue and yellow ones at his left.*—It's like that in the picture?—*Yes.*—And that one [card G] . . . ?—*It's that one.*—Explain to me why you think he can see that one.—*Because the red one is on his left, and then the blue and yellow ones on his left.*—They are all on his left? —*No! The red one is on his right, then the blue one and the yellow one on his left.*—And that one [card D] . . . ?—*No, because he isn't there* [pointing to the position occupied by the the the examiner].—And that one [card F] . . . ?—*Because the yellow one isn't there* [i.e., to the left of the blue mountain, in relation to him, on the board].—And that one [card H] . . . ?—*Because the red one would have to be there* [i.e., to the far left, with respect to him, on the board], *the blue one in the middle and the yellow one there* [i.e., to the right on the board]." Etc.

28 (10:0): *Problem 1* (position F). Chooses card A *"because he sees the red one beside the yellow one and the blue one in the back,"* and then rejects all the other pictures, always referring to his own point of view.

17 (6:0): *Problem 2* (position C). Chooses card A, but *"minus the yellow one. He doesn't see the yellow one.*—Tell me why you say that he sees this one [card A].—*Because the red one is there, and the blue one is there, and the yellow one isn't there.* [!]—And that one [card C], why can't he see it?—*Because the man sees the red one on the other side and the blue one on the other* [which is true for the child but not for the man].—And this one [card F] . . . —*The red one is in the right place, but not the blue one* [true of the child, not of the man].—And that one [card B] . . . ?—*The yellow one is in the red one's place, the blue one is too close to the red one.*—And that one [card E] . . . ?—*The blue one is in the red one's place and the red one is on the blue one's place."* Etc.

27 (11:0): *Problem 2* (position C). Chooses card B *"because the blue one is on the right, the red one on the left, and the yellow one on the right,"* which clearly corresponds to the relative positions of the three mountains in relation to the man, but openly contradicts the perspective in the picture which the child has chosen.

These examples are clear and need no comment. Some much less frequent behaviors, however, are even more disturbing. The subject begins by spontaneously choosing a picture which reproduces the man's perspective in whole or in part (e.g., picture F or H in problem 1; picture C or E in problem 2), but he spontaneously rejects this first choice when one of the typically egocentric pictures is presented to him, and he holds to this second choice to the end.

All these children seem able really to anticipate, though in an extremely fragile and temporary manner, the perspective corresponding to the little man's position. At first glance, we might be tempted to include these behaviors among those deriving from a genuine intellectual decentration and to explain the instability of these anticipations by difficulties of minor importance. We could especially offer the hypothesis that using graphic pictures rather than three-dimensional models runs the risk of complicating the subject's task by introducing additional elements of abstraction or transposition. It is precisely these difficulties foreign to the principal task which subjects less adept in dealing with the graphic conventions of distance and depth representation may stumble over. The very ambiguity of some of the children's expressions (e.g., *"the blue one isn't stuck to the red one the way it is in the picture"; "both points of the blue mountain are missing"; "in the picture, the red mountain is higher than the other two";* etc.) suggests the possibility of such a confusion.

However, the results of a control study[2] showed that this factor is not the major source of the subject's difficulties. The control test was administered to a new group of 50 eight-year-old subjects, selected by the same selection criteria used in the main experiment (e.g., sex, level in school). The major modification of the initial technique consisted of replacing the graphic pictures by miniature models with mountains (of modeling clay) about the same size as those in the pictures. In each of these problems, as in the larger experiment, the subject had to select the model best corresponding to the man's perspective. The models were presented one by one (not all together as in the present test) and were on a level with the child's sight. A second, less radical, modification required the child to give a verbal description of the man's perspective before being presented with each series of models. We note that this new form does not affect the difficulty of the test. When we score them by the same classification criteria, the protocols of the two groups of subjects are similarly distributed on the developmental scale, and the few differences are not significant (at the .05 level: Kolmogorov-Smirnov test). There is, however, one unexpected and instructive point which the results of this experiment revealed in stage 1 children. This is the generalized (and no longer episodic or exceptional) nature of the behaviors that consist of giving a perfect description of the man's perspective while selecting the egocentric model. In fact, 85 per cent of all the stage 1 children's responses to the three problems were of this type. If the children examined by the present graphic-reproductions technique were so rarely able to describe the man's perspective when they had chosen the egocentric picture, it is not because they were incapable of doing so, but simply because they were not asked to do so—whence the futility of distinguishing the subjects who spontaneously offer this verbal description from those who do not, as though these two types of behavior corresponded to different levels of development.

What could account for this *décalage* between the child's verbal description of the man's perspective and the systematic choice of the

---

[2] This experiment was conducted with the collaboration of Richard (1962).

egocentric picture?[3] If it is not related to the particular testing technique used in our experiment, as the countertest indicates, this *décalage* probably reflects an intellectual difficulty rather easy to understand. When he tries to describe the mountains visible from the man's point of view, the child may in fact be satisfied with considering them in turn in order to coordinate them with the man one by one. This kind of coordination may require a minimum of intellectual decentration, but this decentration does not approach the complexity of an anticipation which must cover several complementary elements and requiring the simultaneous coordination of multiple dimensions. It is probably because of this succession of partial representations, which he is not required to coordinate, that the stage 1 child often succeeds in describing the man's perspective quite accurately. He fails, on the other hand, in any attempt to coordinate these partial elements into a single system and thus to construct a complete representation of the set of mountains. The narrowness and rigidity of his field of attention keep him from considering all the elements, and he cannot combine them into a single structure which is both stable enough and mobile enough to lend itself to the deductive or anticipatory transformations necessitated by the diversity of problems. Lacking this flexibility, he spontaneously turns to his own perspective, which is already completely structured in his immediate perceptual field; thus he yields to the egocentric illusion without even wondering whether it might be possible to construct a perspective different from his own, which he sees as absolute and which he automatically assimilates to the little man's perspective. Furthermore, since he is unable to distinguish his previous description from his present perception, the subject does not hesitate to justify his choices and rejections by applying the same attributes to the second that he had found to be correct in the first (left-right or before-behind relations), since he is insensitive to the contradictions forced on him by his egocentrism (see for example protocol 27 (11:0), reported above, where the subject accepts picture

3 The *décalage* is not unanalogous to that which was emphasized above in the *Concepts of left and right* test, where we noted that the current use of the terms "left" and "right" does not seem to aid the child's decentration. When the use of these same terms (and of the terms "before," "behind," etc.) goes so far as to induce, in the present test, a correct verbal description of a perspective different from the subject's without reducing the egocentrism of his choices, the problem of the relationship between language and thought becomes still more acute.

B in problem 2 *"because the blue one is on the right, the red one on the left, and the yellow one on the right"*). It is only fair to add that these subjects sometimes become half-conscious of the fact that their explanations are incompatible with the arrangement of the mountains in the pictures (e.g., admission of confusion, signs of hesitation, etc.); but these flashes of awareness have no real effect, and indications are that the subject's persistence in his initial response is much more a question of inability than of laziness or mental economizing.

To summarize the preceding discussions, stage 1 is characterized by the absence of any real decentration. Although the subject's descriptions and explanations may sometimes suggest the beginning of a mental anticipation and a differentiation of perspectives, we need not admit that the process of decentration has really begun and is effectively operating as long as the subject persists in systematically choosing the pictures that reflect his present or previous egocentric perspectives.

Before going on to a description of the behavior at the second stage, we should recall that the present stage is divided into two substages. In substage 1A, the behaviors typical of stage 1 are, in at least one of the three problems, still accompanied by the reactions of incomprehension typical of stage 0. In substage 1B, on the contrary, all three problems produce the various types of egocentric behavior just described. We might question the legitimacy of giving any value to behaviors which were lost in a sea of overt incomprehension at substage 1A. Is there not some danger of misjudging the subject's real abilities and considering certain choices or explanations as genuine, when in fact chance alone might have produced them? In fact, the reverse danger seems to be the more real. The conditions that regulate the classification of protocols (complementarity of choices and rejections within a single protocol, consistency of choices and alleged justifications, etc.) may lead us to include with the various manifestations of incomprehension (and thus in stage 0) some behaviors in which overt egocentrism takes different, less consistent, and less coherent forms, just as real as those in stage 1. Furthermore, the behavior observed in substage 1A children presents such homogeneity and regularity that it is difficult not to give it a positive and definite psychological meaning. Among these behaviors are included, first, the classical reaction of the child who makes an initial effort to deal with the task but judges it to be too difficult and sooner or later reverts to various attitudes of refusal, play, or pure randomness. In a second type of reaction, the incomprehension appears abruptly in the third problem, as though the change in perspective (from A to E) confused the child enough to make him suddenly shake off all his previous convictions. Finally, a last type of behavior in substage 1A is just the opposite of the preceding type: the subject does not appear to understand any of the instructions until the last problem, as though the effects produced by his change in position shed a new light—however diffuse it may still be—on the nature of the task required of him. These are some of the clearly defined and typical reactions of those transitional moments when the behavior includes characteristics of both adjacent levels.

STAGE 2: PARTIAL DECENTRATION

The second stage is characterized by the beginning of a real intellectual decentration. The protocols assigned to this level may or may not be completely free of the radical egocentrism of the preceding stage. When they are, however, the decentration is always only partial or, if it is total, it appears in only one or two problems. On the other hand, when the protocols still contain purely egocentric reactions, these reactions never appear alone but are always accompanied by at least partial decentrations. In sum, the second stage could be defined by a continual oscillation between purely egocentric behavior, partial decentration, and complete decentration. These three kinds of behavior represent nearly equal proportions of all responses at this level; but they combine in very different proportions from one protocol to another. It is this diversity which forms the basis of subdividing the present stage into two substages; we will discuss the differences between the two substages after describing the typical intermediate-level reactions. This description concerns mainly the partial decentration behaviors, because these behaviors are characteristic of children at this level and especially reveal the obstacles encountered by these first efforts at decentration. We can dispense with discussion of the purely egocentric behaviors, characteristic of the preceding stage, which persist in the children of the second stage. We can also give only secondary importance to the total decentration behaviors which we can already observe in the present stage, though they do not generalize to all the problems in the test as they do in the following stage. By referring to protocol fragments taken out of context, we obviously risk obscuring the real quality of the protocols; but this drawback is largely compensated for by a reduction of the text, a clearer description of the partial decentration phenomenon, and a greater diversification of examples.

The achievement of children at the second stage consists, then, of this attempt to anticipate or mentally to construct the man's perspective without previously perceiving it. Such an attempt does not immediately produce perfect and consistent coordination of all the projective relations involved. On the contrary, the child meets insurmountable difficulties, the greatest of which arises from his inability simultaneously to imagine the various left-right and before-behind relations linking the man to the three mountains. He then considers only one of these two projective dimensions and limits his choice to the pictures in which the arrangement of the mountains conforms to the man's perspective along this one dimension. The various manifestations of partial decentration activities may be divided into three major types.

A. The *first* of these types most directly reveals the nature of the projective representations typical of this intermediate level. It consists of simultaneously choosing two pictures in which the arrangement of the mountains is the same with respect to one of the two dimensions, but different with respect to the other. Examples of this type of behavior appear particularly in the first two problems of the test because the subject's change in perspective in the third problem makes it difficult to distinguish clearly, in the case of a double choice (e.g., choice of A and B), what depends on a real partial decentration from what depends on the simple recognition of a previously perceived egocentric perspective. In the first two problems, however, the cases of partial decentration are very easy to uncover. Thus, in the first problem (position F), the subject may choose pictures F and H because the blue mountain is in the background in both of them as it is in the man's perspective; but he then overtly ignores the left-right dimension along which the two pictures systematically reverse the respective positions of the red and yellow mountains. Similarly, in the second problem (position C), the subject may consider pictures C and E to be equivalent because he rightly recognizes that the yellow mountain is impossible to see from the position occupied by the little man and that therefore it should not figure in the picture he selects; but, as he is paying attention only to this particular aspect of the before-behind dimension, he then ignores another aspect of this same dimension by not differentiating between the pictures, one of which (C) puts the red mountain behind the blue one and the other of which (E) puts it in front. The left-right relation need not even be involved, because, in the only two pictures where the yellow mountain is not included, the red mountain is to the left of the blue one. This partial uniformity may perhaps produce an error on the part of the subject who too rapidly generalizes it to all the other relations without being careful to distinguish the two pictures. But the pitfall is not inevitable because this very uniformity may, on the contrary, cause other subjects, sure that all the pictures differ from one another in some respect, to examine more closely the two apparently similar pictures and discover this second aspect of the before-behind dimension. Nor is it certain that these children would have been more reluctant to confuse two pictures in which the red and blue mountains had been arranged differently in left-right terms. The frequently observed confusion in the first problem between pictures F and H is patent proof of this. Finally, a number of children are aware of the difference between pictures C and E but pay no attention to it, as though the disappearance of the yellow mountain were the only important dimension to be considered. In sum, whether it takes the form of general confusion or of conscious indifference, the equivalence which the child recognizes in certain pairs of pictures must arise above all from the fact that he focuses his attention on the most striking aspect of the man's perspective to the exclusion of all others. Below are several excerpts from protocols which beautifully illustrate this first type of behavior.

19 (7:0): *Problem 1* (position F). Chooses card D *"because the man is like that,"* gesturing to the position occupied by the man (i.e., in a straight line with the blue mountain).—"And that one [card G], why can't he see that one?—*Because he is looking straight at the blue one* [i.e., he is opposite the blue one].—And that one [card A] . . . ?—*He isn't in front of the red mountain like I am.*—And that one [card H] . . . ?— *It's that one.*—Explain to me why . . . —*Because he is in front of the blue mountain.*—And that one [card F] . . . ?—*It's that one, too.*—Explain to me . . . —*Because he is in front of the blue one.*"

10 (6:0): *Problem 2* (position C). Chooses card C *"because he sees the blue one and the red one a little bit. The yellow one is behind the blue one.—And that one [card E], you are sure that he doesn't see that one?—Yes . . . No. It's that one. They're both alike.—Explain to me why . . .—The two are the same.—And that one [card F], explain to me why he can't see that one.—Because we can see the yellow one.—And that one [card A] . . . ?—We can see the yellow one.—And that one [card B] . . . ? —We can see the yellow one."*

8 (11:0): *Problem 2* (position C). Chooses picture E *"because the red one is on the right [!] and the blue one is on the left [!] and the yellow one is behind the blue one, we can't see it.—And that one there [picture C], you are sure that he doesn't see that one?—They are almost the same. He sees it, they are the same. There is just this one [i.e., the red mountain] which is "moved back" a little.—Explain to me why he can see that one too.—The mountains can't move! When the little man moves up, he sees the blue one in front of the red one and, when he goes back, he sees it behind the red one.—And that one [card F], explain to me why he doesn't see that one.—He isn't in the right place to see it. Where he is, he can't see the yellow one.—And that one [card A] . . . ?—Because the yellow one isn't in front of the red one, and then the blue one isn't in the right place. And that one [card B] . . . ?—Because the blue one isn't here [i.e., to the left] and also the yellow one is hidden."*

Some children may prefer one of the two pictures which they consider to be equivalent, but the paucity of the alleged justifications and even the absence of some justifications show that this preference is more verbal than real. Here are two examples of this.

52 (9:0): *Problem 2* (position C). Chooses picture E *"because he can't see the yellow one; it is hidden behind the blue one.—And that one [card A], explain to me why he can't see that one.—Because he can't see the yellow one.—And that one [card B] . . . ?—He can't see the yellow one.—And that one [card F] . . . ?—He can't see the yellow one.—And that one [card C] . . . ?—It could be that one, and then the other [i.e., card E].—Explain . . .—There is no yellow one on it.—Which do you think is better [C or E]?—I'll keep to the other one [i.e., E].—Why do you think that one is better?—I have to choose one, you only want one: and, on both of them, we can't see the yellow one."*

1 (7:0): *Problem 1* (position F). Chooses picture F *"because the yellow one is beside the blue one.—And that one [card G], you are sure that he doesn't see this one?—Yes.—Explain . . .—Because the yellow one is beside the red one [i.e., in front of the red one] and it has to be beside the blue one [i.e., in front of the blue one].—And that one [card A] . . . ?— The yellow one isn't beside the blue one, but beside the red one.—And*

that one [card D] . . . ?—*Because the yellow one is behind the red one.*
—And that one [card H] . . . ?—[Reflection] . . . *I don't know."* Obviously
notices that the yellow one is in front of the blue one as in F.

Further examples would be superfluous. It is already obvious
that although he can anticipate the dominant aspects of the various
viewpoints successively offered to the little man, the child at this
level still cannot consider them simultaneously and make all the
projective transformations necessary for an accurate construction
and recognition.

B. This same inability underlies the *second* type of reaction, the
difference being that the subject here designates only one of the two
pictures considered to be equivalent in the preceding type. When
the choice bears on the one which does not reproduce the man's
correct perspective, it is not difficult to recognize the inadequacy
of the subject's decentration. In most cases, the alleged justifications
unequivocally reflect the exclusive importance accorded by the child
to the dominant aspect of the man's perspective. In the first problem,
for example, picture H is preferred because the blue mountain is in
the background; similarly, in the second problem, the choice of picture E is explained by the absence of the yellow mountain; etc. On
the other hand, when the child's preference finally hits the correct
picture, the incompleteness of his projective construction is more difficult to uncover; it is nonetheless real, however, and the egocentric
adherences in the child's protocol testify to this. In both cases, analysis of the reasons given by the subjects in justifying their choices and
rejections is particularly instructive, much more so even than the
behavior of the first type described earlier. This analysis shows in
fact that if the child prefers one of the partially identical pictures,
it is because his efforts at decentration are still shackled by very
strong egocentric resistances. The protocols always include a mixture
of egocentrism and decentration, variously proportioned depending
on the subject, where these two types of reactions may be closely
mixed but more often are simply intertwined and used alternately.
Following are some examples in which the subject reverts to an unexpected egocentrism after giving some responses of partial or even
total decentration.

9 (12:0): *Problem 1* (position F). Hesitates at first between pictures
G and F, then chooses F *"because he sees the blue one in back like that,*

and then he sees these two in front. The mountains are arranged like that.—And that one [picture G], explain to me why he can't see it.— *Because if he could see the yellow one, it would have to be to the right* [i.e., to the right of the man on the board].—And that one [picture A] . . . ?—*Because the blue one would have to be in the middle, the yellow one is on the wrong side, and the red and yellow mountains are stuck together, and that's not how it really is.*" Thus shows himself to be capable of decentration up to this point. However, the egocentric perspective clearly regains the upper hand in picture H following (and probably even in the last picture D). Rejects picture H *"because the blue one would have had to be more in front, then the red one behind the blue one, and the red one would have to be on the other side.*" In sum, he transforms H into A. He perhaps does the same thing in picture D, judged to be incorrect *"because the red one would have to be on the other side, and the yellow one right next to it.*"

30 (9:0): *Problem 1* (position F). Chooses picture H *"because the big red one hides the end of the blue one and the yellow one hides the other end of the blue one.*—And that one [card G], explain to me why he can't see that one.—*Because the yellow one is in front of the red one.*—And that one [card A] . . . ?—*Because the yellow one is in front of the red one.* —And that one [card D] . . . ?—*Because the yellow one, on the card, is hidden behind the red one.*—And that one [card F] . . . ?—*Because the blue one is supposed to be here* [i.e., to the left on the card] *and the yellow one there* [i.e., to the right] *near the red one.*" This last reaction is typically egocentric, the child correcting the correct card F as a function of his own perspective.

1 (11:0): *Problem 1* (position F). Unhesitatingly chooses picture F *"because the blue and yellow ones are to his left, the blue one is behind the yellow one, and the red one is to his right.*—And that one [card G], explain why he can't see it.—*Because it's arranged the same way as when the man was here* [points to A].—And that one [card A] . . . ?—*Because it's like the one I just saw* [i.e., G]. *The red and the yellow ones are to his right and the blue one is to his left. If he were here* [indicates A], *he would see that.*—And that one [card D] . . . ?—*Because he would have to be on your side to see that* [the examiner is actually on the side opposite the child]." In sum, apart from some confusion between A and G, the protocol is perfect up to this point; however, egocentrism reappears in card H, rejected *"because the red one is in the blue one's place and the blue one in the red one's place.*" We could see this as a simple temporary verbal confusion and admit the correctness of his response, substituting the "yellow" mountain for the "blue" mountain in the child's explanation; but the frequency of similar confusions in the whole protocol precludes the hypothesis of a temporary distraction. Thus, in problem 2 (position C), he chooses picture E *"because the red one is to his*

right [!] and the blue one to his left [!] and the yellow one behind the blue." Similarly, in problem 3 (man at B, subject at E), he rejects picture A *"because the blue one* [on the left in the picture] *is in the red one's place* [to the left of the child on the board] *and the yellow one is in front of the red one* [while it is behind the red one on the board in relation to the child]." Etc.

21 (9:0): *Problem 2* (position C). Chooses picture E *"because the yellow one is hidden and the two mountains are not close together* [referring to the distance separating the red and blue mountains in picture E].— And that one [card C], explain why he can't see it.—*Because the blue one would have to be here* [i.e., to the right of the yellow mountain on the board and in relation to the subject]." He thus seems to be trying, rather curiously, to arrange the mountains so that, from his own position, the red and blue mountains appear as in picture C. "And that one [card F] . . . ?—*Because the yellow one is here* [i.e., to the left of the blue one in the picture, without its being clear whether he would rather not see it at all, as in picture E, or to see it on the right as in relation to himself]. —And that one [card A] . . . ?—*That one could be all right.*—Explain to me why he can see it.—*The man is supposed to be here and he would take pictures of the mountains* [he here adopts a clearly egocentric attitude by holding the card in front of him and indicating a position on the left edge as though the card had become the board].—And that one [card B], are you sure he can't see it?—*Yes* . . . [rather unconvinced] . . .— Explain to me . . .—*Because he can't see the yellow one: he is opposite the blue one and the blue one hides the yellow one* [an at least partial decentration, whereas he had just accepted card A despite the presence of the yellow one]." All things considered, the choice of picture E and the rejection of picture B require a minimum of partial decentration (comprehension of the fact that the yellow one must disappear behind the blue one), but egocentrism predominates in the rejection of at least two of the other three pictures.

2 (11:0): *Problem 2* (position C). Chooses picture C *"because the yellow one is behind the blue one, we can't see it.*—And that one [picture B], explain to me why he can't see that one.—*Because that one isn't right, because the yellow one is in back* [i.e., behind the blue one, for the little man].—And that one [picture E] . . . ?—*Because the blue one would have to be on the other side, and the red one would have to be on this side* [probably referring to his own point of view].—And that one [picture A] . . . ?—*Because the yellow one is in back, he can't see it.*—And that one [picture F] . . . ?—*Because the blue one would have to be in front."*

40 (9:0): *Problem 3* (subject at E, man at B). First chooses picture D *"because he sees the yellow one close to the red one."* Changes his mind, however, when he is presented picture B following, and selects the latter

"because he sees the blue mountain close to the red one and the yellow one far away." Then rejects picture I "because the yellow one isn't close to the red one [for the little man]," then picture E "because the man sees the yellow mountain." Finally, in picture A, rejected like the preceding two, he reverts to his initial egocentrism, alleging that "the blue one is supposed to be on the right."

27 (8:0): *Problem 3* (subject at E, man at B). Hesitates at first for a while, then chooses picture B, saying: "It's that one, I think.—Explain to me why you say that the man sees that one.—He sees the yellow one, the red one, the blue one.—And that one [picture I], explain why he can't see that one.—The red one is the biggest [i.e., the most obvious one in the picture].—And that one [picture E] . . . ?—We only see two of them. There [i.e., from the place where the man is located], we see all three of them.—And that one [picture D] . . . ?—There [i.e., in the picture], we only see the yellow one a little bit, and there [i.e., where the man is standing], we see the whole thing.—And that one [picture A] . . . ?—The red one is the biggest [on the card]; then we see all of the yellow one [on the card], and he [the man] sees a little bit of it." Note the implied contradiction in the responses to the last two pictures, precisely because of this reversion to egocentric attitudes in defending the rejection of picture A.

All these examples indicate that the instability of the child's first decentrations most often appears as a continual alternation of thought between decentration and egocentrism. More rare are the protocols in which these two opposing attitudes, instead of appearing alternately, are mixed in such a way that the choice or rejection of a single picture is motivated by considerations of both egocentrism and decentration. The reason for this relative infrequency may be related to the fact that looking for overtly egocentric behaviors easily leads us to ignore a number of other behaviors in which egocentrism may operate without revealing itself in verbal expressions or gestures. For example, when a child chooses a particular picture simply because the picture reproduces an essential and dominant relation in the man's perspective, paying no attention to the other relations, his behavior may easily be explained by his belief in the rigid and absolute character of the projective relations, a belief whereby a transformation of one of these relations should automatically entail the transformation of all the others.

Whatever the case, there are many examples of egocentrism and decentration openly coexisting within a single response. In the second problem especially, where the man is at C, the choice of picture E often depends on these two types of reasons at once: the subject chooses picture E because the yellow mountain should not show (partial decentration) and because both the red and blue mountains must be completely visible (as they are at A). This is why picture E enjoys such great popularity, as we have already seen in the analysis of errors. This is not the place to return to an interpretation of this type of response, but it is appropriate to cite an example where the confusion of the child's two viewpoints appears quite clearly.

46 (9:0): *Problem 2* (position C). Chooses picture E, claiming that *"the blue one is in front of the yellow one* [i.e., hides the yellow one].— And that one [card A] . . . ?—*When he was in my place* [i.e., at A], *that was the one he saw.*—And that one [card F] . . . ?—*The blue one is in front of the two* [i.e., for the man, contrary to picture F where the blue one is in the background].—And that one [card C] . . . ?—*The line in the middle is clear* [i.e., indicates that the area on the board between the two mountains is open] *and here, in the picture, the blue one covers the red one a little bit.*—And that one [card B] . . . ?—*The yellow one is there* [i.e., is not hidden], *and it is not there* [i.e., for the little man]."

A similar though apparently more superficial confusion is observed in subjects who justify their choices by appealing to relations which in fact do not appear on the picture but derive from their own egocentric perspective. Here are short examples of this.

49 (12:0): *Problem 1* (position F). Chooses picture F, explaining that *"the red one is to the right, the yellow one is to the right also* [sic], *and the blue one is in the middle."*

47 (12:0): *Problem 1* (position F). Chooses picture F *"because it photographs the red one, it hides the blue one a little, and the yellow one is to the right* [sic]."

Thus these two children chose the correct picture and accurately described the position of the red and blue mountains in relation to the man, but they reverted to their egocentric perspective when locating the yellow mountain and did not even notice that their description flatly contradicted the picture they had chosen. This is neither a simple verbal confusion nor an accidental error in expression (the first of these two children insisted on saying that the yellow one is to the right "also"). The rest of the questioning shows that, in most of these cases, egocentrism still persists in one form or another. Thus the first of the two subjects cited in the above example, while rejecting picture H in the same problem, justified this rejection by indicating rather paradoxically that the man had to be standing at F in order to have such a view of the mountains, not even noticing that the man was already standing at F.

To complete this inventory of the second type of behavior, we must add the responses of the child who, while giving no overt sign of egocentrism and sometimes selecting the correct picture, defends his choices and particularly his rejections with reasons whose futility or ambiguity leave too many doubts about his real ability to coordinate the various points of view. In the first problem, for example, some children rejected picture H, claiming that in relation to picture F the blue mountain did not have the same shape (which is incorrect), that the yellow mountain was not on the same level as the red mountain (which is also incorrect), or finally that the blue mountain was not at the same distance from the red or yellow mountains (which is incorrect or at least irrelevant, since picture H is simply the mirror image of picture F). Similarly, in the second problem, some children preferred picture C to picture E, claiming that the blue mountain was "stuck" to the red one in this picture, which is very ambiguous since this expression (or similar ones) might just as easily refer to the overlap in the before-behind dimension (i.e., "in front of the red one") as reflect the simple comparative perception of pictures C and E without reference to the man's viewpoint. It is perhaps wiser to see these responses as signs of partial decentration because, instead of emphasizing the necessary projective relations, the subject seems satisfied with looking for reasons that justify his choice after the fact.

It goes without saying that the importance accorded the general structure of the protocols also requires us to include among these responses of the second type all responses in which the subject, after choosing the correct picture and even basing his choice on all the necessary relations, justifies his rejection of the other pictures by expressions which are too vague to reveal whether he could describe the disagreements or find the positions that correspond to the rejected pictures (e.g., *"it isn't the same," "it would have to be different,"* etc.). For one thing, the examples reported up to now have shown that choosing the correct picture is not a sure sign of a complete and stable intellectual construction and that a child's explanation may easily take account of all the necessary relations when it consists of merely describing the picture in front of him. For another thing, it is often in the child's effort to justify his rejections that the egocentric attitudes are revealed or clarified. Thus we must avoid favoring the subject who resorts to descriptions too vague to be incriminating at the expense of the subject who risks making mistakes by trying to justify concretely all his choices and rejections.

Despite their apparent diversity, all responses described under the second type of behavior reflect the basic instability and incompleteness of the child's first intellectual decentrations. We can always find in them an undeniable beginning of differentiation of viewpoints, but this differentiation either is limited to certain partial and salient relations, or succeeds only sporadically and inconsistently in including all of the relations.

C. The *third* type of behavior arises from a very special illusion. A number of children used various ways in order to more easily compare the man's perspective and the perspective presented by each picture: the most advanced of these consisted of placing each picture, in turn, opposite the man and beyond the group of mountains in order to determine which one could be the best visual projection of the mountains in relation to the man, the child leaning slightly toward the man to make the comparison. It is precisely in applying this procedure that several children made mistakes and yielded to the illusion typical of this third type of behavior. Instead of placing the pictures opposite the man, they put them behind him and leaned slightly toward the opposite side in order to recognize the picture best corresponding to the perspective they have when they look at the man and the pictures from across the mountains. The results of this kind of geometry are easy to predict. When the picture that corresponds to the position exactly opposite the man is presented, it is immediately chosen (in the second problem, for example, picture F is preferred to all the others). If none of the pictures corresponds to the perspective opposite that of the man, the subject then prefers the one which most closely approximates it: thus in the first problem (position F), picture D or H is favored, the subject selecting one or the other depending on whether his attention is fixed on the projective left-right relation or on the before-behind relation. Below are several examples.

42 (10:0): *Problem 1* (position F). Chooses picture A first, saying: *"He'll see the blue mountain in the front of him, the red one on his right and the yellow one on his left."* We recognize in this the behavior typical of stage 1 consisting of correctly describing the man's view and choosing the egocentric picture anyway. But, contrary to what we observe in the preceding stage, the questioning leads the child to correct his first choice. "And that one [card G], explain to me why he can't see that." First places the picture behind the man, then explains: *"because he would have to be there* [then indicates position C, which is easily understood if we note that, placed at C, picture G would be the mirror image of the red and blue mountains seen from this position].—And that one [card D] . . . ?—[Again places the picture behind the man] *Because the blue one is on his left, the yellow one is in the middle, and the red one on his right* [a description which the child rightly considers as partially contrary to the man's point of view because placing the picture behind the man reverses the left-right relations].—And that one [card H] . . . ?—[Again places the picture behind the man] *Oh! That's the one!*—Explain to me . . .—*Because the red one is to his right, the blue one is in the middle, and the yellow one is to his left* [a description which the child recognizes this time as perfectly conforming to the man's perspective, for the same reason which led him to reject card F].—Then tell me why the one you just chose a little while ago isn't right.—*Because it would have required him to be there* [indicates position E, still exactly opposite to that from which he really could have seen picture A]."

51 (9:0): *Problem 2* (position C). Chooses picture F, corresponding to the position exactly opposite the one occupied by the man. Asked to explain his choice, he places the picture behind the man and then points to each of the mountains on the board, and then in the picture, pointing out the agreement each time: *"Because the red one is there, the blue one is there, and the yellow one there."* For each of the following pictures, he does not take the trouble to put the picture behind the man, but his explanations unequivocally show that he is following the same principle each time.—"And that one there [card E], explain why he can't see that. —*Because there are just two mountains.*—And that one [card A] . . . ?— *He would have to be there* [indicates near position D, but several centimeters toward the inside of the board].—And that one [card B] . . .— *Because the man would have to be like this* [indicates position F more or less, but a little closer to the yellow mountain]." In sum, in the last two cases, the position selected is very nearly the opposite of the position corresponding to the picture presented to him.

As this last excerpt indicates, it is not necessary for the subject to try openly to place the pictures behind the man in order to be misled by this reversal of perspectives. In fact, it is only afterward that the subject in the example resorts to this procedure, in order to justify his choice of picture F without having to go into long explanations; but, even though he never repeats the gesture, the nature and consistency of his responses reflect the generality of his reasoning.

It may be surprising to see this third type of behavior express itself in the choice of picture F in the second problem, when such a choice usually reflects (see the preceding stages) the subject's lack of comprehension or his tendency to select any picture whatever. It is undeniable that almost all subjects who chose picture F when the man was at C reveal total incomprehension, as is seen also in the incoherence (or even absence) of reasons invoked to justify their choices and rejections. In fact, it is exceptional (only six subjects, including the last one in the example) for the rest of the protocol to be consistent enough and explicit enough to give this type of response a characteristic of genuine partial decentration.

It remains to describe briefly a last type of intermediate reactions. They are not sufficiently widespread (only five cases) to constitute a clearly defined category and they superficially resemble the behavior of the third group discussed above because, like this group, they produce responses easily attributable to egocentrism. This is the case with the child who rejects each picture in turn and whose massive rejection, rather than relying on fantasy-related reasons as in the children of stage 0 (e.g., *"the mountains on the cards aren't pretty," "the man isn't looking at them"*), derives instead from a true intellectual dissatisfaction. The child has created an image of the view facing the little man; but, because this image includes both egocentrism and decentration, the child cannot find a single picture that satisfies his requirements and he is thus compelled to reject all of them. Here is a very clear example of this.

38 (8:0): *Problem 2* (position C). Examines pictures one by one by placing each one opposite the little man, across the mountains, and facing them, finally concluding: *"The right card isn't there.*—That one [card F], you are sure he doesn't see that one?—*Yes . . . because the blue one is in back.*—And that one [card A] . . . ?—*The yellow one is in front of the red one.*—And that one [card B] . . . ?—*The blue and the yellow ones are in front.*—And that one [card C] . . . ?—*There isn't a yellow one.*—And that one [card E] . . . ?—*There is no yellow one."*

The only trace of egocentrism in this protocol concerns the child's inability to anticipate the disappearance of the yellow mountain behind the blue one. In all other respects, the order in which he would like to see the three mountains corresponds exactly to the man's perspective. In the imaginary (and objectively impossible) picture on which he bases his successive rejections, the blue mountain had to be in the foreground (see the rejection of picture F) and the red one in the background (see the rejection of picture B). As for the yellow mountain, whose possible absence he does not seem to notice, he insists that it not be in front of the red one, nor even on the same plane as the blue one (see the rejection of pictures A and B). Thus this type of confusion is basically comparable to that of all the intermediate-level behaviors described earlier; we can easily see in them the mixture of egocentrism and decentration typical of the second stage.

These three groups of typically intermediate reactions do not exhaust the range of behaviors observed in stage 2, for they account for only 30 per cent of all responses to the three problems in the test. The rest of the responses are, in nearly equal proportions, either fully egocentric (36 per cent) or fully decentrated (33 per cent). In some subjects these extreme responses are the only ones made, without a single typically intermediate response being included, a little as though the mixture of egocentrism and decentration in these children took on a special form of instability or mobility, which is reflected in constant oscillations between these two extreme attitudes rather than in the adoption of a unique and steady attitude, equally dependent on both egocentrism and decentration.

It should be unnecessary here to describe the completely egocentric responses which are still scattered among the protocols assigned to the present stage; they are identical in all respects to the similar responses already described in the preceding stage. On the other hand, we should at once define the responses of full decentration which are found here for the first time; but we can be satisfied for the moment with a general description of these decentrations. For a fuller account of these responses, as well as of the various forms which they can assume, it is better to wait until the study of stage 3, when the process of decentration is generalized to all problems.

Complete decentration is recognizable first by the choice of the picture which exactly reproduces the man's perspective. It can happen that the child's choice is not immediately correct; but, when the examiner presents him with the rejected pictures one by one and asks him to justify each rejection, the child recognizes the correct picture and changes his choice. The choice of the correct picture, however, is not always accompanied by an explicit coordination of all the projective relations concerned. It is, then, the general effect of the protocol which allows us to differentiate the subjects whose choice of the correct picture may be explained by efforts at partial or still incomplete decentration and those whose behavior, despite appearances of partial decentration, nevertheless implies a real ability to consider all the necessary projective relations. It is rather unusual, in fact, for children to mention spontaneously all the elements which they actually use in their initial choice. Their first explanations almost always resemble the typically intermediate level because they emphasize only the partial aspects of the man's perspective. But, unlike what we observe in the intermediate behavior, the successive presentation of all of the pictures initially judged to be incorrect produces no difficulty in subjects who are really capable of complete decentration and does not induce the reappearance of egocentric attitudes. It simply provides the subject with the opportunity to reexamine his initial response and thus to demonstrate the flexibility of his coordinations. In sum, if each of the explanations offered allows the intervention of only one element of the man's perspective, the total of the explanations includes express references to all the projective relations (left-right and before-behind) linking each mountain to the miniature observer. Thus it is the explicit use of all the projective elements concerned and the total absence of egocentric confusion which clearly reveal the quality of the subject's coordinations.

Finally, we must briefly mention the distinction between substages 2A and 2B. The distinction is justified particularly by the size of the differences between protocols in the relative frequency of the three categories of possible responses (pure egocentrism, partial decentration, total decentration). Even though all children whose responses are neither completely egocentric nor completely decentrated are classified at stage 2, it is quite obvious that there is a whole range of behaviors between these two extreme poles; their diversity reflects the progression which the child must follow in his progressive conquest of projective space. It is in order to mark at least some of the major steps in this construction and also to guarantee a greater homogeneity in the classification of protocols that it is helpful to divide this intermediate level into two substages.

Substage 2A (108 subjects) is reserved for children whose efforts at decentration are the most poorly sustained and the least efficient. These children are all capable of reconstructing, at least once, some of the projective relations inherent in the man's perspective; but they never (54 subjects, or 50 per cent) manage, or do so only once (54 subjects, or again 50 per cent), to coordinate all the projective relations. Most of their responses include the egocentrism which it is so difficult for them to disengage themselves from. In fact, in 67 subjects of substage 2A, we still observe two overtly egocentric responses accompanied either by partial (41 subjects) or complete (26 subjects) success. Furthermore, in 34 other subjects of the same substage, the only completely egocentric response is surrounded by either two partial successes (10 subjects) or one partial success and one complete success (24 subjects). Finally, the remaining seven subjects avoided any fully egocentric response and confined themselves either to three partial successes (three subjects) or two partial successes and one complete success (four subjects). The great variety of these intermediate behaviors could even suggest the existence of additional substages; but these various possible levels do not actually correspond to any real and systematic change in the progression of chronological ages. We should probably interpret this variety merely as the expression of the instability typical of all intermediate behavior. The same child may, at any given moment, readily succeed in imagining in whole or in part certain viewpoints different from his own and then, at another moment, revert to purely egocentric attitudes. The distribution of these various reactions depends on accidental conditions, such as the time of the examination, the subject's attention or interest, the type or tone of the questions asked him, etc. All these factors might call into question a diagnosis (or a classification) based on an instrument which is so easily subject to the influence of chance circumstances; but it is as an effort to reduce this influence that the present classification avoids making spurious refinements and combines contemporary but apparently quite different behaviors.

Substage 2B (53 subjects) is similar to the preceding stage in all respects but one: the subjects are capable of two total decentration responses (out of three), while those of substage 2A succeeded with none or with only one. The choice of this criterion may seem arbitrary, and theoretically it would be at least equally legitimate to require only one total decentration response instead of two in defining substage 2B. But the criterion is justified at least by the fact that there is a significant difference (at the .05 level: Kolmogorov-Smirnov test) between the distribution (by age) of subjects who manage only once or not at all to give a total decentration response and that of subjects who do so twice; the difference between those who have only one success and those who have none is not significant. That is why it is legitimate to assume that the criterion is not purely artificial but touches a real psychological difference in the child, corresponding to genuine progress in the development of his system of perspectives.

Thus substage 2B is characterized by complete success with two out of three problems and by a partial failure (31 subjects) or absolute failure (22 subjects) with the third. It is interesting to note that 59 per cent of these partial or absolute failures concern the second problem (man placed at C); this finding was predictable from the results reported above (Chapter XV) concerning the relatively low number of total successes observed with this problem. However— and the paradox is worth mentioning—it is this same problem which, in substage 2A, most often produces partial successes (50 per cent of all partial successes). In sum, this problem is both easier and more difficult than the others. It is easier because it includes certain aspects which the children seem to grasp rather easily (i.e., by substage 2A), such as the overlap or concealment of the yellow mountain by the blue one; at the same time it is more difficult because it also includes certain aspects which complicate and hinder its perfect solution. Once the principle of the disappearance of the yellow mountain behind the blue one has been understood, the child completely ignores the other elements of the projective before-behind relation and is then naturally induced to consider two of the pictures presented to him to be equivalent, or to designate only one of them, but in a purely arbitrary manner.

STAGE 3: OPERATIONAL COORDINATION

Stage 3, which is achieved by only 40 of all the subjects tested, is characterized by an operational coordination of all the projective relations involved in the test. The child is able to recognize the picture which corresponds exactly to the man's perspective in each problem, and his explanations contain explicit references to all the left-right and before-behind relations that define the position of the mountains, each in relation to the other two and all three in relation to the little man. And in addition, the child's initial choice is almost always the correct one. It can happen that the initial choice is erroneous, as is the case with 8 per cent of the responses; but with the examiner's very first questions or the mere presentation of the correct picture, the child very soon recognizes his error, and his explanations then leave no doubt about the accuracy of his representation of the man's perspective. Here are two short examples.

34 (11:0): *Problem 2* (position C). Chooses picture E *"because he sees the blue one and the red one. The yellow one is hidden by the blue one. —And you are sure that this one* [card C] *isn't the one he sees?—Yes . . . no . . . that one is the right one.—*Explain to me why he sees that one.*— Because the blue one is in front of the red one. The other card is wrong because the blue one is behind the red one."* Etc.

42 (9:0): *Problem 2* (position C). Examines each of the pictures in turn and concludes: *"There isn't any.—*Look carefully.*—There isn't any, because the blue one would have to be in front of the yellow one. That one* [card B] *is most like it: only the blue one is misplaced. If the man were in your place, he would see that* [card C] *or that* [card E].*—*Then that one [card B] is the one he sees?*—No, not that one.—*Explain it to me . . .*—Because the blue one would have to be here, in front of the yellow one.—*And that one [card A] . . . ?*—No, not that one, he* [the man] *would have to be here* [position A]. *I think it's this one* [card C].*—*Explain to me why . . .*—Because the yellow one is hidden, the way he sees it; and the yellow one is to the right.—*And that one [card F] . . . ?*— No, not that one, because he would have to be here* [position F].*—*And that one [card E] . . . ?*—No, not that one, because he would have to be in your place. This is the one* [card C] *that he sees here, and not that one* [card E] *because they aren't made the same. On that one* [card C] *the blue one hides the yellow one, and on that one* [card E] *the red one hides the yellow one."*

In more than one respect, this juxtaposition of completely decentrated and still-egocentric responses is not unlike the behavior at the intermediate level. In particular it recalls the case of the subjects who chose the correct picture, justifying their responses with an accurate description of all the projective relations involved, and then reverted to partial or even total egocentrism in explaining the rejection of the alternative pictures. But despite these similarities, these two types of behavior are radically different. The behaviors classified at stage 3 hardly leave any doubt about the subject's ability to form an accurate image of the changes in perspective entailed by the man's movement around the board, regardless of the subject's frequent hesitations at the beginning. In the preceding stage, on the contrary, the subject's difficulty in justifying the rejection of some of the pictures (particularly when these pictures partially conform to the man's perspective) probably betrays the still-incomplete character of the subject's attempted decentrations. The correctness of his choice may perhaps be explained as a happy coincidence favored by the limited number of pictures sharing the same partial characteristics, and the relevance of the initial explanation may be due simply to a factual description of the picture which was selected.

Be that as it may, it is important to give several clear examples of behavior typical of stage 3, where the subject's choice is immediately fixed on the correct picture (sometimes with surprising speed) and where this choice is clearly based on operational considerations.

4 (12:0): *Problem 1* (position F). Immediately points to picture F, saying: "*He sees the red one on his right, the yellow one on his left, and the blue behind the red and yellow ones, in the middle.*—And that one [card G], explain to me why he doesn't see it.—*Because the yellow one isn't* [i.e., should not be] *in front of the red one and the blue one isn't in the yellow one's place.*—And that one [card A] . . . ?—*Because the yellow one is not in front of the red one and the blue one isn't in the yellow one's place.*—And that one [card D] . . . ?—*Because the red one isn't in the yellow one's place, and the yellow one behind the red one, and the blue one isn't in the red one's place.*—And that one [card H] . . . ?—*Because the red one isn't in the yellow one's place and the yellow one in the red one's place, and the blue one isn't exactly like that: it has to be a little more to the side.*"

11 (11:0): *Problem 1* (position F). Chooses card F "*because the red one is on the right; the yellow one is to the left and beside the red one; the blue one is behind the yellow one.*—And can you explain why he

can't see this one [card A]?—*He would have to be here* [in A].—And that one [card H] . . . ?—*The red one has to be to the right; the yellow one should be to the left.*—And that one [card G] . . . ?—*The yellow one is supposed to be here in front of the blue one; and the red one beside the yellow one.*—And that one [card D] . . . ?—*The blue one has to be on the left; the yellow one has to be on the left in front of the blue one; the red one has to be on the right, beside the yellow one."*

Problem 2 (position C). Chooses card C *"because the red one is on the left, beside the yellow one; the blue one is on the right, but since the blue one is bigger than the yellow one, he can't see it.*—And that one [card E], explain to me why he can't see that one.—*The blue one would have to be in front of the red one.*—And that one [card B] . . . ?—*There would have to be no yellow one and the blue one would have to be on the right.*—And that one [card A] . . . ?—*The red one has to be on the left, the blue one on the right in front of the yellow one, and so no yellow one.*—And that one [card F] . . . ?—*The red one has to be on the left, the blue one on the right in front of the red one; we're not supposed to see the yellow one."*

17 (11:0): *Problem 3* (subject at E, man at B). Chooses card B *"because the blue mountain is most in front of him; the red one is a little more to the rear and it's hidden a little bit by the blue one: the yellow one is more to the right side than the others and not as close as the other two.*—And that one [card A], explain to me why he doesn't see that one.—*That's the one when he takes the picture from the front* [i.e., from A].—And that one [card D] . . . ?—*He's supposed to see the blue one first and there* [on the card] *it's the red one; and also the blue one is in the yellow one's place.*—And that one [card E] . . . ?—*He is supposed to see all the mountains; there, he sees only two and they aren't in the right place.*—And that one [card I] . . . ?—*The blue one is in back, the red one is in front, and the yellow one is in back, too."*

These examples are particularly clear in that the child's very first explanation unequivocally demonstrates each time that all the projective relations have been considered in his choice. But we should mention that this is neither a sufficient nor a necessary indication of a complete operational coordination. It is not sufficient because the description of the intermediate level showed that some children can easily yield to egocentric preoccupations after having both chosen the correct pictures and described the man's perspective with all the details we could expect. And it is unnecessary because a number of children at stage 3, not going into all the elements responsible for their initial choice, give explanations which are comparable in all respects to those of subjects at the preceding level in that they are limited to partial aspects of the man's perspective. However, the child's reasons for rejecting one after another of the alternative pictures in each problem—and especially the picture which in each case is the most critical because it is the least different from the correct one—reveal that he ignores none of the essential projective relations, and that the lack of precision noted in the initial choice reflects simply a lack of verbal fluency rather than of operational ability. Several protocol excerpts will show this.

34 (11:0): *Problem 1* (position F). Chooses card F, saying: *"He sees the red one and the yellow one in front, then the blue one behind in the middle* [an explanation which is also true for picture H].—And that one . . . ? [card G]; explain to me why he can't see it.—*The yellow one would have to be in the blue one's place, and then the blue one in the middle.*—And that one [card H] . . . ?—*The yellow one is in the red one's place, and the red one in the yellow one's place.*—And that one [card D] . . . ?—*The blue one would have to be in the yellow one's place* [i.e., in the middle].—And that one [card A] . . . ?—*The blue one is in the yellow one's place, and the blue one would have to be behind in the middle."*

4 (12:0): *Problem 2* (position C). Chooses card C *"because he can't see through the blue mountain. He doesn't see the yellow one which is hidden behind the blue one* [seems to take account only of the disappearance of the yellow mountain].—And that one [card E], explain to me why he can't see that.—*Because the red one isn't in front of the blue one, and the blue one behind the red one.*—And that one [card F] . . . ? —*Because the yellow one is not on that side in front, nor the red one on the other side, nor the blue one behind both of them.*—And that one [card A] . . . ?—*Because the red one isn't in the yellow one's place, nor the yellow one in front of the red one, nor the blue one on the other side.*—And that one [card B] . . . ?—*The yellow and red ones are in the right place, but the blue one is on the wrong side."*

44 (11:0): *Problem 3* (subject at E, man at B). Chooses card B, saying: *"He sees the blue one first, then the yellow one on the other side; and after that, the big red one in back* [an explanation which is also true of card A].—And that one [card A], explain why he can't see that one.— *The red one should be in back of the blue one.*—And that one [card E] . . . ?—*Because there isn't any yellow one.*—And that one [card D] . . . ? —*The yellow one is in back of the red one.*—And that one [card I] . . . ? —*The red one is in front, then it should be in back."*

Thus, unlike the intermediate-level subjects, these children can all defend their choices and their rejections in a consistent and complementary fashion, without confusing their own perspectives with that of the little man. They are classed, therefore, at stage 3, just as are the subjects whose coordination of perspectives is obvious from the first choice.

The preceding examples do not adequately illustrate the diversity of strategies used by subjects at this stage in explaining how the pictures and the man's perspective agree and how they differ. In most of these samples, in fact, the subject's strategy consists of adopting the man's perspective as a stable reference position and emphasizing the points on which each of the (incorrect) pictures is incompatible with this perspective (e.g., *"on the card, the red mountain is in front of the others and he sees it behind the others,"* etc.). To this sort of explanation must be added at least two others which some children used either exclusively or in combination with the preceding type. In the *first* of these two types of explanation, it is the picture instead which is used as a norm by the subject, who then proceeds to designate or to describe the positions which the mountains would have to occupy in order to give the man the corresponding view. In other words, the subject corrects the set of mountains as a function of the pictures, rather than the reverse. The *second* type consists of directly looking for the position that corresponds to each of the alternative pictures. Thus the subject corrects neither the pictures nor the set of mountains: instead, he considers them as elements determined by the only variable element in the situation—that is, the (virtually multiple) position of the man— and he then focuses his mental operations on this one element. More than all the others, this strategy reveals that the child can conceive of projective space as a system of possible viewpoints which is subject to laws determined by related transformations. In a certain sense, it is as though the subject could no longer see a single correct picture among other incorrect ones; on the contrary, all the alternative pictures correspond, for him, to as many possible perspectives, and each perspective is related to a particular position of the man and is recognizable by the projective relations included in the picture. It is not surprising that this strategy is really the only one that favors identification of the absurd pictures (perspectives which are impossible without a rearrangement of the elements) among those presented in the first and third problems. The reason for this is simple. As long as he tries to correct the incorrect pictures in order to make them conform to a particular perspective or, conversely, to change the arrangement of the mountains in order to make them conform to a particular picture, the subject will not notice the difference between an absurd picture and an incorrect (but possible) picture; for example, the moment a particular picture does not exactly reproduce the man's perspective, the subject may have to correct or change almost all the elements, though the importance of the changes is not related to absurdity as such but rather to simple inaccuracy. The nuance is naturally overlooked by the subject who is not trying to make a particular position correspond to each picture. This is not to say that this strategy invariably guarantees the discovery of the absurd pictures, since the coordination of positions and pictures may include errors, and the most frequent of these consists of relating an impossible picture to a real position. Thus, in the first problem (position F), the three main positions variously assigned by the subjects to picture H (red mountain in the foreground to the left, yellow mountain in the foreground to the right, blue mountain in the center and behind the other two which partially overlap it) are distributed in the following manner, in order of preference: (a) the corner between positions E and F (i.e., a position from which the man can see the red mountain on his left); (b) position C (where the yellow and red mountains are to the right and left of the man, respectively); (c) position A or G (where the yellow mountain is to the right of the man). In the third problem, the positions assigned to picture I (red mountain in the foreground flanked by the yellow one to the right and the blue one to the left, both partially covered by the red one) are always next to the red mountain, whose presence in the foreground is considered as an essential and exclusive factor by the subject.

This type of error in the explanations offered for rejecting a particular picture is not observed only with the absurd pictures: it is also seen in the rejection of the incorrect (though possible) pictures; but the positions selected are almost never very far from the actual positions, so that the errors can be partially accounted for by the imprecision of gesture or language, by the subject's overlooking certain details, etc. Thus the subject could justify rejecting two different pictures (e.g., A and B, A and G, D and E) by designating a single position, not paying attention to the rather marked differences between the pictures in each of these pairs. Basically, whether they concern the absurd or the possible pictures, all these errors reflect the same tendency to use only rarely all the projective relations represented in the different pictures in locating the corresponding positions. This strategy is reminiscent of that of subjects at the preceding stage, who were apparently led by the belief in the rigidity of projective relations to assume that the correct reproduction of a particular projective relation must *ipso facto* entail the correctness of all the others. The same phenomenon seems to occur here: for example when a child compares position C to picture H, it is as though he were interested only in putting the red mountain to the left of the little man and the yellow mountain to the right, without worrying about the blue mountain, whose correct position would be completely determined by the other two. The same type of error occurs when, instead of looking for the position that corresponds to a given picture, the child tries to arrange the mountains as they would have to be for the picture in question to be visible to the man. It is frequent, then, for the rearrangement to deal with only one of the dominant projective relations to the exclusion of all others. The following example is especially clear.

21 (12:0): *Problem 1* (position F). Chooses picture F *"because he sees the red mountain there* [pointing to the red mountain on the card], *the yellow mountain there and, a little farther away, the blue mountain in the back* [still pointing to them on the card].—And that one [card G], explain to me why he can't see that one.—*Because there isn't any space between the red one and the yellow one.*—And that one [card A] . . . ?— *If that one were the right card, the yellow mountain would be there."* He then takes the yellow mountain and goes to place it between position F and the corner of the board which is closest to the red mountain, without moving the blue one at all. The red one and the yellow one are then to the right of the little man, the yellow one covering the red one as on card A; but the blue one is to the left in the background, while it is on the same level as the yellow one on card A. "And that one [card D] . . . ?—*If he could see that one, the blue one would be here and the yellow one would be there."* Interchanges the yellow and the blue ones, so that the man then sees the yellow one behind the other two as on card D; is not aware of the fact that the left-right order of the red and blue mountains now contradicts card D.

At first glance, these various errors could be combined with those which are typical of the intermediate level. On closer examination, however, it seems that excluding these subjects from stage 3 would

be to treat them more severely than those who give verbal explanations without fully discussing the differences between the rejected
pictures and the man's perspective. For example, when these subjects
emphasize only one point of disagreement (e.g., *"the red mountain
is on the left on the card, and for him it's on the right"*), they should
not be judged harshly because actually only one disagreement is
enough to compromise the correctness of the whole structure. The
same strategy is used by subjects who commit errors (e.g., designation of an incorrect position, inadequate modifications of the elements on the board, etc.) in justifying the rejection of the incorrect
pictures. Basically, their search for a position or for a new arrangement conforming to the rejected picture may stop as soon as a
particular element of the position or the proposed arrangement contradicts the correct picture while agreeing with the rejected picture,
and further analysis is considered neither necessary nor useful.

In sum, just as in the preceding stage, the subjects at stage 3 may
rely on only partial projective relations (e.g., incomplete verbal explanation, suggesting a position which only partially conforms to the
rejected picture, inadequate rearrangement of the mountains, etc.)
in explaining their choices and rejections. But this nonmentioning
of all the projective relations concerned is no longer due to the
subject's basic inability to coordinate all of them in making his
choices and rejections; rather, it is the result of simple concerns with
mental economy which appear only in the justification of the choices
and rejections, because any further analysis is not considered necessary
once enough agreements and disagreements have been established.
This superiority of stage 3 subjects over those of the preceding
stage is seen first in the complete absence of the egocentric considerations so often present in the protocols of subjects at the intermediate level. It is also obvious when we stop to consider the totality
of the subject's responses to a single problem. In stage 3 subjects, we
can always find an internal coherence and integration—which stage
2 subjects never demonstrate—whereby both the left-right and
before-behind projective dimensions are coordinated to one another,
instead of being simply juxtaposed; this coordination is reflected in
the fact that these subjects show no difficulty whatever in giving
complementary responses (implicit up to this point) when they have
to use an apparently ignored relation or further define a previously
mentioned relation.

Finally, a last type of rather frequently observed behavior at stage 3 consists of placing each picture opposite the man so as to determine, for any particular perspective, whether the arrangement of the elements in the picture coincides with that of the elements on the board. We recall that some subjects at the preceding level attempted to use a similar strategy; but, unable to understand the geometry of the situation, their application of it produced systematic errors. Instead of placing the pictures opposite the man, they placed them behind him or, more specifically, in his position, and they themselves adopted the opposite position in order to determine the agreement of the picture with the board. In sum, because each picture is supposed to reproduce the man's perspective, these subjects could imagine nothing better than bringing the "perceived object" as close as possible to the "perceiving subject"—that is, substituting the former for the latter by placing the picture so that it "looks at" the arrangement on the board just as the man does. This confusion between the "subject" and the "object" (between the "looker" and the "looked at") no longer exists among stage 3 subjects. These children always place the picture opposite the man (at either the near or the far side of the board) and then consider it as a sort of screen (or plane) on or through which are projected the imaginary lines that link the man's gaze and the object. If the obstacles encountered by this pencil of rays correspond in the picture and on the board, the subject judges the picture to match the man's perspective; in the case of noncorrespondence, he can immediately recognize the nature and extent of the disagreement. We might perhaps feel that the use of such a strategy unduly facilitates the solution of the problems and that it would have been better to prohibit it. It seems, however, that the very discovery of such a technique—with the obvious condition that it be correctly applied and that the child not be allowed to move around—in itself implies a degree of projective structuring which could define accession to the last stage, assuming that the instructions had encouraged the child to look for this sort of strategy. In the present conditions of the test, the child's spontaneous use of the strategy can constitute at most an important sign of operational coordination.

At the conclusion of this necessarily long and laborious description, suffice it to mention that the three stages of development proposed here are fairly comparable to Piaget's in content and order of succession. In both cases, we find an initial stage of pure egocentrism (Piaget's stage IIA and stage 1 above) which slowly yields to a final stage of complete decentration (Piaget's stage III and stage 3 above). Between these two extreme levels is a whole range of intermediate behaviors. Piaget was able to distinguish among these a relatively low level (stage II) characterized by still fruitless attempts at decentration, and a higher level at which the child is capable of real but still incomplete decentration. In the present test these two of Piaget's intermediate levels (IIB and IIIA) were not so clearly distinguishable. This is why the early coordinations typical of our stage 2 are defined instead in terms of various combinations of decentration and egocentrism (e.g., responses all partially decentrated, responses completely or partially decentrated with or without still-egocentric responses, etc.), excluding only the totally egocentric or totally decentrated protocols from this intermediate stage. The only more precise discrimination possible at this transitional level is based on the number of totally decentrated behaviors in a single protocol (stage 2A: one or no decentration; stage 2B: two decentrations).

It is important also to emphasize the slowness which characterizes the development of this ability to coordinate perspectives, a coordination which only a small proportion (28 per cent) of the children at twelve years could effect. There is no need to discuss the slight delay which seems to affect the age of accession to the last stage of the present test in relation to the corresponding ages (from nine or ten years to eleven or twelve years) mentioned by Piaget and Inhelder. The *décalage* is not pronounced and may be related to differences in testing techniques (e.g., Piaget and Inhelder's apparatus was much larger and included cues which could favor the correct choices) or to the nature of the samples (number of subjects in each age level, intellectual level in comparison with that of the general population, etc.). It would be helpful, however, to avoid a possible misunderstanding about the delayed nature of this development. The fact that the operational coordination of perspectives is not yet mastered by the age of twelve years could suggest that this ability derives from formal thought. This would probably be the case if the test required the subject to consider two different systems of relations at once and to go into operations of multiplicative composition, compensation or reciprocal cancellation, etc. Still referring to projective concepts, we will recall, for example, the various methods used by Piaget (Piaget and Inhelder, 1948; Inhelder and Piaget, 1955) in studying the development of the child's spatial representations in the projection of shadows. If we ask the subject simply to recognize or sketch the shape of shadows projected by a cardboard disk variously oriented toward a light source, success with the task requires no more than the logical multiplication of the constituent elements of a single system of projective relations. On the other hand, if the subject must instead, as in the second study cited, equalize the shadows projected by two rings of different sizes by varying the distance between these rings and the light source, the operations must then concern two systems at once—the projected shadow is directly proportional to the distance separating it from the ring and inversely proportional to the distance separating it from the light source— and the subject must engage in proportioning activities (at least qualitative, if not metric) in order to guarantee the necessary compensation between the effects produced by each of the two systems. This kind of operational compensation belongs to formal thought. It is obvious that the *Coordination of perspectives* test has none of this internal complexity. In its present form, it hardly requires more than the kind of simple operational reversibility, limited to a single system, whereby the subject must be able to (a) conserve the relative positions of the elements of the system despite any particular change of viewpoint, an achievement which implies at least the operations of vicariousness or reciprocity of perspectives; (b) place these elements in a one-to-one correspondence along two projective dimensions simultaneously, an achievement which does not surpass the operations of logical multiplication of order or position relations.

Although it does not yet derive from the formal level,[4] the coordination of perspective required in the present test nevertheless attains a degree of complexity which places it in the last period of the concrete operational stage. To emphasize this complexity, we need only mention why the *Coordination of perspectives* test is the most difficult of our four tests of the child's ability to conceive

4 Nor should we be misled by the fact that this operational coordination of perspectives requires the establishment of a projective system in which all the various possible viewpoints intervene. This concept of "possible" is a long way from the one that characterizes formal thought (Inhelder and Piaget, 1955)—where it is the possible which conditions the real—and still represents only the virtual extension of the subject's real actions or operations dealing with a single system of relations.

projective space. If the easiest of these tests is the *Construction of a projective straight line* test (last stage attained by 7:5 years), the reason is probably that the subject's task amounts to the simple discovery of aiming behavior. This behavior consists merely of placing the homogeneous parts of one and the same object in a single projective dimension (before-behind) and in relation to a single observer along one line extending the observer's gaze and free of the distortions suggested by the board's outlines. Thus it is evident that this sort of straight line may, in principle, be constructed in the same way in any direction in space. The *Localization of topographical positions* test, on the contrary, is more complex (last stage reached at the age of 9:8 years), because the subject must be able to coordinate, along two projective dimensions at once (left-right and before-behind), the relations that link the elements of a single structure (a miniature landscape) to each other and each in relation to an external observer, despite the reversal in perspective entailed by the 180 degree rotation. Though more difficult than the preceding test, this test is still relatively simple in relation to the following tests (*Concepts of left and right* and *Coordination of perspectives*). Locating the positions is, first, greatly simplified by topological cues (neighborhood, enclosure, etc.) which may spare the subject the need to imagine the reversal of one of the two dimensions concerned. Besides this, the variation in perspectives is reduced to a minimum (a single over-all 180 degree rotation) and the subject has only to recognize the position of an object in relation to several others which retain their present position on the reversed board. The correct localization thus seems to require mental representations which are less complicated than the basically similar representations necessary for identifying the correct picture in the *Coordination of perspectives* test, where the subject must simultaneously rearrange several objects in relation to an observer successively placed in different positions. The *Concepts of left and right* test, the third in difficulty (last stage reached at 10:11 years), is both easier than the one after it and more difficult than the two before. Referring only to the last problem, which deals with the relative position of three objects lined up on the table in front of the subject, the increased complexity of this test is seen first in the fact that the coordination required of the subject, though limited to a single projective dimension, can rely on none of the topological cues which were so useful in the preceding test, and the egocentric cues can produce systematic errors in the relative position of the middle object. Furthermore, in specifically requiring coordination of the objects themselves (e.g., *"Is the pencil to the left or to the right of the plate?"*), the test requires a form of decentration or relative objectivity which amounts, as it were, to considering the objects as so many virtual observers; this decentration is reflected in the necessary distinction between "to the left" (or "to the right") and "to the left of" (or "to the right of"). Finally, the difficulty of this test particularly concerns the two questions on the middle object, questions whose solution requires a purely relative decentration whereby a single object can be, for a single observer, both to the left of one of the two lateral objects and to the right of the other.

Finally, if the *Coordination of perspectives* test is the most difficult of the four, this is because it in fact combines the difficulties raised by the others: plurality of the projective dimensions to be coordinated; plurality of the perspectives produced by the numerous objects to be coordinated and by the diversity of the observers or the positions of a single observer; absence or inadequacy of reference points or topological cues (using these cues in the present test would lead instead to systematic errors); complexity of the mental operations required by reconstructing the perspectives corresponding to the different alternative pictures; etc. And despite the differences among them, all these tests remain theoretically interrelated, as the general analysis in the following chapter should demonstrate quite clearly.

Chapter XVII

General Analysis

The present work would be incomplete without a general analysis of the five tests covered in the preceding chapters. The fact that these tests were all taken by the same subjects makes it possible to make comparisons whose significance and theoretical meaning are much less equivocal than if each test had been administered to different groups of children, as was necessarily the case with Piaget's original tests.[1] This kind of general analysis cannot have the same interest as would the general analysis of the results obtained on the complete battery of 27 tests administered to the same subjects; but although it is limited to the five spatial representation tests, a general analysis can provide new elements for interpretation, and in particular it can lead to some generalizations about the development of the concept of space in the child.

Based mainly on the relationship between behaviors observed in the different tests, this analysis considers first the *general question* of whether there is some sort of cohesiveness in the child's progressive elaboration of the various spatial concepts covered in the five tests. Two *particular questions,* more specifically related to Piaget's hypotheses and partially discussed in the preceding chapters, will then be examined in the more general context of all five tests. The first asks whether there actually is a "topological" period in the development of the child's spatial concepts—that is, a period during which representational space would be exclusively a matter of the qualitative relations inherent in each object or in each particular configuration (relations of neighborhood, enclosure, continuity, etc.) without yet referring to a system of viewpoints or of coordinates.

[1] It seems that the current standardization of Piaget's tests by Vinh-Bang and Inhelder (personal communication) is also given to different groups of subjects.

The second question concerns the egocentrism of child thought. We know how important this primitive attitude is for Piaget's explanation of intellectual development: unable to differentiate subject from object, egocentrism ignores the multiplicity of possible viewpoints and confuses the infinitely varied aspects presented to the subject by external reality. The spatial concepts of a projective nature, which are more widely and specifically explored in the present work than are the other spatial concepts (four of the five tests explicitly deal with it), are particularly suited to proving the existence of these primitive modes of thought. The construction of projective concepts requires differentiating the perspectives as well as coordinating them in an objective general system in which the subject's own temporary viewpoint is no longer the only one operating and becomes merely one perspective in a system of possible perspectives. Separate analysis of the four tests covering the projective aspect of space has already brought out the most obvious manifestations of the egocentrism of the first projective concepts. The additional information provided by the general analysis of these tests deals especially with the extension or generality of this mental attitude in a single child, when this child has been presented successively with several different problems requiring, in varying degrees, a rejection of this exclusive centration on his own point of view (however unconscious it may have been).

INTERNAL (INTERTEST) CONSISTENCY OF THE SUBJECTS

The basic question consists of determining the degree of consistency in the behavior of subjects taking all five tests, each test covering a particular aspect of the development of spatial representations. We need not emphasize the practical implications of this question. We can easily imagine that if we found a strong degree of consistency among the tests, the psychological diagnoses of the practician in this field would be greatly simplified, since a maximum of certainty would be guaranteed by a minimum number of tests. But it is the theoretical importance of the question that makes it imperative—however difficult it may be—to assess the degree of internal consistency shown by subjects in a group of tests which are both different and similar. In fact, the problem raised by this question of consistency is directly related to the more general question of the unity of intellectual functioning. We know that, for Piaget, the progressive coordination of the subject's actions concerning the multiple aspects of reality eventually produces general intellectual structures (the "groupings" of concrete or formal thought). We know also that, again according to Piaget, the elaboration of these structures obeys certain evolutionary laws which are concretely expressed in a succession of increasingly complex stages or levels. The general economy of these laws depends on the gradually perfected elimination of an initial egocentrism, favoring a constantly increasing objectification or socialization. Referring to the particular domain of space, this progression toward decentration can take the form of a gradual structuring of spatial concepts which would at first be based on elementary topological relations alone, before the addition of projective and Euclidian considerations (complementary to each other). If Piaget's general model conforms to reality, we should find a marked consistency in the behavior of subjects who took a group of different tests specifically covering these general developmental dimensions or mental structures—dimensions and structures which a classification by stages attempts to recognize in the confusing variety of particular behaviors.

The unity or internal consistency of intellectual development is perhaps not the central concern of the Geneva school; but it seems that it has always been at least implicitly believed to be necessary. We have already made a full analysis elsewhere (Pinard and Laurendeau, 1969) of the nature of these group structures which, according to Piaget, constitute one of the most rigorous conditions of the concept of stages; we have also emphasized that this structural character varies with the observational scale (intraconceptual or interconceptual) and with the developmental level (simple stage or major period) referred to. It should suffice to recall here the Geneva team's insistence on the correspondence of the steps marking the development of various concepts, a correspondence that refers to the functional or structural equivalence of the mental processes in question as well as to the synchronism of their appearance. Inhelder and Piaget (1959), for example, emphasize the interdependence and developmental synchronism of seriation and classification systems (additive and multiplicative). They specify that these four types of structures "become operational at roughly the same period" and that, although "there are certain minor differences depending on the extent to which the content of a problem lends itself to imaginal representation, . . . they do not invalidate our main thesis" (p. 279); they see this agreement as "one of the weightiest arguments in favor of an operational conception of intelligence" (p. 195). Piaget and Inhelder (1963) further extend the application of the developmental synchronisms, claiming first that the numerical structures develop along steps which are "surprisingly parallel" (p. 134) to those observed in the elaboration of the class and relations structures, even adding that "the infralogical operations develop at the same age and in a direct parallel with the logiconumerical . . . operations" (p. 136).

We know the extreme instability of the empirical observations on which such vast generalizations are based. It often happens that two types of behavior are considered to be related to each other simply because they theoretically belong to a single intellectual structure and actually appear at approximately the same ages, even when one of these two types of behavior is observed in one group of subjects and the other in a different group. And if a difference is found between the ages when these behaviors appear in a single group of subjects, it is immediately seen as a horizontal *décalage;* we know that the nature and operation of this type of *décalage* are still so poorly understood that they easily become a rather disquieting source of comfortable and quasi-irrefutable post-factum explanatory factors. If such *décalage* were at least shown to appear in an identical pattern in all children, it might be possible to recognize their explanatory value and place them among the psychological variables whose appearance (however real) would be unpredictable as long as experimental studies have not been able to determine their structure and concrete implications. This regard for rigor, however, lies outside the concerns of the Geneva theoreticians, and thus we may be inclined to think that they are more immediately interested in the internal coherence of their explanatory system than in its empirical verification.

It is perhaps as a reaction against this lack of rigor that other authors, when testing Piaget's position on the unity of intellectual functioning, implicitly reject any reference to horizontal *décalages* and accept as evidence only the synchronism of the child's acquisitions. Applied to the interpretation of empirical findings, this sort

of rigor can sometimes go so far as to ignore the most elementary
aspects of the theory they are trying to test. Dodwell (1963), for
example, shows no reluctance in concluding that Piaget's stages (of
spatial concepts) are not even approximately verified in reality; this
conclusion is based on the fact that most of his subjects (from 42 to
85 per cent, depending on the test) fall within a category of "mixed"
behavior, to which he relegates subjects whose responses to a presumably homogeneous series of problems are neither always correct
nor always wrong. We need only examine the details of his tests
to see the weakness of his argument. The so-called homogeneous
problems in each of his tests are hardly all at the same level of internal complexity: some of these problems may be solved by a
process of as yet very rudimentary intuitive regulation (e.g., lining
up the objects along a straight line parallel to one side of a rectangular table) and others, on the contrary, imply the use of genuine
operations (e.g., lining up objects along a straight line joining the
mid-points of two adjacent sides of the same rectangular table). In
fact, rather than challenging the stages identified by Piaget in this
area, the differences in difficulty observed by Dodwell may serve
instead to confirm their existence, since the differences refer precisely to the various levels of solution corresponding to Piaget's
stages. The results reported by Dodwell never include real horizontal
décalages: the successive mastery of his various test situations is in
fact achieved by various strategies—a variety which is easily overlooked when the analysis is too superficial and too readily assumes
that similar behaviors must always be explained similarly, regardless
of the conditions in which they appear.

   If Dodwell's study clearly illustrates the methodological inadequacies and the oversimplification of conclusions derived from a too-
hasty examination of a complex and intricate system, we obviously
should conclude nothing either about the quality of other of Dodwell's works in related areas (e.g., 1960, 1961, 1962), or about the
orientation adopted by those who up to now have attempted to verify the synchronism of the intellectual mechanisms related to the
concepts of general structure advocated by Piaget (see especially
Kofsky, 1966; Lovell and Slater, 1960; Mannix, 1960; Lunzer, 1960;
Smedslund, 1964; Wohlwill, 1960b). Most often, in fact, the analysis
is not limited solely to the responses to each problem (or question)
in a single test that is designed to identify the various levels in the

development of a particular concept (or operation) in a single experimental situation. The analysis instead focuses on the general steps or stages of functioning that correspond to the various response patterns in each of several tests. The objective of such an analysis is thus to determine whether the same subject is always located at the same level of development in tests that require the action of either a single concept (or operation) inserted into different concrete situations, or several different concepts or operations (with or without modifications in the concrete situation) whose equivalence or theoretical complementarity suggest either an absolute developmental synchronism or a regular sequence.

Although this latter type of approach is better adapted to the requirements of Piaget's system than is the type of analysis previously discussed, it cannot be applied unreservedly because horizontal *décalages* at any moment can conceal the presence of a synchronism or alter a genuine developmental sequence. Analyzing the consistency of intellectual behavior by restricting ourselves simply to operations which in principle are synchronous or are derived from each other does not guarantee the equivalence of the concrete tests and situations used in reaching these operations. It may seem surprising that none of the authors mentioned above has considered invoking *décalages* related to the material, the instructions, etc., to explain at least partially the distance between the expected synchronisms or sequences and the asynchronisms and confusions actually observed. Only Smedslund and Kofsky sometimes seem aware of the limits imposed on their experimental schema by the patterns of more or less controllable variables likely to produce these horizontal *décalages*. They attempt to minimize the influence of these variables, Kofsky by using the same material (a set of geometric shapes) in his 11 classification tests, Smedslund by basing his most definite conclusions on a comparison of the two tests most closely related in content (transitivity and conservation of lengths). As useful as they may be, these precautions are still quite inadequate, since differences in content hardly exhaust the possible sources of horizontal *décalages*. We may recall, in this respect, the numerous factors referred to by Piaget and Szeminska (1941) in explaining, for example, the lack of synchronism observed in several tests of cardinal coordination. They mention "the words used, the length of the instruction given, [the] more or less concrete character [of each test], the relationship between the instructions and the individual experience of the child, the number of elements involved, the intervention of numbers the child knows, etc., etc." (p. 149). They conclude—and this conclusion is somewhat disconcerting since it applies even to a very limited domain—that the *décalages* which they observed are such "that we never succeed in measuring understanding of this [cardinal] correspondence in its pure state and that the understanding is always with respect to a given problem and given material" (p. 149).

In truth, it may seem illogical to regret that so many authors give no place to horizontal *décalages* in their explanations of developmental asynchronisms while reproaching Piaget for having made too easy use of them. The present state of knowledge of horizontal *décalages* explains these extreme attitudes. For one thing, it is impossible to question the existence of such *décalages*. Too many facts have confirmed them in various ways and on numerous occasions, particularly in the areas of physical quantities (matter, weight, volume), spatial dimensions (lengths, surfaces, geometric volumes), etc. Thus we are no more justified in systematically ignoring them than we are in unfairly invoking them each time the empirical observations contradict the theoretical predictions. For another thing, however, as regrettable as the reticence and weakness of Piaget's theory on this particular problem may be, the ignorance still surrounding the nature, necessary components, conditions, limits, and precise meaning of these *décalages* makes it impossible to form any systematic prediction about their actual effect or about the order of appearance of intellectual behaviors; consequently, it is impossible to resort to the synchronism or temporal seriation of these behaviors in testing Piaget's positions on the consistency of intellectual development. This should clearly indicate how necessary and urgent it is to confront the problem directly. Assuming that it may still be considered useful to examine whether the order of appearance of various behaviors is the same in all children before solving the general question of the *décalages,* we should at least be aware of the partial, provisional, and purely descriptive nature of such an examination, trying neither initially to predict nor then to explain the order of appearance of these behaviors in detail. It is only in this last perspective that the analysis of the consistency of subjects given all five spatial tests of the present work will be presented. This analysis deals first with the agreement of the developmental scales in each of these various tests. It is followed by a scalogram analysis which allows us to see to what extent the individual protocols agree with the chronology of the steps established by combining the stages and substages of all five tests.

AGREEMENT OF THE DEVELOPMENTAL SCALES

The question of the consistency of intellectual functioning cannot be solved directly simply by analyzing the agreement of the five developmental scales. For one thing, as soon as we admit the possible presence of horizontal *décalages* between even very similar tests (e.g., conservation of liquids or of solids) as well as the possible absence of *décalage* between even very dissimilar tests (e.g., inclusion of classes or conservation of surfaces), it becomes impossible to determine the theoretical implications of the empirically observed concordances or discordances for the question of the unity of mental functioning. Thus we would be no more correct in arguing from an actual synchronism between two tasks to the existence of an internal connection between them than we would be in arguing from a lack of synchronism to the absence of an internal connection between the same tasks. This is why the results derived from our proposed analysis of the agreement between the five scales will be considered merely as indicative rather than as conclusive. With this analysis, it will also be important to emphasize the often unnoticed drawbacks inherent in applying the usual correlation methods to problems of developmental psychology.

Since we are dealing with classificatory scales having relatively few levels, Kendall's tau coefficient is probably the kind of correlation that can most simply and directly express the degree of agreement between these scales. Table 59 gives the correlations obtained first between the five tests themselves, compared two at a time, and then between these tests and chronological age. Before examining these results more closely, we must explain why the number of subjects varies from one correlation to another. These variations are due mainly to the fact that the easiest tests were not given to the oldest subjects (e.g., from ten to twelve years), nor the most difficult to the youngest subjects (e.g., from two to four years), and that each correlation must obviously be limited to subjects taking the same tests. On the other hand, in each correlation, subjects judged impossible to classify in one or the other of the two tests had to be

Table 59

Correlations (Kendall tau) between the five tests covering various spatial concepts and between each test and chronological age

	Projective straight line	Topographical localization	Left and right	Perspectives	Chronological age
Stereognostic recognition	$.673^{(2)}$ (N=462)	$.669^{(3)}$ (N=466)	$.416^{(6)}$ (N=382)	$.475^{(5)}$ (N=429)	$.770^{(1)}$ (N=687)
Projective straight line		$.563^{(4)}$ (N=384)	$.368^{(8)}$ (N=201)	$.454^{(7)}$ (N=239)	$.677^{(2)}$ (N=522)
Topographical localization			$.464^{(6)}$ (N=283)	$.548^{(5)}$ (N=327)	$.691^{(3)}$ (N=563)
Left and right				$.506^{(6)}$ (N=373)	$.532^{(6)}$ (N=383)
Perspectives					$.608^{(5)}$ (N=437)

(1) 2:0 to 12:0 years; (2) 2:0 to 10:0 years; (3) 3:0 to 12:0 years; (4) 3:0 to 10:0 years; (5) 4:6 to 12:0 years; (6) 5:0 to 12:0 years; (7) 4:6 to 10:0 years; (8) 5:0 to 10:0 years.

excluded for the same obvious reason. Examination of Table 59, then, reveals that the correlations range from .368 to .770. The correlations seem to be highest among the three tests of *Stereognostic recognition of objects and shapes, Construction of a projective straight line,* and *Localization of topographical positions:* they do not differ significantly from one another, and the correlations between these three tests and the other two are almost all significantly lower. Furthermore, the correlations between chronological age and each test are consistently higher than the intertest correlations. It seems, however, that the degree of agreement is generally quite satisfactory, since Kendall's tau always gives lower values than the more usual coefficients.

It would clearly be unfair to accept these indices of agreement as evidence of a more or less close internal psychological connection between the various behaviors compared in each instance. It is hardly necessary to emphasize that we could obtain at least equally high indices by comparing, between 2:0 and 12:0 years, developmental measures from disparate areas having no internal and obvious connection, as though correlating, for example, a measure of height or weight and a measure of the level of spatial conceptualization. In sum, when two attributes of the organism develop in a parallel fashion during the period selected for observation, it is obvious that the correlations between these two attributes are often positive. And the longer the selected period of development, the higher the correlations will be, admitting an increase in the range of measures which are taken. The results obtained here offer clear examples of this natural phenomenon. We need only examine the figures in Table 59 to note that the obtained correlations increase with the number of age levels included in the calculations. This same heterogeneity influences both the absolute value and the order of the correlations between each test and chronological age.

The role of the age range in the correlation level raises various universally admitted difficulties which have often been mentioned. These difficulties are easily believed to affect only the interpretation of the correlations, and it is usually felt that the standard statistical precautions (e.g., partial correlations, etc.) should smooth them out and justify this type of analysis. It seems, however, that these statistical precautions cannot make up for all the deficiencies inherent in using correlation techniques in a developmental study which is intended to analyze the relationship between two developmental phenomena. We may in fact ask whether using partial-correlation techniques to control for the influence of the age range does not also exclude an essential aspect of the question of whether two concepts develop concomitantly. In truth, excluding the "developmental" factor itself, whose very characteristics we are trying to define, amounts to asking the rather absurd question of whether the development of a particular concept is as strongly tied to that of a second concept when their common developmental dimension is excluded. In other words, it is not easy to see how, after choosing chronological age as the variable that provides the range necessary for a rational application of correlation techniques (over other variables such as intellectual aptitude, rhythm of development, etc.), we are justified in eliminating this same variable and resorting instead, in order to express a relationship between two developmental phenomena, to a statistical index which has been numerically reduced by this limitation in age range.

A second reason for hesitating to use correlation techniques concerns the fact that, even assuming that the technique does not affect the significance of the observed indices, the nature of the relationship reflected by it is poorly suited to the objectives of developmental psychology. What it expresses particularly, in fact, is the

covariation of two phenomena. Since time, in all that it implies
(e.g., maturation, exercise, physical and social experience, etc.), is
the main variable in developmental psychology, it follows that the
covariation of two phenomena is obviously defined by the synchronization of two developments. This dimension is surely not
the only one nor the most important one involved. The filia-
tion of two behaviors, their reciprocal dependence or their complementarity, the substitution of one for the other, etc., are many
kinds of relationships which developmental psychology pays more
attention to than to synchronism, because they favor a more comprehensive and more refined interpretation of the facts. We know
that synchronism, as such, is not an index of any developmental
relationship; it expresses no more than a genetic coincidence between two variables, a coincidence which we could easily be tempted
to assimilate to some form of internal or functional connection. Nor
would it be at all correct, in examining the results given in Table
59, to imagine that the tests yielding the highest intercorrelations
are psychologically more closely related than are those measured by
tests yielding lower intercorrelations. In fact, the correlation level
is directly determined by the age range in each case. If, for example,
there is a strong correlation between the *Stereognostic recognition
of objects and shapes* and *Construction of a projective straight line*
tests, it is not so much that the concepts involved are more similar
than others, as simply that the development of these concepts begins
and is achieved at about the same time in both cases. On the other
hand, the low correlation between the *Construction of a projective
straight line* and the *Concepts of left and right* tests seems to depend
less on an absence of internal relationship than on the marked
décalage between the two concepts, the development of the first being completed when the second has barely begun to appear.

All things considered, then, the correlation technique seems
rather poorly suited to the usual objectives of developmental psychology. In any case, it cannot answer the question whether there is
some sort of internal cohesion between the various spatial tests
analyzed in this work. At most, it might help to specify (and quan-
tify) the importance of the synchronism or asynchronism suggested
by the rough comparison of the developmental scales (and the ages
of accession to each level of these scales). It would hardly be helpful to use partial-correlation methods in eliminating the influence

of the diversity of chronological ages since this would deprive the developmental analysis of its properly developmental dimension, and also because these partial correlations would express merely the degree of chronological agreement (or temporal overlap) between two genetic phenomena artificially fragmented and ordered in successive and independent age levels.

SCALOGRAM ANALYSIS

Probably the simplest and most direct way of discovering whether the various spatial concepts develop with a minimum of consistency or coherence is to proceed with a scalogram analysis. Unlike the correlational analysis, the scalogram analysis is not intended to determine whether there is a precise relationship between various tests (or concepts), and its validity does not depend on the synchronic or asynchronic character of the observed phenomena. The calculated indices show only whether a chronological seriation of levels, derived from an analysis of all the protocols, applies equally to individual protocols. The only question it can really answer is whether the various steps in the development of a set of behaviors, all hypothetically belonging to a single universe of content, are reached in a regular rather than a chance order; it cannot indicate the causes of the observed regularities or irregularities, because it cannot refer to specific postulates concerning the possible types of relationships between the concepts (or tests) to be scaled. However, we should not see this limitation as an argument against the use of this method; quite the contrary, the innumerable gaps in psychological knowledge of intellectual development make any overprecise hypotheses quite premature, and therefore very empirical methods of analysis are recommended.

So that the scalogram analysis can simultaneously cover all the stages established in the five tests, we must first combine them into a single chronological sequence. The age of accession to each level of the scale establishes this order of succession and delimits the exact intersections and overlaps. By calculating the number of exceptions in each protocol in relation to this scale, we can then determine the degree of reproducibility of the whole. The calculated index is then corrected by Jackson's PPR formula (see White and Saltz, 1957), which reduces its value as a function of the level that would be observed if the analysis covered a group of tests equal in difficulty to these tests but having no psychological relationship among themselves. When the PPR is at least .70, the set of behaviors may be considered as scalable, the different levels of the scale being reached in a sufficiently regular order that they may be considered to constitute a homogeneous universe of contents.

Applied in this way to the 26 levels of the scale formed by the progression of behaviors in the five spatial tests, the scalogram analysis yields a reproducibility index of .931 and a PPR of .755.[2] In all probability, then, the various steps marking the development of the five concepts considered here are reached by most children in the order established by the group analysis, and the various *décalages* revealed in this group analysis are found in most of the individual protocols. However, we must point out that this analysis covers only 170 protocols, all belonging to children between 5:0 and 12:0 years of age, because it is only at these ages that subjects took all the tests. We must also mention that the subjects who had been considered as unclassifiable (in one or the other of the five developmental scales) were not included in the analysis. Although the number of protocols finally retained is quite enough to guarantee the validity of the indices, two kinds of objections may arise.

The first concerns the partial and perhaps unique character of the developmental period to which this analysis is confined. If, for example, the period extending from 5:0 to 10:0 years were more favorable than the earlier period in terms of the regularity and coherence sought in this analysis, the significance of the conclusions would be considerably reduced. The objection loses some of its importance when we recall that this period from 5:0 to 10:0 years is characterized by significant transformations related to the appearance of operational structures. In other respects, however, the objection seems to be a serious one. For example, we need only consider the capacity of children in this period to show efforts at sustained attention, the uniformity of intellectual knowledge and activities favored by school attendance, etc. The best way to examine this objection without departing from the empirical results is to extend the analysis to a greater age range, even though this will mean reducing the number of tests (or levels) to be combined. By retaining the three tests taken by all subjects from 3:0 to 10:0 years *(Stereognostic*

---

[2] If we exclude the first five levels, reached by all the children considered in the analysis, the indices fall to .915 and .705 respectively.

recognition of objects and shapes, Construction of a projective straight line, Localization of topographical positions), we produce a scale with 17 levels which can determine the reproducibility of a group of 348 protocols. The indices yielded by this new analysis rise to .951 (reproducibility) and to .823 (PPR), which still appears to be quite satisfactory.

The second objection concerns the subjects who were excluded from the (initial) analysis because they were impossible to classify in one or another of the tests. These aberrant protocols (130 of them) might in fact seem to be the most likely to introduce irregularities in the succession of steps. This possibility seems even greater when we recall that it was because they did not conform to the transitivity rule (success with the most difficult problems and failure with the easiest) in the developmental scale of any one of the tests that some of these nonclassified protocols were considered as aberrant. If these subjects' performance is already inconsistent in a limited sequence of similar tasks, this is an even greater reason for us to expect the same inconsistency in a more complex series of less homogeneous tasks. To exclude these protocols from the analysis, then, would be to favor the reproducibility hypothesis. The relative infrequency of such protocols might suggest that they are due mainly to accidental factors; however, it seems questionable not to integrate them into an analysis whose objective is precisely to determine whether the number of exceptions to the transitivity rule exceeds the number explainable by accidental factors. In sum, in line with this objection, the exclusion of these particular protocols would have the indirect effect of guaranteeing, at the beginning, a reproducibility rate which is higher than the actual rate.

The best way to deal with this objection consists, again, of turning to the empirical results to see how the addition of these protocols could change the results of the scalogram analysis. This integration is easy to make because, for four tests out of five (excepting only the *Coordination of perspectives* test), the various stages are defined by success with groups of problems which are clearly defined in each instance. Thus—if we can temporarily ignore the inconsistency of such a classification—we could consider that a subject has reached stages 2A and 3A (but not stage 2B) of the *Localization of topographical positions* test if he succeeds with the required proportion of the seven easiest problems, before and after the landscape is rotated, and if he misses the five most difficult positions even when the landscape is not rotated. Of the 130 protocols excluded from the analysis, only 30 can be added in this way to the 170 already included. For most (55) of the other protocols, the responses to at least one of the five tests are impossible to classify for reasons unrelated to the lack of transitivity (e.g., obvious incomprehension of the instructions, refusal to submit to the requirements of the experimental situation, the examiner's clumsiness, etc.). Elimination of the other 45 protocols, on the other hand, is required by the fact that in none of these cases could the subject take all five tests.[3] The results of this third scalogram analysis, done on 200 protocols, are scarcely any different from the first analysis. The size of the obtained indices (reproducibility: .925; PPR: .736) seems to indicate that adding the 30 subjects with particularly aberrant protocols does not destroy the scale's reproducibility.

It would obviously be going too far to conclude, from the above results, that the spatial behaviors explored by the five tests are all interdependent or related to a single universe of psychological content (the concept of space) whose unidimensional character would thus be reflected in the necessary coherence of the behaviors. A less ambitious conclusion would be that the five tests are related to a single psychological dimension despite the diverse concrete situations and the variable levels of difficulty. Although this limitation makes it more realistic, the conclusion still seems to go beyond the results. We know in fact that the scalogram analysis rests mainly on a non-reciprocal implication between the homogeneity (or unidimensionality) of the measured attributes and the reproducibility (or regularity) of the behaviors. The temptation is great, however, to see this implication as an equivalence, forgetting that the regular succession of behaviors may be related to causes other than the homogeneity of the measured variable. Perhaps more than in any other domain, a

---

[3] This is explained in a purely accidental fashion. Following the initial plan of the experiment, in fact, children of 9:0 and 10:0 years did not have to take the *Stereognostic recognition of objects and shapes, Construction of a projective straight line,* and *Localization of topographical positions* tests. Analysis of the first results obtained on subjects of 7:0 and 8:0 years required us to revise our optimistic predictions—based on preliminary experiments—and include subjects of 9:0 and 10:0 years. Instead of eliminating the subjects of these two age levels who had already taken several tests, it seemed more appropriate to substitute new subjects who met the same basic selection criteria (age, level in school, etc.). The procedure presents no obstacles when the results are analyzed test by test; but it obviously prohibits, for these cases, any sort of individual analysis covering all five tests.

developmental analysis can reveal an admirable regularity in the appearance of behaviors that have no immediate relationship to each other (e.g., learning to walk, to draw, to read, to count, to drive a car, etc.), simply because these behaviors occur far enough apart for inversions in the order of succession to be improbable. Thus, in principle, it would be fallacious to conclude a necessary link between the concepts of reproducibility and homogeneity. In the present case, however, it clearly seems that the observed coherence is explained mainly by the homogeneity of the measured variable. For one thing, the levels of the scale are too close together for the theoretically possible inversion rates to be consistently reduced; for another thing, Jackson's PPR is specifically designed to reduce the reproducibility index by taking account of the inversions which were made improbable by the distances between levels. In sum, we may think that the observed reproducibility is not an artifact but actually reflects the unity or homogeneity of the psychological dimension covered by the five tests.

This first point made, it remains to try to specify or determine the limits of this presumably homogeneous dimension. We must refrain here from immediately stating that we are dealing with a well-defined and well-characterized concept of space. In fact, there is as yet no proof that the observed coherence is not due to the fact that, rather than applying to one area only, the stages of development of the behaviors in each of these tests are instead the expression of a more general intellectual construction that goes beyond the limited framework of spatial concepts to encompass most, if not all, of mental development. In other words, we could offer the hypothesis that the observed coherence is explained not by the fact that the tests cover spatial concepts alone, but rather by the fact that they involve intellectual activities which would nearly always be equivalent in form regardless of the particular content of the tasks. While not improbable, the hypothesis is risky and exceeds the limits of the one which instead reserves behavioral consistency for more limited domains, such as that of spatial concepts. Basically, it questions the very existence of the domains of structuring so often referred to by Piaget in justifying his horizontal *décalages*—whence the interest in comparing these two extreme possibilities, at least in order to avoid misinterpreting the results, if not to choose between the two hypotheses.

A direct way of making this comparison is to determine the degree of reproducibility of a set of behaviors when the scalogram analysis is extended to both spatial and other concepts. Assuming that a set of behaviors extended in this way is reproducible, it would be likely that the coherence observed in the spatial behavior analyzed above refers to a level of mental structuring which goes beyond the limited area of spatial representations. The domain selected for this new analysis is that of causal thinking, an area which also includes five tests[4] given to the same subjects and which has already been systematically analyzed elsewhere (Laurendeau and Pinard, 1962). Before combining these five tests with the five spatial-representation tests, it is important to determine whether the behaviors observed in the causality tests are themselves scalable. This first analysis, bearing on the protocols of 437 subjects between 4:0 and 12:0 years, shows that the behaviors in question are not scalable in this way (reproducibility: .917; PPR: .688); they become so, however, when the *Concept of life* test is excluded from the total set (reproducibility: .926; PPR: .726). If we then integrate the succession of behaviors observed in the other four causality tests into the scale already established by the five spatial tests, the new scalogram analysis covering the 161 subjects (from 5:0 to 10:0 years) who took all nine tests yields an insufficient reproducibility index (reproducibility: .895; PPR: .675). We might think that these reproducibility rates are related more to the number than to the nature of the tests included in the analysis, since increasing the number of tests would naturally result in multiplying the levels of the scale and increasing the possibilities of inversion or irregularity. In other words, we might have observed the same lack of reproducibility by adding other spatial tests instead of the causality tests. Though plausible at first glance, this kind of explanation must be rejected for at least two reasons. First, the number of tests compared is surely not the determining factor, since the five causality tests, equal in number to the spatial tests, were not scalable. Second, the diversity of areas seems more important than the number of tests because, even when we combine just six tests (three spatial tests and three causality tests)[5] instead of the nine in-

---

[4] The *Dream*, the *Concept of life*, the *Origin of night*, the *Movement of clouds*, and the *Floating and sinking of objects*.

[5] Spatial tests: *Stereognostic recognition of objects and shapes*, *Localization of topographical positions* and *Coordination of perspectives*. Causality tests: the *Dream*, the *Origin of night* and the *Movement of clouds*.

cluded in the general analysis, the reproducibility index is still not high enough for this set of behaviors to be scalable (reproducibility: .913; PPR: .672).

In sum, since the results do not seem to be the effect of a statistical artifact, the most likely conclusion is to recognize that the spatial tests and the causality tests cover different sets of mental representations, each of these sets having its own internal consistency with no real connection between the two. Thus it seems that mental structuring should be limited to these specific areas rather than generalized to the various forms of intellectual activity accessible to the child at a particular point in his development. As a matter of fact, however, this sort of conclusion would be premature. It is true that the statistics just reported clearly suggest this sort of model, in which the spatial concepts and the causal concepts constitute two different homogeneous domains, each being clearly articulated but having no close relationship to each other; still, we could not reject the alternative hypothesis without dangerously overstepping the limits inherent in our observations and techniques. Two reasons in particular lead us to reserve judgment on this.

As concerns the area of causality, first, the presumed homogeneity is most problematical because it was necessary to eliminate one of the five tests in order to attain an adequate level of reproducibility. If we are perhaps justified nonetheless in speaking of unidimensionality or functional homogeneity, it is probably because the irregularities of the *Concept of life* test are more closely related to flaws in the questionnaire itself, and in the resulting classification of the protocols, than to the nature of the mental representations or the beliefs produced by it. Of the five tests that deal with precausal thinking, it is in this one that the subjects are least induced to reflect on their own assertions and the limits of their beliefs. Never, for example, are the subjects openly faced with the contradictions often implied in the sequence of their responses and justifications. For this reason, the questioning is relatively superficial, so that this test is even more susceptible than the others to sociocultural influences and more directly dependent on the child's common or even purely academic knowledge. In this respect, it is interesting that of all the tests used by Boisclair[6] on Martinique children, the *Concept*

6 In preparation.

of life test is the only one that yields divergent results: the delay of the Martinique children in relation to Montreal children is at least eight years in this test, while in all other tests of any kind (e.g., pre-causality, concept of time, of space, of chance, etc.) the delay is never more than four or five years. These imperfections in the *Concept of life* questionnaire affect the quality of the developmental scale related to this concept: the scale includes only three levels, and the transitivity of these levels leaves much to be desired in statistical terms as well as in psychological terms (see Laurendeau and Pinard, 1962).[7] In sum, the fact that animistic beliefs related to the concept of life are poorly integrated with other forms of precausality (artificialism, realism, etc.) should perhaps be attributed to accidental reasons of this sort. Such an interpretation, however, must be purely conjectural so long as it is not confirmed by tests which are better adapted to the study of animistic concepts.

Even assuming that the precausal concepts are as homogeneous as the spatial concepts, the fact that it is impossible to combine these two sets of mental representations does not in itself preclude the possibility that the cohesion in each of these groups (and in particular in the spatial tests) may be due to a more general structuring factor which encompasses almost all mental activities. By their very nature, in fact, the spatial concepts analyzed in this study are a long way from the precausal beliefs analyzed in the preceding work. We know that, according to Piaget himself, the former belong to real and concrete thinking while the latter refer to verbal thinking which has no necessary and direct relationship to action.[8] In this perspective, then, we should not be surprised to find that two such different domains develop quite independently. Nor should we be tempted to generalize the results of this comparative analysis to all spheres of intellectual activity, for it is always possible—if not probable— that the analysis (still to come) of other tests taken by the same sub-

---

[7] In two out of three levels, the criteria which the children used in distinguishing the living from the nonliving are exactly the same (autonomous movement or anthropomorphic attributes), the only difference being that the children at level 2 unduly attribute these virtues to the nonliving as well as to the living, while those of level 3 reserve them for animals and/or plants. The distinction may often be superficial and may reflect a lack of specific knowledge rather than a flaw in the concept of life as such.

[8] It may be necessary to specify that we are dealing here with the concept of causality studied in Piaget's first works and not spatiotemporal (physical) causality as such, which clearly belongs to action-thinking and whose ultimate level is undeniably operational (see Inhelder and Piaget, 1955; Piaget and Inhelder, 1951; etc.).

jects and dealing with clearly operational concepts (e.g., quantity, time, speed, etc.) may reveal a high degree of internal homogeneity and suggest that they may be naturally integrated into the spatial concepts analyzed here.

With these reservations in mind, the only possible conclusion is that the progressive structuring of spatial concepts occurs in a constant order of succession but that this cohesion and regularity is lost when the analysis is extended to a more complex group including both the (verbal) causality tests and the spatial tests. It may be well to emphasize that the cohesion or regularity mentioned here does not at all imply a developmental synchronism. On the contrary, it is quite consistent with the continual *décalages* that characterize accession to the different levels of structuring topological, projective, or Euclidian concepts, even when the only source of variation is the diversity of concrete situations to which a single type of concept must be applied. In fact, such a cohesion requires only that the same *décalage*—when there is a *décalage*—occur in most of the subjects. The importance of this sort of regularity is that it testifies to the existence of a certain form of organization of intellectual operations. The details of this organization are still almost completely undefined, but the discussion of the following two questions should clarify this a bit.

TOPOLOGICAL CHARACTER OF THE FIRST SPATIAL CONCEPTS

Piaget's hypothesis about the topological character of the child's first spatial concepts was amply discussed in Chapters II to X: the empirical results reported at that time seem to confirm Piaget's major position on this question. Thus it will not be necessary to return to this question except to bring together the particular aspects discussed with each test where topological concepts were involved. We have seen that in three of the five tests the earliest behaviors depend on spatial relations which are limited to the internal elements of a single perceptual configuration (or image representation), these elements not being coordinated with any system of viewpoints or of coordinates. The various tests presented to the child have emphasized particularly the importance of the topological relations of neighborhood (e.g., *Localization of topographical positions, Construction of a projective straight line),* of continuity and discontinuity (e.g., *Stere-ognostic recognition of objects and shapes),* and of surrounding or enclosure *(Localization of topographical positions).* With the concepts of order and separation, these relations constitute the basic dimension of topological geometry. In agreement with Piaget's intuitions, then, there would be a pre-Euclidean and preprojective level of spatial conceptualization, based exclusively on elementary topological concepts. We must elaborate this statement, however, since it could have quite diverse meanings and thus lend itself to empirical predictions which are quite different in scope. We shall mention here only two of these possible meanings, attempting to show how and to what extent our results may justify the alleged priority of the topological relations.

EXISTENCE OF A PURELY TOPOLOGICAL LEVEL OF REPRESENTATION

A first interpretation would be that if there is a period of development where spatial representations are limited to elementary topology, each of the developmental scales of the tests analyzed above should include a level of functioning characterized by exclusively topological responses. This sort of inference seems quite legitimate and correct, but we should qualify it with certain reservations.

A. In the first place, since we are dealing with the child's very first mental representations, we could expect to discover a purely topological level of functioning only if we tested very young subjects—that is, subjects who are still in the process of constructing their first spatial concepts. This condition is so obvious that we need not elaborate it here, although certain authors (e.g., Dodwell, 1963) sometimes seem to be unaware of it. In the experiment reported here, for example, it would have been futile to expect that tests like *Concepts of left and right* and *Coordination of perspectives* each could produce a level of development characterized by a purely topological type of discrimination, since the youngest subjects to take these tests were already four or five years old. And in these two cases we could just as well reverse the causality relationship and instead recognize that, if the youngest subjects were not given these tests, it is because the very nature of the problems and their mode of presentation so limited the range of possible responses as to virtually preclude topological concepts. Thus, the solutions which the *Concepts of left and right* test can produce must rely on more or less structured projective concepts when they no longer reflect a pure and simple incomprehension of the terms used in the questions. In other words, as long as the child is still at the preprojective level, which we suppose to be dominated entirely by topological considerations, the terms "left" and "right" used in the questions have no point of reference in his thinking and thus have no real meaning for him, and he is reduced to more or less explicit signs of incomprehension. Similarly, in order for the questions in the *Coordination of perspectives* test to be at all intelligible and to produce any coherence, the subject must have already been aware of the selective role of the observer's viewpoint in perceiving the groups presented to him, however undifferentiated this awareness may be. As long as he still considers that everything is visible from every point, the subject cannot select the one picture that represents all the elements of the situation, as he is requested to do, without the influence of some considerations irrelevant to the spatial relations themselves (e.g., choice of the picture in which his preferred mountain—say, the red one—is the largest; choice of the picture placed closest to the little man; etc.). Actually, however, this test is not fully comparable to the *Concepts of left and right* test, for topological preoccupations are found in several responses at the first levels of the scale (e.g., relations of continuity-discontinuity which probably influence the rejection of a particular picture under the pretext that the open space separating the mountains does not appear in the picture; undifferentiated neighborhood relations which perhaps influence the few cases where the subject indiscriminately accepts all the pictures, claiming that the mountains are next to each other in all of them; etc.). These primitive topological concepts, however, are never the only ones operating: they are always subordinated to projective intuitions (the most rudimentary of which is the egocentric assimilation of all perspectives to the subject's own perspective), and these intuitions themselves are indispensable to an understanding of the instructions.

B. In addition to this first reservation, whereby the search for an exclusively topological level of functioning must be limited entirely to the tests taken by the youngest subjects, the above findings demand a second reservation. In two of the three tests which reached the child's very first spatial concepts, the hypothesis of the primacy of the topological over the projective and Euclidian was directly confirmed. The *Construction of a projective straight line* test in fact produces a developmental scale whose first levels include behaviors which are based exclusively on neighborhood relations. Likewise, the first stages observed in the *Localization of topographical positions* test are characterized exclusively by concepts of order, enclosure, and neighborhood. In the third test *(Stereognostic recognition of objects and shapes)*, on the contrary, there is no stage which is defined by a generalized confusion of all the homeomorphous shapes (i.e., topologically identical despite Euclidian differences) and by an ability to distinguish only the topologically dissimilar shapes. The general analysis clearly shows that the differentiation of topological relations is slightly easier or earlier than the curvilinear-rectilinear relationship: but the protocol analysis does not allow us to distinguish these two levels, largely because of the testing conditions. This is why the first stages of the scale are characterized by the simultaneous discrimination of both the topological continuity-discontinuity relation (the only one really used in this test) and the Euclidian curvilinear-rectilinear relation. In our opinion, however, this fact alone is not enough to call into question the existence of a purely topological level of spatial representation in this test, for two major reasons.

First, if the Euclidian nature of curvilinearity-rectilinearity is so early recognized, that is probably because its concrete realization in the material of a stereognosis test (e.g., objects to be identified by touch) may offer important elements of discrimination even to a mind which still attends only to the topological dimensions of space. Unlike the curvilinear shapes (circle and ellipse), the rectilinear shapes with right angles (square and rectangle) present a sort of irregularity—if not a real "discontinuity"—as to the quality of the neighborhoods that relate the points constituting the outlines. Similarly, the constituent points of the triangle as well as the projections marking the perimeter of the crosses and stars encourage tactile exploration (and the correlative representations) to assimilate these figures to open figures, as though these figures were made of lines whose ends never meet. In other words, unlike what he will be capable of later, the very young child does not perceive these figures as closed contours delimiting continuous surfaces, but rather as more or less thick lines whose direction is sometimes interrupted, as when he happens to touch an open or discontinuous figure. Although the idea may appear contradictory, it would thus be the topological concepts themselves which would explain the differentiation of the simplest Euclidian relations. It may not be necessary to specify that these first topological concepts in the very young child still lack any abstract formalization or specification; they remain implicit and poorly defined, the child being unaware of the importance he accords them in identifying certain qualities of objects and shapes, whether these qualities are really topological or whether they are Euclidian but partially assimilated to topological relations.

In the second place, the persistence of some confusions of heteromorphous figures—confusions which disappear only with or after the appearance of the first Euclidian concepts—does not necessarily mean that the child is incapable of topological discriminations. The observed confusions may be very easily explained by the incomplete and partial nature of the tactile exploration, as is so often seen in the direction of the errors; the youngest subjects, in fact, readily choose a figure that lacks one or another attribute of the figure that was touched (e.g., choice of the closed ring, or the disk with one hole, for the open ring), but rarely make the reverse confusion of choosing a figure having an attribute which the touched figure does not have (e.g., choosing the open ring for the closed ring). When the intent is to determine which types of relations are effective in the child's tactile exploration and first spatial representations, it stands to reason that the only clues to consider are those deriving from the child's actual exploration and not those that theoretically could be provided by a complete exploration. In other words, we must try to dissociate what belongs to the content of a spatial relation from what refers instead to the method adopted in apprehending a spatial reality. Of course, these two aspects are closely related since the movements of tactile exploration are, on the one hand, stimulated and oriented by spatial concepts which are already formed or which are in the process of formation and, on the other hand, provide these same concepts with the elements they need in order to continue and develop. This type of interaction between two aspects of a single process does not preclude the obvious possibility that the confusion between two homeomorphous figures, rather than reflecting the child's inability to conceive topological relationships, arises simply from the gaps in tactile exploration (which may be so limited that the child does not reach the parts of the object where the crucial topological attribute is found).

C. A last reservation should be briefly mentioned. It again concerns the existence of an exclusively topological level of functioning, but it has to do with the meaning and significance of this exclusiveness. To assert the preponderance or exclusiveness of topological considerations in the child's first spatial representations is to do more than assert the existence of a developmental level characterized by behavior which never requires genuinely projective or Euclidian concepts; this does not at all preclude, however, the possibility that topological concepts are associated, in the solution of one or another particular problem, with different sorts of cognitive elements—perceptual elements, for example—and thus produce behaviors which seem to go beyond the purely topological level of mental representation. In the *Construction of a projective straight line* test, for instance, the child can succeed in lining up a series of elements by using simple neighborhood relations before being able to integrate them or subordinate them to some system of viewpoints or coordinates, provided he uses a perceptual guide (e.g., the edge of the table) to improve his construction. It is precisely this perceptual guide which provides the child with the complement he needs to orient his action and which he still cannot provide himself. The objective situation makes up, so to speak, for the lack of spatial representation so that, in this particular case, the combination of representational elements and perceptual elements may allow the child to construct a straight line which seems better than a simple topological line. However, we need only remove this perceptual guide—or require the child to make his straight line in a direction other than that suggested by the perceptual element—to see that the spatial representation, left to its own resources, does not go beyond the level of simple neighborhoods. In the same way, in the *Localization of topographical positions* test, the topological preoccupations (neighborhood and enclosure) are very soon associated with perceptual or intuitive elements (symmetry, gesture imitation, etc.) and, later, with orientation relations; but these relations are very primitive or, in any case, are preprojective because they are linked to the egocentric point of view of which the child is, by definition, unaware. In one or the other of these two cases, it hardly seems questionable that the spatial concepts proper to these levels are purely topological, since the added elements are not conceptual but rather derive from the domain of figurative structures and, in particular, from perception.[9]

Bearing the above three reservations in mind, we may conclude that the results of the present experiment confirm the first interpretation of the primacy of the topological over the projective and the Euclidian. In each of the three tests administered to subjects less than five years old, the lower levels of the developmental scales are defined by exclusively topological spatial concepts.

GENERALITY OF TOPOLOGICAL CONCEPTS

It remains to examine the second possible interpretation of this priority of topological concepts. Assuming that there is a period of development when spatial representations are purely topological, it should follow that the behavior of a single child in several different (spatial) tests always reflects this same exclusiveness of topological concepts during this period. We can then try to determine the extent to which this influence is confirmed by the combined analysis of all the tests. This general analysis is necessarily limited to the only three tests which could be administered to subjects less than five years old; it can be done in two ways—either by examining the chronological overlap of the stages corresponding to the period of pure topology in each test, or by calculating the number of subjects located at these same stages in all three tests. In order to make either of these analyses, however, we would first have to determine the exact limits of the periods to be considered as purely topological in each of the three scales. It is practically impossible to establish these limits with the desired precision. For one thing, it is not easy to differentiate the most primitive forms of projective and Euclidian concepts from the perceptual elements which can be associated with the representational elements in the child's solutions. Besides, like the topological concepts themselves, the projective and Euclidian

9 We know that, for Piaget (e.g., 1936, 1937; Piaget and Inhelder, 1948), perceptual space itself is characterized by a priority of the topological over the projective and Euclidian. Study of the relationships between perception and intelligence (Piaget, 1961) shows also that even though perceptual space and sensorimotor space develop in a strictly synchronous and solidary fashion, the development of perceptual space is ahead of conceptual or representational space. Perception is in fact already able to apprehend projective and Euclidian relations, as seen in the very early development of spatial constancies and discriminations, while representational space is still exclusively limited to topological considerations.

concepts do not abruptly appear at a given moment in development; they go through a long period of development, whose beginnings are very difficult to determine because these concepts are at first very unstable and only slightly differentiated.

It seems impossible to determine with any certainty, for each of the three tests, when the purely topological period begins and when it is over; but comparisons may still be valid and instructive inasmuch as we can at least establish certain general limits which are fairly comparable from one test to another. Thus, in the *Stereognostic recognition of objects and shapes* test, it seems reasonable to have the "topological" period correspond to stages 2A and 2B, since it is at this level that the discrimination of geometric shapes is based on characteristics which we have decided to call elementary (see Chapter IV), referring both to the topological relations proper and to the curvilinear-rectilinear relation—this latter discrimination, as we have seen, being similar to the topological discriminations. Stages 1A and 1B, where only the familiar objects are recognized owing to the simplicity of the visuomanual coordinations, are excluded along with stages 3A and 3B, at which recognition of geometric shapes is based on increasingly Euclidian characteristics (number and size of sides, parallelism, etc.). In the *Construction of a projective straight line* test, stages 1A and 1B are already defined by arrangements based exclusively on neighborhood (sinuous lines) and thus would correspond to the purely topological period. Stages 2A and 2B following, on the other hand, are still neither projective nor Euclidian since the subject constructs his straight lines solely by relying on perceptual clues. The behaviors at this level are mixed, since perceptual activities and topological concepts are intertwined, but the projective (or Euclidian) concepts necessary for unconditional success with the straight lines have not yet appeared. Thus the "topological" period in this test covers stages 1A and 1B, where neighborhoods alone are considered, as well as stages 2A and 2B, where topology is allied with perception in order to compensate (for better or worse) for the lack of projective representations. As for the *Localization of topographical positions* test, stage 1 includes subjects who mainly used topological neighborhood and enclosure relations, often adding the perceptual aspects of static symmetry or dynamic symmetry (copying the examiner's gesture). At stages 2A and 2B, behavior is still basically inspired by topology and symmetry. It is true that the subject, by relying on his egocentric perspective, uses at least one reference point outside the objects themselves, which is the necessary condition for the development of projective concepts; but, because egocentric perspective is by definition unaware of itself, its action is hardly more highly developed or more efficient than that of the perceptual cues themselves (still egocentric), to which it may then be rightly assimilated.

If we admit that the periods thus delimited in each of the three tests are characterized by topological spatial representations, it is possible to compare the ages that correspond to these periods to determine the degree of overlap between the three periods. Figure 19

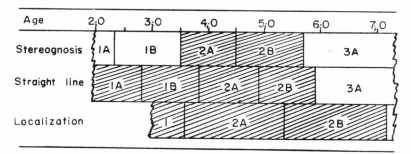

Figure 19. Age range of the stages of the *Stereognostic recognition of objects and shapes, Construction of a projective straight line,* and *Localization of topographical positions* tests. For each of these tests, the shaded area indicates those stages which correspond to a topological level of functioning.

shows that there is in fact a common period of time when the three tests yield purely topological behavior and that this common period lasts more than two years (from 3:6 to 5:8 years). We note that the lower and upper limits of this phase of overlap are in fact determined by the *Stereognostic recognition of objects and shapes* test, where the purely topological responses appear later and disappear earlier than in the other two. The delayed appearance of these responses is probably due to the rather unusual character of the experimental situation, to which the youngest children have some trouble adjusting. Their early disappearance, also, may simply reflect the fact that the Euclidian concepts necessary for solving this task are simpler than the corresponding concepts in the other two tests. Whatever the cause, these *décalages* are quite natural and should not lead us to ignore the considerable overlap of the three topological periods. It goes without saying that the exact limits of the observed overlap depend directly on the number and nature of the tests. If we changed the experimental apparatus or added new tests to examine other aspects of elementary spatial representations, we should expect the extent of this overlap to be modified. It is unlikely, however, that it would completely disappear. The fact that the comparison already covers three tests, rather different from one another in specific content and in their experimental situation, strongly suggests that we are dealing with a real phenomenon, one which is difficult to reduce to a mere coincidence based on superficial factors like overhomogeneity of responses.

The preceding analysis is, however, still very crude. It does not, for example, give the proportion of children who are classified at a purely topological level in all three tests. The brief analysis which follows dwells on this particular aspect of the problem. Obviously, only the subjects who took all three tests, with the further exception of subjects who were judged unclassifiable in one of them, can be included in this study of internal consistency. Taking these two restrictions into account, the protocols included in the analysis number 348, and all belong to children between 3:0 and 10:0 years of age.

The simplest way to examine the consistency of these protocols is to regroup the subjects according to their responses to all three tests at once, after having divided the total period of development in each of these tests into three comparable subperiods, which we may call pretopological, topological, and posttopological, respectively. Table 60 gives the results of this new classification. We note (row 5) that 26 per cent of the subjects (92 out of 348) are classified at the topological level in all three tests. Since the time of complete overlap of the three topological periods represents 31 per cent (26 months out of 84: see Figure 19) of the interval separating the lower limit (3:0 years) and the upper limit (10:0 years) of the subjects included in this analysis, we might see the 26 per cent of perfectly homogeneous cases as proof that the overlap indicated by the global analysis is not only a group phenomenon but holds for individuals as well. However, in order to be justified in seeing a connection between these two percentages, we would have to assume that the subjects are distributed in an equal number at all age levels and that

Table 60

Distribution of subjects by response level in the *Stereognostic recognition of objects and shapes* test (SR), the *Construction of a projective straight line* test (SL), and the *Localization of topographical positions* test (TP): pretopological level (Pre), topological level (Topo), or posttopological level (Post) (Ages: 3:0 to 10:0 years; N=348)

Test			Chronological age										Total
SR	SL	TP	3:0	3:6	4:0	4:6	5:0	6:0	7:0	8:0	9:0	10:0	
1. Pre	Pre	Pre	1										1
2. Pre	Topo	Pre	2	1									3
3. Pre	Pre	Topo	1		2	1							4
4. Pre	Topo	Topo	22	20	11	4	2	1					60
5. Topo	Topo	Topo	12	16	27	17	12	4	4				92
6. Post	Topo	Topo		1	1	4	9	5	4	1			25
7. Post	Post	Topo				2	3	5	8	9	5	1	33
8. Post	Post	Post					2	7	17	25	17	10	78
9. Pre	Post	Topo	1	1	1	1	1		1				6
10. Pre	Topo	Post			1								1
11. Topo	Pre	Topo	2	1		2							5
12. Topo	Topo	Pre	1	2									3
13. Topo	Post	Topo	1	2		4	5	2	2	1	3		20
14. Topo	Topo	Post				1		1			1		3
15. Topo	Post	Post							5	2			7
16. Post	Topo	Topo			1			2		2	1	1	7
Total			43	44	44	36	34	27	41	40	27	12	348

these age levels themselves are equally separated in the scale. We know that these two conditions are not met: for one thing, the age levels are separated by six-month intervals before 5:0 years and by twelve-month intervals after that and, for another thing, the limiting conditions governing the reclassification of the subjects destroy the numerical balance of the age groups.

Therefore, in order to determine whether the consistency of these 92 subjects reflects a particular period of development characterized by purely topological spatial representations, the most direct way is again to use a criterion used several times in this study in establishing the transitivity of the levels of a single developmental scale. Table 60 reports the results necessary for the analysis. The various behavior patterns reported in the upper portion of the table (first eight rows) constitute a scale extending from an initial exclusively pretopological period (row 1) to an entirely posttopological period (row 8). Between these two extreme limits is a series of six intermediate levels; their order and content are determined by the overlap of the three tests described in Figure 19 above. The reader will note that the group of exclusively topological behaviors is located nearly in the middle (row 5) of the 8 categories of the scale.[10] Table 60 presents this scale in the order determined by the group analysis, distributing the subjects by age level in each of these categories. The one-to-one comparison of these various distributions will allow us to answer the major question whether the distribution of purely topological behaviors (row 5) differs significantly from the adjacent distributions and thus reflects the existence of an exclusively topological period of spatial representations.

Before going on to this comparison, however, it is important to consider briefly the basic question whether the number of exceptions to the sequence determined by the group analysis is not so high as to compromise the value of the scale and deprive all comparisons of any significance. In fact, the same Table 60 (rows 9 to 16) shows that 52 (or 15 per cent) of the 348 subjects are classified in these categories of exceptions. The results of a scalogram analysis applied to all protocols, however, are reassuring: the reproducibility index is .978 (and the PPR .918).[11] Once this preliminary condition is met, we can then determine whether the pattern of exclusively topological responses in the three tests (row 5 of Table 60) is a genuinely distinct step in the scale. The Kolmogorov-Smirnov test clearly shows that the distribution representing the development of this type of behavior differs significantly from the two adjacent distributions (at the .01 level) and from all the others. Thus, at least in the frameworks limited to the three tests used here, the hypothesis of a purely topological level of spatial representations seems to be supported: at a particular point in development, topological considerations are the only ones operating, despite the relative diversity of these tests.

GENERALITY OF EGOCENTRIC ATTITUDES

One last question to be discussed concerns the generality of the child's egocentric attitudes. The question is raised in nearly the same

10 In fact, patterns 2 and 3, while ordered in the table, should be considered as equivalent because the results (see Figure 19) do not allow us to determine in which test the topological concepts first appear (*Construction of a projective straight line* or *Localization of topographical positions*).

11 If the scalogram analysis already made on the same three tests yields considerably lower indices, it is obviously because the responses given to each of the tests were classified on a more refined developmental scale than the present division into only three levels.

terms as the one concerning the exclusiveness of topological relations and will be examined in the same way. The reader may recall that in three of the five tests (*Localization of topographical positions, Concepts of left and right,* and *Coordination of perspectives*) the subject's first solutions are overt admissions of egocentrism, the subject's own point of view being the only reference point used in locating the objects and judging their relative positions. Following this period of unconscious and total egocentrism, all three tests include a period of partial decentration when the subject sometimes gives up his own perspective for a different one, on the condition that this new perspective requires only a few simple transformations. Thus the point of view of a person facing him is more accessible than that of an observer placed beside him at an angle of 90 degrees in relation to him because the first entails only a simple reversal of the left-right dimension, while the second requires instead the translation of the left-right dimension into the before-behind dimension (and vice versa). Similarly, it is easier for the child to imagine a perspective other than his own when the change affects only one of the projective dimensions rather than two (or three) at once. These various difficulties are obviously due to the fact that even though the subject's point of view loses its exclusiveness during this transitional period, it is still dominant and remains so as long as all the possible perspectives are not integrated into a perfectly articulated system. It is by its insertion into this total system that the subject's own point of view can serve as a central reference point for coordinating the projective transformations, rather than being a kind of refuge to which the subject turns (more or less consciously) when the projective transformations become too numerous or complex.

When the transformation from a subjective mode of projective representation, based exclusively on the subject's own perspective, into an objective mode characterized by the complete relativity of perspectives has been seen in nearly identical form in three successive tests, it is hardly possible to doubt the importance of the concept of egocentrism in the description and explanation of the child's primitive spatial concepts. However, we can still ponder the degree of consistency or generality of this egocentric attitude and ask especially whether intellectual development includes a period when this egocentrism invades, so to speak, all of the child's spatial representations. Phrased in this manner, the question implies the same reservations and leads to the same impasse as the question of the generality of topological relations, discussed in the preceding paragraphs. In fact, when we admit the existence of horizontal *décalages* concerning the relative complexity of the tests, it becomes futile to attempt to determine the existence of an exclusively egocentric period or to stake out its boundaries. No attempt of this sort can produce easily generalizable results, because they would always be strictly conditioned by the number and nature of the tests in question.

Granting this, there remains the possibility of approaching the problem from a more limited angle and asking, for example, whether the egocentric attitudes observed in the three tests are sufficiently structured or articulated to express a consistent mode of conceiving reality. It would be inconsistent to expect the egocentric behaviors to appear and disappear at the same time when group analysis reveals clearly different levels of complexity from one test to another. Equally, in order to establish the existence of a genuinely egocentric form of mental organization, egocentric types responses must appear and disappear in the individual protocols in a sequence conforming to the order of difficulty established in the group analysis. In the absence of such consistency, it may be necessary completely to forgo referring to egocentrism in describing the lower level of responses and, instead, to consider this level simply as responses which are easier and more accessible to the child—but we would still have to account for this ease and accessibility! Should we insist on retaining the concept of egocentrism, we would then have to see it as no more than a very specific type of reaction whose manifestations are too sporadic to reflect a generalized mental attitude.

Once again, it is the scalogram analysis which can best reveal the degree of consistency of the egocentrism responses in the three tests where this type of response is most manifest. To carry out this analysis, we must begin by regrouping the stages already established for each of these tests, this time taking egocentrism as the exclusive criterion. This regrouping leads each time to a scale with three levels: (1) *pre-egocentrism:* the subject does not follow the instructions (stage 0 of all three tests), or depends entirely on topological relations without referring to a single reference point outside the objects (stage 1 of the *Localization of topographical positions* test); (2) *egocentrism:* the egocentric point of view is the only one operating in the location of topographical positions (stages 2A and 2B), in the definition of left and right (stages 1A and 1B), and in the representation of perspectives visible to an observer walking around a group of mountains (stages 1A and 1B); (3) *postegocentrism:* the awareness of perspectives other than his own leads the subject to make efforts at decentration; the success of these efforts is at first very relative and is limited by the complexity of the transformations (stage 3A of the *Localization of topographical positions* test; stage 2 of the *Concepts of left and right* test; stages 2A and 2B of the *Coordination of perspectives* test), but ends in the full coordination of all possible viewpoints (last stage in each of the three tests). Figure 20 gives this regrouping, showing the respective extensions of these three response levels in each of the three tests.

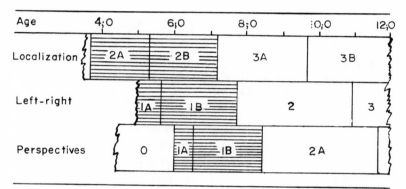

Figure 20. Age range of the stages of the *Localization of topographical positions, Concepts of left and right,* and *Coordination of perspectives* tests. For each of these tests, the shaded area indicates those stages which correspond to an egocentric level of functioning.

It is from this regrouping that the intraindividual analysis of the protocols can help answer the question of the extent to which the egocentrism observed in the three tests has a minimum of consistency and marks a particular period in the development of the child's spatial concepts. Table 61 provides the principal elements of this analysis by indicating, by age, first the distributions of protocols conforming to the sequence of levels marking the development of behavior observed in all three tests at once (first section: rows 1 to 7), and then the distributions of the protocols which are exceptions to this sequence (second section: rows 8 to 11). The first section reports in detail the subject's response level in each test, using the

Table 61

Distribution of subjects by response level in the *Localization of topographical positions* test (TP), the *Concepts of left and right* test (LR), and the *Coordination of perspectives* test (CP): pre-egocentric level (Pre), egocentric level (Ego), or postegocentric level (Post) (ages: 5:0 to 12:0 years; N=274)

Test			Chronological age								
TP	LR	CP	5:0	6:0	7:0	8:0	9:0	10:0	11:0	12:0	Total
1. Pre	Pre	Pre	2	1							3
2. Ego	Pre	Pre	11	6	1	1				1	20
3. Ego	Ego	Pre	10	7	4	1					22
4. Ego	Ego	Ego	2	8	6	2	2				20
5. Post	Ego	Ego		1	7	6	1	2	2	1	20
6. Post	Post	Ego		1	6	7	1	7	3	2	27
7. Post	Post	Post			5	9	16	15	16	17	78
8. +/−	=	=	4	2	2	3	4	1		2	18
9. =	+/−	=	4	1	1	1			2		9
10. =	=	+/−	2	1	4	4	1	1			13
11. ?	?	?	9	9	7	6	6	1	3	3	44
Total			44	37	43	40	31	27	26	26	274

three categories described earlier: pre-egocentrism (Pre), egocentrism (Ego), or postegocentrism (Post). To avoid the detailed enumeration which would be demanded by the great diversity of response patterns (14 distinct types, of which seven appear less than five times), the second section of the table uses instead a condensed classification: the protocols are divided according to the point where the exception is located. For instance, the −/+ sign indicates that the subject's solution in the corresponding test is lower or higher than the equivalent solutions (hence the = sign) given in the other two tests. The question marks (?) reflect the ambiguity of the cases (44 out of 84) in which the exceptional responses cannot be precisely located (e.g., Pre-Ego-Post pattern).

Table 61 reveals that only 190 (or 60 per cent) of the 274 protocols submitted to this analysis conform to the sequence established by the group analysis. Rather deceptive at first glance, this result seems to question the authenticity of the sequence itself as well as the existence of a homogeneous or consistent mode of thought underlying these various behaviors. However, when we go on to analyze the scale's reproducibility the indices are .955 (reproducibility) and .783 (PPR).[12] Thus it seems that the number of protocols which

---

[12] These results are not at all surprising, since the scalogram analysis of the five tests itself yields high indices despite the even greater refinement of the scale. What is difficult to understand here, then, is that the reproducibility indices are so high despite the considerable number of aberrant protocols.

are exceptions to the sequence is not in itself an absolute index of the scalability of a set of behaviors, and that we should always consider the size or importance of the exceptions. In this case, these exceptions are almost always due to minimal errors, so that the reproducibility rate is not radically affected.

Comparative analysis of the distributions corresponding to each behavior pattern reported in Table 61 reveals that the distributions of subjects classified at the egocentric level in all three tests (row 4) differ significantly from all the others (at the .05 level: Kolmogorov-Smirnov test), except from the immediately preceding one (row 3). This exception, however, is not at all disturbing, and may be due to the fact that the distributions obtained in the first three levels are truncated. If the comparisons could include subjects of less than 5:0 years, it is likely that the greater range of the distributions could eliminate the exception. Pending additional data on this particular aspect, and with this reservation in mind, it seems reasonable to conclude that, at least in the development of projective spatial concepts, the egocentric attitude is regular enough to suggest that it reflects a genuine and consistent form of mental organization.

Appendix

Detailed Description of the Tests

STEREOGNOSTIC RECOGNITION OF OBJECTS AND SHAPES

MATERIAL

First phase

Eleven common objects: comb, key, wooden block, penny, safety pin, ball, pencil, pair of scissors, spoon, button, glass; one card picturing all 11 objects (20 x 22 cm.); one rectangular piece of cardboard (28 x 36 cm.), as a screen.

Second phase

Twenty-four shapes cut from stiff cardboard, two of each of 12 shapes: square, disk with one hole, closed ring, irregular cross, triangle, open ring, rectangle, Greek cross, circle, open rectangle, four-cornered star, disk with two holes (see Figure 1, p. 43); one card picturing all 12 shapes (20 x 22 cm.); one rectangular piece of cardboard (28 x 36 cm.).

Third phase

Twenty-four shapes cut from stiff cardboard, two of each of 12 shapes: circle, Maltese cross, square, ellipse, four-cornered star, rectangle, triangle, irregular quadrilateral, Greek cross, trapezoid, six-cornered star, rhombus (see Figure 1, p. 43); one card picturing all 12 shapes (20 x 22 cm.); one rectangular piece of cardboard (28 x 36 cm.).

440

INSTRUCTIONS

First phase (recognition of common objects)

Place the rectangular piece of cardboard, which will serve as a screen during the whole test, vertically on the table in front of the child. Then say:

> We're going to play a game with this. Listen carefully, you must stay behind it and you must not look. You just have to put your hands on the other side, like this [*take the child's hands and place them behind the screen*]. All right, now I'm going to put things in your hands and then you try to tell me what they are. You are going to tell what they are only by touching them with your hands. You are only going to touch them, and then you are going to find what they are.

A. *First trial*

Put the *comb* in the child's hands, making sure that he does not see it beforehand. Then say:

> Okay, what is it? Can you tell what it is?

Note the child's response and also indicate how he manipulates the object (passive or active exploration). Even if the response is not the correct one, remove the object immediately and keep it hidden from the child's view. Present each of the objects to him in this way, in the following order: *key, wooden block, penny, safety pin, ball, pencil, pair of scissors, spoon, button, glass.* Ask him each time:

> What is that? Try to tell by touching it with your hands. Don't look; find it only with your hands.

Note the child's response each time and indicate how he manipulates the object. Do not make any correction if the child makes a mistake. *If the child correctly recognizes the whole series of objects,* proceed at once to the second phase. *If the child makes one or several mistakes,* go on to the second trial.

B. *Second trial*

Leave the screen in front of the child and say:

> We are going to change our game a little bit now. Look, I have here a very pretty picture with all kinds of things on it [*show the*

child the card on which all the common objects are pictured]. You see, there are pretty things drawn in the picture. Okay, now I am going to put something in your hands again, and then you are going to try to find a thing just like it in the picture.

Then put the *comb* in the child's hands and say:

> Okay, take this in your hands, don't look, and try to find the same thing that you have in your hands on the card. What do you have in your hands? Is there something just like it in the picture? Show it to me.

Note carefully the child's response and indicate how he handles the object (passive or active exploration). Even if the response is not the correct one, remove the object immediately and keep it hidden from the child's view. Present him with each of the objects successively in this way, in the following order: *spoon, pencil, glass, safety pin, wooden block, penny, key, ball, pair of scissors, button*. Ask each time:

> What is that? Is there something just like it in the picture? Show it to me.

Note the child's response each time and indicate how he handles the object. *Make no corrections* if the child makes mistakes. Then go on to the second phase of the test without any further trials.

Second phase (recognition of shapes of a topological character)
Show the child the card representing all 12 shapes, and say:

> Look at this picture: there are many sketches on it. We are going to play the same game as before. You are going to stay behind this again so you can't see [*put the screen vertically in front of the child*], then you are going to put both hands on the other side, just the way you did before [*take the child's hands and place them behind the screen*]. I am going to put things in your hands and then you will show me things just like them in the picture. You are only going to touch them, you are going to tell what they are only by touching them with your hands; then you are going to show me the ones just like them in the picture.

A. *First trial*
Put the *square* in the child's hands, making sure that he does not see it beforehand. Then say:

Okay, hold that. What is it? Is there something just like it in the picture? Show it to me.

Note the child's response and indicate also how he handles the object (active or passive exploration). Even if the response is not correct, remove the object immediately and keep it hidden from the child's view. Then present him with each of the shapes in the same way, successively and in the following order: *disk with one hole, closed ring, irregular cross, triangle, open ring, rectangle, circle, Greek cross, open rectangle, four-cornered star, disk with two holes.* Ask each time:

What is it? Is there something just like it in the picture? Show it to me.

Note the child's response each time and indicate also how he handles the object. Make no corrections if the child makes mistakes. *If the child correctly recognizes the whole series* of shapes, go on to the third phase immediately. *If the child makes one or several mistakes,* go on to the second trial.

B. *Second trial*

Remove the card and replace it with the second set of shapes. Arrange these shapes exactly as they are on the card. Leave the screen in front of the child and say:

Now, we're going to change our game a little bit. You see, I have put all of this on the table. I am going to put things in your hands again; you are going to tell what they are without looking, and then you are going to show me if there is something just like them on the table.

Put the *square* in the child's hands and say:

Okay, take this and try to find something just like it. What do you have in your hands? Is there something just the same on the table? Where is it? Show it to me.

Note the child's response and indicate also how he handles the object (active or passive exploration). *Do not let the child handle the objects which are on the table.* Ask him only to point to them with his finger. Even if the response is not correct, immediately remove the object touched and keep it hidden from the child's view.

Present him with each of the objects successively in the same way, in the following order: *open rectangle, closed ring, triangle, disk with two holes, open ring, four-cornered star, disk with one hole, irregular cross, rectangle, circle, Greek cross.* Ask him each time:

> Okay, take this in your hands, don't look, and try to find the same thing on the table as you have in your hands. Show me the same things on the table.

Note the child's response each time and indicate also how he manipulates the object. Make no corrections if the child makes mistakes. Then go on to the third phase of the test without any additional trials.

Third phase (recognition of shapes of a Euclidian character)

Present the card picturing all 12 shapes to the child and proceed in exactly the same way as in the second phase.

In the first trial, present the shapes in the following order: *circle, Maltese cross, square, ellipse, four-cornered star, rectangle, triangle, irregular quadrilateral, Greek cross, trapezoid, six-cornered star, rhombus.*

In the second trial, present the shapes in the following order: *circle, triangle, square, Maltese cross, rectangle, six-cornered star, trapezoid, Greek cross, ellipse, four-cornered star, rhombus, irregular quadrilateral.*

CONSTRUCTION OF A PROJECTIVE STRAIGHT LINE

MATERIAL

Eight miniature lampposts (8 cm. high); two toy houses (1.5 x 2 cm. at the base); one rectangular piece of cardboard (26 x 35 cm.); one circular piece of cardboard (diam.: 34 cm.).

INSTRUCTIONS

Problem 1

Place on the table within reach of the child the *rectangular cardboard,* the two houses and the eight lampposts, saying:

> Now we're going to play another game. See, this [*the cardboard*] is a field. In the field, I place two houses [*put them on the card-*

board as in section 1 of Figure 2, p. 117]. Now, we have to put the
"lights" between the two houses. The lights have to be put there so
it will be lit up. The lights are here [*point to the lampposts*]. Do you
know what a straight line is? Okay, look [*draw a straight line in pencil
on a piece of paper*], this is a straight line, a straight road. And this
[*draw a curved line*], is this a straight line? And this [*draw a crooked
line*], is this a straight road?

Now you know what a straight line or a straight road is [*explain
further, if necessary, the difference between a straight line (or a
straight road) and a curved, crooked, zigzag, etc., line (or road)*].
Okay, now you are going to put the lights between the two houses.
But pay close attention: you must make a row (line, road, etc.) that is
very straight, a row that starts at one house and makes a very straight
road to the other house. Put them here, between the two houses, and
arrange all the lights to make a very straight row.

Do not trace the straight line between the two houses with the
finger. Make sure that the child understands the instructions, and
repeat them when necessary. Let the child work and *do not stop
him if he makes a mistake*. Note carefully in what order and where
the child places his lampposts. When the child is finished, whether
he has succeeded or not, ask him:

Are you finished? Is your row of lights very straight? Are you sure
it isn't bent anywhere?

Note his response and his corrections if he makes any. Then go
on to problem 2 without any further trials.

Problem 2

Dismantle the line which the child has made, put all the lampposts back together, beside the cardboard, and say:

Now, you are going to make another nice line with the lights.
See, I am putting the houses here [*arrange them as in section 2 of
Figure 2*]. Okay, now the houses are farther apart. But you must still
arrange the lights and make a very straight row between the houses,
a row that starts at one house and makes a very straight path up to
the other one. Do just as before, make a nice straight line with the
lights.

Do not trace the straight line between the two houses with the
finger. Make sure that the child understands the instructions, and

repeat them when necessary. Let the child work and *do not warn him if he makes a mistake.* Note carefully in what order and where the child places his lampposts. When the child has finished, whether he has succeeded or not, ask him:

Are you finished? Is your row of lights very straight? Are you sure it isn't bent anywhere?

Note his response and his corrections if he makes any. Then go on to problem 3 without any further trials.

Problem 3

Dismantle the line the child has made, put all the lampposts back together beside the cardboard, and arrange the houses as in section 3 of Figure 2. Then proceed as in problem 2.

Problem 4

Dismantle the line the child has made, put all the lampposts back together, then replace the rectangular cardboard with the *circular cardboard.* See that the cardboard projects about 10 cm. over the edge of the table (see Figure 4, p. 128). Arrange the houses as in section 4 of Figure 2 and then proceed exactly as in problem 2.

Problem 5

Dismantle the line which the child has made, put all the lampposts back together beside the cardboard, and arrange the houses as in section 5 of Figure 2. Then proceed exactly as in problem 2.

Problem 6

Dismantle the line which the child has made, put all the lampposts back together beside the cardboard, and arrange the houses as in section 6 of Figure 2. Then proceed exactly as in problem 2.

LOCALIZATION OF TOPOGRAPHICAL POSITIONS

Material

Two landscape boards (see Figure 14, p. 173), 35 x 47 cm.; 10 houses (two identical series of five): one red (base: 7.5 x 2.5 cm.; height: 3.5 cm.); one yellow (base: 4.5 x 2.5 cm.; height: 3.5 cm.); three of different colors (blue, green, and yellow) but the same size (base: 1.5 x 1.0 cm.; height: 2.0 cm.); two little men of modeling clay (about 3 cm. high).

INSTRUCTIONS

Problem 1

A. *Examples*

Place the two landscape boards on the table in front of the child, and arrange them so that they face the same direction for the child. Then say:

> Now we are going to play another game. You see, we have two pictures that are alike. Here, there is a road for automobiles and, on the other picture, there is a road just like it. Then, here there is a railroad track for trains to travel on and, on the other picture, there is another one just like it. So you see, the two pictures are just alike. Now, if you like, I will take this picture here [*point to board a, to the left in relation to the examiner*] and you will have this picture over here [*board b*]. That one [*board a*] is mine and that one [*board b*] is yours.
>
> Now, we are going to put houses on our pictures. We will put the houses the same way on both pictures. See, here I am putting a red house. Now you should put a red house on your picture. There should be one at the same place so that the two pictures will be just alike [*place the two houses with red roofs in the position where they are in Figure 14*].
>
> Now, we are going to put another house there, one with a yellow roof [Etc.].

In this way, arrange all the houses which appear in Figure 14, on each of the two boards. Then make the child notice the identity of the boards, saying, for example:

> You see, now the two pictures are still just alike. You have houses just like mine and they are in the same place as mine are.

Present the two little men to the child, saying:

> See, I have a little man and I give you one just like mine. Now, I am going to put my man in my picture; and then after that, you are going to put your man in the same place in your picture. You must put your man just the way mine is. See, I am putting my man on the red house [*put it there*]; then you do the same thing; put

your man on your red house, put him in the same position, in the same place.

Allow the child to place his man himself. However, if the child does not place his man on the red roof or if he does not seem to understand the instructions, place his man for him, saying, for example:

See, he goes there. Now he is at the same place as mine, he is placed just the way mine is. Do you understand?

Once the child has clearly understood, present the second example, saying:

Now, watch carefully. I am putting my man on my yellow house [*put him there*]. You do the same thing I am doing: put your man in the same place, in the same position as mine. Put him just like mine on your picture.

If the child still does not understand what he is supposed to do, or if he does not place his man correctly, put it there for him and again explain the identity of the two positions. *Before going on to the problems themselves, make sure that the child fully understands the instructions.* Repeat them when necessary and repeat the preceding examples. *But avoid placing the man in other positions than on the red roof and on the yellow roof.*

B. *Problems*

Once the instructions have been understood, the examiner places his man, on board *a*, successively in the positions indicated in Figure 14 and in the order A, B, L, C, F, H, E, D, J, K, G, I. Ask the child each time to locate his man in the same way on his board, saying, for example:

See, now I am putting my man here. You do the same thing; put your man in the same place on your picture; put your man in the same position so he will be just like mine.

While placing the man, *never give any verbal indications* such as these: "in front of the red house and near the road," "on the road," "near the railroad tracks," etc. Simply say: "I am putting him here (there, etc.)."

For each position *indicate on the observation sheet* the position where the child places his man. Note carefully *whether the child makes several tentative moves or whether he places him immediately* in a position which he immediately finds to be correct. If there is any trial and error, *note the successive positions* in which the man is placed, but clearly indicate the final position. Never suggest to the child that he has incorrectly placed his man. If he has placed him poorly, or even if he has placed him correctly but doubts his response, always make only neutral remarks or evasive responses: e.g., "What do you think? Do you think he is in the right place?" Etc.

Problem 2

A. *Examples*

Remove the two men, leave the houses arranged in the same way on both boards, but turn board *a* 180 degrees, saying to the child:

> Now, I am turning my picture because I can see better that way. You see, it is still just like yours but it is turned. I still have a road the way you do [*point to it*], a railroad track for the trains, a red house, a yellow house, etc. [*pointing to them one after another*]. Okay, now, I am going to put my man on my picture again; then you put yours in the same place as mine, just like mine, at the same place in your picture. See, watch: I am putting my man on the red house. Put yours in the same place, in the same position in your picture.

Allow the child to work. If he does not understand, or if he does not put his man on the red house, put it there for him, saying:

> Watch, this is where he goes. There, he is in the same place as mine. Do you understand?

Repeat the instructions when necessary, giving *an example with the yellow roof* also if necessary.

B. *Problems*

Once the child understands the instructions, the examiner successively places his man, on board *a*, in the same positions as in problem 1 but in the order B, D, G, A, L, E, K, I, J, H, C, F. Ask the child each time to locate his man the same way on his board. *Never give any verbal indications,* but simply say that he is placed "here" or "there," etc.

With the first mistake, but *only for the first problem* (position B), correct the child, saying:

> Pay close attention. You see, I placed my man here [*designating the correct position on board a*]; then you should place yours there [*designating the corresponding position on board b*]. See, I am putting your man there [*place it correctly*]. You see, now he is at the same place as mine. Pay close attention: it is hard because my picture is turned now. Okay, you understand? Always try to put your man at the same place as mine, in the same position as mine on your picture.

Then go on to position D. Make no more corrections. If there was a correction at position B, indicate this on the observation sheet. Enter all the child's responses just as in problem 1. Never suggest to the child that his man is incorrectly placed.

CONCEPTS OF LEFT AND RIGHT

MATERIAL

Six various objects: wooden cube, miniature cow, toy lampposts, miniature boat, miniature plate, pencil; one sheet of paper (21 x 25 cm.) as a base; one rectangular piece of cardboard (28 x 36 cm.) which serves as a screen.

INSTRUCTIONS

During the whole test, the child must be placed *beside the examiner,* except for section 2 where the examiner and the subject are standing and facing each other.

Section 1 (designation of the subject's body parts)

Make sure that the child is paying attention and ask him the following questions successively, noting the child's response (gesture) each time.

(a) Show me your right hand.
(b) Show me your left leg.
(c) Show me your right ear.
(d) Show me your left hand.

(e) Show me your right leg.

(f) Show me your left ear.

Section 2 (designation of parts of the examiner)

The examiner stands up and asks the child to stand up and face him. First make sure of the child's attention, then ask him successively each of the following questions, noting each of the child's responses (gestures).

(a) Show me my left hand.

(b) Show me my right ear.

(c) Show me my left leg.

(d) Show me my right hand.

(e) Show me my left ear.

(f) Show me my right leg.

Section 3 (relative position of three objects)

Problem 3a (uncovered objects)

Place the sheet of paper on the table, in front of the child; then arrange the *block*, the *plate*, and the *pencil* on this sheet (from left to right in relation to the examiner and to the subject, who are sitting side by side). Secure the child's attention and ask him successively each of the following questions, noting his responses verbatim each time.

(a) Is the pencil to the left or to the right of the plate?

(b) Is the plate to the left or to the right of the block?

(c) Is the block to the left or to the right of the pencil?

(d) Is the pencil to the left or to the right of the block?

(e) Is the plate to the left or to the right of the pencil?

(f) Is the block to the left or to the right of the plate?

Problem 3b (hidden objects)

Place the screen vertically in front of the child so that he can no longer see the objects on the sheet of paper. Then replace the three objects used in the preceding problem with the following three objects: the *cow*, the *lamppost*, the *boat* (from left to right in relation to the examiner and to the subject). Arrange these objects while taking care that the child does not see them. Then say:

> Now, you have to pay very close attention. You see, I am putting this [*the screen*] here so that you can't see what is on the paper right away. I took away everything that was there before and I put some other objects (toys) there. In a minute, I'm going to remove the piece of cardboard so you can see; but afterward I'm going to put it back and I will ask you questions to see if you can remember how the objects are arranged on the paper. Now, you have to pay very close attention, you are going to look at the objects so you can remember afterward how they are arranged. Pay close attention because I'm only going to let you see them for a very short time.

Remove the screen and let the child look for about 15 seconds (time to count to 15, rather slowly). After this time, replace the screen in front of the objects and ask the child each of the following questions, noting his response each time.

(a) Is the cow to the left or to the right of the light?
(b) Is the light to the left or to the right of the boat?
(c) Is the boat to the left or to the right of the light?
(d) Is the cow to the left or to the right of the boat?
(e) Is the light to the left or to the right of the cow?
(f) Is the boat to the left or to the right of the cow?

COORDINATION OF PERSPECTIVES

MATERIAL

Three cones of thin cardboard: one red one (diam.: 20 cm.; height: 11.5 cm.); one blue one (diam.: 14 cm.; height: 7.5 cm.); one yellow one (diam.: 9 cm.; height: 5 cm.); one piece of green cardboard (52 x 52 cm.) on which three circles showing the position of the cones are marked; nine cards (14 x 18 cm.) illustrating the three cones from various perspectives (see Figure 18, p. 315); one little man of modeling clay (maximum height: 3 cm.).

INSTRUCTIONS

Place the three cones on the green cardboard (at the three positions indicated by the circles) and place the arrangement in front of the child so that the yellow cone (small) is to his right, the blue cone (medium) is to his left, and the red cone (large) is behind the other two. Explain the material to the child, saying:

Now, we are going to play with some mountains (tents, huts, etc.). You see, I have three mountains: a red one, the biggest one; a blue one, a little smaller; and then the yellow one which is very small. I also have a little man [*show the modeling-clay man*]. You can see how small he is. So the mountains are very big for him, because he is very small.

The man, right now, is going for a walk around the mountains, and he is going to take some pictures of the mountains. He has his camera with him and he wants to take pictures of the mountains. Now, you have to guess what will be in the pictures that the little man is going to take.

EXAMPLE

Put the man at A (see Figure 17, p. 314), just in front of the child, and say:

Watch, I am putting the man here. Now, what does the little man see? What will the photograph look like when he takes it.

Then present cards A and D, and say:

Try to find which of these pictures the little man sees when he is like this.

Let the child work. When he has made his choice (correct or not), explain the problem to him in the following way:

You see, the man is placed right in front of you. So he sees the same thing that you do: he sees the red mountain in the back, and the blue one to the left here, and then the yellow one to the right, here. So you see, he sees this picture [*designate card A*]. On this picture, the red one is in the back, then the blue one is to the left, and the yellow one is to the right, in front of the red one. On the other picture [*show card D*] the red one is in front of the yellow one, and the blue one is on the wrong side. To see it like this, he would have to go somewhere else, do you understand?

Repeat these explanations if necessary, but refrain from adding to those which were selected. In particular, never say to the child which position corresponds to card D, and, above all, *never place the child at position D* in order to show him that card D corresponds to a possible point of view.

First part (recognizing the card)

Problem 1

Put the man at F (Figure 17) and say:

Now the man is there, and he is taking a picture.

Present cards G-A-D-F-H (arranging them in that order in front of the child in a horizontal line, card G being the first one on the right in relation to the child). Then say:

Now you see that I have some pictures of the three mountains. You are going to tell me which of these photographs the man is going to take when he is placed there [*designate the man placed in F*]. Show me the picture that the man sees when he is there.

If the child wants to move so he can better see what the man sees, it is absolutely necessary to keep him from doing so. Note carefully which picture(s) the child chooses.

(a) *If the child proposes a single solution,* question him first on the card which he selected as the right one:

Explain to me why you say that he can see that one.

Note his explanation carefully. Then ask him, successively pointing to each of the cards which he considered to be wrong:

And that one, you are sure he doesn't see that one? Explain to me why he can't see that one.

Note verbatim all of the child's responses and always make sure he justifies his responses.

(b) *If the child proposes several solutions,* first ask him:

Which one is the best one of all? Explain to me why that one is the best.

Note his explanation carefully. Then take each of the cards which he chose at first, but which he rejected when he chose the best one, and ask for each one:

And that one, you just chose it a little while ago. Why do you think that it's not right, why do you think that the man doesn't see that one?

Finally, take each of the cards which the child had just considered as the wrong ones and ask for each one:

Explain to me why he doesn't see that one.

Note all the child's responses verbatim.

Problem 2

Place the man at C (Figure 17) and proceed as in the preceding problem, but *this time present cards E-C-F-A-B* (placing them in that order in front of the child and in a horizontal line, card E being the first one on the right in relation to the child).

Problem 3

First ask the subject to place himself at E (beside the examiner), saying, for example:

Now, you are going to sit beside me to see the mountains the way I see them. What do you see when you are here? Make yourself very small like the little man [*encourage the child to bend down*] and look at the mountains very carefully so you can tell me what you see. Which mountains do you see?

Note the child's response and, if he says he sees three mountains (when in reality he sees only two of them), do not insist further.

Then put the man at B (Figure 17) and proceed as in the preceding problems, but *this time present cards B-I-E-D-A* (placing them in that order in a horizontal line in front of the child, card B being the first one on the right in relation to the child).

Second part (locating the man)

Ask the child to return to A, saying, for example:

Now, you are going to go back to the place where you were before and we are going to play another game. Now, you are going to take the little man. I am going to show you the pictures and you are going to try to find where the little man was when he took the pictures that I am going to show you. You are going to look very carefully at the picture that I am going to show you and then you will place the little man in the place where he has to be to take a picture like that.

Problem 1

Present card C and say:

Look very carefully at this picture and put the little man where he was when he took this photograph. Put the man where he has to be to see the mountains like this.

If the child wants to move so he can find the correct position more easily, do not let him do so. Note the exact position where the child places his man and, if he places him successively at several positions, indicate very clearly the order and the location of these successive positions. If the child places his man in the center of the board or right at the foot of one of the mountains, instead of putting him on the edge of the cardboard base, allow him to do so and make no comment.

(a) *If the child places his man at a single position,* simply ask him:

Explain to me why you put the little man there. Tell me how you know that the man sees the same thing as in the picture.

(b) *If the child places his man at several positions successively,* note them first, and then ask him simply:

Which place is best, do you think? Choose the best of all. Explain to me why you think that is the best place.

Note all the child's responses verbatim.

Problem 2

Present card F and proceed as before.

Problem 3

Present card B and proceed as before.

Problem 4

Present card E and proceed as before.

Problem 5

Present card I and proceed as before, except if the child notices that the card is wrong. In that case, ask him to explain why such a photograph is impossible.

Bibliography

Ames, L. B. & Learned, J. (1948), The development of verbalized space in the young child. *J. Genet. Psychol., 72:*63-84.

Becker, W. C. (1962), Developmental psychology. *Ann. Rev. Psychol., 13:*1-34.

Bell, R. Q. (1965), Developmental psychology. *Ann. Rev. Psychol., 16:*1-38.

Benton, A. L. (1959), *Right-Left Discrimination and Finger Localization.* New York: Hoeber Harper.

——— & Menefee, F. L. (1957), Handedness and right-left discrimination. *Child Develpm., 28:*237-241.

——— & Schultz, L. M. (1949), Observations on tactual form perception (stereognosis) in preschool children. *J. Clin. Psychol., 5:*359-364.

Binet, A. (1911), Nouvelles recherches sur la mesure du niveau intellectuel chez les enfants d'école. *Année psychol., 17:*145-201.

——— & Simon, T. (1908), Le développement de l'intelligence chez les enfants. *Année psychol., 14:*1-90.

Brown, R. (1965), *Social Psychology.* New York: Free Press.

Bruce, M. (1941), Animism *vs.* evolution of the concept "alive." *J. Psychol., 12:*81-90.

Bruner, J. S. (1964), The course of cognitive development. *Amer. Psychol., 19:*1-16.

——— (1966), On cognitive growth: II. In: *Studies in Cognitive Growth,* ed. J. S. Bruner, Rose R. Olver, Patricia M. Greenfield, et al. New York: Wiley, pp. 30-67.

Cénac, M. & Hécaen, H. (1943), Inversion systématique dans la désignation droite-gauche chez certains enfants. *Annales médico-psychol., 1:*415-419.

Coleman, R. I. & Deutsch, C. P. (1964), Lateral dominance and right-left discrimination: a comparison of normal and retarded readers. *Percept. Motor Skills, 19:*43-50.

Cutsforth, T. D. (1933), An analysis of the relationship between tactual and visual perception. *Psychol. Monogr., 44*:125-153.

Dodwell, P. C. (1960), Children's understanding of number and related concepts. *Can. J. Psychol., 14*:191-205.

—— (1961), Children's understanding of number concepts: characteristics of an individual and of a group test. *Can. J. Psychol., 15*:29-36.

—— (1962), Relations between the understanding of the logic of classes and of cardinal number in children. *Can. J. Psychol., 16*:152-160.

—— (1963), Children's understanding of spatial concepts. *Can. J. Psychol., 17*:141-161.

Elkind, D. (1961a), The development of quantitative thinking: a systematic replication of Piaget's studies. *J. Genet. Psychol., 98*:37-46.

—— (1961b), Children's discovery of the conservation of mass, weight, and volume: Piaget replication study II. *J. Genet. Psychol., 98*:219-227.

—— (1961c), The development of the additive composition of classes in the child: Piaget replication study III. *J. Genet. Psychol., 99*:51-57.

—— (1961d), Children's conception of right and left: Piaget replication study IV. *J. Genet. Psychol., 99*:269-276.

—— (1962), Children's conception of brother and sister: Piaget replication study V. *J. Genet. Psychol., 100*:129-136.

—— (1964), Discrimination, seriation, and numeration of size and dimensional differences in young children: Piaget replication study VI. *J. Genet. Psychol., 104*:275-296.

Ewart, A. G. & Carp, F. M. (1963), Recognition of tactual form by sighted and blind subjects. *Amer. J. Psychol., 76*:488-492.

Fisher, G. H. (1965), Development features of behaviour and perception. I: Visual and tactile-kinesthetic shape perception. *Brit. J. Educ. Psychol., 35*:69-78.

Flavell, J. H. (1963), *The Developmental Psychology of Jean Piaget.* Princeton: Van Nostrand.

Flickinger, A. & Rehage, K. J. (1949), Building time and space concepts. *Yearb. Nat. Coun. Soc. Stud.* (Washington, D.C.), *20*:107-116.

Galifret-Granjon, N. (1960), Batterie Piaget-Head (tests d'orientation gauche-droite). In: *Manuel pour l'examen psychologique de l'enfant,* Fascicule I, ed. R. Zazzo. Neuchâtel et Paris: Delachaux et Niestlé, pp. 24-56.

Gibson, E. (1963), Perceptual development. In: Child psychology, Part 1, ed. H. W. Stevenson, J. Kagan & C. Spiker. *Yearb. Nat. Soc. Study Educ., 62:*144-195.

Gibson, J. J. (1950), *The Perception of the Visual World.* Boston: Houghton Mifflin.

——— (1966), *The Senses Considered as Perceptual Systems.* Boston: Houghton Mifflin.

Gouin-Décarie, T. (1962), *Intelligence and Affectivity in Early Childhood.* New York: International Universities Press, 1966.

Harris, A. J. (1957), Lateral dominance, directional confusion, and reading disability. *J. Psychol., 44:*283-294.

Hatwell, Y. (1959), Perception tactile des formes et organisation spatiale tactile. *J. de Psychologie, 56:*187-204.

Head, H. (1926), *Aphasia and Kindred Disorders of Speech.* London: Cambridge University Press.

Hermelin, B. & O'Connor, N. (1961), Recognition of shapes by normal and subnormal children. *Brit. J. Psychol., 52:*281-284.

Huang, I. & Lee, H. W. (1945), Experimental analysis of child animism. *J. Genet. Psychol., 66:*69-74.

Inhelder, B. & Piaget, J. (1955), *The Growth of Logical Thinking from Childhood to Adolescence.* New York: Basic Books, 1958.

——— ——— (1959), *The Early Growth of Logic in the Child (Classification and Seriation).* New York: Harper, 1964.

Ittelson, W. H. (1960), *Visual Space Perception.* New York: Springer.

Kagan, J. & Henker, B. A. (1966), Developmental psychology. *Ann. Rev. Psychol., 17:*1-50.

Klingberg, G. (1957), The distinction between living and not living among 7-10-year-old children, with some remarks concerning the so-called animism controvery. *J. Genet. Psychol., 90:*227-238.

Koffka, K. (1935), *Principles of Gestalt Psychology.* New York: Harcourt, Brace.

Kofsky, E. (1966), Developmental scalogram analysis of classificatory behavior. *Child Develpm., 37:*191-205.

Laurendeau, M. & Pinard, A. (1962), *Causal Thinking in the Child.* New York: International Universities Press.

Lovell, K. (1959), A follow-up study of some aspects of the work of

Piaget and Inhelder on the child's conception of space. *Brit. J. Educ. Psychol.*, 29:104-117.

———— (1961), *The Growth of Basic Mathematical and Scientific Concepts in Children.* London: University of London Press.

———— Healey, D. & Rowland, A. D. (1962), Growth of some geometrical concepts. *Child Develpm.*, 33:751-767.

———— Shapton, D. & Warren, N. S. (1964), A study of some cognitive and other disabilities in backward readers of average intelligence as assessed by a non-verbal test. *Brit. J. Educ. Psychol.*, 34:58-64.

———— & Slater, A. (1960), The growth of the concept of time: a comparative study. *J. Child Psychol. Psychiat.*, 1:179-190.

Lunzer, E. A. (1960), Some points of Piaget's theory in the light of experimental criticism. *J. Child Psychol. Psychiat.*, 1:191-202.

Maccoby, E. E. (1964), Developmental psychology. *Ann. Rev. Psychol.*, 15:203-250.

Mannix, J. B. (1960), The number concept of a group of E.S.N. children. *Brit. J. Psychol.*, 30:180-181.

Medinnus, G. R. & Johnson, D. (1966), Tactual recognition of shapes by normal and retarded children. *Percept. Motor Skills*, 22:406.

Meyer, E. (1935), La représentation des relations spatiales chez l'enfant. *Cahiers de pédagogie expérimentale et de psychologie de l'enfant*, 8. Geneva.

———— (1940), Comprehension of spatial relations in preschool children. *J. Genet. Psychol.*, 57:119-151.

Page, E. I. (1959), Haptic perception: a consideration of one of the investigations of Piaget and Inhelder. *Educ. Rev.*, 11:115-124.

Peel, E. A. (1959), Experimental examination of some of Piaget's schemata concerning children's perception and thinking, and a discussion of their educational significance. *Brit. J. Educ. Psychol.*, 29:89-104.

Piaget, J. (1924), *Judgment and Reasoning in the Child.* New York: Harcourt, Brace, 1926.

———— (1926), *The Child's Conception of the World.* New York: Harcourt, Brace, 1929.

———— (1927), *The Child's Conception of Physical Causality.* London: Routledge and Kegan Paul, 1951.

———— (1936), *The Origins of Intelligence in Children*, 2nd ed. New York: International Universities Press, 1952.

———— (1937), *The Construction of Reality in the Child.* New York: Basic Books, 1954.

———— (1941), Le mécanisme du développement mental et les lois du groupement des opérations. *Arch de Psychologie (Genève), 28*:215-285.

———— (1947), *The Psychology of Intelligence.* London: Routledge and Kegan Paul, 1950.

———— (1949), *Traité de logique.* Paris: Colin.

———— (1950), *Introduction à l'épistémologie génétique.* Tome I: *La pensée mathématique.* Paris: Presses Universitaires de France.

———— (1955), Perceptual and cognitive (or operational) structures in the development of the concept of space in the child. *Proceedings of the Fourteenth International Congress of Psychology* (Montréal, 1954). Amsterdam: North-Holland. (Summary.)

———— (1961), *Les mécanismes perceptifs.* Paris: Presses Universitaires de France.

———— & Inhelder, B. (1948), *The Child's Conception of Space.* London: Routledge and Kegan Paul, 1956.

———— ———— (1951), *La genèse de l'idée de hasard chez l'enfant.* Paris: Presses Universitaires de France.

———— ———— (1963), Les images mentales. In: *Traité de psychologie expérimentale,* Fascicule VII: *L'intelligence,* ed. P. Fraisse & J. Piaget. Paris: Presses Universitaires de France, pp. 65-108.

———— ———— & Szeminska, A. (1948), *The Child's Conception of Geometry.* London: Routledge and Kegan Paul, 1960.

———— & Morf, A. (1958), Les isomorphismes partiels entre les structures logiques et les structures perceptives. In: *Etudes d'épistémologie génétique.* Vol. VI: *Logique et perception,* ed. J. S. Bruner, F. Bresson, A. Morf & J. Piaget. Paris: Presses Universitaires de France, pp. 49-116.

———— & Szeminska, A. (1941), *The Child's Conception of Number.* London: Routledge and Kegan Paul, 1952.

Pinard, A. & Laurendeau, M. (1966), Le caractère topologique des premières représentations spatiales de l'enfant: examen des hypothèses de Piaget. *J. int. de psychologie, 1*:243-255.

———— ———— (1969), "Stage" in Piaget's cognitive developmental theory: exegesis of a concept. In: *Studies in Cognitive Develop-*

ment: Essays in Honor of Jean Piaget, ed. D. Elkind & J. H. Flavell. New York: Oxford University Press, pp. 120-170.

Reingold, H. L. & Stanley, W. C. (1963), Developmental psychology. *Ann. Rev. Psychol., 14*:1-28.

Richard, H. (1962), *Contre-vérification expérimentale d'une étude sur la mise en relation des perspectives.* Unpublished M.A. thesis, Université de Montréal.

Ross, A. O. (1954), Tactual perception of form by the brain-injured. *J. Abnorm. Soc. Psychol., 49*:566-573.

Royer, D. (1964), *Copie de geste et recherche de symétrie dans une épreuve de localisation de sites topographiques.* Unpublished M.A. thesis, Université de Montréal.

Russell, D. H. (1956), *Children's Thinking.* Boston: Ginn.

Shemyakin, F. N. (1959), Orientation in space. In: *Psychological Science in the U.S.S.R.,* Vol. I, B. G. Anan'yev et al. Washington, D.C.: U.S. Joint publications research service, 1961, pp. 186-255.

Sinclair de Zwart, H. (1967), *Acquisition du langage et développement de la pensée.* Paris: Dunod.

Smedslund, J. (1964), Concrete reasoning: a study of intellectual development. *Monogr. Soc. Res. Child Develpm., 20*(93):1-39.

Strauss, A. A. & Lehtinen, L. E. (1947), *Psychopathology and Education of the Brain-Injured Child.* New York: Grune & Stratton.

Terman, L. M. (1916), *The Measurement of Intelligence.* Boston: Houghton Mifflin.

———— & Merrill, M. A. (1937), *Measuring Intelligence.* Boston: Houghton Mifflin.

Vernon, P. E. (1965), Environmental handicap and intellectual development: Part I. *Brit. J. Educ. Psychol., 35*:9-20.

Wallach, M. A. (1963), Research on children's thinking. In: Child psychology, ed. H. W. Stevenson, J. Kagan & C. Spiker. *Yearb. Nat. Soc. Study Educ., 62*:236-276.

Wapner, S. & Werner, H. (1957), *Perceptual Development: An Investigation within the Framework of Sensory-tonic Field Theory.* Worcester: Clark University Press.

Werner, H. (1948), *Comparative Psychology of Mental Development,* rev. ed. New York: International Universities Press, 1957.

White, B. W. & Saltz, E. (1957), Measurement of reproducibility. *Psychol. Bull., 54*:81-99.

Wohlwill, J. F. (1960a), Developmental studies of perception. *Psychol. Bull., 57*:249-289.

—— (1960b), A study of development of the number concept by scalogram analysis. *J. Genet. Psychol., 97*:345-377.

Worchel, P. (1951), Space perception and orientation in the blind. *Psychol. Monogr., 65* (No. 15, Whole No. 352).

Zaporozhets, A. V. (1965), The development of perception in the preschool child. In: European research in cognitive development, ed. P. H. Mussen. *Monogr. Soc. Res. Child Develpm., 30* (No. 2).